Supply Chain
Management
using
Microsoft Dynamics AX

2016 Edition

Other Books by Scott Hamilton

Warehouse Management Using Microsoft Dynamics AX 2012 R3,
Visions Inc. (2015)

Discrete Manufacturing Using Microsoft Dynamics AX 2012,
Visions Inc. (2012)

Food Products Manufacturing Using Microsoft Dynamics AX 2012,
Visions Inc. (2012)

Managing Process Manufacturing Using Microsoft Dynamics AX 2009,
Visions Inc. (2010)

Managing Wholesale Distribution Using Microsoft Dynamics AX 2009,
privately published (2010)

Managing Lean Manufacturing Using Microsoft Dynamics AX 2009,
Visions Inc. (2010)

Managing Your Supply Chain Using Microsoft Dynamics AX 2009,
Printing Arts (2009)

Managing Your Supply Chain Using Microsoft Dynamics AX 4.0,
Printing Arts (2007)

Managing Your Supply Chain Using Microsoft Axapta 3.0, McGraw-Hill (2004)

Managing Your Supply Chain Using Microsoft Navision, McGraw-Hill (2004)

Maximizing Your ERP System, McGraw-Hill (2003)

Managing Information: How Information Systems Impact Organizational Strategy (with Gordon B. Davis), Business One Irwin (1993).

Supply Chain Management
using
Microsoft Dynamics AX

2016 Edition

Scott Hamilton, Ph.D.

Print ISBN 978-0-9884976-4-1
eBook ISBN 978-0-9884976-3-4

The front cover photo depicts the waves on the north coast of Kauai in Hawaii, and was taken by the nationally-recognized photographer Doug Peck (www.douglaspeckphotography.com).

Contents

Chapter 11   Sales Order Processing   249

Chapter 12   Purchase Order Processing   303

Preface

The target audience for *Supply Chain Management using Microsoft Dynamics AX: 2016 Edition* consists of those individuals involved with the operational and supply chain aspects of managing a manufacturing or distribution business. The book contents cover two major options currently available for using AX. One option is labeled "Dynamics AX 2012," and the book focuses on the business logic within the most recent version of AX 2012 R3. The other option represents a new release labeled the "new Dynamics AX," with functionality based on the proven business logic of AX 2012 R3. The two options provide the same supply chain management functionality with some slight differences, so that the book contents apply to both options.

Four previous books similarly focused on supply chain management using AX, especially for discrete manufacturing/distribution businesses. Each previous book covered a major software version but they could just as easily been titled different editions. The first three books were titled *Managing Your Supply Chain*, and they represented the 2004 Edition (for AX 3.0), the 2007 Edition (for AX 4.0), and the 2009 Edition (for AX 2009). The fourth book was titled slightly differently to indicate the focus on SCM in Discrete Manufacturing, and it represented the 2012 Edition (for AX 2012).

A trail guide and topographic maps provide essential information when exploring any unknown territory. They identify the most important features of the landscape and provide insights about key considerations and trail variations. Similar essentials apply to those exploring the use of an ERP system to run their business. As a trail guide, this book identifies the most important features of the embedded conceptual models and business processes related to supply chain management using AX, and provides insights about key considerations and variations. The same major topographical features apply to AX 2012 R3 and the new Dynamics AX.

The scope of book topics was influenced by book length considerations. These are described in the Introduction chapter about the "Prior Research and the Scope of Book Topics." One key aspect concerns the significant amount of additional functionality related to the Advanced WMS approach to warehouse management, which necessitated a companion book to reduce book length. The companion book is titled *Warehouse Management using Microsoft Dynamics AX.*[1]

Many people helped in completing this book. They included Deb Skoog, Elise Kling Marty and Sandra Krzyzaniak in preparing the book. Many people contributed insights and feedback during the months of prior research for this 2016 edition of a trail guide, and to the previous editions.

The book reflects my interpretation of how to use Microsoft Dynamics AX. Errors of omission and commission, and any misunderstandings, are hopefully minimized.[2] Corrections and suggestions are welcome, as well as additional case study examples. Please send to **ScottHamiltonPhD@aol.com**.

Each day of writing was started with the following prayer:

> Creator of all things, give me a sharp sense of understanding, a retentive memory, and the ability to grasp things correctly and fundamentally. Grant me the talent of being exact in my explanations, and the ability to express myself with thoroughness and charm. Point out the beginning, direct the progress, and help in the completion.

---

[1] The currently available version of the companion book was written for AX 2012 R3, but it also applies to those using the New Dynamics AX because only a few minor changes were introduced. The minor changes are covered in this book, such as workspaces related to warehouse management.

[2] The book is for information purposes only. The author, publisher and Microsoft make no warranties, expressed or implied, in the presentation of information.

Chapter 1

Introduction

A primary challenge for many manufacturing and distribution firms involves effective implementation and use of an ERP system for managing their supply chain. Learning the capabilities of your ERP software package provides a foundation for effective usage, and re-thinking previous ways of doing business. This book focuses on how Microsoft Dynamics AX[1] supports supply chain management in discrete manufacturing and distribution.

The book contents cover two major options currently available for using AX. One option is labeled "Dynamics AX 2012", and the book focuses on the business logic within the most recent version of AX 2012 R3. The other option represents a new release labeled the "new Dynamics AX", with functionality based on the proven business logic of AX 2012 R3. The two options provide the same supply chain management functionality with some slight differences, so that the book contents apply to both options. The book identifies the slight differences such as the new variations in user experience and the new workspace capabilities.[2] Beneath these look and feel changes, the two options share the same embedded conceptual models and business processes.

The targeted reader includes those individuals implementing or considering Dynamics AX as their ERP system, as well as those providing consulting assistance. This chapter starts with suggestions for the targeted reader, and describes the scope of book topics. It also covers several aspects of terminology and navigation, and highlights the use of business process modeling (BPM) diagrams as a learning tool. These considerations are reflected in the following sections within this chapter.

1. Suggestions for the Targeted Reader
2. Organization of the Book Chapters

---

[1] Dynamics AX is a registered trademark of Microsoft. This book employs the term "AX" for short.
[2] A shortened term such as "New AX" provides a simplified way to refer to functionality within the new Dynamics AX. One alternative for the shortened term could have been "AX 7" since it represents a well-known term used in the past. This book will employ the shortened term "New AX" when applicable.

3. Reasons for Reading the Book
4. Prior Research and Scope of Book Topics
5. Terminology Used in the Book
6. Variations in the User Experience and the use of Workspaces
7. Business Process Modeling (BPM) Diagrams as Learning Tools
8. Summary of Case Studies

1.1 Suggestions for the Targeted Reader

The targeted reader consists of those individuals responsible for supply chain management at manufacturing and distribution firms. In particular, it is intended to assist professionals implementing or considering Dynamics AX as their ERP system as well as those providing consulting assistance.

The book contents have been segmented to support several categories of targeted readers, so that you can focus on just the relevant sections and chapters for your learning objectives. Several learning objectives are summarized in Figure 1.1 and described below. The suggestions reflect the organization of book chapters so that it may be helpful to view this information first (Figure 1.2). The learning objectives for AX veterans are also addressed, such as a summary of new capabilities relative to a starting point of the older AX 2012 version.

Initially Learn AX New users can benefit from a quick overview of how the whole system fits together, especially in a linear sequence of topics that build on each other. This quick overview consists of approximately 100 to 130 pages, although this can vary based on the type of operation and level of user interest. As a starting point, you may want to read about common scenarios in the next chapter that reflect your dominant business models, including the description of a baseline model of operations (Section 2.2).

The linear sequence starts with several foundation topics. The fundamentals of modeling inventory locations represent a critical foundation topic. The other foundation topics include the definition of material items, BOMs and routings for manufactured items, product costing, and the coverage planning data to model SCM decision-making. The sequence continues with the definition of S&OP game plans and the use of master scheduling logic to coordinate supply chain activities in several business processes. Subsequent chapters cover these key business processes related to sales orders, purchase orders, transfer orders, production orders, warehouse management and quality management. Appendix A summarizes the suggested chapters and sections for initial learning of AX.

Figure 1.1 Typical Learning Objectives about
Supply Chain Management using AX

Learning Objective	Estimated Pages
Initially Learn AX	100-130
Learn Business Processes and their Variations	
Selectively Learn AX Capabilities	
- SCM for a Manufacturing Business	80-180
- SCM for a Distribution Business	70-170
- S&OP Scenarios and Master Scheduling Logic	50
- Warehouse Management	30-40
- Quality Management	25
Reference Book to Confirm/Extend AX Knowledge	
Incrementally Learn the New Capabilities	
- Starting from AX 2012	30-40
- Starting from AX 2012 R3	5-10

For AX Veterans (bracket indicating the last three rows)

Learn Business Processes and their Variations Numerous business processes are illustrated within the book, as summarized in a subsequent section (Section 1.7). The explanation of each business process starts with a basic model that reflects the key constructs and embedded conceptual models within AX. The typical steps and role responsibilities are illustrated using BPM diagrams. The basic model provides a baseline for explaining key considerations and variations in the business process, thereby supporting a "+1" learning approach.

Selectively Learn AX Capabilities Some readers may want to focus on selected topics related to their job responsibilities, functional area or type of business. As one approach, the table of contents provides a starting point for identifying the relevant topics, and estimating the learning effort based on page counts. Other examples for selective learning are illustrated in the following points.

Learn SCM for a Manufacturing Business Several chapters focus on the unique requirements of a manufacturing business. These topics include item definition, bills of material, routings, calculated costs, and coverage planning data for manufactured items, the S&OP scenarios, and the use of production orders, subcontracted production and configuration technologies. The explanation of these manufacturing topics consists of approximately 180 pages, and a quick overview consists of 80 pages.

Learn SCM for a Distribution Business   The targeted reader in a distribution business can skip the above-mentioned topics related to manufacturing, and just focus on topics related to distribution. These topics include item definition, costs and coverage planning data for purchased items, the S&OP scenarios, and the use of sales orders, purchase orders and transfer orders. The explanation of these distribution topics consists of approximately 170 pages, and a quick overview consists of 70 pages.

Learn S&OP Scenarios and Master Scheduling Logic   One of the cornerstones for effective supply chain management consists of sales and operations planning (S&OP) game plans, and the related use of master scheduling logic. The AX term "master scheduling logic" has different synonyms that may be more familiar -- such as planning calculations, MRP logic and DRP logic -- and it often represents one of the most complex aspects of system usage. The book includes an extended explanation of this topic (Chapter 10) consisting of approximately 50 pages. The interested reader should also review the chapter about coverage planning data to model SCM decision-making (Chapter 9), which consists of approximately 25 pages.

Learn Warehouse Management   A separate chapter summarizes the two major options for warehouse management in approximately 20 pages (Sections 16.3 and 16.4), and covers several related topics such as Inventory Status. The companion book about "Warehouse Management using AX" provides in-depth explanations of these two options (in 200+ pages). The interested reader may need the companion book in order to accomplish their learning objectives.

Learn Quality Management   A separate chapter covers the integration of quality management and supply chain management (Chapter 17), and consists of approximately 20 pages.

Reference Book to Confirm/Extend AX Knowledge   This book attempts to explain most of the SCM-related capabilities within AX, and a typical implementation only employs a subset of these capabilities. Many readers find it useful as a reference book to confirm or extend their AX knowledge. It is often helpful to read another viewpoint to complement your hands-on learning and research into the user documentation, blogs and other sources of information. Readers of my previous books have commented about their usefulness as reference information, and it is hoped the current book serves a similar purpose.

Incrementally Learn the new Capabilities starting from AX 2012 A knowledgeable person about the older AX 2012 version can focus on just the sections that provide incremental learning of new capabilities. Appendix B summarizes the incremental differences between AX 2012 and the new versions, and identifies the relevant sections providing more detailed explanations. The most significant changes are related to the Advanced WMS approach to warehouse management. Excluding these changes related to Advanced WMS, the incremental learning consists of 30-40 pages and represents a 5-10% change in overall SCM functionality.

Incrementally Learn the new Capabilities starting from AX 2012 R3 A person already knowledgeable about AX 2012 R3 can focus on just the differences in the new Dynamics AX, such as the new workspaces. Appendix C summarizes these incremental differences and identifies the relevant sections providing more detailed explanations. In summary, this incremental learning consists of 5-10 pages.

1.2 Organization of Book Chapters

The book chapters and the sections within a chapter provide a linear sequence for learning AX and reflect four major groupings. The groupings consist of foundation topics, sales and operations planning, key business processes, and additional topics, as summarized in Figure 1.2.

Figure 1.2 Organization of Book Chapters

Chapter	Foundation Topics	Key Business Processes	Chapter
2	Common Scenarios	Sales Order Processing	11
3	Modeling Inventory Locations	Purchase Order Processing	12
4	Definition of a Material Item	Transfer Order Processing	13
5	Bill of Material Information	Production Order Processing	14
6	Resources and Routings	Subcontracted Production	15
7	Product Costing	Inventory & Warehouse Management	16
8	Serial and Batch Number Tracking	Quality Management	17
9	Coverage Planning Data to Model SCM Decision-Making		

Sales & Operations Planning	Additional Topics	
10 S&OP and Master Scheduling	Multicompany Supply Chain	18
	Configuration Technologies for Custom Product Manufacturing	19

Legend: ☐ = The chapter summarizes a companion book about Warehouse Management using AX.

1.3 Reasons for Reading the Book

Firms involved with a system selection process may be considering Dynamics AX as a candidate package and this book can help provide a vision of an integrated system and evaluate system fit and needed customizations. The book can help businesses involved in implementing and using AX by accelerating the learning process, identifying the basic business processes and variations, reducing user resistance to change, and identifying ideas for improved system usage. For those providing AX consulting services, this book can accelerate the learning process, expand the scope of knowledge, and improve situational fluency. In addition, it can help those with previous AX experience learn the new capabilities within AX 7. Figure 1.3 summarizes these reasons for reading the book.

Figure 1.3 Reasons for Reading the Book

	Manufacturing Firm	Consultant or Solution Provider
Overall Goal	Improve firm performance through effective supply chain management systems	Improve customer service through increased knowledge of AX
System Selection	Provide vision of an integrated system Evaluate system fit and needed customizations	Accelerate learning process Gain knowledge of new functionality Reduce new employee ramp-up time Improve situational fluency Improve training and consulting efforts Prescribe business businesses Support gap/fit analyses Improve customization efforts
Implementation and Use	Accelerate learning process of new system Suggest business processes Take advantage of new business models rather than just replicate previous system Provide ideas for improved system usage Reduce user resistance to change Reduce implementation costs, time and risks	

1.4 Prior Research and Scope of Book Topics

The book focuses on supply chain management of discrete products in manufacturing and distribution companies, and this focus guided the prior research and the scope of book topics.

Prior Research Several steps of prior research were undertaken to understand the supply chain management requirements of discrete products and the AX functionality to support those requirements. With respect to AX 2012 R3 (as well as previous AX versions), these steps included participation in training classes, webinars, and conference sessions; reviews of the existing training materials, e-learning lessons, user documentation and sales demo materials; reviews of blogs and articles; discussions with users, development personnel, and field consultants; and hands-on testing for thousands of use cases that reflected common requirements in manufacturing and distribution. With few exceptions, only those capabilities personally tested and proven were included in the book contents.[3] The same approach was also undertaken for my previous books about Dynamics AX. The discussions with experienced field consultants helped identify the dominant business practices at current users. On-going opportunities to consult with current users have supplemented this understanding.

The prior research concerning the new Dynamics AX has been following similar steps. This included participation in pre-release webinars and conferences, discussions with leading experts and Microsoft team members, reading the currently available information, and hands-on testing of hundreds of use cases. These same use cases were previously tested for AX 2012 R3, thereby supporting a comparative analysis of the two options. The book contents reflect my prior research up until the beginning of the year 2016.

The prior research about SCM requirements included my consulting and teaching experiences with discrete manufacturing firms across the past three decades. These experiences included responses to numerous RFPs (requests for proposal) for an ERP system, face-to-face consulting engagements with several hundred firms, and teaching executive seminars, APICS certification classes, MBA courses, and user group sessions. My understanding is continually being supplemented by staying abreast of the current literature and discussions with various thought leaders about using ERP systems in discrete manufacturing.

One aspect of prior research involved a focus on the embedded conceptual models and business processes within standard AX functionality, and my analysis of the evolving functionality across multiple software releases (as documented in previous books). They provide a foundation for explaining system capabilities in the language of AX. The navigational details of the end-user experience may differ -- whether using customized forms, web-based applications, workspaces or hand-held devices -- but the embedded conceptual models and business processes still apply.

Scope of Book Topics The book topics focus on supply chain management, and the selection of book topics was shaped by several factors. First, the selected topics excluded the integrated accounting applications -- such as payables,

---

[3] The prior research and hands-on testing for AX 2012 R3 reflect the software capabilities through the CU9 release.

receivables, general ledger, payroll and human resources -- except for key intersection points with SCM.   Second, several SCM-related topics were excluded because of book length considerations -- such as lean manufacturing, project-oriented operations, service-oriented operations and retail operations – although they are mentioned in several places. Each of these excluded topics merit a separate book, much like my separate books about warehouse management and process manufacturing. The excluded topic of non-stock purchases reflects the focus on material items. Third, a few topics were excluded because they could not be personally tested and proven within the budgeted time.

The book length considerations precluded screen shots.[4] Other important topics of system development and usage were also excluded, such as business intelligence, security, and the customization capabilities within the AX development environment.

Contributions to the AX Body of Knowledge The body of knowledge related to Microsoft Dynamics AX consists of several levels and components. The foundation level consists of the software, documentation and training materials provided by Microsoft. Additional contributions to the AX body of knowledge build on this foundation. In terms of the book's contributions, I have attempted to summarize the relevant information with an integrative viewpoint of how the whole system fits together to support supply chain management -- especially in a discrete manufacturing business. The book explains the embedded conceptual models and business processes, and provides prescriptive guidance.

1.5 Terminology Used in the Book

The terminology associated with many aspects of supply chain management can vary widely between companies and ERP systems. It is often difficult to clearly understand the meaning of a term -- such as inventory status, reservations, shipments, work orders, and sales or purchase agreements -- without a lengthy discussion about its significance.

As much as possible, this book consistently uses the same terminology to describe the conceptual models and software functionality within AX. In most cases, the book's terminology reflects the names employed by the AX software, such as the names of forms, tabs, fields, and buttons. However, it sometimes reflects generally accepted terms or alternative phrasing to clarify understanding.

---

[4] One argument against screen shot examples is that many companies tailor the standard screens, and the displayed information is also affected by license key activation. As one example of a book with screen shots, see "Using Microsoft Dynamics AX 2012, 4th Edition" by Andreas Luszczak.

One difficulty in terminology stems from the book's attempt to explain two different options for using AX, consisting of the new Dynamics AX and AX 2012 R3. The embedded conceptual models and business processes within the two options are fundamentally the same for supply chain management topics, but there are slight changes illustrated in Appendix C. The book uses the new term when known, otherwise it uses the terminology from AX 2012 R3.

Other difficulties in terminology stem from the AX design. One example involves the AX approach to enterprise- and company-level information about an item. AX employs two different constructs and their identifiers -- termed the product number and the item number -- to define the enterprise and company-level information about an item. The product number provides a unique identifier for enterprise-level information about products, and you release a product to a company to create an item number which acts as the identifier for company-level information. As an explanatory approach, the book generally employs the terms enterprise-level and company-level information about an item, as summarized at the beginning of the chapter about the definition of a material item (Section 4.1).

Another example of terminology difficulties concerns the AX design for supporting mixed mode environments. There are several key differences between production orders and batch orders (and the related BOM and formula information), where batch orders primarily apply to process manufacturing. Another variation of a mixed mode environment involves kanban orders and the support for lean manufacturing. However, the topics about process manufacturing and lean manufacturing fall outside the book's scope because of book length considerations.

One other terminology issue concerns the different options for warehouse management within AX, where the two major options represent completely different conceptual models. Several terms have been used to identify the different options, as described at the beginning of the chapter about warehouse management (Section 16.1). For simplicity's sake, the two major options are termed the basic approach and advanced approach to warehouse management. They can also be termed the "WMS I" approach and "WHS" approach respectively, which reflects the Microsoft acronyms.

1.6 Variations in the User Experience and the use of Workspaces

This book focuses on the embedded conceptual models and business processes within standard AX. The user experience and navigational details may differ -- whether using customized forms, workspaces, web-based applications, or hand-held devices -- but the embedded conceptual models and business processes still apply. This section briefly summarizes the variations in user experience and the use of workspaces.

Variations of the User Experience The standard menu structure and user-defined favorites provide commonly used approaches for navigation. When using the new Dynamics AX, the links within workspaces provide another approach for navigating to commonly used tasks. An additional approach – termed "search for a page" – enables you to specify the desired topic, review a list of applicable forms, and then navigate to a selected form.

Use of Workspaces Workspaces represent one variation in the user experience when using the new Dynamics AX. [5] Workspaces provide an aggregation of tasks related to a specific role. Many of the currently available workspaces provide summarized information with drill-down to details, and they provide links for navigating to commonly used tasks. Some identify needed actions and simplify the reporting of actions taken. Illustrative examples include needed actions to update incomplete data or needed approvals for a new item.

Almost half of the 30+ currently available workspaces apply to the SCM-related topics within the book, as summarized in Figure 1.4. Separate sections describe the workspaces related to item definition (Section 4.18), product costing (Section 7.14), master scheduling (Section 10.18), sales orders (Section 11.17), purchase orders (Section 12.14), production orders (Section 14.16), warehouse management (Section 16.6) and configuration technologies (Section 19.8). Other workspaces are mentioned in the context of defining resources (Section 6.2) and employee competencies (Section 6.4). It is anticipated that additional workspaces and related functionality will become available as the software evolves.

---

[5] The workspace functionality replaces several capabilities in AX 2012 R3, such as role-centered pages and the employee portal. The role-centered pages were built on the deprecated Enterprise Portal capabilities which have been replaced by the new web client platform. The new platform supports the use of workspaces - and the related definition of workspace patterns to support different devices - for navigating to commonly used tasks. For example, a workspace pattern can be specified for a list page, where the number of displayed columns needs to reflect the size of the device.

Figure 1.4 Examples of SCM-Related Workspaces

Design	Released Product Maintenance Product Readiness Cost Administration Product Variant Model Definition	S&OP	Master Planning
Sell	Sales Order Processing & Inquiry Sales Return Processing	Produce	Production Floor Management
Procure	Purchase Order Preparation Purchase Order Receipt & Follow-up	Warehouse	Outbound Work Planning Outbound Work Monitoring Cost Administration Cost Analysis

1.7 Business Process Modeling (BPM) Diagrams as a Learning Tool

One of the book's primary objectives consists of learning the embedded conceptual models and business processes within standard AX. In many implementations, these business processes can help the project team gain an overall understanding of system usage and each team member's roles, enabling them to envision new business practices and the real need for customizations. Almost every chapter includes Business Process Modeling (BPM) diagrams about basic business processes. These basic processes provide the foundation for more extended explanations and for covering major variations. Figure 1.5 illustrates many of the business processes within the book, and Figure 1.6 identifies the primary roles involved in the business processes. These roles correspond to the standard roles within AX.

BPM diagrams are primarily used as a learning tool within this book, and my diagrams do not adhere exactly to the BPM standards. The diagrams employ a limited number of symbols to keep things simple. For example, three symbols are used to denote "And", "Or" and "Any, None, or All". A fourth symbol for an "Event" indicates an automatic action within AX, which helps explain some of the behind-the-scenes functionality. The BPM diagrams indicate a sub-process using a bold border.

Figure 1.5 Examples of Business Processes

Design	Define a material item Define an item's bill of material Define a production resource Define an item's routing Define a configurable item Define a product configuration model	**S&OP**	Maintain S&OP game plans Run master scheduling task Calculate safety stock requirements
Sell	Process a sales order Process a sales quotation Process a customer return Process a direct delivery order Process a special order	**Produce**	Process a production order Report picking using Advanced WMS Report labor using MES capabilities Process a rework order Define a subcontracted service Process subcontracted production
Procure	Process a purchase order Process a purchasing RFQ Process a return to vendor Process a transfer order	**Warehouse**	Pick/ship a sales order Receive a purchase order Pick/ship a transfer order Receive a transfer order Picking for a production order Receive a production order Perform cycle counting
Quality	Report inspection for purchase receipt Report inspection for production		

Figure 1.6 Example Roles for the Business Processes

Design	Product Designer Process Engineer Cost Accountant Engineering Manager	**S&OP**	Sales Manager Master Scheduler
Sell	Customer Service Rep Sales Manager	**Produce**	Production Planner Production Supervisor Machine Operator Production Manager
Procure	Purchasing Agent Payables Clerk Purchasing Manager	**Warehouse**	Receiving Clerk Shipping Clerk Warehouse Worker Warehouse Planner Warehouse Manager Transportation Coordinator
Quality	Quality Manager Quality Control Clerk		

1.8 Summary of Case Studies

Case studies illustrate how the AX software functionality applies to many different industries and scenarios that represent discrete manufacturing and distribution. These industries are described in the next chapter (Section 2.1), along with a baseline model of operations that applies to most scenarios (Section 2.2). Each chapter includes case studies applicable to the topic, and a complete list of case studies is provided at the end of the book.

Chapter 2

Common Scenarios

Manufacturing and distribution firms share many similar requirements in supply chain management of discrete products. Each environment will also have some industry-specific and company-specific requirements. In order to illustrate how Dynamics AX addresses these requirements, this chapter summarizes the industries representing discrete manufacturing and distribution, describes a baseline model of operations, and provides some common scenarios. A baseline model of operations provides a foundation for simplified explanations about how to use Dynamics AX to manage the business, and about variations to the baseline model. The common scenarios build on this baseline model, as described in the following sections within the chapter. Many of the common scenarios illustrate variations in discrete manufacturing, and a separate section focuses on the variations of distribution scenarios.

1. Industries Representing Discrete Manufacturing and Distribution
2. Baseline Model of Operations
3. Material- versus Routing-Intensive Production Process
4. Make-to-Stock versus Make-to-Order Production Strategies
5. Configure-to-Order Custom Product
6. Engineer-to-Order Custom Product
7. New Product Development
8. Multisite and Multicompany Operations
9. Subcontracted Production
10. Lean Manufacturing
11. Polymer Molded Products
12. Equipment Installation and Maintenance
13. Printed Circuit Boards in a CTO Product
14. Variations of S&OP Game Plans
15. Variations of Distribution Operations

The common scenarios include related case studies, and additional case studies throughout the book highlight other common scenarios.

2.1 Industries Representing Discrete Manufacturing and Distribution

The nature of manufacturing and distribution of discrete products applies to a broad spectrum of industries, ranging from industrial equipment and automotive components to aerospace and electronics.   The standard industry classification (SIC) codes provide more detail about illustrative industries within the broad spectrum.

Industrial equipment often comes to mind when considering different industries involved with discrete products, as illustrated by the following categories of products.

◆ Special and large machinery
◆ Oil, gas and mining machinery
◆ High tech machinery
◆ Commercial and OEM machinery and parts
◆ Refrigeration and service industry machinery
◆ Metalworking machinery and equipment

Other industries involved with discrete products include the following.

◆ Aerospace manufacturing
◆ Automotive components and aftermarket parts
◆ Shipping and railroad vehicles
◆ Transportation equipment
◆ Audio and video equipment
◆ Communications equipment
◆ Computer equipment
◆ Household appliances
◆ Optical media
◆ Measurement and control instruments
◆ Electrical components

The spectrum of discrete products includes many other industries not mentioned here.

2.2 Baseline Model of Operations

A baseline model of operations represents the common use of Dynamics AX and the dominant business practices within discrete manufacturing and distribution businesses. It provides a foundation for simplified explanations about how to use Dynamics AX to manage the business, and for explaining variations to the baseline model. In summary, the baseline model focuses on a single AX company with one or more AX sites (and their related AX warehouses) with standard products identified by an item number. Inventory is tracked by site, warehouse and bin location, with inventory replenishment logic at the site/warehouse level. Sales prices and purchase prices are typically companywide, although they can optionally reflect site- or warehouse-specific prices. Each manufactured item requires bill of material information, with optional definition of routing data. The following points provide more detailed explanations about the baseline model of operations.

Single Company and AX instance The baseline model consists of a single company using a single AX instance. Some scenarios involve multiple companies within one instance and possible partitioning of these companies within the database. A multicompany supply chain is treated as a variation to the baseline model, and covered as a separate chapter (Chapter 18).

Multiple Inventory Locations Identified by an AX site and AX Warehouse Each physical location is typically identified by an AX site and an associated value for a "site" financial dimension. The site-specific financial dimension supports financial reports by site. Each AX site has one or more AX warehouses, and different warehouses are employed to support in-transit inventory on transfer orders. The use of AX sites and AX warehouses to model different inventory locations involves several considerations (Chapter 3). Each AX warehouse has one or more bin locations, although use of bin locations is not mandatory. The definition and use of warehouse locations differ significantly between the basic and advanced approach to warehouse management (Chapter 16).

Multiple Business Units within one Company Identified by an AX Financial Dimension In many cases, different items represent different lines of business that require financial reports by business unit. The business units are identified as different values for a "business unit" financial dimension. The appropriate value of this financial dimension is assigned to the relevant items, thereby supporting financial reports by business unit.

Material Items Identified by Item Number Material items are identified by an item number.   Configurable items (and the use of configuration Ids) are treated as a variation to the baseline model, and covered as a separate chapter (Chapter 19). In some cases, an item may be identified by an item number and one or more additional fields termed variant codes (Section 4.16), but these cases fall outside the baseline model of operations.

Bill of Material for a Manufactured Item A bill of material (BOM) defines the product structure for a manufactured item.   In some cases, the product structure can be defined by a formula (especially in process-oriented operations), but a detailed explanation of formula information and related batch orders falls outside the book's scope.

Routing Information for a Manufactured Item Routing information can be optionally defined for a manufactured item, where routings also require the definition of production resources, resource groups and master operations. The routing information involves special considerations for modeling subcontracted production.

Standard or Actual Costing for Material Items Each material item must be assigned an inventory valuation method reflecting a standard cost or actual cost method.   With standard costing, a costing version must be defined for standard costs, and each material item must have an item cost record for each site with inventory.

Inventory Replenishment Logic Applies to the Site/Warehouse Level Replenishment logic is defined by an item's coverage planning data, and applies to the site/warehouse level.

Batch and/or Serial Numbers for a Material Item The use of batch and/or serial numbers is treated as a variation to the baseline model, and covered as a separate chapter (Chapter 8).

Standard Roles within Dynamics AX The baseline model employs the standard roles within Dynamics AX to support role-based security. You assign users to these standard roles, and the predefined privileges for each role may be adjusted.   For example, the privileges for the purchasing agent role include maintenance of purchase orders and vendor information. The standard roles are also reflected in business process diagrams throughout the book that illustrate typical business processes.

2.3 Material-versus Routing-Intensive Production Process

A basic variation in discrete manufacturing involves a material-intensive versus routing-intensive production process. A routing-intensive production process is characterized by a multi-step routing for a manufactured item, and the value-added costs comprise a high percentage of the product costs. Typical examples include the production processes for castings, steel bar or steel block. A material-intensive production process is commonly characterized by a single routing step for a manufactured item, and the material costs comprise a high percentage of the product costs. Typical examples include assembled products. The routing data may not even be defined in cases with an extremely simple production process. Figure 2.1 illustrates two different product structures and associated routing data for a material-intensive versus routing-intensive production process.[1]

Figure 2.1 Material- versus Routing-Intensive Production

End-Item A		
30 ┼ Final Assembly		

Assembly B	Part
20 ┼ Assembly	

Subassembly C	Part
10 ┼ Subassembly	

Part D	Part

Material-Intensive

End-Item X	
100┼ Assembly	

Housing	
90 ┼ Wash	
80 ┼ Deburr	
70 ┼ Groove	
60 ┼ Face Drill	
50 ┼ Machine Bore	

Intermediate	
Ea	
40 ┼ Shot Blast	
30 ┼ Normalize	
20 ┼ Forge & Trim	
10 ┼ Crop	

Steel Block	
Kg	

Multi-step Routing

Routing-Intensive

Dynamics AX supports both of these basic variations. There are slight differences in defining and using multistep routings. For example, the multistep routing may reflect a linear progression of operations (as illustrated in Figure 2.1) or a network, and an operation can require a hard link with the previous

---

[1] The example for a routing-intensive production process actually represents an automotive part and its associated operations, but the specifics are unimportant. The example is simply intended to illustrate a multistep routing.

operation. Another example involves the slight differences in kanban orders for a multistep routing. Other examples apply to an outside operation in a multistep routing, since it requires coordination of the supplied material and the finished item, especially when multiple outside operations require coordination with multiple subcontractors.

2.4 Make-to-Stock versus Make-to-Order Production Strategies

Another basic variation in discrete manufacturing involves the choice of production strategies as part of the S&OP game plans for an item. The two classic production strategies are termed make-to-stock (MTS) and make-to-order (MTO). A MTO strategy may involve linkage between the end-item's sales order and its related supply orders. For example, you can establish linked orders by first creating a production order from a sales order line for the end-item, and then scheduling this production order to automatically create the linked production orders for components (termed reference orders). The reference orders reflect BOM information about components, where a BOM line type of *pegged supply* indicates a make-to-order component and a BOM line type of *vendor* indicates a buy-to-order component. Figure 2.2 illustrates how to create linkage between a sales order line item and a production order, and the impact of the BOM line type on creating linked production orders and linked purchase orders for components.

Figure 2.2 Make-to-Order Product with Linked Orders

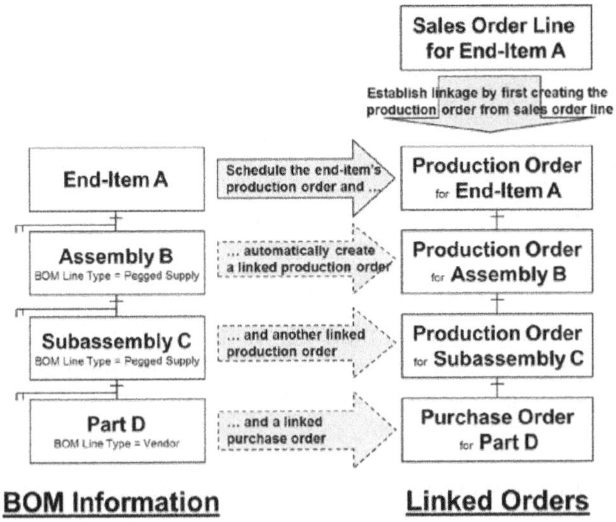

Both of these production strategies apply to lean manufacturing scenarios, with fixed kanbans for MTS products and sales event kanbans for MTO products. It is worth noting that sales event kanbans can be automatically created from the sales order line (without requiring a separate step), and line event kanbans for MTO components are also automatically created (much like reference orders). You designate line event kanbans as part of the kanban rules for components rather than using the BOM line type for components. A subsequent section illustrates a common scenario for lean manufacturing (Section 2.10).

Other production strategies include make-to-order without any link to the sales order, as described in a subsequent chapter about S&OP game plans (Section 10.1).

2.5 Configure-to-Order Custom Product

Many custom product manufacturing scenarios can be modeled as a configure-to-order (CTO) product. When entering a sales order or quote for a CTO product, for example, a configuration technology provides prompts and responses that can be translated into the necessary components and operations for a unique configuration Id. Standard AX functionality supports several different configuration technologies. A common scenario for a CTO product using the constraint-based configuration technology is summarized in Case 2.1. Chapter 19 provides further explanation of this approach to a configuration technology.

Case 2.1: Constraint-Based Configuration Technology for CTO Products An equipment manufacturer had several product lines representing multi-level configure-to-order custom products. Figure 2.3 illustrates the product structure for one product line consisting of a configurable end-item and configurable components. It also indicates the names of options (termed attribute types) for required, optional and common options, and the items representing each option's alternatives (termed attributes).

In this simple example, the configurable items consist of the end-item "Equipment Product Line ABC" and the two variations of the base unit (labeled Basic and Deluxe). Product configuration models representing each configurable item must be defined, and then assigned to the relevant item with validity dates. As requirements evolve over time, a different model would be defined and then assigned to the configurable item with different validity dates, so that a given configurable item would have several versions of a product configuration model with non-overlapping validity dates

Figure 2.3 Product Structure for Configurable Equipment

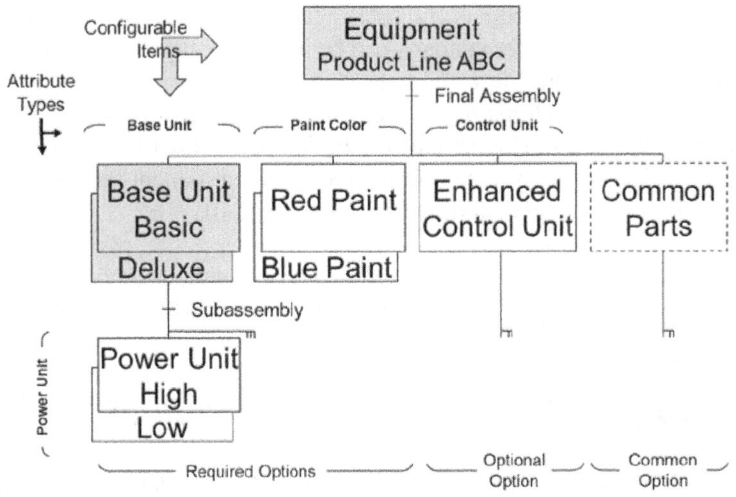

A product configuration model defines the user interface (UI) prompts and responses needed to configure the product, and maps them to the needed components and operations. It also identifies any configurable components and their product configuration models. After using the model such as configuring a sales order line, it automatically creates a unique configuration Id -- and the associated BOM and route versions -- for each configurable item in the product structure. It also assigns this configuration Id and the BOM/route versions to the sales order line. The BOM and routing information can now be manually maintained, so that the product configurator model does not have to result in 100% of the detailed information.

2.6 Engineer-to-Order Custom Product

An engineer-to-order product typically requires significant engineering time to design the product, and to define the product structure and new items. These engineering activities can be budgeted and tracked against a project, and even charged to the customer based on a time-and-material or fixed-price basis. The finalized design typically evolves over time, so that the definition of item and BOM information also evolves over time. While the design evolves, it is critical to define and order the items representing long lead time materials. These items can be identified within a skeleton BOM to help coordinate supply chain activities.

The top levels of the product structure for an ETO product can be modeled as configurable items or as regular items with BOM versions defining the components. They can also be modeled as subprojects, where the item requirements for the subproject specify the components. Case 2.2 illustrates the use of subprojects for modeling the top levels of the product structure and for managing the engineering time.

Case 2.2: External T&M Project to Design and Build an ETO Product

A manufacturing company produced engineer-to-order machines requiring significant engineering design time prior to building a machine, and installation services after delivery of the machine. For a typical ETO machine, the engineering manager defines an external time-and-materials (T&M) project consisting of three subprojects reflecting engineering design, final assembly of the machine, and installation services. Figure 2.4 illustrates the typical project and subprojects.

Figure 2.4 External Project to Design/Build an ETO Machine

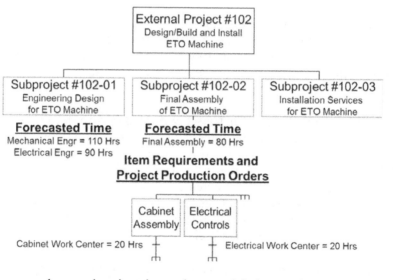

In this example, a subproject is used to model the top level of the product structure, with forecasted time requirements for a production resource (representing the final assembly work center) to perform final assembly of components. An item requirement is defined for each first level component -- such as the cabinet assembly and electrical controls -- and a project production order is generated for each item requirement. This approach provides direct linkage between a project's item requirement and the corresponding project production order.[2]

In this example, the subproject for engineering design has a simple work breakdown structure consisting of several activities (not shown in the figure), and the forecasted time requirements for mechanical engineers and electrical engineers are defined for each activity.

In many cases, a detailed project quotation must be prepared and then accepted by the customer prior to designing and building the ETO machine. The detailed quotation reflects a work breakdown structure of activities, and each activity has forecasted requirements for items and resource hours. After customer acceptance and confirmation of the project quote, the details about item forecasts are transferred to the actual project as item requirements, and the hour forecasts are also transferred.

2.7 New Product Development

New product development is oftentimes undertaken for internal purposes and results in a prototype. Alternatively, the development efforts may be undertaken for a specific customer with requirements for invoicing the customer much like an ETO product. Case 2.3 summarizes the use of an internal project for new product development.

Case 2.3: Internal Project for New Product Development New product development at a discrete manufacturer often entails producing a prototype of the manufactured item, and additional costs associated with engineering time and related expenses. Figure 2.5 illustrates an internal project for developing a prototype. The project's item requirement is specified for just the end-item, which has a multi-level bill of material and routing information. This information is used to calculate the cost of the end-item and its manufactured components, and to coordinate supply chain activities.

The project's forecasted time requirements include engineering time by three major groups of engineers: design engineers, lab technicians and test engineers. The project also has forecasted expenses (such as travel and consulting fees) that will be incurred during prototype development.

---

[2] This example represents one approach for managing production of the top levels an ETO product structure. Another approach employs configurable items for the top levels, as described in Case 2.1.

Figure 2.5 Internal Project for New Product Development

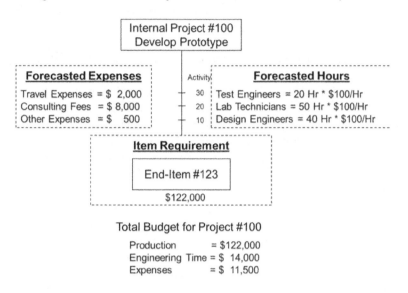

Total Budget for Project #100

Production   = $122,000
Engineering Time = $ 14,000
Expenses   = $ 11,500

Several project categories provide segmentation of costs related to expenses and resource time. As illustrated in Figure 2.5, the expenses were segmented into three project categories (travel, consulting fees, and other) and the hours were segmented into three categories (design, lab, and test). These project categories help segment budgeted and actual costs for analysis and reporting purposes. Figure 2.5 also illustrates the use of activities for the forecasted hours, where the activities are simply labeled 10, 20, and 30 in this example.

2.8 Multisite and Multicompany Operations

Many businesses involved in manufacturing and distribution have inventory at multiple physical sites and transfers between sites. Transfers between sites can be managed using transfers orders or intercompany orders, depending on the grouping of physical sites into companies. These two approaches are summarized below and in Case 2.4.

◆ *Transfer Orders.* Transfer orders represent a two-step approach to transfer material between two sites/warehouses in the same company. The two-step approach means that one transaction records the shipment and a second transaction records the receipt, with tracking of in-transit inventory in a transit warehouse. A one-step approach can also be used, typically when a short transportation time does not require tracking of in-transit inventory. The one-step approach means that one transaction records the shipment, with automatic receipt of the shipped quantity. As an alternative to transfers orders, you can use a transfer journal to record movements between locations.

◆ *Intercompany Orders*. Intercompany orders can be used when both companies exist within the same Dynamics AX instance, so that placing a purchase order with an intercompany vendor will automatically create a corresponding sales order in the sister company, and vice versa. Intercompany orders require setup information about items and also about the vendors and customers representing the sister companies. For example, a product must be released to both companies in order to support intercompany trading, and the item's company-level information must be defined in both companies.

Master scheduling across a multicompany supply chain involves sequencing considerations. Master scheduling logic within AX applies to a single company, which means the master scheduling task should first be performed for the top-tier company. This generates planned intercompany demand that communicates requirements to the second-tier company, which represents an up-stream company within the supply chain.[3] The process must be repeated for additional up-stream companies. To simplify this process, you define a sequence of companies that will be considered by an intercompany master scheduling task.

Case 2.4: Coordination across a Multisite and Multicompany Supply Chain A global manufacturer consisted of multiple companies, and transfers between companies. As shown in Figure 2.6, a simplified example consists of two different companies representing a manufacturing company and a distribution company. In the manufacturing company, an intermediate item produced at one manufacturing site was transferred to another site (via transfer orders) for producing the end item. The manufacturing company sold the end-item to domestic customers. The end-item was also transferred to a different company's distribution center for sales to foreign customers. The primary coordination tools across the multicompany supply chain consisted of planned intercompany demand as well as intercompany purchase orders and sales orders.

---

[3] The term upstream provides a relative reference within a supply chain indicating a source of raw material, whereas the term downstream indicates the direction of the end-customer.

Figure 2.6 Coordination across a Multicompany Supply Chain

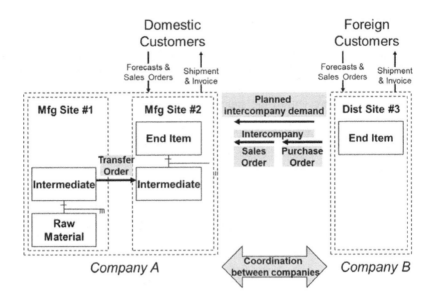

2.9 Subcontracted Production

Subcontracted production has many variations that reflect the options for handling supplied material and finished items, the options for modeling an external operation, and other factors. Other factors include the identification of AX sites and warehouses involved in subcontracted production, and the significance of a single order for subcontracted production.

A key issue for subcontracted production includes the inventory visibility of supplied material and the finished items at subcontractor locations. A common scenario with inventory visibility is summarized in Case 2.5. This scenario employs a single-level BOM to identify the supplied components, and the routing consists of a single external operation. The supplied components are stocked at the subcontractor. A production order provides coordination for the subcontracted production. The finished quantity is reported at the subcontractor site (which triggers backflushing of supplied components), and then transferred to a different site such as a distribution center or manufacturing plant. This approach provides improved visibility and coordination of subcontracted production. A subsequent chapter provides further explanation of subcontracted production (Chapter 15).

Case 2.5: Subcontracted Production with Supplied Components A discrete manufacturer produced several finished goods at subcontractors, and stocked the supplied components at the subcontractor via transfer orders or direct deliveries from suppliers. A given product could be produced at more than one subcontractor so that site-specific BOMs were defined. As illustrated in Figure 2.7, the site-specific BOM for finished good "Product-A" identified two supplied components -- labeled "Component #1" and "Component #2" -- with a warehouse source representing the subcontractor warehouse. The site-specific BOM also included a component representing the "Subcontracted Service for Product-A," which reflects the AX approach to modeling subcontracted production. This item defines the value-added costs for the subcontracted service, and provides the basis for approved vendors and purchase price agreements. In addition, the purchase order for this subcontracted service is generated by and directly linked to the production order for the parent item. Hence, subcontracted production involves the dual constructs of a production order and its associated purchase order for coordinating the supply chain, as shown in the left side of Figure 2.7.

Figure 2.7 Subcontracted Production with Supplied Components

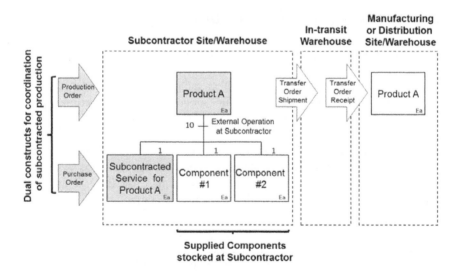

In this example, a single purchase order receipt transaction (for the subcontracted service) also updates the finished quantity for the production order (which triggers backflushing of supplied material). The finished quantity at the subcontractor location is then transferred to a manufacturing plant or distribution center.

2.10 Lean Manufacturing

Lean manufacturing approaches often involve several types of changes, such as changes in factory layout and conceptual viewpoints. One example of a change in conceptual viewpoints involves a production flow, which defines the sequence of activities to produce an item (and replaces the routing information). Another example involves kanban rules, which define how to generate kanban orders for items within the product structure. These conceptual viewpoints are illustrated in Case 2.6 about using kanban orders for a make-to-order product built from stocked components.

Case 2.6: Kanban Orders for a Make-to-Order Product As part of a lean manufacturing operation, a family of make-to-order products were produced from stocked components. The production flow consisted of two work cells and the related activities for subassembly and final assembly, an activity to withdraw material from the stockroom, and warehouses representing the stockroom, the lineside supermarkets at the two cells, and the shipping area. The top part of Figure 2.8 illustrates this production flow viewpoint. The bottom part of Figure 2.8 illustrates the kanban rule viewpoint. Kanban rules determine how to generate kanban orders for items within the product structure -- displayed sideways for showing the correlation between the BOM and the production flow.

Figure 2.8 Kanban Orders for a Make-to-Order Product

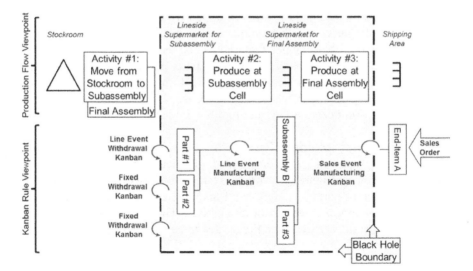

The purchased parts representing the stocked components were received into the stockroom. These deliveries (not shown in the figure) can be coordinated by purchase orders. The lineside supermarkets were replenished using line event withdrawal kanbans (for Part #1) and fixed withdrawal kanbans (for Part #2 and Part #3). After withdrawal, the component inventory was no longer tracked because it was transferred across the black hole boundary, and its value was charged to work-in-process for the value chain. The figure displays the black hole boundary (with a heavy dashed line) and the work-in-process (in light grey shading).

A sales order for the end-item triggered automatic creation of a sales event manufacturing kanban for the end-item (with delivery to the shipping area), which also triggered a line event manufacturing kanban for its key component of the subassembly (with delivery to the lineside supermarket for the final assembly cell). This triggered the line event withdrawal kanban for Part #1. These kanban orders simply provided coordination with no inventory impact until receipt of the end-item within the shipping area. The kanban receipt updated the end-item inventory (after being transferred across the black hole boundary), and the end-item's standard cost was deducted from work-in-process for the value chain.

2.11 Polymer Molded Products

Many discrete manufacturers produce polymer molded items as components for other products. One of the unique aspects of polymer molding involves the nature of a mold, since the mold is often designed with multiple cavities in order to produce multiple parts. Another unique aspect involves the reclaim from the molding process, since the scrapped material can be melted down for reuse in the molding process. The generation of multiple parts and reclaim from a single production process must be modeled using the formula approach to product structure, since they represent co-products. Case 2.7 illustrates the formula information and co-products for polymer molded products.

Case 2.7: Polymer Molded Products A discrete manufacturing firm produced several types of polymer molded products which represented key components of their end items. A simple example consists of a single mold to produce two different parts -- a right-hand and a left-hand part -- and the two parts require secondary processing for assembly. The formula and routing for this simple example are shown in the Figure 2.9 and explained below.

Figure 2.9 Example Formula for a Polymer Molded Product

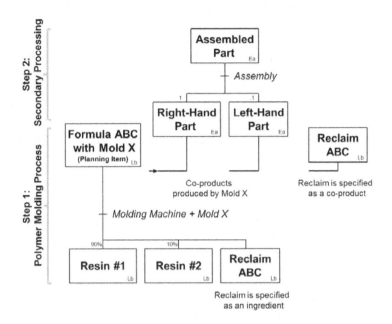

The product structure in Figure 2.9 indicates several item numbers in the formula information, such as Resin #1, Right-Hand Part, and Assembled Part. A key concept is the planning item "Formula ABC with Mold X," since this item provides the basis for defining ingredients, resource requirements, and co-products of a molding process. It is used for planning purposes but is not actually produced.

The first step involves an injection molding machine and the relevant mold (labeled Mold X in the figure). The ingredients for Formula ABC consist of different pelletized resins that must be melted and combined. In this example, the mold consists of two cavities for producing a right-hand and left-hand part, which are identified as co-products within the formula. In addition, the formula indicates that reclaim is a reusable co-product of the molding process, and the reclaim can be used as an ingredient. The second step involves an assembly operation to assemble the right-hand and left-hand parts.

The routing operation for producing the molded parts typically defines the machine cycles that are needed to produce the expected items from a mold. For example, a machine that employs a mold may require 2 cycles to produce a quantity of 10 items. In this case, you define the resource's *batch capacity* as 10. In the operation, you define a *factor* of 2 for the required cycles per batch.

2.12 Equipment Installation and Maintenance

Many manufacturers and distributors provide value-added services such as installation, repair and periodic maintenance, where services are performed by field service personnel or internal service facilities. The most common examples reflect firms that sell and service equipment, such as computer products, home appliances and industrial equipment. A service order provides the basic tool for defining requirements and reporting actual consumption of material and technician time. Common synonyms include a service work order or service call.

Different examples of service orders reflect the differences between field service and internal service facilities. Field service examples include equipment installation, upgrades, and preventive maintenance, which typically reflect scheduled activities with predefined requirements for material and labor. These scheduled activities (and their requirements for material and labor) can be defined within a service agreement, which provides the basis for periodic generation of service orders. Ad hoc activities such as equipment repairs or other emergency situations cannot be scheduled in advance, and the material and labor requirements can be difficult to anticipate. Examples for internal service facilities -- such as a repair department -- include equipment repairs on a customer return or service work on a customer-supplied piece of equipment.

Service orders build on the foundation of project information, where you typically create and assign a unique project to each service order. Case 2.8 describes a typical example for a service order for equipment installation, and its related external time-and-material project.

Case 2.8: Service Order for Equipment Installation An equipment manufacturer employed service orders to install equipment at the customer site. The service order was typically created as part of sales order processing, since the sales line identified the equipment to be installed. The key information for an example service order is summarized in Figure 2.10 and described below.

Figure 2.10 Example Service Order for Equipment Installation

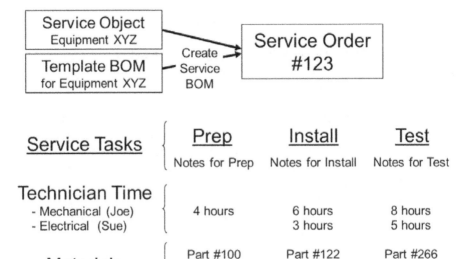

In this example, the service manager assigned a service object (identified as Equipment XYZ in the figure) to the service order, and attached a template BOM (reflecting the bill of material for Equipment XYZ) to create a Service BOM. The Service BOM enables a technician to easily review product structure information should the installation require replacement parts. The service manager also assigned three service tasks (labeled Prep, Install and Test) to the service order, and prepared detailed notes about each task. Finally, the service manager created service order line items that identified the anticipated requirements for materials and the technician's time, and the line items were assigned to the relevant service task. The installation required two types of technicians (mechanical and electrical), and the line items for technician time were assigned to employees (shown as Joe and Sue in the figure). The technicians reported actual consumption of materials and time against the service order line items, and also signed off on the completion of each line item. The signed off completions provide the basis for generating an invoice proposal for billing the customer.

2.13 Printed Circuit Boards in CTO Products

Printed circuit boards often represent key components for discrete manufacturers of equipment and machines. They may also represent the primary end-items for some manufacturers. The production process for printed circuit boards can be modeled by bill of material and routing information, and coordinated by production orders, as illustrated by Case 2.9.

Case 2.9: Printed Circuit Boards in CTO Products   A manufacturer of electronic control units produced configure-to-order products consisting of several printed circuit board (PCB) assemblies placed in a frame and enclosure. Each sales order defined a configuration of different PCB assemblies and options (such as labels and power cord), and the delivery date reflected capable-to-promise logic. Many of the PCB assemblies had high-volume demand and some had infrequent demand. A sales quotation was typically required, which was then converted to a sales order.

As illustrated in Figure 2.11, a PCB assembly was produced from a raw board and various electronic components such as capacitors and resistors. The figure shows two PCB assemblies for the configuration. The production process for a PCB assembly involved a surface mount technology (SMT) line for populating the board, a hand solder operation and then testing. There were four SMT lines, and a given PCB assembly could be produced on any of the lines. Prior to a production run on a selected SMT line, the reels of batch-controlled components were moved from the stockroom for mounting on the SMT line, and the raw boards were moved to the start of the line. After the production run, the reels of unused components were moved back to the stockroom.

Some components were added to the board during the hand solder operation, as illustrated by Resistor-3 in the figure.

The completed PCB assemblies were placed in a frame as part of a final assembly operation for the configured product, and other selected options were added (such as the labels and power cord). The completed CTO product was then shipped to the customer.

The manufacturer currently used production orders (and the associated BOM and routing information) to coordinate production, but they were transitioning toward the use of kanban orders (and the associated production flow information) as part of their lean manufacturing initiatives.

Figure 2.11 Printed Circuit Boards for CTO Product

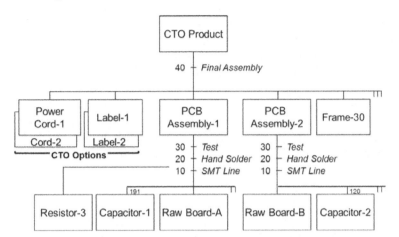

2.14 Variations of S&OP Game Plans

One of the cornerstones for effective supply chain management in a manufacturing or distribution business consists of effective sales and operations planning (S&OP) game plans. They provide the basis for running the business from the top, and build on the models of the organization's supply chain and decision-making logic. The process typically starts with the definition of all demands for the firm's salable items, and results in S&OP game plans that drive supply chain activities to meet those demands. The nature of an S&OP game plan depends on several factors, such as the need to anticipate demand for an item, the item's primary source of supply, and the need for linkage between a sales order and the item's supply order. Demand forecasts are often used to anticipate demand.

Most manufacturing firms have several dominant business models that require different approaches to the S&OP game plans. Typical variations in the dominant business models include make-to-stock, make-to-order and configure-to-order production strategies, as illustrated in Case 2.10. Other variations requiring a different approach to the S&OP game plans include the inventory stocking levels in a multisite or multicompany distribution network, the use of projects in project-oriented operations, and the use of kanban orders in lean manufacturing operations.

Case 2.10: S&OP Game Plans for Make-to-Stock and Make-to-Order Products   The dominant business models at an equipment manufacturing company currently consisted of make-to-stock products (about 25% of business volume), make-to-order products (about 70%) and spare parts (about 5%). They identified each make-to-order product with a unique item number, and produced them from stocked components to reduce delivery lead times.   They were planning a significant shift toward configure-to-order products (to about 50% of business volume) to satisfy the many variations of customer requirements. Each CTO product would be identified by an item number and configuration ID that was created as part of using a product configurator during entry of a sales quotation or sales order. These CTO products would be primarily produced from stocked material, but several specialized requirements would be identified as buy-to-order or make-to-order components. Each of these dominant business models involved a different approach to S&OP game plans.

2.15 Variations of Distribution Operations

The broad spectrum of distribution operations includes many different variations. At its simplest, a distribution operation may consist of a single site and the purchasing and sales of stocked products. Additional variations include multisite operations, including those representing a distribution network and/or a multicompany supply chain. Other variations include special orders and direct delivery orders, light assembly or kits, and installation or service requirements. Some scenarios may involve purchasing of configured items, or the use of subcontractors to produce finished items. Other scenarios involve a combination of distribution centers and manufacturing plants.

The book contents cover many of these variations in distribution operations, and multiple case studies illustrate the variations. The suggested book sections for those readers focused on distribution were summarized at the beginning of the book (Section 1.1).

Chapter 3

Fundamentals of Modeling Inventory Locations

The definition of physical sites containing inventory represents a key part of modeling any supply chain. The fundamental options for modeling these physical sites involve the use of AX sites and AX warehouses within a legal entity. In this book, we will use the generic term of *physical site* or *inventory location* for conceptual explanations, and the terms *AX site* and *AX warehouse* when explaining system-specific functionality. In addition, we will use the term *bin location* when referring to the locations within an AX warehouse.

The model of inventory locations has multiple impacts. It impacts the definition of items, bills of material, resources, routings, product costs, coverage planning data and S&OP game plans. It impacts the business processes related to inventory, such as sales orders, purchase orders, transfer orders and production orders. These impacts are covered throughout the book, and a subsequent chapter provides more detailed explanations about inventory and warehouse management. However, the fundamental options for modeling inventory locations are introduced now, and the chapter consists of the following sections.

1. Major Variations of Modeling Inventory Locations
2. Unique Considerations about using AX Sites
3. Unique Considerations about using AX Warehouses

A graphical portrayal of the inventory locations – termed the operations infrastructure – identifies the multi-level structure of AX warehouses within AX sites and legal entities.[1]

---

[1] The operations infrastructure can be viewed from the workspace titled Resource Lifecycle Management.

3.1 Major Variations for Modeling Inventory Locations

The wide variety of scenarios for supply chain management can be distilled into a few major variations for modeling inventory locations within AX. Several key factors differentiate the nature of these variations, such as the number of AX instances, the number of legal entities related to the inventory locations, and the AX approach for modeling an inventory location. Another key factor involves the need for transfers between inventory locations and the solution approach for coordinating transfers. The most common variations and the key factors are summarized in Figure 3.1 and described below.

Figure 3.1 Major Variations for Modeling Inventory Locations

	Major Variations		
	#1	**#2**	**#3**
	Autonomous Sites Without Transfers	**Multiple Sites With Transfers**	**Multicompany Supply Chain**
Number of AX Instances and Partitions	One		
Number of Companies (Legal Entities)	One		Multiple
AX Approach for Modeling an Inventory Location	Considerations about using an AX Site and AX Warehouse for Modeling an Inventory Location		
Need for Transfers Between Inventory Locations	No	Yes	
AX Solution Approach for Coordinating Material Transfers	N/A	Transfer Orders	Intercompany Purchase Orders & Sales Orders

The simplest variation consists of a single AX instance and partition, and a single legal entity with one or more inventory locations. The locations may reflect autonomous sites without transfers, or they may reflect a distribution network with transfers between locations. Subsequent chapters provide further explanation about transfer orders and the related use of in-transit warehouses (Chapter 13), and the coverage planning data for generating planned transfer orders (Section 9.7). This simplest variation represents one aspect of the baseline model of operations described in the previous chapter (Section 2.2).

Transfers between locations in a multicompany supply chain represent a more complex variation. Transfers can be coordinated by intercompany purchase orders and sales orders, and by master scheduling logic that generates planned intercompany demand. A subsequent chapter provides further explanation about these capabilities in a multicompany supply chain (Chapter 18).

All of these variations involve several considerations about using AX sites and AX warehouses for modeling inventory locations. As one consideration, you can specify whether site-specific or warehouse-specific pricing (or companywide pricing) should apply to an item's sales prices or purchase prices. You define these policies within the Storage Dimension Group assigned to the item, as described in the next chapter (Section 4.4). Some unique considerations only apply to an AX site or an AX warehouse, as described in the next two sections within this chapter.

Several variations represent less common scenarios and are not included in Figure 3.1. For example, a given enterprise may employ two or more AX instances, where intercompany trade between locations in each instance can be handled by the Data Import/Export capabilities within AX.[2] The same capabilities also apply to intercompany trade when one of the companies employs a different ERP system than AX. A single instance can also be partitioned with one or more companies in a partition, thereby isolating the information as if separate instances were being used. These other variations fall outside the book's scope.

3.2 Unique Considerations about using AX Sites

Each physical site is typically modeled as an AX site with one or more AX warehouses. An AX site has several unique aspects that are not applicable to an AX warehouse, as summarized below.

Financial Reporting by AX Site Each AX site can have an associated value for a "site" financial dimension, thereby supporting profit and loss statements by site. This approach involves some setup information about the relevant financial dimension on the Dimension Link form, such as the financial dimension for department. The possible values for department must be defined (one for each site) and the applicable value must be assigned to each site. At that point in time, you can activate the financial dimension link.

---

[2] The Data Import/Export framework replaces the Application Integration Framework (AIF) capabilities in previous AX versions such as AX 2012 R3.

Site-Specific BOM and Routing Information for a Manufactured Item
The BOM and routing information for manufactured items can vary by AX site.

Site-Specific Standard Costs for an Item The assignment of an item's standard cost can vary by AX site, especially when standard costing applies to the item. Stated another way, each material item must have an item cost record for each site with inventory. As a special case, an item may be assigned a zero value for its standard cost at a given AX site.

Site-Specific Labor Rates and Overhead Rates Labor rates and overhead costs can vary by AX site in manufacturing scenarios.

Site-Specific Policies for Quality Orders The automatic generation of quality orders within a business process -- such as production or purchase receiving -- provides a key tool for quality management. These policies can be site-specific or companywide.

Other Production Data related to an AX Site An AX site is assigned to a resource group and its related resources, so that the resources within the group are assumed to be in close proximity to each other. An AX site is also assigned to a production unit, which can determine the warehouse source of components for producing an item.

Some Limitations related to Manufactured Items One limitation applies to manufacturing scenarios with a product structure that spans more than one AX site. More specifically, the warehouse source for a manufactured item's components and the destination warehouse for the item's production order must be within the same AX site. When a product structure spans two AX sites, for example, this limitation often means that an item stocked or produced at one AX site must be transferred to a warehouse within a different AX site in order to use it as a component.

The same limitation applies to the standard cost calculations and inquiries for a manufactured item, since these can only span a single AX site. In order to avoid this limitation, some scenarios will use multiple AX warehouses within a single AX site to model different inventory locations.

3.3 Unique Considerations about using AX Warehouses

Each physical site is typically modeled as an AX site with one or more AX warehouses, as noted in the previous section. The assignment of an AX warehouse to an AX site cannot be changed after posting inventory transactions for the warehouse, so that the initial assignments must be carefully considered. Several unique aspects apply to AX warehouses.

Use of the Basic versus Advanced Approach to Warehouse Management The choice of a warehouse management approach can be warehouse-specific, and a subsequent chapter provides more detailed explanation about these options (Section 16.1). In summary, a warehouse-specific policy about "use warehouse management processes" works in conjunction with a similar item-related policy to determine whether the basic or advanced approach to warehouse management will be used. The two different approaches have different conceptual models for managing inventory. Examples of these differences include the definition of bin locations within a warehouse, the use of reservation logic, and the impact on business processes involving inventory such as sales orders, purchase orders, transfer orders and production orders.

Warehouse Source of Components for a Manufactured Item The warehouse source of components can be defined in several different ways based on BOM/routing information for a manufactured item, and a subsequent chapter provides more detailed explanation about these options (Section 5.5). A component's warehouse source indicates where to pick the item for a production order.

The warehouse source must reflect the previously-mentioned limitation about a product structure than spans more than one AX site. This consideration is especially important in scenarios with subcontracted production, as discussed in a subsequent chapter (Section 15.1).

Significance of a Transit Warehouse The need for a transit warehouse only applies when using transfer orders, so that you can track the in-transit inventory. You designate a transit warehouse when creating it, and assign a transit warehouse to each ship-from warehouse. A subsequent chapter provides further explanation of transfer orders and the use of transit warehouses (Chapter 13).

Significance of a Quarantine Warehouse   The need for a quarantine warehouse only applies when using the Basic Inventory approach to warehouse management, and when using quarantine orders for reporting inspection.   A subsequent chapter about quality management explains the variations for reporting inspection (Section 17.3).

3.4 Executive Summary

The definition of inventory locations represents a key part of modeling any supply chain, and there are several fundamental options for modeling these locations within AX.   These options include the use of AX sites and AX warehouses to model inventory locations, and use of the basic versus advanced approach to warehouse management at a given AX warehouse.   This chapter reviewed the major variations for modeling inventory locations, and highlighted several considerations about using AX sites and AX warehouses.   The choices about these fundamental options are introduced at the beginning of the book because they have multiple impacts described in subsequent chapters.

Chapter 4

Definition of a Material Item

Information about material items provides the foundation for managing supply chain activities in distribution and manufacturing environments. A comprehensive common database about item information must satisfy requirements stemming from multiple stakeholders to avoid the problems associated with multiple nonintegrated files. The stakeholders include sales, purchasing, warehouse management, quality and accounting, as well as engineering and production for manufactured items. Other stakeholder considerations include customers, vendors, industry standards, intercompany coordination, international operations and web-based applications. The multiple stakeholders often have differing requirements concerning the definition of an item.

This explanation focuses on material items identified by an item number. In AX terminology, this means you initially define each item by assigning a Product Type of *Item* and a Product Subtype of *Product*, which indicates the item identifier consists of just an item number. In addition, each item must be treated as a stocked product based on a policy within the Item Model Group assigned to the item.

A typical business process to define a material item provides a starting point for further explanation about key aspects of item information. The typical process requires an understanding of enterprise- versus company-level information about an item. Key aspects include the significance of the storage dimension group assigned to an item, the use of item templates, considerations about descriptive information and units of measure, and the companywide versus site- and warehouse-specific information for an item. These topics are reflected in the following sections within this chapter.

1. Enterprise- versus Company-Level Information for an Item
2. Typical Business Process to Define a Material Item
3. Essential Data for using a New Item within AX
4. Significance of the Storage Dimension Group for an Item
5. Using Templates for Partially Populating Item Information
6. Descriptive Information about an Item
7. Unit of Measure Considerations for an Item
8. Significance of the Production Type for a Material Item
9. Additional Information for a Purchased Item
10. Additional Information for a Manufactured Item
11. Additional Information for a Salable Item
12. Company versus Site/Warehouse Information for an Item
13. Inventory Costing and Financial Reporting for Items
14. Significance of the Item Group for an Item
15. Alternative Item Identifiers
16. Item Identification using an Item Number and Variant Codes
17. Other Types of Items
18. Workspaces Related to Item Definition

4.1 Enterprise- versus Company-Level Information for an Item

The business process for defining a material item requires an understanding of enterprise-level versus company-level information within AX, whether you manage one or multiple companies within an AX instance. In summary, the concept of enterprise- versus company-level information has been implemented within AX using two different constructs and their identifiers -- termed the product number and the item number. The product number provides a unique identifier for enterprise-level information about products, whereas the item number provides the unique identifier for company-level information about items. The enterprise-level information consists of just a few key policies and some descriptive information, whereas all other item information is defined at the company level. Two key forms are employed to maintain product and item information: the Products form (for product information) and the Released Products form (for item information).

Enterprise-Level Information for an Item In addition to the designated Product Type (of *Item*) and Product Subtype (of *Product*), the key aspects of enterprise-level information for a material item include the product number, the product name and extended description (and their translations if applicable), and unit of measure conversions (if applicable).

One aspect of enterprise-level information involves the default values for two key fields – about the Storage Dimension Group and Tracking Dimension Group -- that represent essential company-level information. A subsequent section explains the essential information for a new item (Section 4.3).

Other aspects of enterprise-level data will be covered in the applicable chapter. For example, the assignment of a National Motor Freight Code is required to support bill of lading information when using the Advanced WMS approach to warehouse management (Section 16.4). The assignment of one or more product categories to a product number can support different purposes, such as creating sales order lines via selection from a sales hierarchy (Section 11.3) or creating purchase order lines via selection from a purchase hierarchy (Section 12. 3). A product category also provides one basis for discount percentages defined within a sales agreement or purchase agreement (Sections 11.7 and 12.6).

Two Approaches for Defining an Item The conceptual model of enterprise- versus company-level information gives rise to two different approaches for defining items, termed the multi-company approach and the single-company approach.

◆ *Multi-company approach to defining items.* You employ a two-step process to initially define a product and then release the product to a selected company. Releasing the product creates an item number that matches the product number, and you maintain the company-level information for the item number. You can apply a template to partially populate the item information.

As an example, a given item may be manufactured in one company and sold to a sister company that represents a distribution operation, so that the product needs to be released to two different companies. The multi-company approach supports the concept of a centralized engineering function, where centralized engineering may apply to one or more companies.

◆ *Single-company approach to defining items.* You employ a one-step process to simultaneously create product and item information, which automatically releases the product to the company. The one-step process allows you to specify a template (to partially populate the item information) when initially defining the item, or to apply a template later. This one-step approach can also be used in a multi-company environment to initially create a product and auto-release it to one company.

The identifiers for a product number and item number are typically assigned the same value.   For example, releasing a product to a selected company automatically creates an item number that matches the product number. The one-step process also supports the assignment of the same identifier. If needed, you can optionally override the item number for a company, thereby supporting a company-specific identifier.[1] Deleting an item number from a company simply removes its authorization for the company; it does not delete the product number.

4.2 Typical Business Process to Define a Material Item

The business process for defining a material item requires an understanding of enterprise-level versus company-level information within AX, as described in the previous section. The conceptual model of enterprise- versus company-level information gives rise to two different approaches for defining a material item, termed the multi-company approach and the single-company approach.   Both approaches are included in the typical business process to define a material item.   The business process starts with a request for a new item, where a product designer role typically has the responsibility for initially defining the product and item information. The process ends with the approval of the new item. The steps within the business process are summarized in Figure 4.1 and described below.

Create Product Number and Define Enterprise-Level Data for an Item
In a multicompany approach, the product designer within a centralized engineering group initially creates a product number and defines its enterprise-level data.   The enterprise-level data includes the product name, extended description and several other policies. Specifying the policies about batch/serial tracking (aka the Tracking Dimension Group) and the Storage Dimension Group means they are mandated for all authorized companies.

Release Product to a Company and Create Item Number In a multi-company approach, the product designer within a centralized engineering group releases selected product numbers to one or more companies, which automatically creates the item number within each company. After the release step, the product designer (within the local company) assigns several essential fields that must be populated prior to using the item.

---

[1] You can override a different value for the item number (after it has been released to a company) using the rename capability, or when creating an item number and product number using the single-company approach.

When you attempt to release a product that has already been released to the selected company, the system prevents release and provides a message about the problem. The message can be viewed on the Open Product Release form, or optionally displayed as a message, so that you can correct the problem. The message must be manually deleted from the Open Product Release form.

Figure 4.1 Typical Process to Define a Material Item

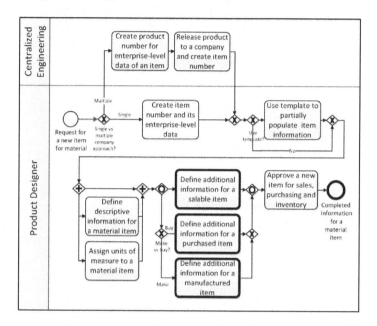

Create Item Number and Define its Enterprise-Level Data The product designer employs a single-company approach to create a new item number and define its enterprise-level data. The enterprise-level data includes the product number, product name and extended description, and several other policies. A template may be specified when creating an item in order to partially populate item information. Subsequent maintenance of enterprise-level data employs the product number, otherwise the product designer maintains all other aspects of item information for the item number (aka a released product).

Use template to partially populate item information The product designer employs a template as a short-cut approach to partially populate item information, either when creating a new item or by applying it afterward. The product designer creates a template from an existing item number, and designates it as a personal or shared template.

Define descriptive information for an item The product designer defines the item's description (and an extended description) as part of its enterprise-level information. Language-specific translations can also be defined. The descriptive information may also include documents, such as notes, Word files or other file formats.

Assign units of measure to an item The product designer assigns the inventory unit of measure (UM) to an item. The item's inventory UM is used to display inventory balances, define costs, and calculate replenishment. An item may have additional units of measure for purchasing, sales or warehouse purposes, which may require item-specific UM conversion factors with the item's inventory UM.

Define additional information for a salable item The sales manager defines the sales pricing and possible discounts for a saleable item. The sales manager may also define sales agreements for blanket sales orders, trade promotions for customers, and the start dates for selling and shipping a new product.

Define additional information for a purchased item The definition of information for a purchased item involves several activities performed by different roles. The purchasing agent defines an item's approved vendors, purchase prices and planning data. The accounting manager defines the item's accounting information and inventory valuation method (standard versus actual cost), and the cost accountant defines an item's standard cost. If applicable, the quality control manager defines the item's testing requirements and the policies for batch and/or serial tracking.

Define additional information for a manufactured item The definition of information for a manufactured item involves several activities performed by different roles. The product designer defines an item's bill of material. The process engineer defines the routing for an item. The production planner defines the item's planning data. The accounting manager defines the item's accounting information and inventory valuation method (standard versus actual cost), and the cost accountant calculates the cost of a manufactured item. If applicable, the quality control manager defines the item's testing requirements and the policies for batch and/or serial tracking.

Approve a new item for sales, purchasing and inventory You can define restrictions (aka stopped flags) about item usage within a company, so that removal of the restrictions represents an item approval step. The restrictions consist of three policies to prevent purchase orders, prevent sales orders and prevent inventory transactions for an item.

Additional Steps in the Typical Business Process The typical process often includes additional steps or slight variations. The following example is not shown in Figure 4.1 so that the diagram does not become too complex.

◆ *Define additional item information for warehouse management purposes.* The need for additional item information depends on whether you employ the basic or advanced approach to warehouse management. A subsequent chapter provides further explanation about these two major options (Chapter 16), but the key issue is summarized here. The definition and assignment of a Storage Dimension Group determines whether an item can "use the warehouse management processes", which entails additional item-related policies such as the Reservation Hierarchy and the Unit Sequence Group for an item.

4.3 Essential Data for using a New Item within AX

The typical process to define a material item involves many different fields and policies, and different roles have responsibility for this data. However, several company-level policies represent the absolute minimum information in order to use a new item within AX. These policies are termed *essential* item data. The essential data are listed in Figure 4.2 and described below. Two of the policies can be mandated by enterprise-level policies, and two policies only apply to a WMS-enabled item. You can optionally perform a "validation" to determine whether these policies have been specified for an item, and a message displays whether any essential item data is missing.

◆ *Storage Dimension Group for an Item.* The Storage Dimension Group assigned to an item consists of several policies which can be broadly segmented into two groups. One group of policies involves considerations about site, warehouse and bin locations, and a second group is related to the basic versus advanced approach to warehouse management. Most scenarios only require a few user-defined Storage Dimension Groups. A subsequent section provides further explanation of the Storage Dimension Group policies (Section 4.4).

When assigned to an item at the enterprise level in a multicompany scenario, the Storage Dimension Group represents a global policy that will be inherited and mandated for the item at all applicable companies. Otherwise, a blank value means each company can assign their own Storage Dimension Group to the item. The most common approach employs a blank value at the enterprise level.

Figure 4.2 Essential Data for using a New Item

Type of Item Information	Level of Information	
	Enterprise	Company
Item Identifier	Specify Product Number	Inherit Item Number
Product Name	Specify Product Name	N/A
Storage Dimension Group for an Item	Specify as an Enterprise Policy or	Inherit the Enterprise Policy or
Tracking Dimension Group for an Item	Leave Blank	Assign the relevant Dimension Group to Item
Item Model Group		Assign an Item Model Group to Item
Item Group	N/A	Assign an Item Group to Item
For WMS-Enabled Item — Reservation Hierarchy		Assign a Reservation Hierarchy to Item
For WMS-Enabled Item — Unit Sequence Group		Assign a Unit Sequence Group to Item

Legend: ⇨ = Release product to a company when using a multicompany approach to item definition

◆ *Tracking Dimension Group for an Item.* The policies within a Tracking Dimension Group identify the need for tracking batch numbers or serial numbers (or both) for an item. Most multicompany scenarios will assign it to an item at the enterprise level so that it is mandated for all applicable companies. In any case, each company can have a different basis for the assignment of batch numbers or serial numbers. A subsequent chapter provides further explanation of batch and serial tracking considerations (Chapter 19).

◆ *Item Model Group.* The Item Model Group assigned to an item consists of multiple policies with a wide variety of impacts. The key policies for a material item include identifying the item as a stocked product and the assignment of an inventory valuation method. The valuation method determines whether actual costing or standard costing applies to an item, and a subsequent chapter provides further explanation of product costing for supporting standard or actual costs (Chapter 7).

Given the wide variety of policies within an Item Model group, it is easier to provide further explanation within the relevant context. For example, the policy about enforcing approved vendors for a purchased item will be further explained in the context of purchase order processing and approved vendors (Section 12.2). Most scenarios only require a few user-defined Item Model

Groups because of similarities in the applicable policies for different groups of material items.

◆ *Item Group.* The applicable G/L accounts are embedded in the Item Group assigned to the item. Additional G/L accounts related to standard cost items must be specified as part of a posting profile, where the account number assignment may reflect an Item Group or Cost Group or both. A subsequent section provides further explanation about the significance of the Item Group (Section 4.14).

◆ *Reservation Hierarchy.* A Reservation Hierarchy only applies to a WMS-enabled item, and indicates how to handle reservation logic at WMS-enabled warehouses. More than one user-defined Reservation Hierarchy may be needed to support the differing reservation logic for normal items versus serialized or batch-controlled items. A subsequent chapter provides further explanation about the applicability of the Reservation Hierarchy for WMS-enabled items and the advanced approach to warehouse management (Section 16.4).

◆ *Unit Sequence Group.* A Unit Sequence Group only applies to a WMS-enabled item, and indicates how to handle an item's UM for warehouse management transactions at WMS-enabled warehouses. For example, an item may have four different units of measure (such each, box, carton and pallet) with applicable UM conversion factors, and the four different UM are defined as part of a Unit Sequence group. Alternatively, an item may have just one unit of measure (such as each), but the item still requires a Unit Sequence Group with a single UM value. More than one user-defined Unit Sequence Group may be needed to support the differing UM values for different items. A subsequent section provides further explanation about unit of measure considerations for an item (Section 4.7)

4.4 Significance of the Storage Dimension Group for an Item

A user-defined Storage Dimension Group represents one aspect of the essential information that must be assigned to an item, and it consists of several policies which can be broadly segmented into two groups. One group of policies determines the use of site, warehouse and bin locations, and a second group is related to the basic versus advanced approach to warehouse management.

Policies related to the use of Site, Warehouse and Bin Location Most scenarios will track an item's inventory by site, warehouse and bin location, while other scenarios simply require site and warehouse. The related policies can reflect the following considerations.

◆ Indicate mandatory entry of the site and warehouse (and bin location) for inventory transactions, and prevent entry of a blank value.

◆ Indicate the need for financial tracking of an item's inventory by site and warehouse, or simply by site.

◆ Indicate whether an item's coverage planning policies apply to the site or the site/warehouse.

◆ Indicate whether an item's purchase prices will represent companywide or site/warehouse-specific values.   The selected choice is displayed when defining purchase price trade agreements.

◆ Indicate whether an item's sales prices will represent companywide or site/warehouse-specific values.   The selected choice is displayed when defining sales price trade agreements.

Two additional policies for a Storage Dimension Group are termed Warehouse-Specific Setup. One policy indicates whether the warehouse is a mandatory entry on inventory-related transactions such as sales order line items. The second policy (termed Primary Stocking) indicates whether you want to lock the specified warehouse when reserving the item's inventory, otherwise the system allows overrides for reserving from a different warehouse.

Policies related to the Basic versus Advanced Warehouse Management The policy "use warehouse management processes" indicates a WMS-enabled item, and automatically results in use of the Inventory Status and License Plates. These two dimensions within a Storage Dimension Group are not available for any option which does not include the "use warehouse management process" policy. A subsequent chapter about warehouse management provides further explanation of Inventory Status (Section 16.2) and License Plates (Section 16.4).

4.5 Using Templates for Partially Populating Item Information

A template can be used to automatically populate many aspects of the company-level information for an item, thereby simplifying the item definition process.[2] The following guidelines describe the creation and use of an item template.

♦ *Create template based on a released product.* A template can only be created from a selected item on the Released Products form (in edit mode). The desired template information should be populated for the item prior to creating the template, and the template name should reflect the nature of the information. Most firms will employ several templates that reflect their dominant business models for items. A simplistic example would be a template for a material item with batch tracking and an inventory UM of kilograms; another example would be a template for a material item with an inventory UM of each and no batch tracking.

When creating a template, you designate whether it represents a personal template or shared template. Personal templates are only available to the user who created the template, whereas a shared template can be accessed by any user.

♦ *Applying a template to an already-released product.* Applying a selected template will update the item information for the selected item. The initial step involves selecting the relevant item on the Released Products form, and then applying the template. This approach allows you to release products and then mass update the newly-created item numbers.

♦ *Applying a template when creating items via the single-company approach to item definition.* You select the desired template as part of the Create Product dialogue.

Some aspects of item information cannot be updated from a template, since they reflect additional tables that must be populated. For example, this includes lead times and order modifiers (defined on the Default Order Settings form), and item costs for a specified costing version (defined on the Item Price form). Figure 4.3

---

[2] Dynamics AX provides two basic approaches to templates which differ in their creation and use. The item template represents the unique approach in terms of how you create it, and how it can be applied after creating an item. All other templates employ a different approach to creation, and they can only be used when you initially create a record (such as a new customer or a new delivery mode). They cannot be applied after you create a record.

provides additional examples of item information that can and cannot be populated by item templates.

Figure 4.3 Examples of Item Information Populated by Templates

Category of Information	Populate via Template	Cannot Populate via Template
Engineering	Production Type	
Planning	Coverage Group	
Inventory Management	Inventory UM Storage Dimension Group Tracking Dimension Group Reservation Hierarchy * Unit Sequence Group *	Item-specific UM conversions Physical dimensions of different UM for item Policies for planned transfer orders
Manufacturing		Order quantity modifiers for production Production lead time
Procurement	Company-wide preferred vendor Buyer responsibility Default purchasing UM	Approved vendors for item Vendor item number Purchasing lead time Order quantity modifiers for purchase orders
Sales	Default sales UM Alternative product for sales	Customer item number Order quantity modifiers for sales orders
Accounting	Item Group (G/L account numbers) Financial dimension for item Item Model Group (Std vs Actual Cost)	Standard cost for an item
Quality Management	Batch numbering policy Serial numbering policy	Product testing requirements for an item Batch attributes for an item

4.6 Descriptive Information about an Item

Several types of descriptive information can be defined for a product and an item. This includes the enterprise-level information such as the Product Name and Extended Description, as well as company-level information such as physical dimensions.

Product Name and Extended Description The descriptive information for a product number consists of two fields -- for a product name and an optional extended description -- that represent enterprise-level data for an item. The Product Name field is a fixed length field where the number of characters can be easily expanded. The Extended Description field consists of unlimited descriptive text. Language-specific translations can be defined for both fields. The item's extended description is automatically inherited by a sales order line or purchase order line, and it can be optionally overridden.

Document Handling Capabilities (aka Attachments) The document handling capabilities apply to products and items, and allow entry of extended text using a document type of "Note". Other document types include Word files, Excel spreadsheets, images and various file formats. One or more documents can be attached to a product or an item. These document handling capabilities apply to more than just items; they apply to almost every construct within AX, ranging from master files and setup information to orders and invoices.

A document type of note has several additional characteristics. A note document related to an item number can be inherited by a sales line or purchase line for the item; a note document can also be added manually to the line item. In addition, you can designate whether a note document relates to internal or external purposes. For example, an external note document assigned to a sales line or purchase line can be optionally printed on order documents, as defined by the form setup policies for each type of document. The ability to create types of note documents -- and then assign the note type to a note -- can be creatively used for classification purposes, such as note types related to customer instructions about delivery or material handling.   These classifications can then be used to selectively print the type of note document. The effective use of notes is further described as a key consideration for sales orders (Section 11.3) and purchase orders (Section 12.3).

The document handling capabilities are also used to support MSDS documents for regulated products, and to support printing of these documents with a sales order packing list or invoice.

4.7 Unit of Measure Considerations for an Item

Considerations about an item's unit of measure (or UM for short) are important for multiple groups within a company, including purchasing, sales, engineering, production, and warehousing. Each group sometimes has unique requirements for an item's UM, The unit of measure codes and the assignment of an item's authorized UM represent enterprise-level information, whereas other UM considerations represent company-level information. These considerations are reflected in the following topics within the section.

- ◆ Definition of Unit of Measure Codes
- ◆ Inventory UM for an Item
- ◆ Authorized UM for an Item
- ◆ Weight/Volume and Physical Dimensions for an item's UM
- ◆ Default UM for Sales or Purchases of an Item
- ◆ UM Considerations for the Advanced WMS approach

Definition of Unit of Measure Codes The unit of measure codes represent enterprise-level information that is language specific. The codes for two different systems of units – metric units and US standard units – are automatically loaded into AX, along with the unit conversion factors (such as grams per kilogram). Additional units of measure must be defined (such as box and case), and the UM conversion factors are often item specific (such as the number of items per box).

Inventory UM for an Item Each item requires one UM for costing and inventory purposes. This is termed the inventory UM or base UM. An item's inventory UM is reflected in its inventory balances, replenishment calculations, product costs, and many of the inventory transactions. It is also reflected in the definition of BOM and routing information for a manufactured item, where component quantities and time requirements are typically expressed per the item's inventory UM. The inventory UM for an item cannot be changed after you report inventory transactions, so the assignment of an inventory UM requires careful consideration.

Authorized UM for an Item The item's inventory UM represents an authorized UM for the item. Any other UM must be authorized before it can be used for the item. An authorized UM means it has a UM conversion factor that ties it back to the item's inventory UM. Standard UM conversions apply to UM codes representing metric or US standard units, such as conversions between kilograms, grams, and milligrams. Additional UM codes such as box and case may need to be defined, along with their UM conversion factors for an item. When entering transactions for an item, you can view an item's authorized UM in the drop-down list for the UM field.

Weight/Volume and Physical Dimensions for an item's UM An item's weight/volume and physical dimensions can be defined via two options. As the preferred option, you define this information for one or more of the item's authorized UM (including the item's inventory UM) using the Physical Dimensions form. The volume is automatically calculated based on the physical dimensions.   Alternatively, you can define this information for just the item's inventory UM using the Released Products form. The first option represents a greater level of specificity for the source of information used by the system, and it can automatically populate the fields maintained by the second option. The weight, volume and dimensions have an implied unit of measure (such as pounds, cubic inches and inches), which means that a consistent interpretation should be applied to the values.

Default UM for Sales or Purchases of an Item You can optionally specify an item's default UM for sales orders and purchase orders. These represent companywide defaults for the item with the following impacts.

◆ *Default UM for Sales Orders.* An item's default sales UM applies to the definition of its order quantity modifiers for sales orders (for a minimum, multiple, maximum, and standard order quantity). The item's default sales UM and order quantity modifiers are normally reflected in a manually entered sales order line. However, when you specify a sales agreement for the sales order, the item's sales UM will default to the sales agreement.

◆ *Default UM for Purchase Orders.* An item's default purchase UM applies to the definition of its order quantity modifiers for purchase orders (for a minimum, multiple, maximum, and standard order quantity). The item's default purchase UM and order quantity modifiers are normally reflected in a manually entered purchase order line. However, when you specify a purchase agreement for the purchase order, the item's purchase UM will default to the purchase agreement.

Many items only require a single unit of measure. In these cases, you can simplify system usage by assigning the same UM to the item's inventory UM and to the item's default UM for purchase orders and sales orders.

UM Considerations for the Advanced Approach to Warehouse Management The advanced approach employs license plates, where the assignment of a license plate ID often reflects a physical pallet. The term "physical pallet" will be used to simplify the explanation. An item typically has a standard quantity per physical pallet. You must define the UM conversion when the standard quantity is greater than one, such as the number of pieces per pallet. Some items involve additional UM conversion factors, such as pieces per box and boxes per physical pallet.

These UM considerations must be reflected in the Unit Sequence Group assigned to the item, which defines several warehouse policies related to the use of mobile device transactions -- especially for receipts. You typically define several Unit Sequence Groups reflecting the common UM considerations related to your products, and then assign the applicable group to each item. For example, the group should include a UM code that represents an item's inventory UM and another UM code representing a physical pallet. Several additional policies apply to the UM codes within a Unit Sequence Group. For example, by identifying the UM code that represents a physical pallet for the item (and an item's standard quantity per physical pallet), the system will suggest the number of license plates when receiving a large number of pieces.

4.8 Significance of the Production Type for a Material Item

The assignment of a *Production Type* to a material item impacts how the item can be used. The production type indicates whether an item is manufactured or purchased, and whether a manufactured item employs the BOM or formula approach to product structure information. Most scenarios in discrete manufacturing will only use a BOM approach to product structure, and the following two values for a production type.[3]

◆ *None.* A production type of *None* indicates the item represents purchased material. You cannot define BOM or routing information for the item, or create production orders for the item.

◆ *BOM.* A production type of *BOM* indicates a manufactured item, and you can define bill of material and routing information for the item. The item can also be purchased.

The production type of an item can be changed from *None* to *BOM*. However, changing it from *BOM* to *None* has an additional impact because the item can no longer have BOM information, so that the Master BOMs assigned to the item (if any) will be automatically removed.

The production type provides one indicator of whether an item is manufactured or purchased. However, the actual make/buy indicator is embedded in the *planned order type* for the item. For example, the planned order type indicates whether master scheduling logic should generate planned production orders or planned purchase orders. The planned order type of production also indicates that cost calculations should consider an item's BOM/routing information.

---

[3] The other possible values only apply to process manufacturing scenarios. A value of *Formula* indicates a manufactured item, where you define its product structure using the Formula approach rather than the BOM approach. The other three values support manufacturing scenarios involving a *Co-Product, By-Product* and/or *Planning Item.*

4.9 Additional Information for a Purchased Item

A purchased item is typically indicated by its primary source of supply of planned purchase orders (as part of the item's coverage planning data). However, purchase orders can be created for any material item.

The definition of information for a purchased item involves several activities performed by different roles, such as the purchasing agent, cost accountant and quality manager. Various aspects of defining a purchased item are summarized in this section, along with references to more detailed explanations provided throughout the book.

- Define and enforce approved vendors for an item (Section 12.2)
- Define purchase prices and discounts for an item using trade agreements (Section 12.5) or blanket purchase orders (Section 12.6)
- Define planning data for a purchased item (Section 9.3)
- Assign a cost group to a purchased item (Section 7.3)
- Define standard costs for a purchased item (Section 7.4)
- Define serial or batch tracking policies for an item (Sections 8.1 and 8.3)
- Define batch attributes for an item (Section 8.5)
- Define testing requirements for an item (Section 17.4)

Some scenarios define a category hierarchy for procurement purposes, where the hierarchy consists of different nodes that reflect a classification of purchased products. This is commonly termed a procurement category hierarchy, and you assign purchased products to the relevant node (aka the product category). This information can be used in several ways. For example, you can automatically create purchase order lines via selection of products from a purchase category hierarchy, or define a purchase agreement and an associated discount percentage based on a total commitment value for a specified product category. The product categories can also be used for purchase spend analysis.

4.10 Additional Information for a Manufactured Item

A manufactured item is typically indicated by its primary source of supply of planned production orders (as part of the item's coverage planning data). However, production orders can be created for any material item with an approved BOM.

The definition of information for a manufactured item involves several activities performed by different roles, such as the product designer, process engineer, production planner, cost accountant and quality manager. Various aspects of defining a manufactured item are summarized in this section, along with references to more detailed explanations provided throughout the book.

- ◆ Define the bill of material for a manufactured item (Chapter 5)
- ◆ Define the routing for a manufactured item (Chapter 6)
- ◆ Define the BOM and routing for a subcontract manufactured item (Chapter 15)
- ◆ Calculate standard costs for a manufactured item (Section 7.7)
- ◆ Calculate planned costs for a manufactured item (Section 7.9)
- ◆ Define planning data for manufactured item (Section 9.5)
- ◆ Define serial or batch tracking policies for an item (Sections 8.1 and 8.3)
- ◆ Define batch attributes for an item (Section 8.5)
- ◆ Define testing requirements for an item (Section 17.4)

With the current AX design, a product must be released to a company before you can define its BOM information as part of the company-level information for the manufactured item.

4.11 Additional Information for a Salable Item

Some scenarios define a category hierarchy for sales purposes, where the hierarchy consists of different nodes that reflect a classification of salable products. This is commonly termed a sales category hierarchy, and you assign salable products to the relevant node (aka the product category). This information can be used in several ways. For example, you can automatically create sales order lines via selection of products from a sales category hierarchy, or define a sales agreement and an associated discount percentage based on a total commitment value for a specified product category. The product categories can also be used for sales analysis purposes.

Other aspects of defining a salable item are summarized in this section, along with references to more detailed explanations provided throughout the book.

◆ Define sales price trade agreements (Section 11.6)
◆ Define sales agreements for blanket sales orders (Section 11.7)
◆ Assign the start dates for selling and shipping a new product (Section 11.3)
◆ Manage direct delivery orders for a purchased item (Section 11.8)
◆ Manage special orders for a purchased item (Section 11.9)
◆ Manage a production order linked to a sales order (Section 11.11)

4.12 Company versus Site/Warehouse Information for an Item

The concept of company- versus site/warehouse-specific information applies to several aspects of item information. The concept is introduced now, and subsequent chapters provide more detailed explanations. Figure 4.4 summarizes some of the major examples of company versus site/warehouse information.[4]

Figure 4.4 Companywide versus Site/Warehouse Information for an Item

	Type of Information	Company-Wide	Site-Specific	Warehouse-Specific
		Level of Information		
Basic	Item Identifier	Yes	N/A	
Basic	Inventory UM	Yes	N/A	
Costing	Costing Method (Standard vs Actual)			
Costing	Standard Cost for Item	N/A	Yes	
Costing	Actual Cost for Item	N/A	Yes	
Planning	Approved Vendor	Yes	N/A	
Planning	Primary Source of Supply	Specify (Act as default)	Override the default	
Planning	Coverage Group (Set of Policies)	Specify (Act as default)	Override the default	
Planning	Preferred Vendor	Specify (Act as default)	Override the default	
Planning	Purchasing Lead Time			
Price	Purchase Price Trade Agreement	Yes		
Price	Sales Price Trade Agreement	Yes		
Mfg	BOM for a Manufactured Item	Yes	Yes	N/A
Mfg	Routing for a Manufactured Item	N/A	Yes	N/A

---

[4] The figure does not include the enterprise-level information about the basis for item identification (item number) and the nature of the item (tangible material), as previously illustrated in Figure 4.2.

The companywide item information includes the item identifier and inventory UM.   Other aspects of an item can reflect companywide information, or site- and warehouse-specific information.   For example, an item's companywide information includes the costing method for standard versus actual. An item's standard costs can only be maintained as site-specific information, whereas an item's actual costs can be tracked by site or warehouse.

The companywide information for a purchased item includes its approved vendors. It also includes the default values for the item's coverage planning policies -- such as the preferred vendor -- which can be overridden as site/warehouse-specific policies.   In addition, the applicability of sales and purchase trade agreement information can be companywide or site/warehouse-specific, as defined by the policies embedded in the Storage Dimension Group assigned to an item.

A manufactured item produced in more than one site can have a companywide BOM that applies to all sites, or it can be site-specific. In contrast, the routing for a manufactured item must be site-specific, and resources must be site-specific.

4.13 Inventory Costing and Financial Reporting for Items

Several item-related policies impact inventory costing and financial reporting for items. These policies include the inventory valuation method, the item group, and the financial dimension assigned to an item, as described below.

Inventory Valuation Method   Item costs provide the basis for valuing inventory transactions. An item's costs can be based on a standard costing or actual costing method (such as FIFO, LIFO, and weighted average cost), as defined by the costing method policy embedded in the Item Model Group assigned to the item. Chapter 7 provides further explanation about maintaining standard costs and actual costs.

G/L Accounts and the Item Group The Item Group assigned to an item defines the G/L account numbers impacted by the item's inventory transactions. For example, some of the key G/L accounts include inventory, revenue, cost of goods sold (COGS), and purchase price variances. The item groups and their G/L account numbers do not need to reflect product lines when using a financial dimension for items. For example, the value for the item's financial dimension supports revenue, COGS and inventory by product line.

The item groups assigned to purchased items typically have a parallel with the cost groups assigned to these same items. Cost groups serve a slightly different purpose, since they provide cost group segmentation in the calculated costs of manufactured items. The cost groups also provide an alternative approach for assigning G/L account numbers related to standard cost variances, as illustrated in Case 7.8. A subsequent chapter about product costing provides further explanation about the significance of cost groups (Section 7.3).

The item group can serve several other purposes in addition to the assignment of G/L account numbers, as summarized in the next section. These other purposes often result in multiple item groups with the same G/L account numbers.

Financial Dimension assigned to Items The combination of a financial dimension value and G/L account number provide the basis for financial reporting. With a product line dimension, for example, you define the possible values for different product lines. The applicable value for a product line can then be assigned to an item, which will be inherited by any item-related transaction. On a sales line, for example, the financial dimensions could reflect the customer type and product line, where the product line value gets inherited from the item and the customer type gets inherited from the customer.

The assignment of a financial dimension for a business unit has special significance when assigned to an item, since it supports financial reporting by business unit.

Financial dimensions can also be assigned to other entities such as customers, vendors, and sites to support multidimensional reporting. For example, the financial dimension assigned to sites (with a different value for each site) supports financial reporting site by site.

4.14 Significance of the Item Group for an Item

The primary rationale for assigning different item groups to items is to support the assignment of G/L account numbers, as described in the previous section. However, the item group can be used in multiple contexts that may be parallel with (or different from) the assignment of G/L account numbers. The multiple contexts often justify the definition of multiple item groups with the same G/L account numbers. The following examples summarize the major contexts.

Item Groups for Similar Salable Items The item group has multiple purposes related to similar salable items, as illustrated below.

◆ *Forecasting a Group of Items (aka Planning Bill).* A forecast can be defined for an item group rather than an individual item. This method employs a user-defined template (termed an *item allocation key*) that spreads out a total quantity across several items based on a mix percentage per item. The applicable items are typically assigned the same item group,

◆ *Sales Analysis by Item Group.* As one example, a pivot table inquiry provides multi-dimensional sales analysis based on sales by item group and customer group.

Item Groups for Similar Manufactured Items The Item Group may represent similarities in the items' production process. As the primary example, you can define the applicability of a master operation to a subset of manufactured items with the same Item Group. The Item Group also provides one basis for the applicability rules related to overhead formulas (Section 7.6). For example, the overhead formulas for material-related overheads can differ for different groups of manufactured items.

As additional examples, you can filter planned production orders based on the Item Group and maintain coverage planning policies for a group of items with the same Item Group. In addition, you can assign an Item Group to a Master BOM in order to filter a displayed list of BOMs, but this only acts as reference information.

4.15 Alternative Item Identifiers

Several approaches can support an alternative identifier for an internal item number. These approaches include an alternative item number to support bar coding, external item numbers for a customer or vendor, and an external code that represents the identifier for UPC, GTIN or EAN purposes. The item's search name (aka alias) can also be used as an alternative identifier.

Alternative Item Identifier for Bar Coding Purposes The bar code for an item requires an explicit mapping between the internal item number and the bar code digits, even when the bar code digits are exactly the same. The mapping also defines the bar code size and type (such as EAN13 or EAN128/UCC128). If required, the system supports two different bar code identifiers for the same item: one for scanning and one for printing purposes.

Customer or Vendor Item Numbers (aka External Item Numbers) An internal item number can be associated with other item identifiers for sales and purchasing purposes. These are termed external item numbers. Each external item number can be mapped to one internal item number and have a separate description.

♦ *Customer Item Number.* The external item number is specified for a single customer to reflect a customer item number. In some cases, it can be specified for a group of customers (or all customers) to reflect a catalog item number or an industry standard.

♦ *Vendor Item Number.* The external item number is specified for a single vendor to reflect a vendor item number.

GTIN or UPC Number for an Item (aka External Code) Different types of external codes can be defined to represent an industry standard such as the UPC (Universal Product Code) number, EAN (European Article Number) or GTIN (Glaboal Trade Item Number) identifier. You can then define the mapping between an internal item number and the associated identifier for a selected external code.

Alternative Item Identifier for Electronic Transactions Electronic exchange of documents with customers and vendors is supported by various methods such as Microsoft Biztalk. These documents include sales orders and purchase orders. As part of the setup for each type of document, the item identification can be based on the internal item number, the external item number (described above), or the external code (described above).

Search Name (aka Alias) for an Item The search name is displayed in many of the drop-down lookups for an item, and represents an alternative identifier.

4.16 Item Identification using an Item Number and Variant Codes

Some scenarios can benefit from item identification based on the combined identifiers of an item number and one or more additional fields, where each additional field is termed a variant code. In AX terminology, this means you initially define each item by assigning a Product Type of *Item*, a Product Subtype of *Product Master*, and a Configuration Technology of *Predefined Variant*. You also assign a Product Dimension Group to indicate the applicable variant code(s).

Standard AX includes four possible variant codes named size, color, style and configuration.[5] You define the possible values of a variant code for a given item, such the values for an item's color or size. The use of multiple variant codes for a given item also requires definition of the valid combinations of these values. The use of a variant code (and its possible values) represents enterprise-level information of an item.

Several aspects of item information can only be defined for an item number, so that they apply to all of its variants. These item-related fields include the following.

- Inventory UM, and the defaults for Sales UM and Purchase UM
- UM Conversions
- Item Group and the associated G/L accounts
- Approved Vendor
- Assignment to a Product Category
- Batch tracking and the policies for assigning a batch number
- Batch attributes
- MSDS document
- Item characteristics for production sequencing purposes

Other aspects of item information can be defined for each combination of values for applicable variant codes, as illustrated below.

- Vendor item number
- Customer item number
- UPC code or other External code
- Sales prices, based on a policy within the Product Dimension Group
- Purchase prices, based on a policy within the Product Dimension Group
- Standard costs, based on an item-specific policy (termed the "use combination cost price" policy) that enables variants to have a different cost
- Item Coverage policies, such as planned order type, preferred vendor and lead time
- Attachments
- Routing information for a manufactured item
- BOM information for a manufactured item
- Supplies and demands identified by variant

---

[5] When using AX 2012 R3, you can rename a variant code and also create and name additional variant codes. These capabilities do not currently work in the "New AX" release.

4.17 Other Types of Items

The book focuses on items representing material, but many manufacturing and distribution environments also require other types of items. Examples include service items and non-stock material. Another example includes configurable items for custom product manufacturing, as described in a subsequent chapter (Section 19.3).

Item Identification of a Service An item number can represent a service, where you designate a product type of *Service* when initially creating the new item number. You also assign an Item Model Group with a "not stocked product" policy and an actual cost valuation method, and a separate Item Group that represents the services.

Some scenarios involve subcontract manufacturing. The AX approach to subcontract manufacturing employs a separate item number to represent the subcontracted service, where you also define the item as a component within the parent item's BOM. A subsequent chapter explains the definition of items representing subcontracted services (Section 15.3).

Item Identification of Non-Stock Material Item numbers can identify non-stock items, typically representing indirect material used for maintenance, repair, and operations (MRO) purposes. The inventory of non-stock material is not tracked, and standard costs do not apply. You typically define a unique Item Model Group with a "not stocked product" policy and a FIFO valuation method, and assign it to non-stock material.[6] In addition, you typically define a separate Item Group for non-stock material. Trade agreements can be defined for the non-stock material, such as purchase price trade agreements.

4.18 Workspaces Related to Item Definition

Several predefined workspaces are related to item definition, as described in the following summary of each workspace and its applicable functionality.

Released Product Maintenance Workspace This workspace identifies items with a stopped flag for sales, purchasing and/or inventory. Removal of the stopped flags represents an approval step in the typical process to define a material item (Section 4.2). It also identifies recently released products within a user-defined number of days. You can view all released products and create new ones.

---

[6] One implication of a "not stocked product" is that the item cannot be specified as a component in a BOM.

Product Readiness for Discrete Manufacturing Workspace   The Product Readiness workspace has two variations -- one for discrete manufacturing (using the BOM approach to product structure) and one for process manufacturing (using the Formula approach). Both variations identify items with incomplete information or an expected change. An expected change can reflect a product change case for an item. For a manufactured item, the workspace identifies an expected change related to a BOM version expiring within the item's lead time, and it identifies the incomplete information about missing an active BOM version.

The links provide access to information about cases and items (including BOMs and routes), and also routing-related details (such as resources, master operations and mass maintenance of resource requirements). Menu items also provide access for defining a new Master BOM or Route, or a new case.

Cost Administration Workspace   This workspace identifies items with a missing active cost, including standard cost items without an active item cost record. The active cost is typically calculated for manufactured items based on BOM and route information.

This workspace covers additional aspects of cost administration that apply to other chapters, such as identifying production orders with high variances (Section 14.12) and providing links to reports/inquiries about inventory accounting (Section 16.6).

Product Variant Model Definition Workspace   This workspace summarizes several aspects of information about product masters, including the use of predefined variants as part of item identification (Section 4.16). It identifies the product masters that need to be released and product change cases related to items. It identifies items that have not yet been assigned the values for predefined variants, and the items where values have been defined but not yet released. The links provide access to information about the variant codes and possible values. Menu items provide access for defining a new product master or a new case. Additional uses of the workspace apply to other variations of a configuration technology, and a subsequent chapter describes these variations (Section 19.8).

Category and Product Management Workspace   This workspace focuses on the use of product categories, especially for retail purposes. You can view and maintain information about products by category and the released products by category.

4.19 Additional Case Studies

Case 4.1: Customer Supplied Material An item representing customer supplied material was used as a component in a manufactured product. The item was treated just like any other purchased material, except that its site-specific standard costs were assigned a zero value. This approach supported BOM information about the component, and also provided visibility of requirements, coordination via purchase orders, and tracking of receipts, inventory and material usage.

Case 4.2: Product Categories for Sales Purposes An equipment manufacturer defined a three level category hierarchy to support sales-related trade promotions. The lowest level of the category hierarchy -- termed the product category -- was assigned to each saleable product. The category hierarchy represents enterprise-level information for an item. Figure 4.5 summarizes an example of the category hierarchy for sales. As noted in the figure's comments, one level in category hierarchy (the brand level) is also mirrored in the business unit financial dimension assigned to an item number, which represents company-level information and supports financial reports by brand.

Figure 4.5 Example Category Hierarchy for Sales Purposes

Level	Description	Examples	Comments
0	Sales Hierarchy	N/A	
1	Brand	SuperTech	Brand also defined as a Business Unit Financial Dimension, with a value assigned to an Item Number
2	Family	Appliances	
3	Product Category	Blenders	
N/A	Product	12345	Product Category assigned to a Product Number

Case 4.3: Enterprise-Level Policies for Items in a Multicompany Supply Chain A manufacturing/distribution business modeled their multicompany operation using multiple companies within an AX instance, and goods flowed between different AX sites/warehouses in the different companies. As part of the enterprise-level policies for items, they standardized their item identification and product names, the UM conversion factors and NMFC code for each item, and enforcement of batch number tracking and the use of storage

dimensions.   Other company-level policies and data about each item were considered to be the responsibility of each company.

Case 4.4: Variant Codes for Hardware   A hardware manufacturer of screws, bolts and nuts was considering the use of variant codes to replace their current item numbering scheme.   The current scheme used significant digits in the item number to represent a product, its characteristics, and its pack sizes.   For example, the characteristics of a bolt included length, diameter, finish, and head type, and the pack sizes included 10, 100, and 500 counts.   The existing item master had thousands of item numbers reflecting different combinations of these attribute values.   The number of new items was growing to meet customer-specific demand for additional variations.   The proposed scheme consisted of an item number to represent the product (such as a type of bolt) and several variant codes to represent the product characteristics and pack sizes.   The proposed scheme would simply data maintenance about item identification, such as simply adding new values for relevant variant codes and automatically creating new combinations of the values.

4.20 Executive Summary

Item identification, units of measure, and descriptive information represent some of the basic issues for implementing an ERP system in distribution and manufacturing firms.   Item definition involves enterprise- and company-level information, and considerations about companywide versus site/warehouse-specific information.   This chapter included a typical business process for defining material items, and summarized the key aspects of purchased items, manufactured items and salable items.   It covered several aspects of inventory costing and financial reporting for items, especially the significance of the item group assigned to an item.   The chapter reviewed alternative item identifiers, and the use of variant codes for item identification purposes.   Several case studies described scenarios with customer supplied material, product categories, and enterprise-level policies for an item.

Chapter 5

Bill of Material Information

A key aspect of manufactured items consists of product structure information. The product structure is typically modeled by a bill of material (BOM) in discrete manufacturers. The BOM information defines the product design and provides the basis for product costing, material planning, material usage reporting, batch and serial number tracking, and tracking progress through stages of manufacturing. It often reflects considerations about the routing information, such as the material requirements for specific operations.

Standard products have predefined BOM information, whereas custom products typically involve creation of a unique BOM for a configurable item. This chapter focuses on BOM information for a standard product. A subsequent chapter covers the BOM information for a custom product based on the use of a configuration technology (Chapter 19).

This chapter begins with a typical process for defining an item's bill of material. Key aspects of the business process include the definition of BOM versions and BOM lines, and the maintenance of BOM information. Another key aspect involves the relevant option for defining the warehouse source of components. These considerations are reflected in the following sections within the chapter.

1. Typical Process to Define an Item's Bill of Material
2. Master BOMs and BOM Versions
3. BOM Version Policies for an Item
4. BOM Lines for Components
5. Define the Warehouse Source of Components in BOM/Routing Information
6. Order-Dependent BOM for a Production Order
7. Maintain BOM information
8. Maintain BOM Information using a Product Change Chase

71

Dynamics AX provides a second approach for modeling product structure information in process manufacturing scenarios. This is termed the Formula approach rather than the BOM approach to product structure. The Formula approach supports several special cases in discrete manufacturing, such as scenarios involving co-products, substitute components or production sequencing considerations. The Formula approach was illustrated in one of the common scenarios about polymer modeled products (Section 2.11), and in the cases about strip down (Case 5.10) and repair and overhaul of used equipment (Case 5.11). However, further explanation falls outside the book's scope.

5.1 Typical Process to Define an Item's Bill of Material

The typical business process to define an item's bill of material consists of several steps performed by a product designer role. These steps are illustrated in Figure 5.1 and summarized below. As a starting point, the product designer selects the desired item and accesses a separate form in order to create a new BOM version for the item. The new BOM version may involve creation of a new Master BOM or the assignment of an existing Master BOM. The BOM version policies include the effectivity dates. Each BOM line identifies a component and the required quantity. Upon completion of all information, the product designer approves and activates the item's BOM version.

Figure 5.1 Typical Process to Define an Item's Bill of Material

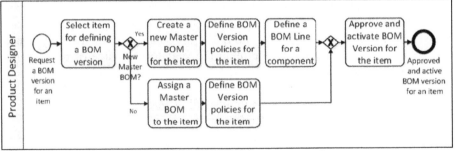

Create a new Master BOM for the Item The creation of a Master BOM typically occurs in the context of creating a new BOM version for a selected item, where the Master BOM is automatically assigned to the item. Each assignment is termed a BOM Version, and an item may have multiple BOM versions, such as different versions that represent site-specific BOMs or planned changes.

Assign an existing Master BOM to the item An existing Master BOM can be assigned to an item, typically reflecting scenarios when the Master BOM has been independently defined beforehand.

Define BOM Version policies The product designer employs the BOM version policies to specify the effectivity dates and to indicate whether the BOM version represents a companywide or site-specific BOM for the item.

Define BOM Line for a Component The product designer uses a BOM line to identify a component and its required quantity. Other considerations include the designated warehouse source of the component, the applicable operation number, and a scrap percentage.

Approve and Activate the BOM Version for the Item The product designer must approve a BOM version before it can be specified for a production order, and an approved version is typically activated for use in planning and costing calculations. Electronic signatures can be optionally employed as part of the approval process.

5.2 Master BOMs and BOM Versions

A master BOM has a unique identifier (termed the *BOM Number*) which can be manually or automatically defined. Manual definition should be used when the identifier needs to be meaningful. The creation of a master BOM typically occurs in the context of creating an item's BOM version, where it is automatically assigned to the item. A master BOM can also be created independently and then assigned to an item. Each assignment of a master BOM to an item is termed a *BOM Version*. A BOM version has several policies indicating the effectivity dates and whether it represents a site-specific or companywide bill of material for the item. Multiple BOM versions can be defined for an item, typically to support the following situations.

◆ Variations between sites producing the same manufactured item
◆ Planned changes with effectivity dates
◆ Revision levels of a manufactured item

◆   Variations that reflect larger production quantities

◆   Alternate bills of material

◆   Prototype or production ramp-up

In summary, a manufactured item can have multiple active BOM versions that reflect different sites, non-overlapping validity periods, and/or different quantity breakpoints. An item can also have approved-but-not-active BOM versions.

An item's BOM version is initially treated as unapproved, which still allows you to calculate the item's costs. It must be approved in order to specify it when creating a production order. Only an approved BOM version can be marked as active. The active BOM version for an item will normally be used in planning and cost calculations.

Electronic signatures can be optionally employed as part of the approval process. For example, you can be prompted for an electronic signature when approving a BOM version, or when designating a BOM version as active. Related situations may also require an electronic signature, such as releasing a production order or reporting the finished quantity for a production order.

5.3 BOM Version Policies for an Item

The BOM version policies serve several different purposes. For example, the policies enable a manufactured item to have multiple active BOM versions that reflect different sites and non-overlapping validity periods. The following explanation covers the key fields in the BOM version for an item.

Site-Specific versus Companywide BOM Versions Specifying a blank site for an item's BOM version indicates a companywide bill of material, whereas a specified site indicates a site-specific bill. The primary difference is that master scheduling logic will use a site-specific BOM version (if it exists) that matches the site of the item's requirements. If a site-specific BOM version does not exist, the master scheduling logic will use the companywide BOM version for the manufactured item. Master scheduling logic will generate an error message if an appropriate BOM version does not exist.

A secondary difference concerns the options for defining the warehouse source of a component. For example, the warehouse source can be manually specified for a site-specific BOM version, but not for a companywide BOM version. A subsequent section provides further explanation about the various options for designating the warehouse source of component inventory.

Effectivity Dates for an Item's BOM Version   The effectivity dates for an item's BOM version can represent planned changes in the item's product structure.   For example, a manufactured item may have two BOM versions -- one valid to date X and the other valid from date X+1 -- to indicate planned changes. A blank value for the starting and/or ending date indicates no limitation.   An item can have multiple active BOM versions with non-overlapping dates.

Quantity Breakpoints for an Item's BOM Version   In discrete manufacturing, the concept of quantity breakpoints does not generally apply to an item's BOM versions although it may apply to an item's route versions.   With different route versions reflecting different quantity breakpoints, for example, you can indicate different equipment for producing a larger production order quantity.   A planned production order will be assigned the relevant route version based on the required quantity.

5.4 BOM Lines for Components

A BOM line is used to define each component of a manufactured item.   Key aspects of a BOM line include the item identifier of the component, the required quantity, the associated operation number, and information about the warehouse source of the component.   This section summarizes several key aspects of defining a component, starting with the different approaches to defining component requirements.

Define Component Requirements as a Quantity   The component's required quantity reflects the variable amount needed to produce the parent item. The required quantity also reflects the specified UM for the component.   This quantity can be entered as a fraction or decimal.   A component's required quantity is normally expressed per a quantity of one parent item, but it can be expressed for a different quantity of the parent item (using the per series field).

Some basic variations to the required quantity include a fixed quantity, the rounding up policy, and planned scrap (expressed as a percentage or a fixed amount or both).   A special case of a component's required quantity reflects a non-linear or step-function relationship, but this does not typically apply to discrete manufacturer.

Define the Component's Required Quantity based on Measurement Calculations   A special case of a component's required quantity involves a calculation formula and measurement information, such as height, width, depth and density.   This approach often applies to cut-to-size components, such as a cut-to-length component where the component quantity depends on the length measurement of its parent item.   In this way, a single master BOM can be assigned to multiple manufactured items and each parent item will have a different measurement for length.

The component's rounding-up policy and multiple take on special significance in this approach. In the just cited example, let's assume the cut-to-length component has an 8-foot length that will be taken from 10-foot steel rod, so that the multiple is 10 and requirements are rounded to increments of 10.

Impact of the Operation Number assigned to a Component   When routing data exists, the operation number assigned to a component provides the key link between the BOM information and the associated operation within the routing. There are several impacts of assigning an operation number to a component. For example, the operation's scrap percentage affects component requirements, and the resource assigned to the operation can determine the relevant warehouse source for picking the component for a production order. These impacts are summarized below.

◆ Align the due date of a component with the start of its associated operation. Components with a blank operation number are required at the start of the production order.

◆ Align the due date of a component with the end of its associated operation, which typically applies to a component representing a subcontracted service.

◆ Calculate component requirements to reflect the scrap percentage of the operation, and its cumulative scrap percentage in a multi-step routing.

◆ Populate the picking list based on the started quantity for a specified operation number (or a range of operation numbers).

◆ Segment the picking list by operation number. A picking list can be generated for all components with the same operation number.

◆ Determine the resource that requires the component in order to support resource consumption logic about the warehouse source of component inventory.

The operation number assigned to a component should correspond to the operation number in the associated route version for the manufactured item. However, the operation number in the routing may not exist in some cases. For example, you can specify a different route version when manually creating a production order, or override the operations in the order-dependent routing.

Warehouse Source of a Component   A component's warehouse source indicates where to pick the item for a production order. There are several options for defining a component's warehouse source using BOM and routing information. The selected option impacts master scheduling logic about material requirements at the component's warehouse, and the related information will be inherited by the Production BOM and ultimately by the picking list journal for a production order.

As one of the simplest options, you can specify the component's warehouse source as part of the BOM line when using site-specific BOMs. Other options employ the "resource consumption" policy for each BOM line, which defers assignment of a warehouse source until a resource (or resource group) has been scheduled for each routing operation. This requires routing information and operation numbers linking BOM lines to specific operations. The next section provides further explanation about the various options for a component's warehouse source (Section 5.5).

Impact of the BOM Line Type   The BOM line type represents a key policy impacting supply chain management. In most cases, it simply designates whether a manufactured component will be treated as a normal item or a phantom item, as described below. However, it can also designate a make-to-order or buy-to-order component.

◆ *Item (or Normal).*   Master scheduling logic will suggest a planned order to satisfy requirements. These orders are not directly linked to the production order for the parent item.

◆ *Phantom.*   A phantom only applies to a manufactured item. The requirements for a phantom component are passed (or blow-through) to its components and routing operations. The impact of blow-through logic becomes obvious in the order-dependent BOM and routing for a production order. The netting logic within master scheduling ignores the phantom's on-hand inventory and scheduled receipts (if applicable), and suggests planned orders for the phantom's components to satisfy requirements.

BOM Line Type for a Make-to-Order or Buy-to-Order Component   The BOM line types of *Pegged Supply* and *Vendor* support make-to-order and buy-to-order components, as described below.

◆ *Make-to-order component.*   A line type of *pegged supply* applies to a manufactured item, and represents a make-to-order production strategy with direct linkage between production orders. That is, a production order for the parent automatically generates a linked order (termed a *sub-production* or *reference order*) for each manufactured component with a line type of pegged supply. [1] The system indicates linkage via the reference fields in each production order, and linked orders can be scheduled separately or synchronized.

The netting logic within master scheduling ignores the component's on-hand inventory and scheduled receipts, since the system assumes the component is being produced just for the parent item's production order. The master scheduling logic will generate planned production orders to provide visibility of requirements, but these planned orders cannot be firmed.

A make-to-order component was previously illustrated in a common scenario for a make-to-order production strategy (Section 2.4). Other sections describe its impact on coverage planning data for a manufactured item (Section 9.6) and common S&OP approaches (Section 10.9).

◆ *Buy-to-order component.* A line type of *Vendor* applies to a purchased item or service, and it represents a buy-to-order component. That is, a production order for the parent automatically generates a linked purchase order (also termed a reference order) for each purchased component with a line type of vendor. [2] Similar to make-to-order components, the system assumes the component is being purchased just for the parent item's production order, and master scheduling logic ignores the component's on-hand inventory and scheduled receipts. Master scheduling logic will generate planned purchase orders to provide visibility of requirements, but these planned orders cannot be firmed.

A buy-to-order component has one other unique feature, since a preferred vendor can be defined for the component as an override to the preferred vendor for the item. When automatically generating a linked purchase order, the system assigns the component's preferred vendor (if defined) or the item's preferred vendor to the purchase order. This line type is commonly used to support purchases of a component that represents a subcontracted service, and a subsequent chapter provides further explanation of subcontracted production (Chapter 15).

A line type of vendor can also be assigned to a manufactured component, and it works just like the line type of pegged supply. As a minor difference, this type of production order is labeled as *vendor* rather than *standard.* For

---

[1] The production order for a make-to-order component is automatically generated when the status of the parent item's production order has been changed from created to estimated, or to a higher status such as scheduled.
[2] The purchase order for a buy-to-order component is automatically generated when the status of the parent item's production order has been changed from created to estimated, or to a higher status such as scheduled.

example, a production order type of vendor could indicate that a subcontractor will produce the manufactured component.

A buy-to-order component was previously illustrated in a common scenario for a make-to-order production strategy (Section 2.4). Other sections describe its impact on coverage planning data for a purchased item (Section 9.4) and purchase order processing (Section 12.4).

Considerations about Planned Scrap   The planned scrap for a component can be expressed as a percentage or a fixed quantity or both. When using routing data, the planned scrap percentage for an operation can also affect the requirements of components associated with the operation. An accumulated scrap percentage may also apply in a multistep routing because of scrap percentages for previous operations. Each order-dependent BOM and routing (for a production order) inherit the scrap factors from the item's BOM version and route version, and these can be overridden. These scrap factors are included in planning and cost roll-up calculations.

Effectivity Dates of an Component   The effectivity dates provide one approach for managing planned changes to BOM information, as described in a subsequent section (Section 5.7).

Position Information for a Component   A component's position information provides reference data that can serve different purposes. For example, it can represent a sequential counter of components, often tied to the find number on drawings. It can identify a grouping of components, such as the material needed for an operation (when routing data does not exist), the delivery area for a group of picked components, or a group representing related parts in the production process. The position field also provides one approach for handling reference designators.

5.5 Define the Warehouse Source of Components in BOM/Routing Information

A component's warehouse source indicates where to pick the item for a production order. There are several options for defining a component's warehouse source using BOM and routing information. The selected option impacts master scheduling logic about material requirements at the component's warehouse, and the related information will be inherited by the Production BOM and ultimately by the picking list journal for a production order. This inherited information can be optionally overridden.

Three basic options are summarized in Figure 5.2 and explained below. These three options reflect the use of a picking list journal for reporting the picked material, which also indicates actual material usage for the production order. Each option involves considerations about BOM and routing information, and the requirements for additional information vary by option.

The fourth option displayed in Figure 5.2 represents a slightly different purpose for the picking list journal, and it must be employed when using the advanced approach to warehouse management. It assumes components will be picked and delivered to a production input location based on work orders for Raw Material Picking, so that the picking list journal is only used for reporting actual material usage from the production input location.

Option #1: Use the specified warehouse on the BOM line for the component   The first option only applies to a site-specific BOM version, and the specified warehouse must belong to the site. After creating a production order for the manufactured item, the component in the Production BOM inherits the component's specified warehouse.

Option #2: Use the default warehouse for the item   The second option does not specify a component warehouse on the BOM line, and requires additional information about the item's default inventory warehouse for each site (as defined in the item's site-specific order settings). After creating a production order, the component in the Production BOM inherits the component's default inventory warehouse for the required site.

A shown in the figure, the first two options do not require routing information, and they represent the most straight-forward approach. In addition, they do not employ the "resource consumption" policy on a BOM line, even when routing information has been defined.

Option #3: Automatically assign an input warehouse based on the scheduled resource and its related production unit   The third option requires routing information and operation numbers linking BOM lines to specific operations. It employs the "resource consumption" policy for each BOM line, which defers assignment of a warehouse source until a resource (or resource group) has been scheduled for each routing operation. A resource group has an assigned production unit, which might be assigned to multiple resource groups with a common warehouse source of components. This is termed the input warehouse for a production unit. After scheduling a production order, the component in the Production BOM inherits the input warehouse associated with the resource group performing the operation.

Figure 5.2 Variations in Warehouse Source of Components

Purpose of Picking List Journal		Pick from Locations in Suggested Warehouse Source of Components			Pick from Production Input Location
		Option #1	Option #2	Option #3	Option #4
		Use specified warehouse on BOM Line for component	Use default warehouse for item	Assign input warehouse based on production unit and scheduled resource	Assign production input location based on scheduled resource
BOM & Route		Site-Specific BOM	Applies to Site-Specific or Companywide BOM		
		Routing Information not Required	Routing Information Required		
Additional Information		BOM Line has no Resource Consumption Policy		BOM Line has Resource Consumption Policy and an Operation Number linked to Routing	
		None	Item's default inventory warehouse for required site	Resource group has an assigned production unit (with its input warehouse)	Resource group (or resource) has an assigned production input location

Legend: ☐ = Supports the Advanced WMS approach to warehouse management

Option #4: Automatically assign a production input location based on the scheduled resource The fourth option represents a different purpose for the picking list journal, as mentioned earlier. It assumes components will be delivered to a production input location which will be identified on the picking list journal for reporting actual material usage from the location. Delivering components to a production input location involves work orders for Raw Material Picking when using the Advanced WMS approach to warehouse management. It involves transfer journals or withdrawal kanbans when using the basic approach to warehouse management.

The fourth option requires routing information and operation numbers linking BOM lines to specific operations, and it also employs the "resource consumption" policy for each BOM line, just like the third option.

You define a location representing each production input location within a warehouse, so that it can be assigned to a resource group or to individual resources within the group. After scheduling a production order, the component in the Production BOM inherits the production input location associated with the resource group (or resource) performing the operation.

It is feasible to assign both a production input location and a production unit to a resource group, but the former will be used by scheduling logic for assigning the location to components in the Production BOM.

5.6 Order-Dependent BOM for a Production Order

An order-dependent BOM (aka Production BOM) refers to the BOM lines attached to a production order. It initially contains the BOM lines inherited from the BOM version used to create the production order. Changes to the order-dependent BOM do not affect the Master BOM. Creation and maintenance of the order-dependent BOM reflect several rules.

♦ Creation of a production order for a manufactured item also creates an order-dependent BOM.

♦ The order-dependent BOM initially reflects the item's BOM version that was used to create the production order. In most cases, this will be inherited from the active BOM version for the delivery date and site on the production order. However, you can manually specify a different BOM version for the item when creating the production order, where the BOM version can be approved-but-not-active.

♦ The order-dependent BOM contains components of a phantom.

♦ You can modify the components in an order-dependent BOM at any time prior to reporting the production order as Ended. For example, you can manually maintain the information, or copy BOM lines from another production order or Master BOM.

♦ A material item can be issued to a started production order even when the component does not exist on the order-dependent BOM. The issued component will be automatically added to the order-dependent BOM with a zero required quantity.

5.7 Maintain BOM Information

The maintenance of BOM information can serve different purposes such as planned changes, and several different approaches can be used. For example, you can directly maintain components in a Master BOM, update the BOM components using the copy function or the mass change function, or employ the graphical design tool within AX. This section covers the maintenance and analyses of BOM information, such as multi-level and where-used inquiries. An alternative approach to maintaining BOM information involves the use of product changes cases, as described in the next section.

Manage Planned BOM Changes using Effectivity Dates   Planned changes to an item's BOM can be managed by (1) the date effectivities for a component or (2) by date effectivities for a BOM version. Figure 5.3 illustrates these two options for managing planned changes, and the starting point of the original BOM. The figure reflects a simplistic bill of material to illustrate the options.

Figure 5.3 Manage Planned Changes to BOM Information

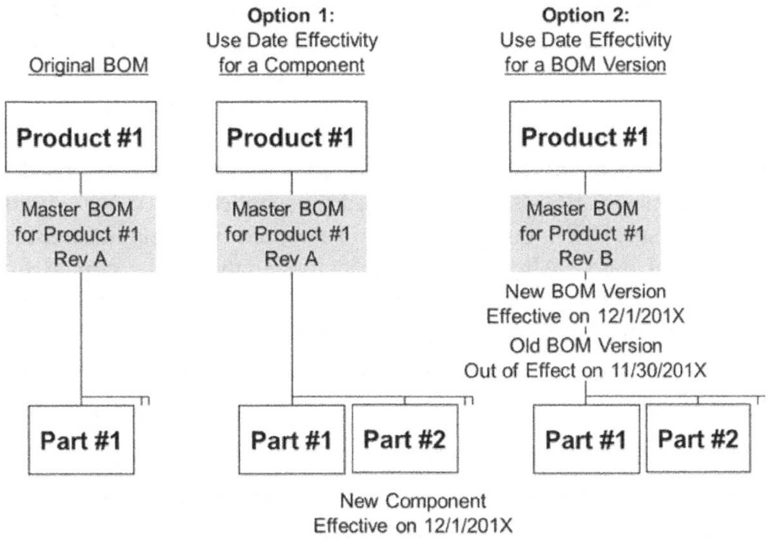

- *Option 1: Use Date Effectivity for a Component.* The first option employs date effectivities for a component. The example shown in the left side of Figure 5.3 illustrates the original BOM for Product #1 with a single BOM version (labeled Rev A) with a single component of Part #1. As shown in the example, a new component Part #2 can be added to the BOM version with a specified effectivity date such as 12/1/201X. A component can also be phased out on a specified date.

- *Option 2: Use Date Effectivity for a BOM Version.* The second option employs date effectivities for a BOM version. Using the example shown in the right side of Figure 5.3, a different Master BOM can be assigned to Product #1 that represents a different revision level (labeled Rev B versus the original Rev A). As shown in the example, you would phase out the assignment of the original Master BOM on the day prior to 12/1/201X, and phase in the assignment of the new Master BOM on 12/1/201X. The new Master BOM contains both Part #1 and Part #2. The approval status and active status for a BOM version provide an additional consideration for planned changes. Removing the approval status or the active status on a BOM version, or phasing out the effectivity date, provides a selective approach to discontinued use.

A third approach to managing planned changes represents a special case, and generally applies to make-to-order custom products. As part of the BOM line information, it employs a specified BOM version for a manufactured component, where the item's BOM version is approved but not necessarily active. This third approach can build on the use of component date effectivities to phase in and phase out specified BOM versions for a manufactured component.

Copying Components to a BOM   A copy function can be used to add components to master BOMs and to the order-dependent BOM for a production order. For a master BOM, components can be copied from another master BOM as of a specified date. Alternatively, the components can be copied from the order-dependent BOM associated with a specified production order. You determine whether the components will add to or replace the existing components. Hence, the copy function can be used multiple times to generate incremental additions.

The copy function also works for an order-dependent BOM. The copy-to information identifies the specified production order number, and the copy-from can be another production order or a master BOM.

Mass Changes to Components based on Where-Used Information
Where-used information provides the basis for a mass replace and a mass add function for maintaining components. You perform a mass change of BOM information using the periodic task *Change BOM Item.* You can select an item to be phased out or replaced, view the affected BOMs, selectively eliminate them from the update or change the required quantity, and then indicate when the new item should be phased in. This approach supports Option #1 for managing planned changes via date effectivities for a component.

Graphical Tools for Maintaining BOM Information   The BOM Designer provides a graphical tool for maintaining information about the BOM versions (and route versions) for an item. The form displays a multi-level product structure with an indented graphical format. You can edit or delete existing components, or add components via drag-and-drop from the displayed list of item master data. This graphical tool is employed in other contexts, such as displaying the BOM information during sales order entry.

Analyzing BOM Information Analysis tools for BOM information include multi-level BOM reports, and a multi-level costed BOM with routing information (based on cost roll-up calculations). The analysis tools also include where-used inquiries about a component item and a master BOM.

There are two other types of where-used inquiries that reflect information about existing production orders and batch tracking. The first type includes single- and multi-level pegging to the sources of demand and supply. The second type includes forward and backward batch tracking throughout the product structure.

5.8 Using a Product Change Case to Maintain BOM Information

An alternative approach to maintaining BOM information involves the use of cases that specifically handle product changes. Cases are typically used to manage issues raised by customers, vendors or employees, as described in a subsequent chapter about quality management (Section 17.8). However, you can assign a case category when creating a case so that it is designated as a product change case. The functionality for a product change case works differently than other types of cases. Each product change case represents an Engineering Change Order (ECO), and you define the items and BOM information affected by the ECO. The shortened term of an "ECO" will be used here as a synonym of the term "Product Change Case."

The key information for using a product change case consists of the associated items and BOM versions affected by the change. A simple-yet-typical scenario consists of an ECO to identify a planned change to an item's BOM version (and the relevant effectivity date). In this scenario, you can create a product change case for an item's existing BOM version. The product change case can then be used to define the new BOM version, and associated it and the new component items to the case. You can subsequently approve and activate the item's new BOM version. Another scenario consists of an ECO to identify a planned change to the BOM version for multiple items, such as replacing an existing component with a new component, and employing where-used information to identify the associated parent items and BOM versions impacted by the change. You can optionally enter detailed notes about the ECO and each associated item and/or BOM version, thereby providing a rationale and history of the changes.

The only required setup information consists of a user-defined case category that has been assigned a category type of Product Change. Most scenarios only need to define one case category, where a typical identifier is *Prod-Chg* or *ECO*. Some scenarios create more than one case category for product change cases, such as indicating different types of ECOs that have different validation criteria.

Each product change case is uniquely identified by a Case ID. After creating a case and a description, you can indicate progress (via the case status of opened, in-process, and closed or cancelled) and case resolution (of accept, reject or none). Some aspects of the functionality for a case do not necessarily apply to its use for ECO purposes. Examples include a case process (which consists of user-definable steps to follow when working on a case), a service level agreement (which defines a guaranteed response time), and knowledge articles.

A product change case can only manage planned changes to the BOM version for a manufactured item; it cannot support planned changes to a component's effectivity dates. While it can be used to support planned changes to the Route version for a manufactured item, this approach is not commonly employed for maintaining routing data.

5.9 Additional Case Studies

Case 5.1: Revision Levels for a Manufactured Item A manufacturer employed the BOM versions to represent the revision levels for a manufactured item, such as revision A, B and C. The inventory resulting from production of different revision levels was treated as interchangeable by master scheduling logic. For reference purposes, the identifier assigned to each Master BOM represented a combination of the item number and revision level. The item's BOM version policies identified the effectivity dates for phasing out (and phasing in) these BOM versions. A complete change in a product was identified by a different item number, since it represented the maxim about changing form/fit/function.

Case 5.2: Warehouse Source of Components A manufacturer produced items at different sites and employed site-specific BOM versions to define the components. The warehouse for each component's inventory was specified as part of the BOM line information. The company felt this approach was the most straight-forward to understand and simplest to maintain, and the warehouse source was not determined by the resource performing the operation. After creating a production order for the manufactured item, the component in the order-dependent BOM inherited the component's specified warehouse.

Case 5.3: CAD/PLM Integration The product designers at a manufacturing company required integration between their computer-aided design (CAD) package and information about items and bills of material.   For standard products, this involved importing information from the CAD package into the master BOM and viewing the CAD drawings via the document handling capabilities. The CAD package was used to generate 3D models (for viewing) and 2D layout drawings, and cut lists for assisting production personnel in completing the work. This integration helped reduce the man-hours to define drawings and bills, and the cost of errors such as production rework, field installation services and customer confidence.

Case 5.4: Kit Items A manufacturing company sold kits of material, where a separate item (and associated master BOM) defined each kit's components. Several types of kits could be sold. One type of kit was priced and sold as a single item, and posting the sales invoice resulted in backflushing of the item's components.   Another type of kit was priced and sold as separate component items. Each sales order line for a kit item was exploded into its components, thereby creating multiple line items with separate prices that were shipped and invoiced separately.   Other scenarios involved the selection of kit components from a predefined list, pricing based on the sum of sales prices for kit components, returns of an entire kit or selected components, and selective printing of kit information on sales-related documents.[3]

Case 5.5: Phantoms for Intermediate BOM Levels A toy company produced and sold cases of toys to retailers, where each case included boxes of the individual toy. Each box represented the consumer unit and an intermediate level of packaging. Each case and box of the toy had separate item numbers, with different UPC codes, weights and measurements. The box with an individual toy was treated as a phantom in the product structure because the packaging line could insert the toy into a box and pack them immediately into cases. It was sometimes stocked or sold separately. Figure 5.4 illustrates the phantom component in the product structure.

---

[3] See www.AXtension.com for additional information about their kitting add-on module for Dynamics AX.

Figure 5.4 Phantoms for Intermediate Packaging Levels

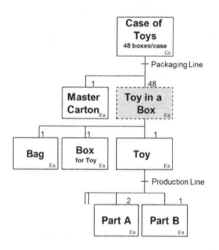

Case 5.6: Light Assembly A manufacturing company performed light assembly for both make-to-stock and make-to-order products, such as packaging purchased materials or painting/finishing items to customer specification. With stocked items, they used an order-less approach (termed the BOM Journal) to report completed units that auto-deducted components. With make-to-order items, a production order was created from (and directly linked to) the sales order line item. Customer specifications were identified on the order-dependent BOM and routing for the production order.

Case 5.7: ECOs and Revision Levels A manufacturing company used Engineering Change Orders (ECOs) to manage changes to their product structure. They required workflow capabilities for an ECO approval process, revision levels for purchased items (reflecting documentation changes) and revision levels for manufactured items (reflecting bill, routing, or documentation changes). The new revision level for a manufactured item, for example, could reflect a non-significant change (such as a new BOM version) or a significant change that required a new identifier for the item. The new identifier consisted of the item number and an additional field to identify a revision level.

Case 5.8: Engineering versus Production BOMs The engineering department wanted to define a separate engineering BOM and then convert it into a BOM for production purposes. They defined a separate BOM version for a manufactured item that represented the engineering BOM. At the appropriate time, it was copied into a different BOM version for production purposes, and it was subsequently approved and activated for production. The starting effectivity date for the BOM version considered current inventories and other factors.

Case 5.9: Cut-To-Size Materials A fabricated products company needed to express BOM requirements in terms of the number of pieces of cut-to-size materials, such as steel rod and sheet metal, but did not want to create item numbers for each unique size. They solved the problem using the calculation formula and measurements for a component's required quantity. One example involved sheet metal purchased in pounds, costed and stocked in 5x10 sheets, and with component requirements expressed in square feet. Each parent item produced from the sheet metal required different height and width measurements, but only one master BOM to calculate the required square footage in sheet-size increments (50 square feet). This approach also identified purchasing and stockroom picking requirements for the raw materials, and provided cut-to-size instructions for production.

Case 5.10: Strip Down of Used Electronics Products A manufacturing company purchased several types of used consumer electronics devices, and stripped them down to obtain reusable parts that could be sold. This required the formula approach (rather than the BOM approach) to model the business, especially the use of planning items for modeling disassembly. Figure 5.5 illustrates the planning item for disassembling one type of used device (Device XYZ), along with its sole component and its multiple co-products of several reusable parts. The expected quantity of each co-product reflected the reusable fraction that could be obtained from used devices. Unusable parts were thrown into a waste container, and the company paid a disposal fee per pound of waste. The item number for this waste was identified as a by-product, with an inventory UM of pounds and a cost reflecting the disposal fee per pound. From an S&OP perspective, the management team defined sales forecasts for the planning items that represented different used devices, and planning calculations identified the expected receipts of reusable parts.

Figure 5.5 Strip Down of Used Consumer Electronics Devices

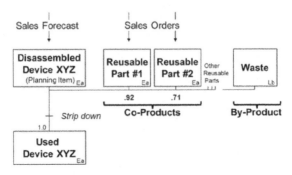

Case 5.11: Repair and Overhaul of Used Equipment A repair-and-overhaul business typically started with a used item, and then went through three phases (strip-down, repair and rebuild) to refurbish the item. Examples of similar businesses include the repair and overhaul of used transportation equipment, engines, auto parts, computers or other types of equipment. The used items often reflect a customer supplied item, a customer return, or purchases of used equipment.

The nature of repair and overhaul typically involves the formula approach (rather than the BOM approach) to model the business. Figure 5.6 illustrates the formula for a typical scenario, where a planning item represents the disassembled equipment, and co-products represent the reusable parts (with a decimal quantity reflecting the fraction that can actually be reused).

In this example, the Used Part-1 must be repaired and Used Part-3 can be "used as is." The figure shows a used assembly (Used Assy-2) that requires repair. However, it could be the starting point for further strip-down, which means it would be the only component of another planning item with co-products representing the expected parts. In many scenarios, inspection of the used equipment may identify the need for a predefined or ad hoc repair procedure. A predefined repair procedure can be modeled as an item number with predefined BOM and routing information, and a production order is used to report completion of the task. Ad hoc procedures are also modeled as an item number, but the required materials and labor are defined in the order-dependent BOM and routing. This example represents combination of the BOM and Formula approaches, since the formula and batch orders for a planning item model the strip-down steps and production orders can model the repair/rebuild steps.

Figure 5.6 Formula for Repair & Overhaul of Used Equipment

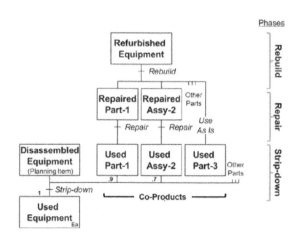

5.10 Executive Summary

Discrete manufacturers typically employ bills of material to model their product structure. This chapter summarized a typical business process for defining an item's bill of material, and described the key information about BOM version policies and BOM lines. It explained the different approaches to maintaining and analyzing BOM information, including the use of product change cases. Several case studies illustrated the use of BOM information, such as integration with a CAD package, engineering change control and kit items.

Chapter 6

Resources and Routings

Routing information provides a model of the processing steps for a manufactured item, expressed as operations that identify the production resource requirements. The routing information also provides the basis for calculating value-added costs, capacity planning and production scheduling of resources, reporting of actual labor and resource usage, and tracking progress through the processing steps. In addition, the bill of material often reflects considerations about an item's routing information, such as the material requirements for specific operations.

A single version of an item's routing may be sufficient in some scenarios, but many scenarios require multiple route versions in order to model variations in the manufacturing process for an item. For example, the route versions may reflect planned changes to the manufacturing process (such as new equipment or a different factory layout) or variations between sites producing the same item.

This chapter covers information about resources and routings. It starts with a typical business process to define production resources, and provides more detailed explanations about several steps in this business process. It also explains the typical business process to define routing information, which builds on an understanding of master routings and their assignment to items. More detailed explanations cover several steps in this business process, such as the definition of master operations and the feasibility of an item's route version. Additional sections explain the maintenance of routing information, scheduling method considerations, and alternatives to the use of routing information. These considerations are reflected in the following sections within the chapter.

1. Typical Process to Define a Production Resource
2. Production Resources and Resource Groups
3. Define Capabilities and Assign to Resources
4. Define Competencies and Assign to Employees
5. Master Routings and Route Versions
6. Typical Process to Define an Item's Routing Information
7. Define Master Operations

8. Define an Internal Operation in a Routing
9. Review Feasibility of Resource Requirements for an Item's Route Version
10. Scheduling Method: Job versus Operation Scheduling
11. Order-Dependent Routing for a Production Order
12. Maintain Routing information
13. Alternatives to the use of Routing Information

When defining routing information -- and the resource requirements for an operation -- there are multiple scenarios involving preferred equipment for producing an item. These scenarios include a dedicated machine (specified as the required resource for the operation) and a machine within an interchangeable group of machines (specified as the required resource group for the operation). Other scenarios may involve a preferred machine based on the required capability or minimum capability, or the production quantity (specified as a different route version with a quantity breakpoint). The chapter explains the solution approaches to various scenarios for preferred equipment.

6.1 Typical Process to Define a Production Resource

The typical process consists of several steps to define each production resource and its resource group. An internal resource often represents a machine, a specific employee, or a type of production worker. It can also represent some other capacity constraint or costing consideration. A resource group represents similar resources in close proximity within the same AX site. A resource or a resource group can then be specified as the resource requirement for a routing operation.

Additional steps may be involved for modeling resource capabilities or employee competencies. Resource capabilities, for example, can be used to model alternate resource logic based on a prioritized list of preferred resources or a minimum level of capability. Employee competencies apply to scenarios with highly skilled employees as a scheduling constraint, where you define an employee competency (such as skills, certifications or courses) as the resource requirement for an operation, and maintain information about each employee's competencies. Figure 6.1 illustrates these steps for three variations of production resources -- representing a machine, a type of production worker or a specific employee -- as illustrated by the three boxes within the figure. The process engineer role typically defines production resources and resource groups.

Figure 6.1 Typical Process to Define a Production Resource

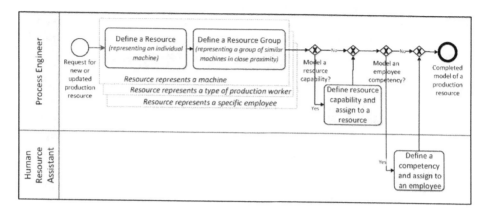

Define a Resource Representing a Machine The process engineer defines a production resource that represents a machine, and assigns it to a resource group that represents similar machines in close proximity within the same AX site.[1] A machine may subsequently be moved to a different site, which can be modeled in terms of validity dates for the assignment of the resource to a resource group. The basic information for a resource includes a calendar of working hours and a designation whether its available capacity should be considered finite or infinite. Since multiple time elements can be specified for performing an operation at the resource -- such as run time, transit time and queue times -- you may also need to designate the scheduling significance of each time element. The relevant costs (aka machine rate code) may also be assigned to the resource, such as the hourly costs for run time and setup time.

Define a Resource Representing a Specific Employee The process engineer defines a human resource to represent an individual employee, and assigns the employee number to the resource. The resource is also assigned to a resource group that represents similar workers in close proximity within the same AX site. An employee may subsequently be assigned to a different resource group, as identified by the validity dates of the assignment. The crew size requirements for an operation can be modeled by specifying the required resource group and the number of required resources.

Define a Resource Representing a Type of Production Worker The process engineer defines a human resource to represent a type of production worker, but does not assign an employee number to the human resource.

---

[1] A scenario involving a unique machine typically requires a resource group with only one resource that reflects the unique machine.

Example identifiers for these resources could be Prod-Worker-1, Prod-Worker-2, and so forth. As noted above for modeling specific employees, you assign each resource to a resource group that represents similar workers in close proximity, and you can model an operation's crew size requirements by specifying the required resource group and the number of required resources.

Define a Resource Capability and Assign to a Resource The process engineer defines resource capabilities and assigns them to resources. A capability can be assigned to one or more resources, and a resource can have more than one capability assigned to it. The process engineer can then define a capability as the resource requirement of a routing operation. When assigning a capability to multiple resources, the process engineer can specify the priority associated with each resource so that the priorities will be considered by the scheduling logic. In addition, the process engineer can define a capability level for a resource, expressed as a numeric value (such as 50 tons for a press). The process engineer can then define the minimum required capability level as the resource requirement for an operation so that the capability levels will be considered by scheduling logic in determining which resource should perform the operation.

Define a Competency and Assign to an Employee A human resource assistant typically defines employee-related competencies such as certifications, skills, and courses, and maintains the assignment of competencies to employees. As an illustrative example concerning certifications, you can define the possible types of certifications and assign a certification (and a starting date for the certification) to employees. The process engineer can then specify a required certification as part of the resource requirements for a routing operation. Similar steps apply to the use of skills and courses as the basis for human resource requirements.

6.2 Production Resources and Resource Groups

Resources and resource groups represent two of the primary approaches for specifying the resource requirements for a routing operation. The other primary approaches include resource capabilities and employee competencies, as explained in subsequent sections. A resource may represent a machine, an individual employee, a type of production worker, a tool, or some other type of capacity constraint or manufacturing cost. It may also represent a tightly linked group of machines or a manufacturing cell that can be treated as single resource.

Each resource must belong to a resource group.[2] A resource group typically represents similar resources located in close proximity within the same site. You can specify a resource or a resource group as the resource requirement for a routing operation.

Identification of Resources and Resource Groups A resource has a unique identifier and description, and a resource group also has a unique identifier and description. Each resource must be assigned to a resource group, and changes in this assignment can be indicated by validity dates.

Type of Resource The common types consist of a machine or human resource, and sometimes a vendor when the scenario involves subcontracted production. Some suggested guidelines for identifying resources and resource groups are provided below.

◆ *Machine.* A machine resource often represents a single machine, but it may also represent a tightly linked group of machines that acts as a single entity for capacity planning and scheduling purposes. The resource capacity for a single machine is typically expressed as one.

  When defining a resource group related to machines (and then assigning machines to the group), the grouping typically represents machines in close physical proximity with similar characteristics in terms of capabilities and operating costs.

  A machine resource is sometimes used to model a miscellaneous area comprised of a mixture of personnel and equipment performing various operations. This provides the basis for defining routing operations, and an approximation of costing, capacity planning, and scheduling considerations. The resource capacity provides an approximation of how many operations can be concurrently processed within the miscellaneous area.

◆ *Human Resource.* A human resource can represent a specific employee (by assigning the employee number) or a type of production worker (by not assigning an employee number). When defining a resource group related to human resources, the grouping typically represents a labor pool or a team of people in close physical proximity with similar characteristics in terms of capabilities and labor rates. In this way, you can model crew size requirements in a routing operation by specifying the resource group and the number of required resources within the group.

---

[2] The Resource Lifecycle Management workspace identifies the resources not yet assigned to a resource group, and supports the assignment to a resource group. The workspace also provides links to related information such as calendars, resource capabilities, and the mass maintenance of resource requirements.

◆ *Vendor.* A vendor resource typically represents a specific subcontractor (with optional assignment of the vendor number) that performs subcontracted production using supplied material. A subsequent chapter provides further explanation of how to model subcontracted production (Chapter 15).

◆ *Tool.* A tool resource is rarely specified unless it represents a critical scheduling constraint. Examples of a tool include a serialized die, mold or re-useable fixture. A tool is typically specified as a secondary resource for performing an operation. A resource group for tooling generally represents several serial numbers of the exact same tool. A tool resource does not support tool inventory management or the tracking of tool cycle usage (e.g., for triggering replacement or rebuild). A serialized tool must be identified as an item to support these purposes.

◆ *Location.* A location resource is conceptually similar to a tool resource, and is rarely specified unless it represents a critical scheduling constraint. One example would a clean room. The clean room would typically be specified as a secondary resource for performing an operation. A resource group could represent several clean rooms. Modeling a location as a resource simply provides a scheduling constraint. Actual inventory locations must be defined in terms of the site, warehouse and bin location.

Guidelines for Specifying a Resource or Resource Group in a Routing Operation Several factors should be considered in choosing whether to designate a resource or a resource group for performing an operation. The following guidelines focus on machines and human resources.

◆ *Specify a Resource for the Operation.* This approach assumes the operation can only be performed at the specified machine, where the operation identifies the machine-specific times and costs. A similar assumption applies to a specified human resource, where the resource represents a specific employee.

◆ *Specify a Resource Group for the Operation* With machines, this approach assumes the operation can be performed on any machine within the group, and the machines have similar run times and cost structures. As part of defining a routing operation, you can optionally specify which machine will provide the default values for cost information and time requirements. The job scheduling logic will assign a specific machine (within the group) to an operation in order to meet the due date.

With human resources, the resource group typically represents a group of employees or production workers with interchangeable skills and similar hourly rates. When defining an operation for the resource group, you can specify the required number of people (aka crew size) for the operation. You can optionally specify which human resource will provide the default values for cost information. The job scheduling logic will assign specific human resources (within the group) to an operation in order to meet the due date and crew size requirements.

Changing the Assignment of a Resource to a Resource Group In a static environment, you assign a resource to a single resource group. In a dynamic environment with changing assignments, you indicate the expiration date for the current assignment, and also indicate the new assignment. For example, a piece of equipment or a person may be moved to a different site, which would be modeled by assigning the resource to a different resource group. Note that a site is assigned to a resource group, and the site applies to all resources assigned to the group.

Production Unit for a Resource Group A user-defined production unit provides one approach for identifying an input warehouse and output warehouse related to production orders at the resources within a resource group. You assign a production unit to a resource group. The use of a production unit to define a component's warehouse source was described in a previous chapter (Section 5.5).

Production Input and Output Locations for a Resource Group The assignment of a production input location to a resource group (or to individual resources within the group) is typically used to support the Advanced WMS approach to production order picking, where a picking work order delivers components to the relevant production input location. The use of a production input location to define a component's warehouse source was described in a previous chapter (Section 5.5). In addition, the assignment of a production output location to a resource group indicates where to place the finished quantities of a production order.

Available Capacity for a Resource A resource's available capacity is defined by two basic factors: the calendar defining the hours of operation and the capacity per hour.

◆ *Hours of Operation.* The calendar assigned to a resource defines the hours of operation (such as 7:00 a.m. to 4:00 p.m.) for each calendar day. The calendar assigned to a human resource typically reflects the relevant shift. Exceptions to this calendar of daily working hours can be specified, such as specifying downtime or overtime.

◆ *Capacity per Hour.* A single resource that can perform one task at a time has a capacity of 1.00 during working hours. However, a resource sometimes represents a number of people or machines, where more than one task can be performed at the same time. The average number of concurrent tasks is termed the *resource capacity.* With a capacity of 5, for example, up to 5 different operations can be scheduled concurrently for each hour of operation.

You calculate a resource's available capacity by performing a periodic task to compose working times. Master scheduling logic considers the available capacity for a resource group based on the sum of available capacities of its related resources.

A third factor -- termed the *operations scheduling percentage* for a resource -- affects how scheduling logic views the resource's available capacity. A scheduling percentage of 80%, for example, means that the master scheduling logic will only consider 80% of the available capacity when assigning loads to the resource. This approach provides flexibility for handling unexpected time requirements at the resource.

Infinite Versus Finite Available Capacity for a Resource A resource's available capacity can be designated as finite or infinite for scheduling purposes. An infinite capacity viewpoint means that scheduling logic ignores existing loads when scheduling a given order, but still considers constraints related to hours of operation and concurrent task capabilities to calculate operation durations. An analysis of resource load versus capacity can be used to identify overloaded periods, so that adjustments can be made to loads or available capacity.

A finite capacity viewpoint means that scheduling logic considers current loads (and the concurrent task capability) for each resource when scheduling a given order. Finite capacity considerations can be optionally included/excluded when performing the master scheduling task or when scheduling individual orders.

Designating Bottleneck Resources for Finite Capacity Planning Purposes The optional designation of a bottleneck resource can improve performance of master scheduling calculations. Additional master plan policies must be defined for the use of bottleneck scheduling and for three time fence policies related to bottleneck scheduling (the finite capacity time fence, the backward capacity time fence, and the bottleneck capacity time fence).

Efficiency   The time requirements expressed in routing operations can be factored up or down based on the efficiency percentage assigned to the resource. The resource's efficiency percentage acts as a default in the resource's assigned calendar. The efficiency for selected working times (such as a lower efficiency for late night hours) can then be manually overridden in the calendar.

Resource Costs   The costs associated with a resource are typically expressed in terms of hourly rates for setup and processing time.[3] That is, you define hourly rates for a cost category, and assign the cost category to a resource. Different cost categories must be defined for each labor rate or machine rate, and different categories may be needed to differentiate the rates related to setup or run time. You also assign a cost group to a cost category, which supports cost group segmentation in the calculated costs for a manufactured item. The costs associated with setup and run times are normally included in the cost calculations. You can selectively exclude these costs based on the policies embedded in the Routing Group assigned to a resource. A subsequent chapter provides further explanation of product costing, and the definition of costs for resources (Section 7.5).

Time Reporting and Auto-Deduction Policies   The time associated with processing and setup can be manually reported or auto-deducted, as indicated by *Automatic Route Consumption* policies embedded in the Routing Group assigned to a resource.

Block Scheduling via Properties   Block scheduling represents one approach to scheduling similar operations together, and involves the use of properties in two ways. First, a property must be assigned to a specified block of working time within the resource's calendar.[4] Second, a property must be assigned to operations. Scheduling logic can then schedule operations with the same property to the designated block of time, thereby helping to minimize setups for similar operations.

Summarized Information for a Resource   You can view summarized information about a resource's available capacity, actual reported time, and the capacity utilization percentage for the current accounting period, current year to date, and the preceding year. A resource's load inquiry summarizes available capacity, expected load, and a capacity utilization percentage for various time increments, such as months and weeks. It also provides drill down to the orders causing the expected load.

---

[3] Costs can also be defined in terms of piece rates for output units. The concept may apply to labor that is paid on a piece rate basis, or to the allocation of overhead costs per unit of output.

[4] Block scheduling requires that the resource must be flagged as having a finite property, and that production orders must be scheduled based on a finite property.

Aggregate Capacity and Loads for a Resource Group The aggregate capacity for a resource group is based on the sum of available capacity for the related resources. The aggregate load for the resource group includes the time requirements for its related resources.   An analysis of aggregate load versus capacity can help anticipate overloaded periods.

6.3 Define Capabilities and Assign to Resources

Capabilities provide one approach for modeling the resource requirements of a routing operation, and they apply to any type of resource. They build on the use of resources described in the previous section. You assign a capability to one or more resources, and a resource can have more than one capability assigned to it. In addition, you specify the required capability for a performing a routing operation.

Each capability has a user-defined identifier and description, and you specify a list of which resources can provide the capability. Conversely, you can assign a capability to resource. The following subsections provide guidelines concerning the definition and use of resource capabilities.

Specify Date Effectivities of the Resource Capability Each resource assigned to a capability can be assigned a starting and ending effectivity date. A resource can be listed more than once with different effectivity dates, typically to represent a capability that cannot be performed for a period of time. When a requirement date for the capability falls outside of the effective period, the resource will not be scheduled.

Assign Priorities to Support Alternate Resource Logic Each resource assigned to a capability can be assigned a numeric priority, where a value of 0 (or 1) represents the highest priority. The priority provides the basis for alternate resource logic in scheduling calculations.[5] That is, the resource with the highest priority will be considered first by the scheduling logic. The resource with the next-highest priority will only be considered when the requirement date cannot be met.

---

[5] A policy - termed *primary resource selection* - determines whether scheduling logic assigns resources based on *duration* or *priority*. Selecting a policy value of *priority* supports alternate resource logic based on priorities. The policy can be company-wide or site-specific, as defined on the Scheduling Parameters or Scheduling Parameters by Site form within the Master Planning setup information.

Specify the Level of Capability to Support Alternate Resource Logic
The level of capability provides an additional basis for determining whether a resource can satisfy the capability. You specify the capability level as numeric value. In a similar fashion, you specify a value for the minimum level needed as part of the resource requirements in a routing operation. The scheduling logic will only consider resources in the list with an equal or higher value than the minimum level needed.

An example concerning presses illustrates how to use these two values. Let's say we have three machine resources that represent a 20-ton press, a 50-ton press, and a 100-ton press. The first step is to define a capability termed Press, and assign the three resources to the capability. The three resources are assigned a capability level of 20, 50 and 100 respectively. As the second step, you assign the minimum level needed to perform a routing operation requiring the Press capability. Let's say the value of the minimum level needed is 40. At this point, the scheduling logic considers the requirement specified for the operation (of 40) in selecting which resource can satisfy the requirement, which means only the 50-ton and 100-ton presses would be considered.

Specify the capability as the resource requirement for a routing operation   One or more capabilities can be specified as the resource requirements for a routing operation. Since the required capability may be satisfied by different resources, you should specify the approximate costs for performing the operation. These hourly rates can be manually specified using the cost category fields, or the cost categories can be initially populated by specifying a "costing resource" for the operation. A subsequent section provides further explanation about defining an internal operation in a routing.

Case 6.1: Preferred Equipment for a Capability

The production supervisor wanted to schedule production using the optimal packaging line (out of the three possible packaging lines). When the optimal packaging line was fully booked, the production could be scheduled on another line. To support this logic, the operation's resource requirements (in the route version for each manufactured item) were defined for a "packaging line" capability, and the capability was assigned to the three packaging lines along with a priority sequence. In this way, the scheduling logic assigns the optimal line to meet the production due date. If the due date cannot be met, the scheduling logic assigns a different line based on the prioritized list.

Case 6.2: Preferred Equipment based on Minimum Capability

The production supervisor wanted to schedule production using the optimal packaging line (out of the three possible packaging lines). One packaging line could only handle small packages, another line could handle small or medium packages (but not large packages), and the third line could handle any package size. To support this logic, the operation's resource requirements (in the route version for each manufactured item) were defined for a "packaging line" capability and a minimum capability level of 1, 2 or 3 (that represented the three package sizes). The capability and a capability level were also assigned to the three packaging lines. In this way, the scheduling logic would only assign production to a packaging line that could meet the minimum required capability. For example, large packages were only assigned to the packaging line that could handle them.

6.4 Define Competencies and Assign to Employees

Some production environments require scheduling of highly-skilled employees with specific competencies, such as a certification, course or skill level. After defining a competency, you maintain the related information about each employee's competencies as part of the employee master information. You also define the competency as one of the resource requirements for a routing operation. This approach to resource requirements only applies to human resources representing individual employees where the employee number has been specified. The following subsections provide guidelines concerning the definition and use of employee competencies.

Employee Skills A skill has a user-defined identifier and description, and also a rating model consisting of a rating and skill level. You assign an actual skill (and a starting date for the skill) to an employee, and an employee can have more than one skill. In addition, you can specify the skill as a resource requirement for performing a routing operation.

Employee Certifications A certification type has a user-defined identifier and description. You assign a certification type (and a starting date for the certification) to an employee, and an employee can have more than one certification. In addition, you can specify the certificate as a resource requirement for performing a routing operation.

Employee Course A course has a user-defined identifier and description. You assign a course (and a completion date for the course) to an employee, and an employee can have more than one course. In addition, you can specify the course as a resource requirement for performing a routing operation.

Employee Self-Service Workspace for Updating an Employee Competency This workspace enables an employee to add information about a skill (and skill level) or a certificate type (and the start and end dates), and to view their registered courses.

6.5 Master Routings and Route Versions

The concept of a master routing enables you to define it once, and then assign it to multiple items with the same production process. When you create a master routing, the identifier (termed a *Route Number*) can be automatically or manually assigned, as defined by the number sequence policy for Route Numbers. Manual assignment should be used when the master routing identifier needs to be meaningful, such as the process specification for a common routing or the item number for an item-specific routing.

After creating a master routing identifier, you can define the associated operations and also assign the master routing to relevant items. Each assignment is termed a *Route Version*, and a manufactured item can have multiple route versions. Each route version must be site-specific, and the associated operations must reflect resources within the site. Master scheduling logic will use an item's site-specific routing version based on the site of the requirement.

Create and Assign a Master Routing There are two basic approaches to create and assign master routings, as described below. Each assignment is termed a *Route Version.*

◆ *Create a new routing for an item*. This approach starts from a selected item (on the Released Products form), where you access its routing information in order to create a new master routing and define its operations. The new master routing is automatically assigned to the item. There is a single approval step, which results in approval of the master routing and the route version.

As an alternative to creating a new master routing for an item, you can assign an existing one to the item. This alternative represents a "new" assignment for an existing master routing; the assignment can also be "deleted". Each assignment requires a separate approval step. The assignment of a master routing to relevant items is also employed in the second approach.

◆ *Create a master routing and assign to items.* This approach starts from the list of master routings (termed the All Routes form), where you create a master routing and its operations, and then assign it to the relevant items.[2] There is an approval step for the master routing, and a separate approval step for each assignment (aka the route version). The creation of a master routing can also originate from the first approach, so that it can be subsequently assigned to other items.

Approved and Active Route Versions   A master routing and a route version must be approved, as described above.   You can optionally employ electronic signatures as part of the approval process, as previously described for approving BOM information.

Only an approved route version for a manufactured item can be marked as active. The active route version for a manufactured item will normally be used in planning and cost calculations. There are several scenarios requiring multiple active route versions for an item, and even multiple approved-but-not active route versions, as described in the next topic.

Rationale for Multiple Route Versions for a Manufactured Item   A manufactured item can have multiple active route versions that reflect different sites, non-overlapping validity periods, and/or different quantity breakpoints. Other route versions may be approved but not active, typically to model an alternate production process.   The reasons for multiple route versions are explained below.

◆ *Routing Variations between Sites Producing the Same Manufactured Item.* The site-specific route versions reflect variations in the resources and operations for producing the item.

◆ *Planned Changes with Effectivity Dates.* The multiple route versions can represent planned changes to the production process, where each route version has a different validity period. For example, a manufactured item may have two route versions to indicate planned changes, where one route version is valid until date X and the other route version is valid starting on date X+1.

---

[2] The assignment of master routings to a manufactured item can be assisted by an attribute (the Item Group) assigned to each master routing. Based on this attribute, the drop-down list of master routings can display the subset with an Item Group that matches the manufactured item.

♦ *Variations due to Order Quantities.* The multiple route versions can represent variations in the preferred production process for larger order quantities, where each route version has a different quantity breakpoint. For example, a route version can reflect use of a faster equipment for producing a large order quantity.

♦ *Alternate Routings.* Additional route versions can represent alternate processes for producing the manufactured item. The alternate would be an approved-but-not-active route version that could be specified for a manually-created production order or rework order. It could also be specified for a sales order line item (for a make-to-order product) or for a BOM line about a manufactured component (for a make-to-order component), so that scheduling logic employs the specified route version rather than the active route version.

♦ *Routings for Prototypes or Production Ramp-up.* A different route version may identify the production process for prototypes or different stages of production ramp-up.

In summary, a manufactured item can have multiple active route versions that reflect different sites, non-overlapping validity periods, and/or different quantity breakpoints. An item can also have approved-but-not-active route versions.

Case 6.3: Preferred Equipment based on Production Quantity

The production supervisor at a manufacturing firm wanted to schedule production using the optimal equipment for small and large order quantities. The large order quantities (over 1,000) were produced on larger faster equipment. To support this logic, two different route versions were defined for the relevant manufactured items, where the quantity breakpoint for one route version reflected 1,000 units. This route version contained an operation with resource requirements for handling a large quantity, and the other route version contained an operation with resource requirements for handling the small quantity. In this way, master scheduling logic will assign the optimal route version to a planned production order based on the required quantity.

6.6 Typical Process to Define an Item's Routing

A typical business process to define routing information builds on an understanding of master routings and route versions. In summary, you define a master routing consisting of one or more operations and assign it to the applicable manufactured items. Each assignment is termed a route version, and the item's route version policies specify the relevant site and validity dates. In many cases, an item may require multiple route versions to reflect planned changes in the production process or variations between sites producing the same item. As part of defining an operation in a master routing, you identify an operation number, the resource requirement, and a master operation identifier. You define these master operations beforehand, so that an operation automatically inherits the resource requirements from the master operation. You can optionally review the feasibility of the resource requirements after completing the assignment of a master routing to an item. You can then approve and activate the item's route version, or simply approve it. These steps and their applicable roles are illustrated in Figure 6.2 and described below.

Figure 6.2 Typical Process to Define an Item's Routing

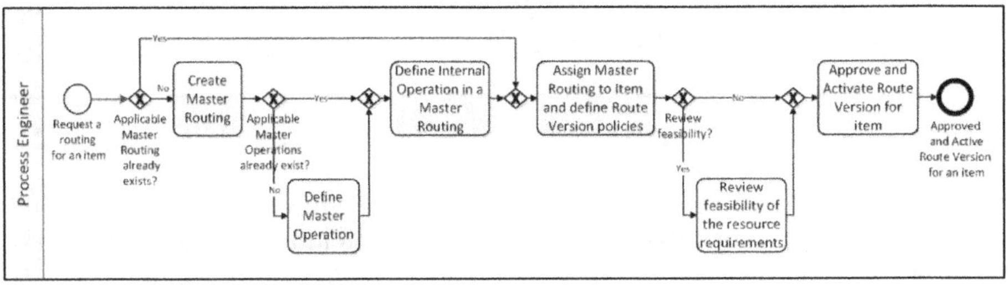

Create Master Routing   The process engineer typically creates a Master Routing and its operations so that it can be assigned to items going through the same production process. As an alternative starting point, the process engineer can start from an item and create a Master Routing, which is automatically assigned to the item.

Define Master Operation   The process engineer employs the Master Operation concept to help minimize data maintenance efforts. By defining the resource requirements and applicability rules of a Master Operation, the process engineer can simply specify the Master Operation identifier in a routing operation, and the operation inherits the resource requirements. A Master Operation may have more than one applicability rule (and its associated resource requirements), such as a different applicability rule for a different group of items.

Changing the resource requirements for the Master Operation will automatically update all applicable operations.

Some scenarios do not employ the Master Operation concept. In these scenarios, the process engineer simply defines a Master Operation identifier without the applicability rule and associated resource requirement. An identifier must still be specified for a routing operation, where the process engineer must define the resource requirements for the operation (since nothing is inherited). However, the system will automatically track use of the Master Operation identifier by creating an applicability rule, such as the specific item number and master routing. In this way, the process engineer can still maintain the resource requirements using the Master Operation form.

Define an Internal Operation in a Master Routing For each operation, the process engineer assigns an operation number, a master operation identifier, the resource requirement, and the time requirements. The operation number can also be specified for relevant BOM components to provide linkage to the routing operation.

Some scenarios have an operation with one or more secondary resources. For example, the secondary resources of a machine operator and a tool may apply to the primary resource of a machine.

Assign Master Routing to item and define the Route Version policies
The process engineer defines an item's route version policies, which include the Master Routing identifier, the relevant site, the validity dates, and an optional quantity breakpoint for a quantity-sensitive route version.

Review feasibility of the resource requirements for an Item's Route Version The process engineer analyzes route feasibility to determine whether applicable resources exist to satisfy the resource requirements of operations in an item's route version. For example, an operation's resource requirements may be infeasible due to lack of an assigned resource group (for a resource), or the lack of capabilities or employee competencies with valid dates. Attempts to activate an infeasible route version result in a soft warning message, and an option to review route feasibility. As a supplemental approach, the process engineer can also analyze availability of applicable resources when defining a master operation or specific operation within a routing.

Approve and Activate Route Version for Item The process engineer approves and activates an item's route version to enable actual usage on production orders and in planning/costing calculations. Attempts to activate an infeasible route version result in a soft warning message, and an option to review route feasibility. The process engineer may approve and activate multiple route versions for an item to reflect different sites, validity periods, or quantity breakpoints. In addition, the process designer may simply approve an item's route version but not activate it.

6.7 Define Master Operations

The concept of a master operation is central to the definition of routing operations within AX. A master operation (termed *Operation*) has a unique user-defined identifier and a description, and you define master operations on the Operations form. The identifier typically has some meaning so that its significance is easily understood, such as an abbreviation for an operation or a process specification number. An identifier for a master operation must be specified for each routing operation. The master operation provides default values for the operation's information such as the required resource and associated time. Changing the values for a master operation will automatically update the information on the associated routing operations, subject to applicability rules.

The applicability rules for a master operation represent a key related concept. In defining a master operation, you can specify one or more sets of data that will serve as default values in a given routing operation. Each set has an applicability rule. For example, a set of data could apply to a specified group of items, and an additional set of data could apply to another group of items. The combination of an applicability rule and a set of data is termed an *Operation Relation.*

The applicability rule can reflect a specific item, a group of items (based on the Item Group) or all items. In addition, the applicability rule can reflect a specific master routing or all master routings. These applicability rules reflect decreasing levels of specificity. When multiple applicability rules have been defined, the most specific level will be used to inherit values from a master operation.

The applicability rule and set of data (aka the Operation Relation) can be specified when you initially define a master operation. The set of data provides default values when the master operation is specified for a routing operation.

Manually overriding the values on a routing operation will automatically create an additional applicability rule for the master operation, and the set of data reflects the manually-overridden values. The new applicability rule indicates the item and master routing in which you performed the manual override. In this way, subsequent changes to the master operation will only affect the one routing operation.

The use of master operations varies from company to company. Many companies already employ the concept of master operations, and they can replicate their current conceptual model within AX. If the concept of master operations does not apply, you can simply create a master operation without any applicability rules or data. When you specify the master operation in a routing operation, no values will be inherited and you must define them. This will automatically create an Operation Relation for the master operation.

6.8 Define an Internal Operation in a Routing

The critical information for an internal operation consists of an operation number, a master operation identifier, the resource requirement, and the time requirements. Previous sections described the various methods for defining a resource requirement and the concept of a master operation. This section explains the other aspects of defining an internal operation. A subsequent chapter explains the definition of an external operation for subcontracted production (Section 15.5).

Operation Number   The operation number provides a unique numeric identifier for each operation within a routing, and the basis for scheduling a serial routing. The system automatically assigns new operation numbers in increments of 10 but this operation number can be overridden. The use of operation numbers has several implications as described below.

◆ *Sequence the operations in a multistep routing.* The operation number itself does not provide sequencing logic. For sequencing purposes, each operation requires additional information about the next operation number, whether you are modeling a serial or parallel sequence.

◆ *Identify the last operation within a routing.* You must identify which operation represents the last operation in a routing (with a value of zero "0" in the Next Operation field). This information is helpful when reporting actual production activity for the last operation, so that reporting the units completed at the last operation can automatically update the finished quantity for the production order.

◆ *Identify the material components required for an operation.* Assigning the operation number to the required material (in the BOM line information) allows master scheduling logic to synchronize material due dates with the operation start date. It provides the basis for calculating the impact of operation scrap percentages on the associated material requirements. It also provides the basis for populating the picking list for a production order based on the started quantity for the operation number.

◆ *Provide an identifier to report actual production activity.* You report actual time and/or unit completions against an order number and operation number.

◆ *Indicate when tests should be performed during production of an item.* The required tests for an item (via the automatic creation of a quality order) can reflect a specified operation number within the routing.

Primary Versus Secondary Resources (Operation Priority)   Each operation requires a primary resource, and most production environments can be modeled using operations with just a primary resource.   Some production environments have operations requiring one or more secondary resources, such as the people and tools for running a machine. The operation's primary resource represents the pacing resource that determines operation duration. The same operation number must be assigned to each secondary resource, and the same time requirements apply because it is not the pacing resource. Operations with the same operation number are termed *simultaneous operations.*

The type of linkage between a primary and secondary resource affects scheduling logic, where the link type can be hard or soft. That is, you can indicate that the secondary resources for an operation must start at the same time as the primary resource (a link type of hard). The alternative allows a time gap (a link type of soft or blank).

Case 6.4: Simultaneous Requirements for a Machine, Operator and Tool

---

One production process at an equipment company required a dedicated machine, a skilled operator, and a specialized mold. In order to model these simultaneous resource requirements for the operation, the route version for each manufactured item contained three lines with the same operation number. The first line identified the primary resource requirement of the machine, since this acted as the pacing resource. The next two lines identified the secondary resource requirements for the skilled operator and the mold tool.

Case 6.5: Use Secondary Resources for Costing Purposes

The routing information for several manufactured items consisted of a single operation that involved a single primary resource representing the equipment and multiple secondary resources representing the different types of labor to run the equipment. The different types of labor were assigned different labor rates and cost groups, and the overheads varied for each type of labor. The secondary resources were used for costing purposes rather than scheduling purposes.

Resource Requirement Each operation must include at least one resource requirement. The resource requirement can be expressed for a resource, a resource group, a resource capability or an employee competency, as previously described.

Resource Quantity The resource quantity indicates the number of resources required to perform the operation. It can be illustrated by a resource group for human resources containing resources that represent individual people. For example, a run time requirement of 3 hours and a resource quantity of 2 people would be interpreted as a total load of 6 hours (for the resource group). The detailed scheduling method creates a load of 3 hours for 2 different resources (people).

Time Requirements Time requirements are normally expressed as hours per unit or units per hour. They can also be expressed in minutes or days (which applies to all time elements for the operation), but cost and planning calculations will convert these time requirements back into hours.[3] This approach to defining time requirements is termed a "standard" resource consumption policy, and you assign the policy to an operation. The next subsection describes some alternate approaches to defining time requirements, whereas this section focuses on the standard approach.

The time requirements are typically defined for run time and optional setup time, but some scenarios employ additional time elements to model the production process. The following considerations apply to the definition of time requirements for various time elements.

◆ *Run Time per Unit* The run time is typically expressed per 1 unit. It can be expressed for a different quantity, such as the run time per 100 units (as defined by the process quantity field). Alternatively, you can define a run

---

[3] Time requirements expressed in hours reflects an "hours per time unit" value of 1. This "hours per time unit" field can also be used to define time requirements in minutes (a value of 1/60 or .0167) or days (a value of 24) or some other user-specified interval.

rate, such as specifying a time requirement of 1 hour and a process quantity that represents the run rate per hour.

◆ *Setup Time*. Setup time represents a fixed requirement before starting the run time for production. Short setup times are typically not defined.

◆ *Changeover Time*. Changeover time represents a fixed requirement after completing the run time for production. It is typically modeled by the "queue after" time element within AX, as described in the next point.

◆ *Other Time Elements for Scheduling and Capacity Planning Purposes.* Other time elements include the number of hours for queue time before and after the operation, and the transit time to the next operation. Many scenarios employ different names for these time elements, such as a changeover time or cooling time rather than a queue time after the operation. Several policies (embedded in the Route Group assigned to the operation) determine the impact of time requirements for these time elements, since they can optionally consume capacity. The impact of route group policies are described in a following subsection.

◆ *Overlapping Operations.* An operation can have a specified overlap quantity (also termed the transfer batch quantity) so that the next operation can start before operation completion.

Alternative Approaches to Defining Time Requirements An alternative approach to defining time requirements may apply to a machine and its machine cycles. The capacity of the machine is expressed as the number of cycles per hour, and the resource requirement identifies the number of required cycles to produce an item. This approach to defining time requirements is termed a "capacity" resource consumption policy, and you assign the policy to an operation. This alternative approach requires the following information.

◆ *Normal Cycles per Hour for a Machine.* The normal cycles per hour are defined in the resource's *capacity* field. An optional capacity unit provides reference information about the run rate -- such as strokes per hour, meters per hour, or pounds per hour -- but has no other significance.

◆ *Required Cycles per Unit for an Operation performed by the Machine.* An operation's required capacity is expressed in cycles per unit, as defined by the factor field. For example, a factor of 10 means 10 cycles will produce 1 unit, whereas a factor of .5 means that 1 cycle produces 2 units. The operation's run time will be calculated based on the required cycles per unit and the machine's normal cycles per hour.

A slight variation builds on the use of machine cycles, and typically applies to a machine using a mold or die to produce a "batch quantity" of an item. This approach to defining time requirements is termed a "resource batch" resource consumption policy, and you assign the policy to an operation. For example, a machine that employs a mold may require 2 cycles to produce a quantity of 10 items. In this case, you define the resource's *batch capacity* as 10. In the operation, you define a *factor* of 2 for the required cycles per batch. This approach would apply to the use of molds for polymer molded products (Case 7).

Another approach to defining time requirements is termed a "batch" resource consumption policy. This is approach is more common in process manufacturing, A typical example involves the use of a kettle to produce an item via mixing, such as using a kettle with a 500 Kg capacity to produce an item with an inventory UM of Kg. In this example, you define the resource's batch capacity as 500 and the run time (such as 2 hours of mixing) indicates the time requirement to produce one batch in the kettle. Hence, a production order quantity of 2000 Kg would require 8 hours, which reflects four batches requiring 2 hours each.

Time Requirements and the Impact of Route Group Policies A route group defines a set of policies that determine how an operation's time requirements will be treated. An explanation of these policies can be grouped into the various time elements, as described below. Most scenarios only require one or two route groups with policies reflecting common business practices. The following explanation covers these common practices and the typical exceptions:

◆ *Run time and setup time.* The costs associated with these time elements are normally included in cost roll-up calculations, and the time elements are normally included in scheduling and capacity planning. In addition, the actual time for run and setup can be manually reported or auto-deducted for a production order.

   The typical exception to these normal business practices occurs when the time requirements should be ignored in cost calculations or planning calculations or both. For example, the time requirements may only apply to capacity planning purposes, so that a separate Route Group should be defined (with policies to ignore setup and run time in cost calculations) with assignment to relevant resources and operations.

♦ *Queue time.* Two different queue times represent the fixed amount of elapsed time that occurs before setup time and after run time. Costs cannot be defined for these time elements. The amount of elapsed time normally reflects the Gregorian calendar (of a 24-hour day and a 7-day week), and it does not reserve capacity of the relevant resource.

The typical exception occurs when resource capacity must be scheduled for queue time. A typical example consists of a resource (such as a kettle or tank) used for an extended period to support fermentation or cooling of its contents. In this case, the Route Group policies must indicate that scheduling and capacity reservations apply to the time elements for queue time. In most cases, the amount of elapsed time will reflect the Gregorian calendar, but it can optionally reflect the working hours in the resource calendar.

♦ *Transit time.* The transit time represents the fixed amount of elapsed time that occurs after performing an operation, where you move material to the next operation. Costs cannot be defined for transit time, and the elapsed time normally reflects the Gregorian calendar without reserving capacity of the relevant resource.

Case 6.6: Burn-In Period after Completing Production

The production process for a manufactured item involved a burn-in period after completing assembly at a final assembly work center. The number of burn-in hours was specified using the "queue after" time element. This approach requires the definition of a Route Group in which "queue after" time is designated as working time (but does not consume resource capacity), and the assignment of this Route Group to the operation performed by the final assembly work center.

Yield Percentage for an Operation The planned yield percentage for an operation affects the required runtime and the materials tied to the operation. The system automatically calculates and displays an accumulated yield percentage for each operation in a routing with multiple operations.

Cost Data for an Operation The cost data for an operation includes the cost categories defining the hourly rates. The cost categories would normally default from the required resource, and can be overridden. You can optionally specify which resource should be used for costing purposes (aka the costing resource) in order to populate the cost categories; the costing resource has no other purpose.

The costs associated with an operation can be optionally ignored in cost calculations, as determined by the policies embedded in the Route Group assigned to the operation.

Reporting Operation Time   The auto-deduction policies for an operation reflect the Route Group assigned to the operation.

Operation Description   The operation description consists of unlimited free-form text, and the optional use of documents such as a Word file or an image.

6.9 Review Feasibility of Resource Requirements

An item's route version may be infeasible due to the lack of applicable resources. When you attempt to activate an infeasible route version for an item, you receive a warning message to prevent activation. The message also provides the option to view information about route feasibility so you can identify which operations do not have applicable resources. This route feasibility information can also be viewed before you attempt to activate a route version.

The Route Feasibility form summarizes the feasibility of the resource requirements for operations within a selected route version for an item. It displays a list of the routing operations, and identifies those operations without an applicable resource as of a specified date. The specified date is relevant because of different validity dates for the assignment of resources to a resource group, the assignment of capabilities to resources, and/or the assignment of employee competencies (for skills, courses and certificates) to human resources representing a specific employee. In some cases, it is helpful to view the feasibility information for a different specified date (within the effectivity dates for the route version) in order to analyze changes in validity dates.

In addition to a specified date on the Route Feasibility form, you must also specify which scheduling method to consider. The feasibility can be different for the two scheduling methods of operation scheduling and job scheduling. For example, the resource requirements for an employee competency (such as skills) only apply to job scheduling. The next section provides further explanation about scheduling method considerations.

The Route Feasibility form provides a starting point for analyzing and correcting those operations without applicable resources. It does not provide sufficient detail to indicate the exact reasons for the problem. The Route Feasibility form can be accessed from the Route form (displaying the Route Versions for an item) or from the Route Details form (for a selected Master Routing).

The availability of applicable resources can also be analyzed for an individual operation, typically in the context of defining a master operation or an operation within a routing.   To support this analysis, you can access the Applicable Resource form for a selected master operation or a routing operation.

A discrete manufacturing firm was implementing a change in equipment that also required skilled operators with the relevant equipment certification. As part of the new route versions for manufactured items produced by the equipment, an operation specified the resource requirements for the new equipment (as a primary resource) and for the employee certification (as a secondary resource). One concern was the match-up between the equipment availability date (defined by the effectivity date for its resource group) and the availability of certified operators (defined by their certification date). This date could be analyzed by reviewing the feasibility of the resource requirements for an item's route version.

6.10 Scheduling Method: Job versus Operation Scheduling

The scheduling logic within AX is slightly different for the two scheduling methods, which are termed *operation scheduling* and *job scheduling*. The term *job scheduling* may be confusing to those people that think of a job as synonymous with a production order or project, but in this context job refers to the individual time elements within an operation.   These time elements can include setup, process and queue times.   The scheduling significance of these time elements is defined within the Route Group assigned to an operation.

The ability to handle detailed time elements represents a primary difference between the two scheduling methods.   A second key difference concerns the detailed information about employee competencies. The job scheduling method can handle these details, whereas the operation scheduling method cannot.   The differentiating factors between the scheduling methods are summarized in Figure 6.3 and explained below.

Figure 6.3 Comparison of Scheduling Methods

		Scheduling Method	
		Operations Scheduling	Job Scheduling
Differentiating Factors	Scheduling Focus	Resource Group	Resource
	Capacity Planning	Detailed (by Resource) and Aggregate (by Group)	Detailed (by Resource) and Aggregate (by Group)
	Scheduling Capabilities		Schedule detailed time elements (aka jobs) Lock a job and synchronize related time elements Assign a resource based on capabilities or employee competencies Support alternative approaches to the definition of time requirements (e.g. via machine cycles) Perform block scheduling via properties Use of Gantt Chart to display production schedule
	Time Granularity	Schedule by date	Schedule by date and time
	Printed Shop Traveler	Route Card	Job Card
	Reporting Operation Time and Unit Completions	Use Route Card Journal	Use Job Card Journal or Route Card Journal
	Computer Processing Time	Faster	Slower

◆ *Job Scheduling Method.* This method supports (1) scheduling the time elements for an operation, (2) assigning resources based on a requirement for capabilities or employee competencies, (3) block scheduling based on a property, and (4) use of a Gantt Chart to display production schedule information. Minor differences include the printed shop traveler, the approach for reporting operation time and unit completions, and computer processing time.

◆ *Operation Scheduling Method.* This method does not support some scheduling capabilities, as mentioned above.

With the master scheduling task, the scheduling logic based on routing data only applies within the time horizon defined by a capacity time fence (expressed in days). You define the capacity time fence as one of the policies within the coverage group assigned to an item, or as one of the policies for a master plan. In most cases, the capacity time fence reflects near-term scheduling requirements (such as a 30 day horizon), although a longer horizon (such as 365 days) would be used to calculate long-term capacity requirements.

6.11 Order-Dependent Routing for a Production Order

An order-dependent routing refers to the routing operations attached to a production order. It is also termed the Production Route. Changes to an order-dependent routing do not affect the master routing. Creation and maintenance of the order-dependent routing reflect several rules, which parallel the rules for maintaining an order-dependent BOM.

◆ Creation of a production order can also create an order-dependent routing.

◆ The order-dependent routing initially reflects the item's route version that was used to create the production order. In most cases, this will be inherited from the active route version for the site and start date on the production order. However, you can manually specify a different route version for the item when manually creating the production order, where the route version can be approved-but-not-active.

◆ The order-dependent routing contains the routing operations of a phantom.

◆ You can modify the operations in an order-dependent routing at any time prior to reporting the production order as ended.

◆ You can copy operations to an order-dependent routing -- such as copying from another production order or a Master Routing -- prior to reporting a production order as scheduled.

◆ Time can only be reported when the operation sequence number exists in the order-dependent routing.

6.12 Maintain Routing Information

Routing information can be maintained using several approaches. You typically maintain multiple master routings in order to support multiple active route versions for an item, and a copy function provides one approach to data maintenance. Other approaches include the master operation concept to support mass updates to routing operations, and a mass update wizard for updating the assignment of resource requirements within master operations. Another aspect of maintaining routing information includes the review of route feasibility, since a routing may be infeasible due to the lack of applicable resources for one or more operations. These approaches to routing maintenance are summarized below.

Maintain Multiple Active Route Versions for an Item Planned changes can be identified by the validity dates assigned to the route versions for an item, so that multiple route versions can be approved and active. Multiple active route versions may also be necessary to support site-specific or quantity-sensitive versions.

Use the Copy Function to Populate Operations in a Master Routing The copy function involves a destination for the "copy to" master routing, and a source for the "copy from" information. Initiating the copy function for a selected master routing will identify the copy to destination. The copy function is also provided when you create an additional route version for an item.

Mass Updates via the Master Operation Concept In order to support mass updates, the applicability rule for a master operation must reflect a group of items (or all items). In this way, changes to the master operation will automatically update the operations that specified the master operation identifier. If an applicability rule only applies to a single item and its master routing, the changes to the master operation only updates the single occurrence. A previous section described the use of master operations (Section 6.7).

Mass Update the Assignment of Resource Requirements within Master Operations A mass update wizard uses information about existing resource requirements within master operations so that you can delete the existing resource requirement, replace it with a different one, or add another resource requirement. The wizard -- termed the Maintain Resource Requirements wizard -- consists of several steps and their associated screens, as described below.

◆ *Step 1: Identify an existing resource requirement based on Search Criteria.* Use the first screen (labeled Search Criteria) to specify the search criteria for existing resource requirements, such as a specific resource or capability. More than one search criteria can be specified. The search criteria can optionally include the identifier of a master operation.

◆ *Step 2: Specify the mass update action.* Use the second screen (labeled Action) to specify whether you want to delete, replace or add to the existing resource requirement. As part of this step, you also indicate the option for where to apply the action. The option would be "routing" information in this scenario, but another option could be the order-dependent routing information (aka production route).[6]

---

[6] The other options include project-related information about resource requirements (termed hour forecasts) and custom product-related information about resource requirements defined in a Product Configuration Model or a Product Model. Chapter 19 describes the configuration technologies for custom products.

♦ *Step 3: Specify the new resource requirement.* The third screen (labeled New Resource Requirements) is only displayed when the action involves adding to or replacing an existing resource requirement.

♦ *Step 4: Review a summary of the proposed mass update.* The final screen (labeled Summary) summarizes the information from the first three steps. You can accept the proposed changes, go back to a previous step and make adjustments, and cancel the proposed mass-update. Accepting the proposed mass update will change the resource requirements within master operations.

Maintain Routing Information using a Product Change Case An alternative approach to maintain routing information involves the use of cases that specifically handle product changes. Each product change case represents an Engineering Change Order (ECO), and it typically applies to maintaining the BOM versions of a manufactured item as described in the previous chapter (Section 5.8). However, it can also be used to maintain the route versions for a manufactured item.

Review Feasibility of the Resource Requirements for Operations within a Routing A key aspect of data maintenance involves reviewing the feasibility of the resource requirements for an item's route version. A routing may be infeasible due to the lack of applicable resources for one or more operations. Section 6.9 previously described how to review the feasibility information.

Analysis Tools for Routing Information Analysis tools for an item's routing information include where-used inquiries about a resource, a master routing and a master operation. They also include a multilevel cost analysis, which shows the cost contributions of resources and related overheads in the calculated cost of a manufactured item.

6.13 Alternatives to the Use of Routing Information

Some production processes are extremely simple and easily coordinated. These scenarios do not necessarily warrant the definition of routing data and the scheduling methods within AX. Some suggested alternatives to the use of routing data include the following.

◆ *Production schedule of production orders.* Attributes of a manufactured item -- such as production group, production pool or property -- can represent the required machine. These attributes are inherited by a production order (and can be overridden), and provide the basis for segmenting the production schedule by machine. This approach replaces a production schedule by resource.

◆ *Capacity planning.* A dummy item number can represent the labor or machine hours for production time, with a unit of measure in hours. You can include this dummy item as a BOM line with a relevant required quantity, so that master scheduling logic can calculate the item's requirements. This approach replaces the use of resources and routings for calculating capacity requirements.

◆ *Value-added costs.* Assigning costs to the dummy item representing labor hours (or machine hours) provides the basis for calculating value-added costs.

◆ *Fixed lead time.* The fixed lead time assigned to a manufactured item will be used by master scheduling logic to determine when components must be available. The fixed lead time should also reflect the significance of a single production order. For example, the production order may reflect a week's worth of production and a Friday due date, so that a one week lead time ensures components will be available beforehand. Alternatively, the production orders may reflect daily granularity, so that a one day lead time should be used.

6.14 Additional Case Studies

Case 6.8: Integration with an Equipment Maintenance Application

The plant manager at a discrete manufacturer wanted to implement an integrated equipment maintenance application, also termed an Enterprise Asset Management (EAM) application. A key issue concerned the coordination between production planning and maintenance scheduling. The plant manager preferred a software module built using the standard AX constructs rather than a separate best-of-breed software package with its own constructs and interface requirements. With standard AX constructs, for example, the spare parts for equipment maintenance could be defined in the item master, procured using requisitions and purchase orders, and tracked via inventory transactions in the same way as other purchased items. Three aspects of integration were especially important. First, the downtime at machines (reflecting planned and ad hoc maintenance) must be identified and coordinated in the production schedules. Second, the triggers for planned maintenance must reflect actual and projected equipment usage. And third, inventory tracking was required for the tools used in maintenance, so that each serialized tool could be easily checked out and checked in.

6.15 Executive Summary

A master routing represents a model of production activities for a manufactured item. Assignment of multiple master routings to an item (termed route versions) can support site-specific variations, planned changes, preferred equipment based on production quantity, and alternate equipment. Each operation within a route version defines the resource requirements and associated time requirements. For example, the resource requirements can be defined for a specific resource, a resource group, a resource capability or an employee competency. The case studies illustrated variations in the use of routing data, such as designating the preferred equipment, integration with equipment maintenance, and simultaneous requirements for a machine, operator and tool.

Chapter 7

Product Costing

Product cost information defines the value of an item's inventory transactions. The primary variations in product costing involve standard versus actual costs, and purchased versus manufactured items. For a manufactured item, the calculation of product costs reflects the item's BOM and routing information. These calculations can be used to project future costs, simulate the impact of cost changes, analyze cost reduction opportunities, analyze profitability, and calculate an item's suggested sales price.

Product cost information represents one of the more complex and critical aspects of an integrated ERP system. As an explanatory approach, we'll start with the foundation of costing versions and the rationale for different costing versions. A costing version contains cost records about items, labor rates and overheads. The foundation also requires an understanding of the terminology about item cost records and cost calculations, and the significance of cost groups. We'll build on this foundation in order to explain costs for purchased items and the cost calculations for manufactured items. These topics and others are reflected in the following sections within the chapter.

1. Summary of Costing Versions
2. Terminology for Item Cost Records and Cost Calculations
3. Significance of Cost Groups
4. Standard Costs for Purchased Items
5. Define Resource Costs via Cost Categories
6. Define Overhead Costs via Overhead Formulas
7. Standard Cost Calculations for Manufactured Items
8. Convert Items to a Standard Cost Model
9. Planned Cost Calculations for Manufactured Items
10. Calculation of a Manufactured Item's Sales Price
11. Order-Specific Calculations of an Item's Cost and Sales Price
12. Summary of Standard Cost Variances
13. Actual Costing
14. Workspaces Related to Product Costing

7.1 Summary of Costing Versions

The primary purpose of a costing version is to define the cost records about items, labor rates and overhead formulas. You designate whether a costing version contains standard costs or planned costs. With a version containing standard costs, the cost records about items define their site-specific standard costs, and the cost records about items, labor rates and overhead formulas are used to calculate a manufactured item's standard cost. A costing version containing planned costs can be used in a standard cost or actual cost environment. It is used for simulation purposes in standard cost environments, where you calculate a manufactured item's planned cost. An actual costing environment can use a costing version containing planned costs to define the labor and overhead costs associated with manufacturing, and to support simulation purposes. Whether the costing version contains planned costs or standard costs, the calculation of a manufactured item's cost creates an item cost record within the costing version. This item cost record enables you to analyze the calculated costs.

A secondary purpose of a costing version involves the calculation of a suggested sales price for a manufactured item. This section summarizes the various purposes of costing versions, especially the use of item cost records. It starts with the rationale for different costing versions for standard costs.

Rationale for Different Costing Versions for Standard Costs The significance of a costing version depends on how you conceptualize your approach for maintaining standard costs. Some example approaches are described below.

◆ *Multiple costing versions represent standard costs for different calendar years (or quarters).* With this approach, you maintain all item cost records within one costing version that represents the current calendar year, and use an additional costing version for maintaining next year's standard costs. You can copy the active cost records from one costing version to create pending cost records in the other cost version, thereby providing a starting point for updating next year's standard costs.

◆ *Multiple costing versions represent site-specific standard costs for different sites.* This approach typically applies to a multi-site operation with transfers between sites, where you define a different costing version for each site. Within a given costing version you only maintain the item cost records for applicable items at the site, ranging from raw materials to end-items. In this way, you can calculate costs for a manufactured end-item within one costing version (that represents a production site), and then copy just the end-items' costs to another costing version (that represents the distribution site). Case 7.4 illustrates this approach to maintaining site-specific standard costs.

♦ *Multiple costing versions represent incremental changes to standard costs.* A costing version can contain the incremental changes to standard costs, such as pending cost records that represent new items or cost changes. The use of separate costing versions for incremental changes is commonly termed the two-version or n-version approach to maintaining standard cost data. This approach takes advantage of the fallback principle for calculating a manufactured item's cost, as described in a subsequent section (Section 7.7). For example, the fallback principle can identify the use of the active costs contained within other costing versions (the n-version approach), or within a specified costing version (the two-version approach). In contrast, cost calculations for item cost records within a single costing version employ a fallback principle of none.

In summary, the rationale for different costing versions depends on how you want to conceptualize your approach to maintaining standard costs. The conceptual approach should be shaped by AX capabilities such as copying costs to another costing version, site-specific costs, the effective date of pending and active cost records, the fallback principle, the policies affecting standard cost calculations, cost calculations within a single site, and calculating costs for items with missing costs. Subsequent sections provide further explanation of these capabilities.

Item Cost Records for Standard Cost Purposes   Standard costing employs one or more costing versions that contain item cost records about each item's standard cost. A costing version typically represents a user-defined time period such as a year or a quarter. For example, three costing versions could represent the three different time periods for years 20X0, 20X1, and 20X2. These examples of a costing version are displayed in Figure 7.1 and described below.

The concept of an annual time period is reflected in the first three costing versions displayed in Figure 7.1, all of which have a designated Costing Type of standard cost. In these examples, we'll assume a current date of December 20X1 and an implementation cutover date that occurred in the previous year of 20X0. Hence, the costing version Std-20X0 contains the initially-loaded item cost records, and the costing version Std-20X1 contains item cost records that were activated on January 1st 20X1. The item cost records for the following year will be defined in costing version Std-20X2, but not activated until January 1st 20X2.

Figure 7.1 Examples of Costing Versions
for Standard Costing Purposes

Identifier of Costing Version	Costing Type	Purpose of Costing Version
Std-20X0	Standard Cost	Contains item cost records for 20X0, plus cost records for labor and overhead formulas
Std-20X1	Standard Cost	Contains item cost records for 20X1, plus cost records for labor and overhead formulas
Std-20X2	Standard Cost	Contains item cost records for 20X2, plus cost records for labor and overhead formulas
Simulated-Cost	Planned Cost	Contains selected cost records for simulation purposes and item cost records generated by cost calculations

A costing version has two blocking policies that constrain the ability to enter and activate cost records. For example, these blocking policies would enforce the frozen standard costs for the costing versions representing the previous and current years, since all cost records have been entered and activated. The Std-20X2 costing version represents next year's standard costs, so the blocking policies should allow entry of cost records but prevent activation. The blocking policy for activation would be removed at the appropriate time to allow activation. The blocking policies would then be enforced again after activation.

Item Cost Records for Calculation of Planned Costs A costing version can be designated as a set of planned costs, such as the Simulated-Cost costing version shown in Figure 7.1. The designation supports several simulation capabilities not applicable to cost calculations based on standard costs, such as indicating a different basis of purchased material costs when performing cost calculations for manufactured items. A subsequent section provides further explanation of cost calculations for a manufactured item's planned cost.

Cost Records related to Resources and Overheads The hourly costs for a resource (termed *Cost Categories*) and the manufacturing overhead costs are defined as cost records within a costing version. The costing version must reflect standard costs to support standard cost environments, although actual costing environments can employ a costing version for standard or planned costs. Subsequent sections provide further explanation about resource costs and overhead costs.

Applicability of Item Cost Records to Actual Cost Items The concept of item cost records has limited applicability to items with actual costing as an inventory valuation method (such as FIFO). In a typical scenario, you may employ a costing version for planned costs, and perform cost calculations for a manufactured item in order to create (and analyze) the item's cost record. Activating this item cost record simply populates an initial value for the item's actual cost, as displayed in the item master. A subsequent section provides further explanation of actual costing.

Calculation of Manufactured Item's Sales Price   You can calculate a suggested sales price for a manufactured item in order to create an item sales price record within a costing version. A subsequent section provides further explanation about calculation of a manufactured item's sales price.

Policies about the contents of a Costing Version   The policies can limit the information contained within a costing version. As noted earlier, you designate whether a costing version contains standard costs or planned costs, and whether it contains cost records for a single site or all sites. In addition, you typically designate that it only contains item cost records so that you do not clutter things up with item sales price records.

Comparing Costs (or Prices) within a Costing Version   The nature of a comparison of item cost records depends on your rationale for different costing versions, and how you enter pending costs with a specified activation date. For a selected costing version, you can use the Compare Item Prices report and its associated dialogue to compare the costs (1) to the pending costs in another costing version or (2) to the active costs as per an effective date. For a set of standard cost data, the report options support calculation of the net change in inventory value. The comparison can also apply to item sales price records or item purchase price records.

7.2 Terminology about Item Cost Records and Cost Calculations

Item cost records within a costing version, and the cost calculations for manufactured items, provide the foundation for standard cost environments. This information is viewed and maintained on several AX forms. However, an explanation using these form names leads to cumbersome English-language sentences.[1] This section summarizes the terminology used in the book and the associated names of AX forms, as shown in Figure 7.2 and described below. The explanation focuses on costing versions containing standard costs, but it also

---

[1] The form name "Item Price" is one example. The name may have originated because several types of information can be viewed on the Item Price form, such as a calculated value for an item's suggested sales price (aka the item sales price record). However, the name does not indicate the primary purpose of viewing/maintaining information about an item's costs.

applies to costing versions containing planned costs (which typically do not require activation of item cost records).

Figure 7.2 Terminology for Item Cost Records and Cost Calculations

Terminology used in Book		Name of AX Form
View an Item Cost Record	For a pending cost For an active cost	Item Price
Manually enter an Item Cost Record	For a pending cost	Item Price
Perform a Cost Calculation	For a single item For an item's BOM version For items within a costing version	Cost Calculation for an Item Cost Calculation for a Costing Version
View Results of a Cost Calculation for an item	View an item cost record View costs segmented by cost group View costs in multi-level format	Item Price Summary Calculation Inquiry Complete Calculation Inquiry
Activate Item Cost Record	For a single item For items within a costing version	Item Price Activate Prices

View an Item Cost Record An item cost record defines an item's site-specific costs within a costing version. The initial entry of an item cost record has a pending status, and activating the cost record changes the status to active. Using the Item Price form, you can view both pending and active item cost records for an item.

Manually Enter an Item Cost Record An item's site-specific costs can be manually entered within a costing version (using the Item Price form) to create an item cost record. The initial entry of an item cost record has a pending status, and activating the cost record changes the status to active. Manual entries typically reflect the site-specific costs for a purchased or transfer item, whereas the item cost record for a manufactured item can be automatically created via a cost calculation.

Perform a Cost Calculation for a Manufactured Item (and Create an Item Cost Record) The cost calculation of a manufactured item's site-specific cost creates an item cost record.[2] You can perform the cost calculation for an individual item or one of its BOM versions. Alternatively, they can be performed for multiple items within a costing version, typically in the context of updating standard costs on a periodic basis. A subsequent section (Section 7.7) provides further explanation about performing standard cost calculations.

---

[2] Previous versions of Dynamics AX employed several different terms for *Cost Calculation* such as the BOM Calculation. The new term reflects additional functionality related to purchased items (such as the calculation of purchased material overheads), whereas the previous functionality only applied to manufactured items.

View Results of a Cost Calculation for a Manufactured Item   The results can be viewed for an item cost record on the Item Price form, which provides access to additional inquiries to view costs in a multi-level format or to view costs segmented by cost group.

Activate Item Cost Record   The initial entry of an item cost record has a pending status and pending effectivity date. Activation changes the status to active, and the effectivity date to the actual activation date. You can activate the item cost record for an individual item, or for multiple items within a costing version.

7.3 Significance of Cost Groups

Cost groups serve multiple purposes. Cost groups are user-defined, and you assign them to items, cost categories and overhead formulas. Their purposes include the segmentation (by cost group) of a manufactured item's calculated costs, the calculation of a suggested sales price for a manufactured item based on cost-plus-markup percentages (by cost group), and the assignment of G/L accounts to standard cost variances (based on the cost group assigned to an item). The definition and purposes of cost groups are described below.

Defining a Cost Group and its Cost Group Type   A cost group has a user-defined identifier and a designated cost group type. The cost group type indicates the purpose and constrains the assignment of a cost group. The assignment of a cost group type of *direct material* to a cost group, for example, means that the cost group can only be assigned to material items. Figure 7.3 summarizes the significance of a cost group type, and provides examples of cost groups.

A cost group type of *undefined* does not constrain the assignment of a cost group. For example, an item number that represents a subcontracted service may require standard costing, which involves assignment of a cost group with a type of undefined (and a Product Type = Item).

Assigning a Cost Group   You typically assign a cost group to purchased items. It may be assigned to manufactured items with standard costing, since the cost group can optionally support segmentation of production-related variances. You also assign cost groups to cost categories and overhead formulas in manufacturing environments. As summarized in Figure 7.3, the cost group type constrains the ability to assign a cost group, such as constraining the assignment of direct material cost groups to items.

Figure 7.3 Significance of Cost Group Type

Cost Group Type	Examples of Cost Groups	Significance for Using the Cost Group
Direct Material	Electrical Fabricated Packaging	The cost group can only be assigned to material items (Product Type = Item)
Direct Outsourcing	Subcontract	The cost group can only be assigned to items identified as a service (Product Type = Service)
Direct Manufacturing	Labor Machine	The cost group can only be assigned to cost categories, which define the hourly costs (or piece rate costs) for a resource
Indirect	Overhead	The cost group can only be assigned to an overhead formula
Undefined	Subcontract *	The cost group assignment is not constrained; it can be assigned to an item, service, cost category or overhead formula.

Legend: * = This approach supports standard costing for an item representing a subcontracted service (Product Type = Item), whereas actual costing must be employed for services (Product Type = Service)

Using Cost Groups for Standard Cost Variances Cost groups represent one factor for the assignment of a G/L account to standard cost variances, such as a purchase price variance or a production-related variance. You define these factors and the relevant G/L accounts on the Posting Profile form. At one extreme, a different G/L account can be assigned to individual item numbers. In most cases, the relevant G/L account will reflect the item group and/or the cost group assigned to an item.[3] Case 7.8 describes purchase price variances based on cost groups.

Using Cost Groups for Segmenting the Calculated Costs of a Manufactured Item Cost groups provide the basis for segmenting and analyzing cost contributions in a manufactured item's calculated costs, such as the cost contributions for material, labor and overhead. Synonyms for cost group segmentation include cost breakdown, cost decomposition, and cost classification. Cost group segmentation serves the following purposes.

◆ Segment costs for different types of material based on the cost group assigned to purchased items. These cost groups represent direct material costs.

◆ Segment costs for different types of resources based on the cost categories assigned to a resource and its operations. Examples include different types

---

[3] A companywide policy (defined on the parameters for Inventory and Warehouse Management) determines whether standard cost variances will be calculated by cost group.

of labor and machines, and differences in setup versus run time. These cost groups represent direct manufacturing costs.

◆ Segment costs related to subcontracted services. The cost group is assigned to the item number representing the subcontracted service. Chapter 15 provides further explanation of subcontracted production.

◆ Segment costs for different types of overheads based on the cost groups assigned to overhead formulas. These cost groups represent indirect costs.

◆ Segment costs by cost group type. The cost group type (such as direct material and direct manufacturing) assigned to each cost group provides supplemental segmentation for reporting purposes.

Information about cost group segmentation for a manufactured item's calculated cost can be viewed on the Summary Calculation Inquiry form, Cost Rollup by Cost Group form, and the Variance Analysis Statement report.

Using Cost Groups for Calculating the Suggested Sales Price of a Manufactured Item Cost calculations can be used to calculate a manufactured item's suggested sales price based on a cost-plus markup approach, where the markup reflects the profit-setting percentages assigned to cost groups. For example, a profit-setting percentage of 50% could be defined for a cost group assigned to purchased material, and a profit-setting percentage of 80% could be defined for a cost group assigned to a cost category for labor operations. A subsequent section provides further explanation about calculating this suggested sales price (Section 7.10).

7.4 Standard Costs for Purchased Items

The standard costs for a purchased item are defined by item cost records within a costing version. Each item cost record is uniquely identified by five key fields. An understanding of these key fields provides the starting point for explaining how to maintain an item's standard cost across time.

Key Fields in an Item Cost Record The standard cost for a purchased item is defined by an item cost record within a costing version containing standard costs. The key fields and other fields in an item cost record are summarized in Figure 7.4 and explained below

◆ *Item Identifier.* The item identifier normally consists of an item number. When the item identifier includes a variant code such as color and size, an item-specific policy (termed *use combination cost price*) determines whether item cost records can be maintained for the various combinations of the item number and variant code(s).

Figure 7.4 Key Fields in an Item Cost Record

	Field	Significance of the Field
Key Fields in Item Cost Record	Item Identifier	The identifier indicates the item number; it sometimes includes variant codes.
	Costing Version	The costing version can contain standard costs or planned costs; this costing type affects the calculation policies for a manufactured item's calculated cost.
	Site	A standard cost item requires an item cost record for each site that stocks the item. Transfers between sites can result in a variance when standard costs differ.
Key Fields in	Effective Date	Initial entry of an item cost record has a pending status and effectivity date. Activation changes the status (to active) and effectivity date (to the activation date). Activating an item's standard cost record revalues existing inventory if costs change.
	Status	An item's active standard cost record is used for valuing inventory transactions. Pending item cost records are used in Cost Calculations based on effectivity date.
	Cost	An item's cost is expressed for its inventory unit of measure. A manufactured item's cost can be calculated or directly entered.
	Other Fields	Charges for a manufactured item reflect the calculated amount of amortized constant costs.

◆ *Costing Version.* A costing version contains cost records for standard costs or planned costs, as indicated by its costing type. The costing type also affects the calculation policies for a manufactured item's calculated cost, since standard costing principles must be enforced for standard cost items.

◆ *Site.* An item's cost record must be defined for each site that stocks the standard cost item. For example, an item purchased (or manufactured) at one site and transferred to a second site will require two item cost records, one for each site. The item's cost at the transfer site can be different, such as an increased cost because of handling and transportation. Transfers between sites when an item's standard costs differ will generate a variance (termed a *cost change* variance).

◆ *Effective Date and Status.* The two fields concerning the status and effective date (also termed the activation date) work together in tandem. The initial entry of an item cost record has a pending status and pending effectivity date. Activation changes the status to active, and the effectivity date to the actual activation date.

A standard cost item can only have one active standard cost record for each site, which will be used for valuing an item's inventory transactions at the site. The concept of one active cost record applies to the item regardless of the associated standard costing version. Activating an item's standard cost record will revalue existing inventory if costs change, and generate a variance (termed a *cost revaluation* variance).

Pending item cost records are used in cost calculations based on their effectivity date, and the future date specified for the cost calculation.

◆ *Cost*. An item's cost is expressed for its inventory unit of measure. A purchased item's cost must be directly entered, whereas a manufactured item's cost can be calculated or directly entered.

◆ *Other Fields*. Price charges -- or *charges* for short -- must be included in an item's cost when the costing version contains standard costs. The primary rationale is that AX employs the charges field to indicate the calculated amount of amortized constant costs for a manufactured item, and the related field (termed price quantity) to indicate the accounting lot size used in the calculations. Ignoring these charges would run counter to standard costing principles.

In terms of purchased items, it is suggested that you enter a zero value for the charges field. The item's standard cost (including charges) is compared to a purchase order price in order to calculate a purchase price variance. You obtain a false variance if you entered a value in the charges field.

You can enter the item cost records and activate individual pending records (using the Item Price form), or activate all pending records within a costing version (using the Activate Prices form).

Maintaining Standard Costs for a Purchased Item   The maintenance of a purchased item's standard cost involves the definition of item cost records within a costing version, as described in the previous subsection. The data maintenance starts with the initial loading of an item's cost prior to system cutover, and subsequent updates reflect a progression through time. For example, you would activate the initially loaded costs, and subsequently enter and activate a pending cost in a costing version that represents next year. You may enter a pending cost in a costing version that represents a simulated cost in order to perform simulated cost calculations for manufactured items.

Suggestions for Copying Item Cost Records   A copy function facilitates preparation of item cost records, such as preparing the next period's standard costs or preparing costs for a new site or a different site. The copy function (embedded in the Copy Costing Version form) focuses on the copy-to costing version, and there are two basic options for the copy-from source. You can copy the item cost records from a specified costing version, or copy the active item cost records regardless of costing version. The item cost records can be selectively copied (such as copying selected item numbers) to populate the copy-to costing version. The item cost records can also be selectively changed as part of the copy process. For example, you can change the costs based on a factor or amount, change the site (thereby creating cost records for another site), or change the effectivity date (thereby creating cost records applicable to a future time period). The newly-created item cost records have a pending status and can be manually maintained.[4] Costs for manufactured items need to be recalculated.

Purchase Price Variances An item's standard cost provides the basis for calculating purchase price variances at the time of purchase order receipt (reflecting the difference with the purchase order price) and invoice entry (reflecting the difference between the purchase order price and invoice price).

7.5 Define Resource Costs via Cost Categories

Cost categories define the hourly costs for a resource and its related routing operations. Common synonyms include labor rate codes and machine rate codes. If applicable, a cost category can also define the piece rate for a resource. The cost categories assigned to a resource will act as default values for its operations. The preparation of cost category information includes the assignment of a cost group. Different cost categories will be needed to support different purposes, as illustrated below.

◆ Assign different hourly costs by resource, such as different costs for various types of labor skills, machines, or manufacturing cells.

◆ Assign different hourly costs for an operation's setup and run time.

◆ If applicable, assign piece rates by resource by assigning a cost category to the output units associated with an operation.

◆ Segment different types of direct manufacturing costs in cost calculations, such as segmentation of labor and machine costs, based on the cost group assigned to cost categories.

◆ Provide the basis for routing-related overhead calculations, such as an hourly overhead amount for a resource.

Definition of a Cost Category The definition of a cost category requires two steps: one step to define a *shared cost category* and a second step to define the *cost category* for production purposes.

The second step requires additional information when the cost category also applies to project-related time estimates and reporting. This additional

---

[4] Several restrictions apply to the copy process. First, the copy process cannot create duplicate item cost records in the copy-to costing version. Second, planned costs can only be copied to another costing version that contains planned costs; they cannot be copied to a costing version that contains standard costs. Third, the copy process does not apply to cost records for cost categories and overhead formulas.

information includes the assignment of a project category group (that supports a transaction type of hours), a line property (that indicates a default value for how reported hours will be charged to a project), and the hourly costs and sales prices associated with a project.

Define Standard Costs for a Cost Category Each cost category has its associated cost records within a costing version containing standard costs. The cost records can reflect site-specific costs or companywide costs. Cost calculations for a manufactured item employ the current active cost records for a cost category, and also consider pending cost records (based on effectivity date) when using a future calculation date. Figure 7.5 summarizes the key fields in the cost record for a cost category.

Figure 7.5 Key Fields in the Cost Record for a Cost Category

Field		Significance of the Field
Key Fields in Cost Record	Identifier	The identifier indicates the cost category (e.g., labor rate code)
	Costing Version	The costing version type can be standard cost or planned cost.
	Site	The cost record for a cost category can be site-specific or company-wide.
	Effective Date	Initial entry of the cost record has a pending status and effectivity date. Activation of the cost record changes the status (to current active) and effectivity date (to the actual activation date). If an existing record has a current active status, activation changes its status to previous active.
	Status	The current active cost record (regardless of costing version) will be used for valuing the estimated and actual time on a production order. Pending cost records are used in cost calculations based on effectivity date.
Cost		The cost represents a resource's hourly cost (for setup and run time), or its piece rate cost (for output quantity), expressed in the local currency.
Other Fields		The cost group assigned to each cost category provides the basis for segmentation of direct manufacturing costs in cost calculations.

The key fields for a cost category are similar to those of an item cost record, but there are several differences. These differences can be highlighted using an example of a labor rate code. The labor rate can be site-specific or companywide, the labor rate can be different for run time and setup time elements (or piece rate). There is also a slight change in handling the cost record status, where activation of a pending cost record changes its status to current active, and also changes the status of an existing record (if any) from current active to previous active.

Define Planned Costs for a Cost Category Planned costs can be assigned to a cost category for simulation purposes. In addition, an actual costing environment typically defines planned costs (rather than standard costs) for a cost category, so that actual costs on a production order can be calculated.

7.6 Define Overhead Costs via Overhead Formulas

The definition of an overhead formula supports the calculation of a manufactured item's overheads (termed *indirect costs*). An overhead formula can calculate different types of overheads for a manufactured item, such as material- or routing-related overheads, or overheads based on the item's weight or volume. Each overhead formula has a unique identifier, and it must be defined as part of the Costing Sheet Setup form. After defining the identifier, you can maintain the cost records associated with the overhead formula.

Define an Overhead Formula within a Costing Sheet Setting up the costing sheet involves defining a format for displaying information about the cost of goods manufactured (COGM) for a manufactured item or a production order. The format (termed a *costing sheet*) segments material, labor and overhead costs based on the cost groups assigned to items, cost categories, and overhead formulas. The definition of a costing sheet format is required to support overhead formulas. An overhead formula can define different types of overheads, as described below.

♦ *Surcharge Percentage for Material-Related Overhead.* An overhead formula for a material-related overhead employs a surcharge percentage. For example, the percentage can be applied to the value of an item's first level components that have a specified cost group. Each overhead formula has an assigned cost group.

♦ *Rate Amount for Routing-Related Overhead.* An overhead formula for a routing-related overhead employs a rate amount. The rate amount will be added to the hourly cost for run time (or setup time) when the operation's cost category has a specified cost group. Each overhead formula has an assigned cost group.

♦ *Per-Unit Amount based on the Manufactured Item's Weight, Volume or Quantity.* The overhead formula (termed an *output unit based* formula) defines a per unit amount that reflects the specified weight or volume for the manufactured item. It can also simply reflect a per unit amount for a quantity of one. The overhead formula does not employ an assigned cost group.

♦ *Per-Unit Amount based on the Component's Weight or Volume or Quantity.* The overhead formula (termed an *input unit based* formula) defines a per unit amount that reflects the weight or volume for the components of a manufactured item. Each overhead formula indicates the applicable cost group of the components.

With each of these approaches, you can optionally define applicability rules within the cost records for the overhead formula, so that an overhead formula only applies to a specific manufactured item or group of items.

Key Fields in a Cost Record for an Overhead Formula You can maintain the cost records for each overhead formula, such as indicating the overheads for different sites, years, and manufactured items. Figure 7.6 summarizes the key fields in the cost record for an overhead formula.

The key fields for an overhead formula's cost record share some similarities to those of an item cost record, but there are several differences. These differences can be highlighted using an example of a surcharge percentage for a material-related overhead. For example, the surcharge percentage can be site-specific or companywide, and vary by manufactured item based on applicability rules. There is also a slight change in handling the cost record status, where activation of a pending cost record changes its status to current active, and also changes the status of an existing record (if any) from current active to previous active.

Figure 7.6 Key Fields in Cost Record for an Overhead Formula

	Field	Significance of the Field
Key Fields in Cost Record	Identifier	The user-defined identifier assigned to a node within the costing sheet
	Costing Version	The costing version can reflect a cost type of standard cost or planned cost.
	Site	The cost record for an overhead formula can be site-specific or company-wide.
	Effective Date	Initial entry of the cost record has a pending status and effectivity date. Activation of the cost record changes the status (to current active) and effectivity date (to the actual activation date). If an existing record has a current active status, activation changes its status to previous active.
	Status	The current active cost record (regardless of costing version) will be used for calculating estimated and actual overheads on a production order. Pending cost records are used in cost calculations based on effectivity date.
	Applicability Rule	The overhead formula can apply to a specific manufactured item, a subset of items (based on item group), or all manufactured items.
Overhead	Surcharge Percentage	The surcharge percentage is used to calculate material-related overheads.
	Rate Amount	The rate amount is used to calculate routing-related overheads.
	Output Unit Based Amount	The per-unit amount applies to the manufactured item's weight or volume, or to a quantity of one.
	Input Unit Based Amount	The per-unit amount applies to the components' weight or volume.

Alternative Approaches to Routing-Related Overheads Several approaches can be used to model routing-related overheads. One approach involves the just-described overhead formula to calculate an incremental overhead cost for an operation's run time or setup time, or its piece rate. A second approach employs a secondary resource for a routing operation, where the secondary resource represents a resource overhead. A third approach applies to cases where overheads can be tied to output units (rather than time), where the cost category assigned to an operation's output quantity can indicate the overhead amount per unit.

Overhead Costs for Purchased Material   The overhead costs for purchased material often reflect internal handling costs or the costs associated with acquisition, such as duties, freight and other landed costs. These overhead costs (termed *purchase indirect costs*) can be calculated as a surcharge percentage of the item's value, or as a per-unit amount based on the item's weight or volume. They are defined within a separate section of the Costing Sheet labeled "Costs of Purchase", much like defining overhead formulas within the Cost of Goods Manufactured section.

7.7 Standard Cost Calculations for Manufactured Items

The cost calculations for a manufactured item will create an associated item cost record within a costing version. The cost calculations require some preparation information about purchased items and manufactured items. The dialogue for initiating the cost calculations varies slightly based on how you initiate them, such as initiating them for a costing version versus a single item. Several policies affect the cost calculations for standard costs, and constant costs will be amortized over an accounting lot size. These topics are included in the following subsections.

◆ Prepare item information for cost calculations
◆ Initiate a cost calculation
◆ Policies affecting standard cost calculations
◆ Amortizing constant costs for a manufactured item
◆ Calculating costs for items with missing costs
◆ Cost calculations using the fallback principle

Prepare Item Information for Cost Calculations   Cost calculations use item master information about purchased components and manufacturing items, as described below.

◆ *Information about Purchased Components.* Each purchased component should have an item cost record containing its standard cost. Each component should also be assigned a calculation group and a cost group. The calculation group assigned to a purchased item defines applicable warning conditions in cost calculations (such as zero cost or a zero component quantity for the item). The cost group assigned to a purchased item provides segmentation in the calculated costs of its parent item.

◆ *Information about Manufactured Items.* Each manufactured item should be assigned a calculation group. The calculation group defines applicable warning conditions in cost calculations, such as the lack of an active BOM version. When a manufactured item has constant costs, you should also assign the accounting lot size for amortizing these constant costs, as described in a subsequent subsection.

◆ *Ignore a Component's Costs in the Cost Calculations.* As part of the BOM line information, you can optionally flag a component so that its costs are not included in the cost calculation of its parent item.

◆ *Ignore a Routing Operation's Costs in the Cost Calculations.* You optionally flag a routing operation so that its costs (associated with run time, setup time or piece rate) are not included in the cost calculation of its parent item. These policies are embedded in the Route Group assigned to the operation.

◆ *Treating a Manufactured Item as a Purchased Item.* An item-specific policy will prevent calculation of the item's costs. This "Stop Explosion" policy is embedded in the Calculation Group assigned to the item.

Initiate a Cost Calculation Initiating a cost calculation involves a dialogue, and the nature of the dialogue varies slightly depending on where you initiate it. The cost calculations can be initiated for a single manufactured item or its BOM version, or for multiple items within a costing version, as summarized in Figure 7.7 and described below.

◆ *Cost Calculation for a Costing Version.* Initiating the cost calculation for a costing version will display a dialogue form so that you can enter relevant information. As shown in the right hand column of Figure 7.7, the dialogue inherits the costing version, and you can optionally select items and employ the where-used concept. [5] Information about the specified site and

---

[5] The concept of where-used updates is motivated by the single-level cost calculation for standard costs, since an item's recalculated cost can impact higher levels within the product structure. This impact on higher levels can also be calculated by performing the cost calculations for all manufactured items.

calculation date can be inherited from the costing version policies or manually entered. Figure 7.7 displays the inherited information and the ability to override the information. As an example, the costing version may contain costs for a specified site so that the inherited site cannot be overridden.

You can also initiate the dialogue for a cost calculation by starting from a selected BOM version for a manufactured item.

Figure 7.7 Dialogue for Initiating a Cost Calculation

Dialogue Information	Initiating a Cost Calculation: For an Item	Initiating a Cost Calculation: For a Costing Version
Key Fields in Item Cost Record: Item Identifier	Inherited	All items or selected items or where-used items
Key Fields in Item Cost Record: Costing Version	User specified	Inherited
Key Fields in Item Cost Record: Site	Inherited from costing version policy; Or manually enter the site and calculation date (if not mandated)	
Key Fields in Item Cost Record: Calculation Date		
BOM Version	Inherit active version for the item and site; Optionally override with an approved version for the item	Inherit active version for the item and site
Route Version		
Calculation Quantity	Inherit the item's accounting lot size; Optionally override the quantity	Inherit the item's accounting lot size
Calculated Cost	Generate an item cost record for the single item	Generate an item cost record for each selected item

Policies affecting Cost Calculations The nature of cost calculations varies slightly depending on whether the calculations involve a costing version for standard costs or planned costs, and the policies that can be inherited from the specified costing version. These policies are explained below.

- *Cost Calculation Policies for Standard Costs.* Cost calculations with standard costs must be restricted by costing version policies because the restrictions ensure standard costing principles will produce accurate consistent results. For example, these mandated restrictions mean that cost roll-up calculations are limited to a single level (termed a single level *explosion mode*), the source of a purchased item's cost data must be from the item cost records within a costing version, and charges must be included in the unit cost of an item. Charges for a manufactured item reflect the calculated amortization of constant costs.

◆ *Cost Calculation Policies for Planned Costs.* Cost calculations with planned costs do not have to follow standard costing principles. This means you can perform multi-level cost roll-up calculations, and the source of a purchased item's cost data can be from item cost records or from another source such as purchase price trade agreements (as specified by an item's calculation group).

◆ *Other Cost Calculation Policies.* Cost calculations can generate warning messages.[6] The messages can also identify other types of information, such as the fallback information (when using the fallback principle), and the items which did not get updated with cost calculations (when updating calculated costs for items with missing cost records).

Amortizing Constant Costs for a Manufactured Item A manufactured item's constant costs reflect operation setup times, the components with a constant quantity (or constant scrap amount), or a component quantity expressed as a step function. The concept of an accounting lot size is used to amortize these constant costs in cost calculations. The item's site-specific standard order quantity (for inventory) acts as the default value for the accounting lot size; the quantity may be greater to reflect a multiple within the order quantity modifiers for the item.[7]

The default value for an accounting lot size is displayed as the calculation quantity when performing a cost calculation for a single item, and it can be overridden. The specified calculation quantity only applies to the parent item. An alternative approach only applies to planned cost calculations, where you specify a make-to-order explosion mode so that the specified quantity acts as the accounting lot size for the parent item and all manufactured components.

The calculated amount of a manufactured item's amortized constant costs is termed *price charges (*or *charges* for short). After calculating a manufactured item's cost, these charges are displayed as two fields identifying the total amount and the accounting lot size (termed the *price quantity* field). These two fields are displayed on the Item Price form. Activating a manufactured item's cost record updates this information on the item master. These charges are always included in the item's standard cost and used for valuing inventory transactions.

---

[6] The warning messages reflect the applicable warning conditions defined within the Calculation Group assigned to items, and you can override these warning conditions in the dialogue for initiating a cost calculation. For example, a warning message can indicate a zero quantity component or the lack of an active BOM version for a manufactured item.

[7] The definition of an item's accounting lot size differs for a formula item, where the formula size for the item's active formula version acts as the default value for the accounting lot size.

Calculating Costs for Items with Missing Costs   The concept of a *missing cost* refers to a manufactured item without a pending cost record (for the relevant key fields). For example, when you prepare item cost records within a costing version for a new period (prior to activation), a pending cost may not yet exist for an item. A missing cost typically reflects a new manufactured item, or an item that requires recalculation because the pending cost record was intentionally deleted. Cost calculations can be performed for just the items with a missing cost record, thereby supporting a net change approach to cost calculations.

When attempting to update costs for items with missing costs, it may be useful to be notified (via messages) that an item already has a pending cost record thereby preventing the desired outcome of updating the missing costs.

Cost Calculations using the Fallback Principle   The fallback principle indicates an alternative source of cost data (for a cost calculation) when an item's cost data does not exist within the specified costing version. Cost calculations for item cost records within a single costing version employ a fallback principle of none. However, several situations can benefit from cost calculations employing a fallback principle of using another costing version or the active cost records. The following situations illustrate use of the fallback principle with standard costs.

◆ *Two-Version and n-Version Approaches to Maintaining Standard Costs.* A costing version can contain the incremental changes to standard costs, such as pending cost records that represent new items or cost changes. The use of separate costing versions for incremental changes is commonly termed the two-version or n-version approach to maintaining standard cost data. In this situation, the fallback principle can identify the use of the active costs contained within other costing versions (the n-version approach), or within a specified fallback costing version (the two-version approach).

◆ *Simulating the Impact of Cost Changes on Standard Costs.* A costing version that represents next year's standard costs can contain pending cost records about selected cost categories, overhead formulas, and/or purchased material. For example, the entry of pending cost records can reflect the anticipated cost changes for critical purchased components and labor rates. In this situation, the fallback principle can identify the use of the current year's costing version, and the cost calculation can create pending cost records for all manufactured items.

Simulations about the impact of cost changes are generally performed using cost calculations with planned costs, where the fallback principle reflects the active standard costs. The cost calculations can be multilevel (rather than single level), and the costs for purchased components can be based on different sources, such as purchase price trade agreements (rather than item cost records).

7.8 Convert Items to a Standard Cost Method

A standard cost conversion refers to changing an item's inventory valuation method from an actual costing approach to a standard costing approach. The conversion process involves performing a prerequisite inventory close, performing several steps during a transition period (defined by a transition start date and a planned conversion date), and then performing the conversion and an associated inventory close at the end of the conversion period.

After successful completion of the conversion process, each item will have a standard cost inventory model and the item's standard costs will be activated. Subsequent inventory transactions will be valued at the item's standard cost. In addition, the system converts the item's physical inventory transactions during the transition period (for receipts and issues) to standard cost as per the conversion date. The system also converts the item's financial on-hand inventory to standard costs, and posts the value difference as an inventory revaluation variance.

You can analyze revaluation variances using the variance analysis report. You can also analyze inventory value before and after the conversion date using the inventory value by inventory dimension report.

7.9 Planned Cost Calculations for Manufactured Items

Cost calculations can be used to calculate a manufactured item's planned cost, where the costing version reflects a costing type of planned cost. One advantage of using planned costs is that cost calculations can be multilevel rather than single level. A second advantage is the capability to create item cost records for purchased components based on information about each item's purchase price trade agreements, and then use these for calculating costs for manufactured items. This capability represents an easier-to-use alternative to a historical AX approach, where you designate the source of cost data for a purchased item (such as trade agreements) within the Calculation Group assigned to the item. Finally, you can creatively use the fallback principle in planned cost calculations, which minimizes data maintenance for simulation purposes.

Source of Cost Data for Purchased Items There are two basic options on the source of cost data for purchased items. You indicate the choice (termed the Cost Price Model) when performing a planned cost calculation.

◆ *Costing Version* (termed Version Cost Price). Costs for purchased items are based on item cost records within a costing version. These item cost records can be automatically created from purchase price trade agreement information, as described in the next subsection.

◆ *Calculation Group.* Costs for purchased items are based on the source of cost data designated by the calculation group assigned to an item. In this case, the source of information can be (1) the item's inventory cost, such as the item's actual cost or active standard cost (2) the item master information about the item's standard purchase price, which can be updated automatically by the last purchase invoice, (3) the manually specified cost on the item master, or (4) the purchase price trade agreement information with the item's preferred vendor. The designated calculation group can reflect a companywide policy, which requires the assignment of a blank value for each component item.[8]

A planned cost calculation employs the active cost records for cost categories and overhead formulas. The cost calculations generate an item cost record for manufactured items within the specified costing version. This item cost record provides the starting point for viewing the cost calculation details, such as viewing the costs in a multi-level format. This item cost record provides reference information, and is typically never activated.

Using Planned Cost Calculations to Create Item Cost Records for Purchased Items based on Purchase Price Trade Agreements
Planned cost calculations can use item cost records within a costing version as the source of costs. In addition, the planned cost calculations can automatically create these item cost records (for purchased items) based on purchase price trade agreements. The cost calculation approach is labeled the Purchase Price Model with the option for Trade Agreements. The approach involves the following steps.

◆ *Identify purchased items.* A purchased item is designated by the planned order type of "purchase order," which can be specified as a companywide or site-specific policy for the item.

---

[8] The companywide policy for a calculation group is defined as part of the parameters for Inventory and Warehouse Management.

◆ *Create item cost records for purchased items.* Planned cost calculations will automatically generate the item cost records for purchased items, but only when you designate the relevant policy (termed "items procured using purchase order") for performing the cost calculation. The associated cost will reflect the item's purchase price trade agreements with its preferred vendor. The associated cost will also reflect a quantity of 1, regardless of quantity breakpoints in the trade agreement. The newly-created item cost records can then be used in planned cost calculations for manufactured items.

The Purchase Price Model has one other option. The option is labeled Item Purchase Price, but a longer phrase would be more informative such as "item purchase price records within the costing version". This approach means that an item cost record will be automatically created based on previously entered information about item purchase price records within the costing version. The approach only works when the costing version allows entry of the item purchase price records.

7.10 Calculation of a Manufactured Item's Sales Price

The alternative approaches to defining an item's sales price are described in a subsequent chapter about sales order processing. One of these approaches employs cost calculations to calculate a manufactured item's suggested sales price based on a cost-plus markup approach or a rolled price approach, as described below.

◆ *Cost-Plus Markup Approach.* The markup reflects the profit-setting percentages assigned to cost groups, where a cost group can be assigned to each purchased item, cost category, and overhead formula. Each cost group can be assigned up to four sets of profit-setting percentages, labeled Standard, Profit 1, Profit 2, and Profit 3. Within the Profit 1 set, for example, a profit-setting percentage of 50% could be defined for a cost group assigned to purchased material, and a profit-setting percentage of 80% could be defined for a cost group assigned to a cost category for labor operations.

◆ *Rolled Price Approach* The rolled price approach only applies to a component. The cost calculation uses the component's standard sales price (rather than its cost) to calculate the manufactured item's sales price.

A policy within the calculation group assigned to a purchased item (termed the *sales price model*) determines whether the component's sales price or cost-plus-markup will be used in the calculation of a sales price for a manufactured item.

A cost calculation can generate an item sales price record (rather than an item cost record) within a specified costing version.[9] The item sales price record provides the starting point for viewing the calculation details, such as viewing costs and sales prices in a multi-level format. An item's sales price record primarily acts as reference information. However, activating an item's sales price record will update the item's standard sales price on the item master, which represents one option for an item's sales price.

7.11 Order-Specific Calculations for an Item's Cost and Sales Price

An order-specific cost calculation typically applies to make-to-order products in the context of a line item on a sales order or quote, and results in a calculated cost and sales price for the line item. It shares many similarities to a cost calculation with planned costs, but it reflects a different purpose and different capabilities. The major differences are summarized in Figure 7.8 and described below.

Figure 7.8 Order-Specific Calculations for an Item's Cost and Sales Price

	Cost Calculation with Planned Costs	Order-Specific Calculation
Primary Purpose	Calculate the planned cost of a manufactured item	Calculate the estimated cost and sales price of a make-to-order product for sales purposes
Key Outputs	Generate an item cost record within a costing version	Generate a calculation record containing the calculated cost and sales price; Transfer the calculated sales price to the order
Key Inputs	Information specified for cost calculation Source of component's cost data within a costing version Source of labor rates and overhead formula within a costing version	Inherit information from originating sales order Source of component's cost data based on calculation code assigned to items Current active costs for labor and overheads
Secondary Purposes	Calculate an item's suggested sales price and generate an item sales price record within a costing version	Simulate an order's calculated sales price using a different set of profit percentages, a different manufacturing site, a different quantity, or a different date.
	Simulate an item's calculated cost using a set of item cost records, or using a source of component's cost data (when calculating planned costs)	

Primary Purpose An order-specific cost calculation is performed in the context of a sales order, sales quotation, or service order line item, typically to calculate an estimated sales price based on a cost-plus-markup approach. An order-specific calculation has the exact same logic as a cost calculation with

---

[9] The costing version must be able to contain item sales price records.

planned costs using the items' calculation group to indicate the source of component costs, an explosion mode of "according to BOM line type", and the current active costs as the fallback principle (for labor rates and overhead formulas).

Key Outputs An order-specific calculation generates a *Calculation Record* containing the calculated cost and sales price. It may be performed multiple times for a single order, such as simulating the calculated sales price using different sets of profit percentages, thereby generating multiple calculation records. The Calculation Results' form displays an item's calculation records. The sales price for a selected calculation record can be transferred to the originating line item.

An order-specific calculation only applies to a sales context. It does not generate an item cost record or an item sales price record within a costing version.

Key Inputs The key inputs for an order-specific calculation initially reflect the values from the originating line item. These initial values include the ship-from site, ship date, order quantity, and the sub-BOM and sub-route (if specified). The initial values can be overridden. In particular, the site can be overridden to reflect a different manufacturing site, which may involve a different BOM version, route version, and costs for material, labor and overhead.

You can specify the desired set of profit-setting percentages, and an explosion mode (of multi-level or make-to-order). The explosion mode impacts the assumption of an accounting lot size for amortization of constant costs.

Secondary Purposes An order-specific calculation has a few secondary purposes, such as simulations of an order's calculated sales price using different sets of profit percentages, a different manufacturing site, and a different quantity or date (which would affect usage of purchase price agreement information). The retention of previous calculations (viewed on the Calculation Results form) also supports comparisons of price.

7.12 Summary of Standard Cost Variances

Several types of standard cost variances can be generated, and each variance will be posted to a relevant G/L account. This section summarizes the variances and definition of G/L accounts.

Purchase Price Variance An item's site-specific standard cost provides the basis for calculating purchase price variances at the time of purchase order receipt (reflecting the difference with the purchase order price) and invoice entry (reflecting the difference between the purchase order price and invoice price).

Cost Change Variance Transfers between sites will generate a cost change variance when there are differences between an item's site-specific standard costs. The variance is generated at the time of receipt for a transfer order. An item's standard cost at two different sites can be different for several reasons. For example, the item's costs may be higher because of the associated transfer costs to another site, or because of different manufacturing or purchasing costs.

Inventory Revaluation Variance Activating an item's standard cost record will revalue existing inventory if costs change, and generate a cost revaluation variance. This variance can also be created when converting to a standard cost model, since conversion of an item's financial on-hand inventory to standard costs will generate a variance for the value difference.

Production-Related Variances Production-related variances are automatically calculated after ending a production order for a standard cost item. The variances reflect a comparison between the reported production activities and the item's standard cost calculation (not to the order's estimated costs). Four types of variances are calculated: lot size variance, production quantity variance, production price variance, and production substitution variance. Similar variances are also calculated for co/by-products. A subsequent chapter about production orders provides further explanation of production-related variances (Section 14.12).

G/L Accounts for Standard Cost Variances Item groups and cost groups represent two factors for the assignment of a G/L account to standard cost variances, such as a purchase price variance or a production-related variance. You define these factors and the relevant G/L accounts on the Posting Profile form.

7.13 Actual Costing

Actual costing provides different approaches for valuing an item's on-hand inventory. Several actual costing inventory models are supported by Dynamics AX, as summarized in Figure 7.9. Each item must be assigned an item model group, which defines the inventory model and related policies. For example, the policy to prevent negative physical inventory should be enforced to avoid calculation problems in actual costing. With the exception of moving average, these inventory models impact an inventory close process, as described in the next two subsections.

Figure 7.9 Actual Costing Methods

Inventory Model	Impact of Inventory Model on the Inventory Closing Process
Weighted Average	Issues will be settled against a summarized weighted average for the month
Weighted Average Date	Issues will be settled against a summarized weighted average for each day
FIFO	Issues will be settled against the oldest receipts within monthly period
LIFO	Issues will be settled against the newest receipts within monthly period
LIFO Date	Issues will be settled against the newest receipts closest to the issue date
Basic Rules for the above Inventory Models	An item's issues will be valued at a running average cost (as of the transaction date). The running average cost reflects the average of the financially updated transactions; it can optionally include physically updated transactions. The user can optionally link (aka mark) a specific receipt to a specific issue transaction.
Moving Average	None. Inventory close only closes the accounting period..

Impact on the Inventory Closing Process Most of the inventory models for actual costing are based on periodic calculations termed *inventory closing and adjustment.* Several basic rules apply to these inventory models, as described below.

◆ An item's issue transaction (such as a sales order shipment) will be valued at a running average cost as of the transaction date. The running average cost reflects the average of the financially updated transactions; it can optionally include physically updated transactions.

◆ The month end closing process will settle (aka match) the relevant receipt transactions to the issue transaction based on the item's inventory model, and adjust the item's issue transaction to the correct cost as of the closing date. The receipt transactions must be financially updated, such as an invoiced purchase receipt or the ended status for a production order.

◆ You can optionally link (aka mark) a specific receipt to a specific issue transaction, which will be used in month-end settlements regardless of the item's inventory model. Marking can occur before or after an issue transaction has been posted.

An inventory closing is normally performed at month end. Each inventory model for actual costing has a slightly different impact on the inventory closing process, as shown in right side of Figure 7.9. The inventory close process will settle issue transactions to receipt transactions based on the inventory model assigned to an item, and create adjustments to the value of on-hand inventory quantities based on financially updated receipts. These adjustments reflect corrections to the running average cost that was originally used to value an inventory transaction. An inventory close prevents users from posting inventory transactions to a prior period, and you can reverse a completed inventory close.

Prior to the inventory closing, you should identify open quantities (via the Open Quantities report) that reflect financial issue transactions that cannot be matched to a financial receipt. A related step identifies excessively high financial receipts that exceed an item's cost and user-specified deviation percentage (via the Investigation of Cost Price for Receipts report). You can then take action on the open quantities and deviations.

Moving Average Cost This approach does not involve the inventory closing process, and primarily applies to purchased material. With moving average, a purchased item's cost is determined at the time of receipt based on its purchase price. If the price differs on the vendor invoice, the difference is proportionally adjusted to current inventory, and any remaining amount is expensed. The approach can apply to a manufactured item, where a production order receipt is valued at the estimated cost for the order, and no adjustments occur after ending the order (even if actual costs differ).

7.14 Workspaces Related to Product Costing

The Cost Administration workspace provides information related to product costing. It identifies items with a missing active cost, including standard cost items without an active item cost record. The active cost is typically calculated for manufactured items based on BOM and route information. The links provide access to several key constructs, such as costing versions, cost categories and the costing sheet.

This workspace covers additional aspects of cost administration that apply to other chapters, such as identifying production orders with high variances (Section 14.12) and providing links to reports/inquiries about inventory accounting (Section 16.6).

7.15 Additional Case Studies

Case 7.1: Cost Segmentation of Manufacturing Costs A discrete manufacturer calculated the total cost for each of their salable products, and employed cost group segmentation to understand their cost structure. The material costs were segmented into different cost groups (such as electrical parts and fabricated parts) and the manufacturing costs were segmented into different cost groups (such as fabrication, subassembly and final assembly).

Case 7.2: Simulate Impact of Cost Changes The cost accountant at a discrete manufacturer wanted to simulate the impact of potential cost changes on the calculated costs of manufactured items. The company had already been maintaining the active standard costs for all items within multiple costing versions, and the active cost records for labor rates and overhead formulas, so that active cost records could be used as the fallback principle in cost calculations. The cost accountant employed a separate costing version containing planned costs to define pending cost records (for selected items, labor rates and overhead formulas) that represented the potential cost changes, and then performed a cost calculation for this costing version to simulate the impact. The resulting item cost records were analyzed using the Complete Calculation inquiry.

Case 7.3: Allocate Overheads based on Material The cost accountant at a discrete manufacturer wanted to allocate overheads based on material, especially since routing information was not defined. An overhead calculation formula was employed to apply a surcharge percentage to the value of components in order to allocate overheads to the manufactured items.

Case 7.4: Maintain Standard Costs in Multisite Operations A discrete manufacturing company had multiple manufacturing sites producing different end-items that were transferred to a distribution site. In order to maintain standard costs, the cost accountant defined multiple costing versions representing the different sites. These costing versions also represented each site's standard costs for the current year, so that the cost accountant defined additional costing versions to represent each site's standard costs for next year. The cost accountant used these costing versions in a three-step approach to maintaining next year's standard costs, as summarized below.

◆ *Step 1: Prepare next year's standard costs at the manufacturing sites.* For each manufacturing site, the cost accountant copied the active cost records from one costing version (representing the current year's standard costs) to create pending cost records within another costing version (representing next year's standard costs) with a pending date of January 1st. The cost accountant updated the pending costs for purchased items to reflect expected cost changes and calculated the costs for manufactured end-items, thereby preparing next year's standard costs as pending cost records.

◆ *Step 2: Prepare next year's standard costs at the distribution site.* The cost accountant copied the pending cost records (for end-items) from the costing versions for each manufacturing site to the costing version for the distribution site. As part of the copying process, the item cost records were marked up by 5% to reflect the freight/handling costs associated with transfers to the distribution site.

◆ *Step 3: Activate next year's standard costs.* On January 1st, the cost accountant activated the pending cost records within the costing versions representing next year's standard costs.

Case 7.5: Calculate Sales Prices based on Cost The sales manager at a discrete manufacturer wanted to calculate a suggested sales price for manufactured items based on a cost-plus-markup approach. The company had already been maintaining a costing version containing the standard costs for all items, labor rates and overhead formulas. The sales manager defined the profit-setting percentages for the various cost groups associated with material, labor and overhead. The sales manager also defined a separate costing version that only contained item sales price records. The sales manager then performed a cost calculation for this costing version to calculate the suggested sales price using a specified set of profit-setting percentages.

Case 7.6: Calculate Sales Prices for a Sales Quotation The sales manager at a discrete manufacturer wanted to calculate an item's suggested sales price for sales quotations, which could then be used to support price negotiation efforts. The sales manager wanted the calculated price to reflect a cost-plus-markup approach and the purchase price trade agreements as the source of cost data for purchased components. As part of entering a sales quotation, an order-specific cost calculation was performed to calculate the suggested sales price, and the suggested price could then be transferred to the sales quotation line item.

Case 7.7: Costing for Precious Metal Components A fabricated products company used several types of precious metal components with purchase prices that could vary widely on a week-to-week basis. They wanted to immediately reflect new purchase prices of the precious metals in each end-item's cost and sales price. Using a standard cost approach, the standard cost of each precious metal was updated after a change in purchase price, and the end-items' costs (and suggested sales prices) were recalculated using cost calculations. The cost changes revalued the existing inventory of components and products, but the company generally carried a minimum level of inventory.

Case 7.8: Purchase Price Variances based on Cost Group   A manufacturer of printed circuit boards defined one item group representing electronic components that was assigned to the relevant purchased items. In addition, the company defined several cost groups for different types of electronic components such as integrated circuit chips and capacitors in order to support cost group segmentation of a manufactured item's calculated costs. These cost groups (rather than the item group) were also used to assign the G/L accounts for purchase price variances.

7.16 Executive Summary

Product cost information supports valuation of an item's inventory transactions using a standard cost or actual cost method. Standard costs for items are maintained in a set of standard cost data termed a costing version. Manufacturers can also maintain labor rates and overhead formulas in a set of cost data, and use cost calculations to maintain the standard costs for manufactured items. In addition, the cost calculations can be used for simulating the impact of cost changes, or to calculate a suggested sales price. These simulations can optionally employ a set of planned cost data, which supports additional options in cost calculations. As an example option, the source of cost data for purchased items can reflect purchase price trade agreements rather than the item cost records within a costing version.

With actual costing methods, an item's actual cost is not maintained in a costing version. An item's actual cost reflects financially-updated receipt transactions such as invoiced purchase orders. For manufactured items, the actual production costs for a production order reflect the active labor rates for routing operations and the overhead formulas, where labor rates and overhead formulas are defined in a costing version. Planned costs for manufactured items can also be calculated and maintained in a set of cost data. The cost calculations can be used for simulating projected costs or the impact of cost changes, or to calculate a suggested sales price. With planned cost calculations, the source of cost data for purchased items can reflect their actual cost or purchase price trade agreement, or item cost records within a costing version.

An order-specific cost calculation can be used in the context of a sales order, sales quotation or service order line item in order to calculate the estimated cost and sales price of a manufactured item, and optionally transfer the calculated sales price to the originating line item.

Several case studies illustrated product costing functionality, such as cost segmentation for a manufactured item, simulating the impact of cost changes, and allocating overheads based on material.

Chapter 8

Batch Number and Serial Number Tracking

Some manufacturing and distribution companies require tracking of serial numbers or batch numbers for a material item, or both. The term batch number is used because Dynamics AX employs the term *lot number* as a system-assigned internal identifier for inventory transactions. A serial number or batch number is typically assigned upon receipt, such as the receipt of a purchase order or the finished quantity of a production order. Subsequent transactions identifying these numbers automatically create tracking history. Several additional capabilities apply to batch tracking for an item, including the vendor batch information, batch attributes and/or batch disposition codes to indicate restricted usage. The following sections of the chapter reflect these topics.

1. Serial Number Tracking
2. Deferred Assignment of Serial Numbers
3. Basics of Batch Number Tracking
4. Vendor Batch Information
5. Batch Attributes
6. Batch Disposition Codes and Restricted Usage
7. Additional Case Studies

Many of these topics also involve quality management considerations such as product testing and quality orders. For example, the test results associated with a quality order can apply to a serial number or batch number. A subsequent chapter provides further explanation of quality management (Chapter 17).

8.1 Serial Number Tracking

Serial number tracking traditionally refers to a unique serial number for each unit of inventory. AX also supports a single serial number for multiple units of an item (conceptually similar to batch number tracking), but this section focuses on serial numbers for individual units. In addition, AX supports two options for a serialized item. The inventory of a serialized item can be tracked, or you can use deferred assignment of the serial number when the item is sold. This section explains the inventory tracking option, and the next section explains the deferred assignment option.

The explanation starts with the identification of a serialized item, the assignment of serial numbers to received material, and the picking and moving of serialized items. Several of these topics involve dual explanations because of differences in the two approaches to warehouse management.

Identify a Serialized Item A serialized item is identified by several policies embedded in the Tracking Dimension Group assigned to the item. One policy indicates that each serial number identifies an individual unit, and additional policies determine whether the serial number assignment must be tracked throughout inventory (the *Active* policy), or deferred until the product is actually sold (the *Active in Sales Process* policy). The deferred assignment approach is further explained in the next section, so that further explanation focuses on tracking inventory of a serialized item. The Tracking Dimension Group has several other policies not typically used for a serialized item, such as sales pricing or coverage planning for specific serial numbers.

The Advanced WMS approach involves an additional consideration, since a serialized item must be assigned an appropriate Reservation Hierarchy that includes the serial number. It is typically placed below the location because it is not relevant for reservation logic.

Typical Inventory Transactions requiring Assignment of a Serial Number The typical transactions include purchase order receipts, production order receipts, RMA receipts and inventory adjustments when tracking inventory by serial number. The transactions differ slightly between the basic and advanced approaches to warehouse management.

◆ *Basic Approach to Warehouse Management:*   A purchased item's serial numbers are typically assigned when reporting purchase order arrival using the Arrival Journal form, although they can also be reported (via a simple inventory transaction) by registering the serial numbers when posting the product receipt for a purchase order. A manufactured item's serial numbers are typically assigned when reporting a production order receipt using the Report as Finished form or its alternatives.

◆ *Advanced WMS Approach:*   A purchased item's serial numbers are typically assigned when reporting purchase order arrival via a mobile device transaction, although they can also be reported via a simple inventory transaction. A manufactured item's serial numbers are typically assigned when reporting the finished quantity via a mobile device transaction, or by using the Report as Finished form or its alternatives.

Several different approaches can be used for assigning a serial number to each unit of an item's inventory, as described in the following points.

Manual Assignment of a Serial Number You can manually assign a serial number to inventory transactions with a quantity of one, so that receipts for a larger quantity must first be split into quantities of one. Manual assignment allows you to enter the existing serial number on received material.

Automatic Assignment using the item's Serial Number Mask A mask can help enforce internal guidelines about assignment of serial numbers to an item, where you place your internal serial number on received material. It represents one policy within the serial number group assigned to the item. The mask may simply reflect a prefix and counter, or include the date, order number, and/or the system-assigned lot id. A second policy determines when to assign the serial number; it is typically assigned when recording arrivals that update inventory balances.

Automatic Assignment using an Ad Hoc Serial Number Mask The existing serial numbers for received material often reflect a pattern. For example, the pattern might consist of the same 10 characters and three unique digits in a numerical sequence, where the three unique digits differentiate the serial numbers. This pattern and automatic numbering for a range of three digit numbers can be defined as part of the ad hoc serial number mask. However, the ability to use an ad hoc mask differs between the basic and advanced approaches to warehouse management.

◆ *Basic Approach to Warehouse Management:* The ad hoc mask and its associated "Create Serial Numbers" dialogue can only be accessed when reporting purchase order arrivals using the Arrival Journal form, or when reporting production order receipts using the Report as Finished form or its alternatives.

◆ *Advanced WMS Approach:* The assignment of serial numbers using an ad hoc mask is not supported by the mobile device transactions for purchase order arrival, RMA arrival or production order receipt. However, the ad hoc mask can be used as part of a client transaction such as the Report as Finished form or its alternatives.

Picking and Moving Serialized Items Serialized items can be picked for sales orders, transfer orders, production orders and returns to vendor, and also moved to different locations. The reporting differs between the basic and advanced approaches for warehouse management.

◆ *Basic Approach to Warehouse Management:* The serial number(s) can be identified when reporting actual picking against a sales order picking list, a transfer order picking list, or a production order picking list. When reporting moves, each serial number requires a separate move transaction.

◆ *Advanced WMS Approach:* The mobile device transactions for picking a serialized item can differ based on the use of license plates and the quantities involved. For example, when a pallet contains multiple serial numbers (say 100 pieces), and the required quantity represent one pallet, you simply report picking of the one license plate. Alternatively, when the required quantity represents a subset of the serial numbers on a pallet (say 3 pieces), you must identify each serial number when reporting the picking work via the mobile device.

A special case applies to raw material picking work for a production order, since an entire pallet or an exact number can be picked to meet the required quantity. It depends on whether the inventory is being picked from a license plate controlled location or not.

When reporting moves, the mobile device transaction for a move can be reported for the license plate ID containing multiple serial numbers (at a license plate controlled location), or for individual serial numbers.

Information about a Serial Number Information about each serial number for an item consists of descriptive text and a manufacturing date. This information can be viewed and maintained on the Serial Numbers form.

Historical Information about Serial Number Tracking The tracking history is automatically maintained based on receipt and issue transactions. This historical information is typically viewed and analyzed using the Item Trace form. It can also be viewed using the Serial Number form, but the simplified format does not support the analysis capabilities of the Item Trace form. You can view historical information about a selected item or serial number, such as forward or backward tracking information using a multilevel indented format. Each entry in the indented format indicates a receipt or issue. An entry can also reflect a transfer.

Serial Tracking on Intercompany Orders When using intercompany orders in a multi-company operation, the serial numbers assigned to the shipped material (on the intercompany sales order) can automatically apply to the received material (on the intercompany purchase order).

Printing Serial Numbers on Documents The serial numbers can be printed on sales and purchase documents based on the form setup policies. For example, the serial numbers can be printed on the sales order packing slip and invoice.

8.2 Deferred Assignment of Serial Numbers

The concept of deferred assignment of serial numbers applies to many different scenarios, where it avoids detailed tracking of serialized inventory but still supports requirements about serial number information. A simple scenario involves deferred assignment at the time of shipment of an end-item. This represents the current capabilities within AX described in this section. A more complex scenario in a manufacturing company involves deferred assignment for a serialized end-item and its serialized components, as illustrated in Case 8.2.

A serialized item is identified by several policies embedded in the Tracking Dimension Group assigned to the item. In particular, the policies provide an option about whether the serial number assignment must be tracked throughout inventory (the *Active* policy), or deferred until the end-item is actually sold (the *Active in Sales Process* policy). This section explains the deferred assignment option, and the previous section explained the inventory tracking option.

With deferred assignment, you register the end-item's serial number(s) when posting the sales order packing slip or invoice by accessing the Serial Numbers form for the line item. You can then scan the serial numbers or manually enter a value. You can also indicate an unreadable serial number (resulting in a null value) and change the assignment of a serial number.

The serial numbers can be printed on packing slips or invoices (just like the inventory tracking option), but the lack of inventory information means that serial number tracking is limited to the related sales order. This also means that a previously shipped serial number cannot be identified on a customer return.

Mobile device transactions for sales order picking cannot be used for reporting deferred assignment (when using the Advanced WMS approach). Deferred assignment must be reported via a client transaction for posting the sales order packing slip.

8.3 Basics of Batch Number Tracking

Batch number tracking is a critical requirement in many scenarios. The use of batch tracking starts with the identification of a batch-controlled item and several related policies. Different approaches can be used to assign an internal batch number to an item's inventory, and to report picking and moves of the inventory. Several of these topics involve differences in the two approaches to warehouse management.

This section focuses on the basics of batch number tracking and subsequent sections cover vendor batch information (Section 8.4) and batch disposition codes and restricted usage (Section 8.5). Some AX capabilities for batch-controlled items are not covered because they do not generally apply to discrete manufacturing, such as shelf-life information, batch attributes, and merging batches.

Identify a Batch-Controlled Item A batch-controlled item is identified by a the Tracking Dimension Group assigned to the item, which must include the batch number. The batch number dimension has several policies that enforce batch tracking for issues and receipts, and optionally support unique requirements such as batch-specific costing and pricing.

A second set of policies (termed the Batch Number Group) determines how the item's batch numbers are created and when they are assigned to inventory transactions for received material. A batch number can be created manually or automatically, and it is typically assigned upon arrival which updates inventory balances.

The Advanced WMS approach involves an additional consideration, since a batch-controlled item must be assigned an appropriate Reservation Hierarchy that includes the batch number. For most discrete manufacturing scenarios, it is placed below the location because the batch number is not relevant for reservation logic.

Typical Inventory Transactions requiring Assignment of a Batch Number The typical transactions include purchase order receipts, production order receipts, RMA receipts and inventory adjustments. The transactions differ slightly between the basic and advanced approaches to warehouse management.

◆ *Basic Approach to Warehouse Management:* A purchased item's batch numbers are typically assigned when reporting purchase order arrival using the Arrival Journal form, although they can also be reported (via a simple inventory transaction) by registering the batch numbers when posting the product receipt for a purchase order. A manufactured item's batch numbers are typically assigned when reporting a production order receipt using the Report as Finished form or its alternatives.

◆ *Advanced WMS Approach:* A purchased item's batch numbers are typically assigned when reporting purchase order arrival via a mobile device transaction, although they can also be reported via a simple inventory transaction. A manufactured item's batch numbers are typically assigned when reporting the finished quantity via a mobile device transaction. An additional policy for the mobile device transaction (labeled "override batch number") allows manual assignment. A manufactured item's batch number can also be assigned by a client transaction using the Report as Finished form or its alternatives.

Several different approaches can be used for assigning an internal batch number as described in the following points. Some scenarios will use manual assignment while others will use automatic assignment, and there are several variations of automatic assignment.

Manually Assign an Internal Batch Number when reporting Receipt Manual assignment is typically used when the internal batch number can be easily scanned or involves significance that cannot be modeled as a batch number mask.

Automatically Assign an Internal Batch Number when reporting Receipt Automatic assignment can be based on a batch number mask, such as a prefix and counter. Alternatively, the mask could reflect the date, order number, and/or system-assigned lot id. Other approaches to a batch number mask may need to be customized to meet requirements for a meaningful batch number.

Automatically Assign Different Batch Numbers when reporting Multiple Receipts for an Order Some scenarios require a unique internal batch number for each receipt of the same order. One example involves partial receipts of the same purchase order line, where the same vendor batch number may apply but the material needs to be tracked by different internal batch numbers. Another example involves multiple receipts of the same production order where each receipt represents a different physical batch. A batch numbering policy (within the Batch Number Group) determines whether to assign the same batch number or a different batch number to each partial receipt.[1]

Automatically Assign Different Batch Numbers based on Fixed Increments   Some scenarios require a unique batch number for fixed increments of a receipt quantity, such as assigning unique batch numbers for every 100 units received when receiving a quantity of 1000. This requirement may reflect the item's packaging characteristics, production characteristics or a quality management consideration. The "per quantity" increment is one of the policies within the Batch Number Group.

Pre-Assign a Batch Number to a Production Order or a Purchase Order Line   Some scenarios involve a pre-assigned batch number. You can manually assign a batch number to a purchase order line or a production order, and the batch number will apply to all receipt transactions.

Picking and Moving Batch-Controlled Items   Batch-controlled items can be picked for sales orders, transfer orders, production orders and returns to vendor, and also moved to different locations. The reporting differs between the basic and advanced approaches for warehouse management.

◆ *Basic Approach to Warehouse Management:* The batch number(s) can be identified when reporting actual picking against a sales order picking list, a transfer order picking list, or a production order picking list.

◆ *Advanced WMS Approach:* The mobile device transactions for picking and moving a batch-controlled item can differ based on the use of license plates and the quantities involved. For example, a license plate may contain one or more batch numbers of a given item, and you can reporting picking and moving of a single license plate.

A special case applies to raw material picking work for a production order, since an entire license plate or an exact number can be picked to meet the required quantity. It depends on whether the inventory is being picked from a license plate controlled location or not.

---

[1] The same batch number will be assigned to partial receipts when the numbering policy (within the Batch Number Group) is simply "assignment on inventory transaction". Different batch numbers will be assigned by specifying the additional policy "assignment upon physical update".

Viewing the Internal Batch Numbers A key form for batch information -- termed the Batches form -- provides a list of all internal batch numbers and the related items. It also displays the batch-related information such as the quality order status and batch disposition code.

Changing Batch Numbers of an Item's Inventory You can change the batch number for an inventory quantity by using the Transfer Journal, much like you would change its bin location or combine inventory in a bin location.

Batch Tracking on Intercompany Orders When using intercompany orders in a multi-company supply chain, the batch numbers assigned to the shipped material (on the intercompany sales order) can automatically apply to the received material (on the intercompany purchase order).

Printing Batch Numbers on Documents The batch numbers can be printed on sales and purchase documents based on the form setup policies. For example, the batch numbers can be printed on the sales order packing slip and invoice.

Historical Information about Batch Number Tracking The batch tracking history is automatically maintained based on receipt and issue transactions. This historical information is typically viewed and analyzed using the Item Trace form. It can also be viewed using the Batches form, but the simplified format does not support the analysis capabilities of the Item Trace form.

You can view historical information about a specified item or batch number, and the on-line inquiry avoids the need for extensive printed reports. In a manufacturing environment, you can view forward or backward trace information using a multilevel indented format that reflects the product structure. Each entry in the indented format indicates a receipt or issue. The batch number for a sales order shipment can be traced backward through the production orders to purchase order receipts. A receipt can also be traced forward.

When using the Advanced WMS approach, the historical information about batch number tracking includes the work order transactions to pick and put the inventory.

Batch Tracking and Serial Tracking for an Item Some scenarios require batch and serial tracking for an item. The two tracking numbers represent separate constructs, and a hierarchical relationship does not exist between a batch number and serial numbers for an item.

8.4 Vendor Batch Information

The vendor batch information normally applies to a purchased item, but it can also be used for other items. The information includes a vendor batch number, a field for the vendor-specified manufacturing date, and two fields for capturing country of origin information. The vendor batch information can be assigned to an item's internal batch number using the Batch Details form, and accessing the Reset Vendor Batch Details form.

Some scenarios assign the vendor batch information when reporting purchase order arrival. It typically involves reporting by the receiving clerk rather than a quality control clerk. This approach requires an additional policy labeled "Vendor Batch Purchase Registration" which is embedded in the Item Model Group assigned to the item.

8.5 Batch Attributes

One or more batch attributes can be assigned to a batch-controlled item, and actual values recorded against the batch numbers for the item. The use of batch attributes requires some setup information, including the definition of batch attributes and assignment of batch attributes to the item.

Setup Information for Batch Attributes The setup information consists of the following steps.

◆ *Define batch attributes.* The identifier and description of a batch attribute are user-definable, and the attribute can be designated as an integer, fraction, date, string, or enumerated list (which requires definition of possible values in the list). When designated as an integer or fraction, the batch attribute must also be assigned values for a minimum, maximum, and increment as well as a tolerance policy. The tolerance policy has two options concerning the actual values for the batch attribute, where the system can provide a warning or prevent entry.

◆ *Define a group of batch attributes.* This approach provides a shortcut for assigning multiple batch attributes to an item, and represents an optional step. The identifier and description of a batch attribute group are user-definable, and one or more batch attributes can be assigned to the group. When an assigned attribute consists of an integer or fraction, the values for the minimum, maximum, increment, and tolerance policy are inherited but can be overridden. For example, the attribute's minimum and maximum values can be overridden each time it is assigned to an attribute group.

♦ *Assign batch attributes to an item.* One or more batch attributes or groups can be assigned to a batch-controlled item using the Batch Attributes by Item form. Those attributes consisting of an integer or fraction will inherit values (such as the minimum and maximum) from the definition of the batch attribute, and these can be overridden to indicate item-specific values.

An additional setup step is needed when using the test results from quality orders to update a batch attribute value, since the test must be mapped to the batch attribute.

Recording Actual Values for Batch Attributes The actual value for an item's batch attribute can be recorded after creation of a batch number. When the batch attribute reflects an integer or fraction, a message provides a warning or prevents entry (based on the tolerance policy) when the actual value exceeds the minimum or maximum. The actual value for an item's batch attribute can also be updated by the validated test results for a quality order. A subsequent chapter about quality management provides further explanation of quality orders (Section 17.4).

Batch Attribute Searching You can search for an appropriate batch based on actual values of the item's batch attributes. This is termed a batch attribute search. A batch attribute search may be used in the context of finding an ingredient for production, or in the context of order entry. For example, a customer may have specific requirements for the values of batch attributes, so that a batch attribute search (and reservation) can be performed as part of order entry.

8.6 Batch Disposition Codes and Restricted Usage

Batch disposition codes often represent a critical tool for quality management because the policies associated with a code can selectively enforce restricted usage.[2] Batch disposition codes represent an optional capability for managing inventory of batch-controlled material.

---

[2] Batch disposition codes represent a different construct than the RMA disposition codes for handling return orders from customers. They are also different than the "combined disposition code" used in the Advanced WMS approach, which reflects the combination of an RMA disposition code and a value for Inventory Status.

This section describes the setup information for batch disposition codes, and the assignment (and reassignment) of a disposition code to an item's batch. Those scenarios that do not require enforcement of restricted usage can define and use a single disposition code that reflects available material without restricted usage.

Setup Information for Batch Disposition Codes The user-defined batch disposition codes must be set up on the Batch Disposition Master form. One batch disposition code should reflect available material, where the disposition status is designated as available. The number of additional codes will depend on the desired variations in restricted usage, where the disposition status is designated as unavailable. The typical requirements for two additional batch disposition codes include (1) non-nettable with all usage restrictions and (2) nettable with some usage restrictions.

The following policies can be assigned to a batch disposition code with an unavailable disposition status, where the policies indicate aspects of restricted usage:

◆ *Nettable*. This policy determines whether inventory will be considered available by master scheduling logic.

◆ *Restricted usage for sales orders*. You can designate one or more of the following policies on restricted usage:

  – Block reservations. This policy prevents reservation of the batch inventory
  – Block picking. This policy prevents picking of the batch inventory.
  – Block shipping. This policy prevents posting of the sales order packing slip of the batch inventory.

◆ *Restricted usage for transfer orders*. You can designate one or more of the following policies on restricted usage. However, you should not block transfers if you intend to return a purchased batch to the vendor, or move the batch to a different location.

  – Block reservations. This policy prevents reservation of the batch inventory for a transfer order.
  – Block picking. This policy prevents picking of the batch inventory for a transfer order.
  – Block shipping. This policy prevents transfer order shipment of the batch inventory.

◆ *Restricted usage for production orders.* You can designate one or more of the following policies on restricted usage:

- Block reservations. This policy prevents reservation of the batch inventory.
- Block picking. This policy prevents picking of the batch inventory.

Assignment of a Batch Disposition Code to an Item's Batch Number

The initial value of the batch disposition code can be automatically assigned to a batch number based on a default value for the item. You define this default value within the Item Model Group assigned to the item. Otherwise, the batch disposition code can be changed as needed.

The assigned value can also be defined as part of the information for quality orders. One value can be defined for a failed validation and another value can be defined for a passed validation, so that validation will update the batch disposition code to the assigned value.

Once an internal batch number has been created, you can manually override the batch disposition code by accessing the Reset Disposition Code form, or by changing the code via a mobile device transaction. A history of changes to a batch's disposition code is automatically maintained by the system, and viewable on the History of Disposition Inventory form.

Summary of Batch Disposition Codes with an Unavailable Status A

summary of batch disposition codes with an unavailable status is shown in Figure 8.1 and described below. An unavailable status provides a form of inventory blocking, and a comparable figure provides a similar analysis of the three Inventory Blocking approaches (Section 17.2). Batch disposition codes can be used in conjunction with all three approaches to inventory blocking, but is most commonly used with quality orders for updating the batch disposition code based on pass/fail results of validation.

A batch disposition code with an unavailable status can be assigned to a batch number at any time. The associated blocking can be removed by changing the code to one with an available status. The expected outcome for inventory (with a code representing an unavailable status) can be designated as nettable or non-nettable. Some of the allowable transactions are impacted by the restricted usage policies, but many are not impacted such as moves and adjustments.

Figure 8.1 Batch Disposition Codes with an Unavailable Status

Considerations	Impacts on Inventory
Create blocking for a specified batch number	Assign a batch disposition code (with an unavailable status) to a batch number
Ability to assign batch disposition code at time of order receipt	Yes
Remove blocking for a batch number	Change the batch disposition code (to one with an available status) for a batch number
Impact of a Batch Disposition code with an unavailable status on master scheduling logic	Nettable or Non-nettable
Allowable transactions for a batch number that has been assigned a batch disposition code with an unavailable status	Restricted usage for sales orders Restricted usage for production orders Restricted usage for transfer order Move Adjustment out Cycle count Return to vendor Create quality order
Additional considerations	Different ways to change the Batch Disposition Code Split the quantity for a batch number to assign different batch disposition codes

The batch disposition code can be changed by a quality order or changed directly (via a client or mobile device transaction). The code can be changed via a rework order for the item's inventory. When needed, you can split the quantity for a batch number into two or more batch numbers in order to assign different batch disposition codes. As another option, a subset of a batch number can be blocked via manual assignment of inventory blocking or a blocked value of Inventory Status.

8.7 Additional Case Studies

Case 8.1: RMAs for Serialized Items A manufacturing company required RMA processing on customer returns of their serialized electronic items. Each serialized number had a 12 month warranty period (from date of sale) for free replacement. The customer identified an item's serial number when requesting an RMA, which was used to verify the applicability of its warranty period. The customer shipped the returned item after receiving an electronic copy of the printed RMA. Items were shipped to a repair facility, which verified the serial number and sent a free replacement (when it was within warranty) or charged for the replacement (when it was not within warranty). The repair facility assigned a disposition to each returned item during an inspection process, which determined whether the item was usable, scrapped, or repairable. A scrapped item could also be stripped down for reusing the high value components.

Case 8.2: Deferred Assignment for a Serialized End-item and its Serialized Components A manufacturing company produced printed circuit boards that were serialized, and then placed in a cabinet that represented a serialized end-item. The boards were continually changed out during the testing process for the end-item. When the fully-tested end-item was completed, the quality manager wanted to record the serial numbers of the actual boards within a serialized cabinet. This information was critical for warranty and quality tracking purposes. As part of a proposed customization, a new option for deferred assignment would be added to the Storage Dimension Group policies, and a new screen and related database would be developed. The new screen would display a multi-level indented BOM format for the end-item and only those components with the deferred assignment option, so that the actual serial numbers could be recorded after production was completed. This serial number information would be retained in a related database. It could also be used to create "objects" for the serialized items (after the product was shipped) in order to support service and warranty purposes.

Case 8.3: Vendor Batch Numbers A manufacturer used several purchased components that were batch-controlled items. At the time of product receipt, the receiving clerks recorded an internal batch number and the vendor's batch number. A bar-coded label with the internal batch number was affixed to the product receipt, and subsequent transactions referred to the internal batch number.

Case 8.4: Country of Origin for Purchased Material A manufacturer used several purchased components from other countries. For a given item, the country of origin was specified as part of the foreign trade information for the item. However, some batch-controlled items were sourced from more than one country. They recorded the country of origin as part of the vendor batch details for each batch of these purchased items. Most cases involved a single country of origin, although a few required two different countries. This information was used to support government reporting requirements about country of origin.

8.8 Executive Summary

Some scenarios require tracking of serial numbers or batch numbers for a material item, or both. An item's batch numbers may also involve vendor batch information, batch attributes and/or batch disposition codes to indicate restricted usage. This chapter summarized how to setup and use serial numbers and batch numbers for an item.

Several case studies illustrated the use of batch number tracking and serial number tracking. These included RMAs for serialized items, deferred assignment for a serialized end-item and its serialized components, vendor batch numbers, and the country of origin for purchased material.

Chapter 9

Coverage Planning Data to Model SCM Decision Making

Planned orders communicate the need to replenish an item's inventory, and are generated by master scheduling logic based on an item's coverage planning data and related S&OP game plans. The coverage planning data (or planning data for short) represents a model of decision making about coordinating the supply chain. The planning data differs for purchased items, manufactured items and transfers. Much of this planning data can be assigned as a companywide policy for an item, and optionally overridden as a site-specific or site/warehouse-specific policy. The key planning data includes the coverage group assigned to an item. Each user-defined coverage group consists of multiple policies such as the applicable coverage code and use of action messages. These messages work in conjunction with planned orders to coordinate supply chain activities to meet the S&OP game plans.

This chapter focuses on coverage planning data and the next chapter covers S&OP game plans and master scheduling. The chapter starts with the significance of coverage groups and the options for a coverage code, and then explains the key planning data for purchased items, manufactured items, and transfers. It addresses several topics within the coverage planning data, ranging from policies about action messages to time fences. These considerations are reflected in the following sections within the chapter.

1. Significance of Coverage Groups
2. Options for a Coverage Code
3. Planning Data for Purchased Items
4. Special Cases for Purchased Items
5. Planning Data for Manufactured Items
6. Special Cases for Manufactured Items

7.   Planning Data for Transfers
8.   Additional Planning Data for the Master Scheduler Role
9.   Maintain Coverage Planning Data for Items
10. Action Messages and Related Policies
11. Messages about Calculated Delays and Related Policies
12. Negative Days and the Rescheduling Assumption
13. Positive Days and Assumptions about Current Inventory
14. Safety Margins
15. Time Fence Policies

9.1 Significance of Coverage Groups

A coverage group consists of multiple policies that provide a model of decision making about coordination of an item's supply chain activities. Each coverage group has a user-defined identifier and name, and a typical company will employ different coverage groups to model the differences in decision-making logic. For example, key aspects of decision-making logic involve the generation of planned supply orders to meet demands, and the use of action messages to coordinate supply orders.

As an explanatory approach, the various policies within a coverage group will be segmented into different topics and covered by different sections within the book. The key policies merit separate sections. Several other policies only apply to the context of a specific business process or special case, so that their significance must be explained within the context. Hence, the various aspects of coverage group policies are summarized here along with references to more detailed explanations.

◆   Options for a coverage code (Section 9.2)
◆   Action messages and related policies (Section 9.10)
◆   Messages about calculated delays and related policies (Section 9.11)
◆   Negative days (Section 9.12)
◆   Positive days (Section 9.13)
◆   Safety margins (Section 9.14)
◆   Time fence policies (Section 9.15 and 10.12)
◆   Demand forecasts for salable end-items (Sections 10.3 thru 10.5)
◆   Demand forecasts for stocked components (Section 10.8)
◆   Status of a production order after firming a planned order (Section 14.12)

As already noted, a typical company will employ different coverage groups to model the differences in decision-making logic. Case 9.1 illustrates a company that started with just a few coverage groups, and then evolved into more coverage groups.

9.2 Options for a Coverage Code

The coverage code represents a key part of the decision-making logic about generating planned supply orders for an item. It is embedded within the coverage group assigned to an item, but its importance merits a separate explanation. The term coverage code has several synonyms and different ERP systems employ different terms and provide different options. Examples of different terms include the reorder policy and the replenishment policy.

The four options for a coverage code include period (aka period lot-sizing logic), requirement, min-max and manual. The most commonly used options include period and requirement. Each option can be characterized by its primary planning data, order quantity modifiers, and a safety stock approach. These options are summarized in Figure 9.1 and described below. The left-hand columns characterize each option in terms of its underlying logic, such as order point or period lot-sizing logic.

Figure 9.1 Options for a Coverage Code

Logic Basis	Coverage Code and its significance	Planning Data		
		Primary Planning Data	Order Qty Modifiers**	Safety Stock Approach
Period Lot Size	**Period** Suggested order quantity covers multiple demands within the period subject to order quantity modifiers	Period Size (in days)	Minimum Multiple Maximum	Minimum Quantity*
Order Driven	**Requirement** Suggested order quantity covers one demand subject to order quantity modifiers		Minimum Multiple Maximum	Minimum Quantity*
Order Point	**Min-Max** Suggested order quantity achieves maximum inventory quantity subject to order quantity multiple	Minimum Quantity* Maximum Quantity	Multiple	N/A
Manual Planning	**Manual** No suggested orders	N/A	N/A	N/A

* = The minimum quantity represents a site/warehouse-specific safety stock quantity, and differs from the order quantity modifiers for a minimum.

** = Three different sets of order quantity modifiers can be defined for an item: for sales orders, purchase orders and for production/batch orders. Planned transfer orders use the order quantity modifiers related to production/batch orders.

Period (also known as Period Lot Size)   When an item's projected inventory reaches zero (or its minimum quantity), master scheduling logic will suggest a planned order with a quantity that covers demands over the period size, subject to order quantity modifiers. The period size reflects the frequency of replenishment (such as daily, weekly or monthly) and different coverage codes must be defined for each period size. Examples of the user-defined values for a coverage code include *Period-1Day*, *Period-7Days* and *Period-30Days*, where the associated period size reflects the frequency of daily, weekly and monthly replenishment.

The item's minimum quantity for a given site/warehouse represents an explicit inventory plan or safety stock. An implied inventory plan reflects the extent to which the order quantity modifiers (for minimum and multiple) inflate the suggested order quantity so that it exceeds the requirements.

Requirement (also known as Order-Driven or Lot-for-Lot)   When an item's projected inventory reaches zero (or its minimum quantity), master scheduling logic will suggest a planned order and quantity that covers each individual demand, subject to order quantity modifiers. As noted above, the minimum quantity and the order quantity modifiers represent explicit and implied inventory plans respectively.

Min-Max When an item's projected inventory falls below its minimum quantity, master scheduling logic will suggest a planned order with a quantity that achieves the item's maximum quantity, subject to an order quantity modifier for a multiple. The projected inventory reflects future demands and scheduled receipts for the item. The values for minimum and maximum quantity are typically specified using a fixed approach, but a variable approach can be used. The fixed approach consists of a single value for each quantity, whereas the variable approach employs a pattern for each quantity such as different quantities for each month to reflect seasonality or trends.   Each pattern is termed a minimum/maximum key.

Manual Master scheduling logic will not suggest planned orders, but it does calculate requirements to support manual planning efforts.

Assignment of the Coverage Code to an Item   The coverage code is embedded within the coverage group assigned to an item. You assign the coverage group as part of the item master information, but it can be overridden as part of the site/warehouse information for an item. Alternatively, you can just override the coverage code (rather than the coverage group) as part of the site/warehouse information for an item.

Order Quantity Modifiers   Three different sets of order quantity modifiers can be defined for an item -- for sales orders, purchase orders and production/batch orders. Planned transfer orders use the order quantity modifiers related to production/batch orders.   These order quantity modifiers involve several considerations for planned supply orders.

◆ *Minimum.* The minimum represents the smallest suggested order quantity.

◆ *Multiple.* The suggested order quantity will always reflect the multiple, even if it exceeds the maximum.

◆ *Maximum.*   The maximum represents the largest order quantity, so that master scheduling logic   will generate multiple planned orders to cover requirements exceeding the maximum.

Some situations require a fixed order quantity, perhaps reflecting considerations about batch tracking, transportation, production or some other factor. In these situations, use the same values for minimum, maximum and multiple so that master scheduling logic will generate multiple planned orders for the fixed quantity.

9.3 Planning Data for Purchased Items

Master scheduling logic will generate planned purchase orders based on an item's planning data. Figure 9.2 summarizes the planning data for purchased items, and highlights the companywide versus site-specific and site/warehouse policies. The information reflects the book's baseline model, where coverage planning applies to the combination of site and warehouse. The bottom of the figure also highlights the four key forms for maintaining an item's planning data. Further explanation covers each aspect of planning data within the figure.

Primary Source of Supply A planned order type of Purchase Order indicates the primary source of supply for an item, so that master scheduling logic will generate planned purchase orders. An item's planned order type (aka default order type) can be specified as a companywide policy, and optionally overridden for a given site/warehouse. For example, a purchased item may be replenished via purchase orders at one warehouse, but replenished via transfer orders at a different warehouse.

Figure 9.2 Key Planning Data for Purchased Items

Key Planning Data	Companywide Policies	Site-Specific Policies	Site/Warehouse Policies
Primary Source of Supply Planned Order Type = Purchase Order	Specify	N/A	Override
Preferred Vendor		N/A	Override
Coverage Group (Set of Policies)	Specify	Override	Override
Purchase Lead Time	Specify	Override	Override
Order Quantity Modifiers for Purchase Orders	Specify	Override	N/A
Buyer Responsibility		N/A	N/A

Form for Data Maintenance: Use Released Products or Default Order Settings — Use Site-Specific Order Settings — Use Item Coverage form

Preferred Vendor   An item's preferred vendor can be specified as a companywide policy, and optionally overridden for a given site/warehouse. It must reflect one of the item's approved vendors when enforcing the policy for approved vendors. Master scheduling logic assigns the preferred vendor to planned purchase orders for the item.

The approach to defining an item's preferred vendor differs slightly for buy-to-order components, or when sourcing to the vendor with the lowest price or delivery lead time. The next section provides further explanation of these special cases for purchased items.

Coverage Group The coverage group consists of multiple policies that provide a model of the decision-making logic about coordination of an item's supply chain activities, as described in the previous section. The companywide policy for an item's coverage group can be overridden for a given site/warehouse. As an alternative approach for overriding the coverage group, you can override selected policies such as the coverage code and period lot size.

Purchase Lead Time An item's purchase lead time can be specified as a companywide policy, and optionally overridden as a site-specific or site/warehouse-specific policy. It is expressed in terms of calendar days unless explicitly flagged as working days. This lead time typically represents the average number of days to receive material after placing a purchase order. It will be used by master scheduling logic to suggest an order date for planned purchase orders. It is also used when manually creating a purchase order to initially calculate the delivery date for the item.

An item's purchase lead time can be optionally specified in purchase trade agreements. However, this information only applies to several special cases described in the next section.

Order Quantity Modifiers for Purchasing The order quantity modifiers consist of a minimum, maximum and multiple. They are expressed in the item's default purchase UM (if specified) otherwise they reflect the item's inventory UM. The order quantity modifiers impact planned purchase order quantities. They are also considered when manually creating or maintaining a purchase order for the item, where a soft warning will be displayed when you enter a quantity that does not meet these criteria. The item's standard purchase order quantity also reflects considerations about these order quantity modifiers, and it acts as a default value when manually entering a purchase order line for the item.

Buyer Responsibility The concept of buyer responsibility provides an organizing focus for communicating the need to synchronize supplies with demands. The concept of buyer responsibility is typically based on the buyer group field; an alternative basis could be the item group field. A user-defined buyer group can be assigned to an item to indicate responsibility for maintaining planning data, whereas the buyer group assigned to a vendor indicates responsibility for coordinating purchases. Master scheduling logic generates planned orders identified with the buyer group associated with the vendor. A purchase order header contains a buyer group that applies to all purchase order line items.

9.4 Special Cases for Purchased Items

The previous section focused on the key planning data for purchased items, and several special cases involve additional considerations. These special cases include buy-to-order components, purchase lead times within purchase price trade agreements, the suggested vendor for planned purchase orders based on lowest price or delivery lead time, purchased items requiring internal production, and the use of default ship-to locations.

Buy-to-Order Component for Material A purchased item can be designated as a but-to-order component in the BOM information of its parent item, where you specify a BOM line type of Vendor. The preferred vendor for a buy-to-order component can be optionally overridden as part of the component information otherwise it reflects the companywide or site-specific preferred vendor for the item.

Master scheduling logic will calculate requirements for a buy-to-order component, and even generate planned orders based on the item's planning data.[1] The logic ignores on-hand inventory for meeting the buy-to-order requirements. However, the planned orders simply provide visibility about these requirements, and they cannot be firmed for creating a purchase order. Instead, the system will automatically create a linked purchase order for a buy-to-order component when you update the status of the parent item's production order, such as updating the status to Estimated or Scheduled. The quantity for the linked purchase order reflects the production order quantity and the BOM information about the component quantity. Deleting the parent item's production order will delete the linked purchased order.

Buy-to-Order Component for a Subcontracted Service The AX approach to subcontracted production employs a buy-to-order component to represent the subcontracted service. The above explanation also applies to these buy-to-order components. A subsequent chapter provides further explanation about purchasing a subcontracted service (Chapter 15).

Purchase Lead Times within Purchase Price Trade Agreements An item's purchase lead time can be optionally specified within the entry for a purchase price trade agreement, such as specifying a longer lead time for a lower purchase price. However, you must explicitly designate usage of this lead time information as part of the entry. When explicitly designated for use, the lead time will be inherited by a manually entered purchase order line that meets the criteria for the trade agreement entry. It will also be inherited by the planned purchase order.

Suggested Vendor based on Lowest Price or Delivery Lead Time Some scenarios will source a purchased item based on price or delivery considerations rather than a preferred vendor. In this case, the preferred vendor field should be left blank in order to support automatic vendor assignment on planned purchase orders based on trade agreement information for lowest price or delivery lead time.[1] The previous point explained the additional consideration for using the purchase lead time associated with trade agreement entry. A subsequent chapter provides further explanation about purchase trade agreements (Section 12.6).

---

[1] You typically assign a coverage code of Requirement or Period to a purchased item that has buy-to-order requirements.
[1] A companywide policy (defined in the Master Planning Parameters form) determines whether master scheduling logic can use the purchase price trade agreement information to suggest a vendor for purchased items (when a preferred vendor has not been specified). A related policy specifies whether price or delivery lead time serves as the basis for suggesting a vendor.

Purchased Items Requiring Internal Production   Some scenarios involve internal production or rework of a purchased item.   Internal production may reflect an intermittent basis or a planned change.   In this case, the item must be designated with a production type of BOM.   The item should also have bill of material information to support the use of production orders.   When you primarily purchase the item, you assign a planned order type of Purchase Order.   You may also need to assign a standard cost reflecting the item's purchase price rather than calculating the item's manufacturing cost.   The cost calculations for higher level items should also employ the item's purchase cost, which requires a *stop explosion* policy in the calculation group assigned to the item.

Default Ship-To Location   You can optionally specify a default ship-to location for a purchased item (consisting of a specified site or a specified site/warehouse), and even mandate use of the ship-to location.   This approach typically reflects a scenario where the purchased item is only used at the specified location.   Alternatively, the default ship-to location can be assigned to a vendor.

9.5 Planning Data for Manufactured Items

Master scheduling logic will generate planned production orders based on the planning data for a manufactured item.   Figure 9.3 summarizes the key planning data for a manufactured item, and highlights the companywide versus site-specific and site/warehouse policies.   The information reflects the book's baseline model, where coverage planning applies to the combination of site and warehouse.   The bottom of the figure also highlights the four key forms for maintaining an item's planning data.   Further explanation covers each aspect of planning data within the figure.

BOM Version   The BOM versions for a manufactured item can be site-specific or companywide.   Master scheduling logic will use an item's site-specific BOM version (if it exists) based on the site of the item's requirements.   If a site-specific BOM version does not exist, master scheduling logic will use the companywide BOM version (if it exists).

Route Version   Master scheduling logic will use an item's site-specific route version (if it exists) based on the site of the item's requirements.   The routing data will be used to calculate the lead time for planned and actual production orders, but only within the capacity time fence employed by master scheduling logic.

Figure 9.3 Key Planning Data for Manufactured Items

Key Planning Data	Companywide Policies	Site-Specific Policies	Site/Warehouse Policies
BOM Version	Specify BOM as Companywide	Specify BOM as Site-Specific	N/A
Route Version	N/A	Specify Route as Site-Specific	
Primary Source of Supply Planned Order Type = Production	Specify	N/A	Override
Coverage Group (Set of Policies)			
Production Lead Time		Override	
Order Quantity Modifiers for Production Orders			N/A
Planner Responsibility		N/A	N/A

Form for Data Maintenance: Use Released Products or Default Order Settings   Use Site-Specific Order Settings   Use Item Coverage form

Primary Source of Supply A planned order type of Production indicates the primary source of supply for a manufactured item, so that master scheduling logic will generate planned production orders. An item's planned order type (aka default order type) can be specified as a companywide policy, and optionally overridden for a given site/warehouse. For example, a manufactured item may be replenished via production orders at one warehouse, but replenished via transfer orders at a different warehouse.

Coverage Group The coverage group consists of multiple policies that provide a model of the decision-making logic about coordination of an item's supply chain activities, as described in a previous section (Section 9.1). The companywide policy for an item's coverage group can be overridden for a given site/warehouse. As an alternative approach for overriding the coverage group, you can override selected policies such as the coverage code and period lot size.

The capacity time fence determines when routing data should be ignored by the master scheduling logic. For example, routing data may be used for near-term scheduling purposes within the next 30 days, and then ignored after the 30 day time fence so that a fixed lead time applies to the manufactured item.

Production Lead Time An item's fixed production lead time (expressed in days) can be specified as a companywide value, and optionally overridden as a site-specific or site/warehouse policy. Master scheduling logic will use this fixed lead time when routing data does not exist, or when ignoring the routing data beyond the capacity time fence. In addition, the fixed lead time can be used to determine the due date of safety stock requirements, and to calculate safety stock requirements based on historical usage (Section 10.7).

Alternatively, routing data can be used to calculate a variable elapsed time for each production order, where several other factors also impact the calculated time (such as order quantity and capacity availability). The calculated time only applies to production orders within the capacity time fence employed by master scheduling logic. In a typical scenario, master scheduling logic will calculate the variable elapsed time in the near-term horizon defined by the capacity fence, and use the fixed lead time beyond this time horizon.

Order Quantity Modifiers for Production   The order quantity modifiers consist of a minimum, maximum and multiple. They are expressed in the item's inventory UM. The order quantity modifiers impact planned production order quantities. They are also considered when manually creating or maintaining a production order for the item, where a soft warning will be displayed when you enter a quantity that does not meet these criteria. The item's standard production order quantity also reflects considerations about these order quantity modifiers, and it acts as a default value when manually creating a production order for the item.

Planner Responsibility   The concept of planner responsibility provides an organizing focus for communicating the need to synchronize supplies with demands. The concept of planner responsibility is often based on the production pool and buyer group assigned to a manufactured item. For example, master scheduling logic generates planned production orders identified with the buyer group, so that a planner can selectively view and mark planned orders for which they have responsibility. In addition, production orders inherit the item's production pool thereby enabling the planner to selectively view orders for which they have responsibility. Changes to the order status of production orders can be based on the production pool, and a planner can selectively view action messages by production pool.

9.6 Special Cases for Manufactured Items

The previous section focused on the planning data for manufactured items, and several special cases require additional considerations. These special cases include phantoms, make-to-order components, and assigning a specific BOM version and/or route version to a manufactured component.

Phantoms A manufactured item can be designated as a phantom component in the BOM information of its parent item, where you specify a BOM line type of *Phantom*. Master scheduling logic will calculate requirements for the phantom and ignore its on-hand inventory. Master scheduling logic will also generate a planned order for the phantom, but the planned order cannot be firmed.

Make-to-Order Components A manufactured item can be designated as a make-to-order component in the BOM information of its parent item, where you specify a BOM line type of *Pegged Supply* (or *Vendor*). Master scheduling logic will calculate requirements for a make-to-order component, and even generate planned orders based on the item's planning data.[2] The logic will ignore on-hand inventory for meeting the make-to-order requirements.   However, the planned orders simply provide visibility about these requirements, and these planned orders cannot be firmed (for creating a production order).   Instead, you automatically create a linked production order for a make-to-order component when you update the status of the parent item's production order, such as updating the status to *estimated* or *scheduled.* The quantity for the linked production order reflects the parent item's production order quantity and the BOM information about the component quantity. Deleting the parent item's production order will delete the linked production order.

Assign a BOM Version or Route Version to a Manufactured Component The assignment of a BOM version to a manufactured component (termed a sub-BOM) will override the normal use of the active BOM version for the item. You can also assign a route version to a manufactured component (termed a sub-route), which will override the normal use of the active route version for the item. The use of sub-BOMs and sub-routes for manufactured components generally applies to custom product manufacturing scenarios.

9.7 Planning Data for Transfers

Master scheduling logic will generate planned transfer orders based on an item's planning data. Figure 9.4 summarizes the key planning data for transfers of an item, and highlights the companywide versus site-specific and site/warehouse policies. The information reflects the book's baseline model, where coverage planning applies to the combination of site and warehouse. The bottom of the figure also highlights the four key forms for maintaining an item's planning data. Further explanation covers each aspect of planning data within the figure.

---

[2] You typically assign a coverage code of Requirement or Period to a manufactured item that has make-to-order requirements.

Figure 9.4 Key Planning Data for Transfers

Key Planning Data	Companywide Policies	Site-Specific Policies	Site/Warehouse Policies
Primary Source of Supply Planned Order Type = Transfer	N/A	N/A	Specify
Refilling Warehouse			
Coverage Group (Set of Policies)	Specify		Override
Transfer Lead Time	Specify transport time between warehouse pairs		
Order Quantity Modifiers for Transfer Orders	Specify	Override	N/A
Planner Responsibility		N/A	N/A

Form for Data Maintenance:	Use Released Products or Default Order Settings	Use Site-Specific Order Settings	Use Item Coverage form

Primary Source of Supply   Replenishment based on transfers must be designated in the item's site/warehouse-specific coverage data, where you indicate a planned order type of *transfer* so that master scheduling logic will generate planned transfer orders. A related field defines the preferred refilling warehouse.

Refilling Warehouse   The preferred refilling warehouse can be defined for transferring individual items to a warehouse (as part of each item's site/warehouse-specific coverage planning policies). Alternatively, it can be defined for an entire warehouse, which indicates that all warehouse inventory will be replenished from one refilling warehouse unless specifically overridden for an individual item.

Coverage Group   The coverage group consists of multiple policies that provide a model of the decision-making logic about coordination of an item's supply chain activities, as described in the previous section. The companywide policy for an item's coverage group can be overridden for a given site/warehouse. As an alternative approach for overriding the coverage group, you can override selected policies such as the coverage code and period lot size.

Transfer Lead Time   The transfer lead time (aka transportation time or transport days) is expressed in calendar days. It can reflect a warehouse viewpoint or an item viewpoint. With a warehouse viewpoint, you specify the transport days between a pair of warehouses on the Transport form. It reflects a companywide policy for all transfers between the warehouse pair. The item viewpoint supports an item-specific transfer time for handling unusual situations, and is defined as part of the item's site/warehouse-specific coverage planning policies. Most scenarios simply use the warehouse viewpoint.

Order Quantity Modifiers for Transfer Orders   The order quantity modifiers consist of a minimum, maximum and multiple. They are expressed in the item's inventory UM. The order quantity modifiers impact planned transfer order quantities.   They are also considered when manually creating or maintaining a transfer order line for the item, where a soft warning will be displayed when you enter a quantity that does not meet these criteria. The item's standard order quantity also reflects considerations about these order quantity modifiers, and it acts as a default value when manually entering a transfer order line for the item.

Planner Responsibility   The concept of planner responsibility for transfer orders is often based on the ship-from or ship-to warehouse, or the buyer group assigned to the item.   For example, master scheduling logic generates planned transfer orders identified with the buyer group and the ship-from/ship-to warehouses, so that a planner can selectively view planned orders for which they have responsibility.

Special Cases for Transfers   Some scenarios have adjacent warehouses where planned transfer orders between the warehouses are used to communicate requirements, but without the need for tracking in-transit inventory.   Actual transfers between warehouses can be handled through a transfer journal rather than a transfer order.   In this case, planned transfer orders can be used to communicate requirements, but firming the planned orders should generate a transfer journal which can be subsequently posted after physically moving the material.   This approach requires a site-specific policy termed "Use transfer journals for movements within site" otherwise firming a planned order results in a transfer order.

An alternative solution approach to this scenario involves a one-step transaction for reporting shipment of a transfer order with automatic receipt at the ship-to warehouse, as described in subsequent chapter about transfer orders (Section 13.2).

9.8 Additional Planning Data for the Master Scheduler Role

A master scheduler role is typically responsible for entering and maintaining the S&OP game plans in most manufacturing companies. In most cases, the master scheduler is also responsible for maintaining the planning data for relevant end-items and even stocked components within the S&OP game plans. An additional aspect of planning data involves forecast consumption logic, as defined by several policies within the Coverage Group assigned to these items. Another aspect involves the delivery date control policy assigned to salable items, such as ATP or CTP logic. The next chapter provides further explanation of forecast consumption logic (Section 10.4) and the delivery date control policy (Section 10.10).

9.9 Maintain Coverage Planning Data for Items

The coverage planning data for an item is spread across multiple forms. These include the Released Product Details form for the selected item and the associated form for Default Order Settings. This information represents companywide policies, and the coverage planning data on the Released Product Details form can be populated via a template. The information on two other forms – termed the Site-Specific Order-Settings and the Item Coverage form -- represent site-specific and site/warehouse-specific policies respectively. As a general guideline, you maintain the coverage planning data at the highest possible level unless warranted; this approach reduces the level of data maintenance.

Information on the Item Coverage form can be maintained directly, or you can use a mass maintenance approach using the Item Coverage Setup form. Use of the Item Coverage Setup form provides several advantages.

◆ View items without any item coverage records, thereby making initial data maintenance easier.

◆ View a subset of items by filtering on the item group or buyer group, or the currently assigned coverage group or storage dimension group.

◆ Use the default settings (of a selected record of one item's coverage data) as the copy basis for initially creating a new record for selected items without data.

◆ Delete the item coverage data records for selected items, so that you have a fresh start at maintaining the data.

9.10 Action Messages and Related Policies

Action messages represent one of the key tools for coordinating supply chain activities to meet the S&OP game plans. However, many companies struggle with effective use of action messages because the volume can easily overwhelm the planner so that the messages become meaningless. This section summarizes the action messages and provides some guidelines for effective usage.

Several action message policies are embedded within the coverage group assigned to an item, and master scheduling logic can generate action messages for planned and actual supply orders. The various types of action messages and related policies are summarized in Figure 9.5. The figure includes information for messages about calculated delays will be covered in the next section.

Figure 9.5 Significance of Action Messages

Type of Message		Significance of Message	Message Filters		
			Suppress	Tolerance	Horizon
Action Messages	Advance	Expedite the order to an earlier date	Yes/No	Advance Tolerance (in days)	Look-Ahead Horizon (in days)
	Postpone	De-expedite the order to a later date	Yes/No	Postpone Tolerance (in days)	
	Increase	Increase order to a suggested quantity	Yes/No	N/A	
	Decrease (or Cancel)	Decrease order to a suggested quantity / Cancel order	Yes/No*		
	Derived Actions Policy	Transfer the action message related to a production order to its component items	Yes/No		
	Delay	Projected completion date does not meet requirement date	Yes/No	N/A	Look-Ahead Horizon (in days)

* = Suppressing the decrease message will also suppress the cancel message.

Summary of Action Messages An action message indicates a suggestion to advance/postpone an order's delivery date, to increase/decrease an order quantity, or to cancel a supply order. Message filters can eliminate unnecessary action messages, such as a look-ahead horizon to limit the number of messages and tolerances for the advance and postpone messages. The look-ahead horizon can be specified within a coverage group, or as one of the policies for a set of master plan data.

In many cases, the "advance" action message reflects the rescheduling assumption about an item, where it is generally easier to reschedule an existing supply order than create a new one. That is, master scheduling logic will generate an advance message for an existing order rather than generating a new planned order to cover a requirement that occurs within a relevant time horizon (such as the item's lead time). A subsequent section provides further explanation of the rescheduling assumption and the definition of the relevant time horizon (Section 9.10).

The action message policy about "derived actions" means that an action message related to a planned or actual production order should be transferred to its component items. It represents a prerequisite for analyzing the multi-level format about action messages using the Action Graph capabilities described in the next point.

Analyzing Action Messages Action messages can be viewed from several different forms for a specified set of master plan data. For example, you can view the action messages for a single item on the Net Requirements form or for all items on the Actions form. The Actions form enables you to apply the suggested action for a selected message, where the applied action depends on the message and the type of supply order, and whether it represents a planned or actual supply order. An associated Apply Action dialogue enables you to specify an additional-but-related impact. When applying an advance message related to production, for example, you can also reschedule the actual production order or indicate the planned production order should be approved. When applying a cancel message for a purchase order line (which will delete the line), you can choose to delete the entire purchase order if it was the last line on the order.

From the Actions form, you can also access the Action Graph form to view a graphic analysis of related action messages for a selected message. The related action messages are displayed in a multi-level format when the selected item reflects any part of a supply chain involving production orders and/or transfer orders. The multi-level format involving production orders requires the "derived actions" policy described in the previous point. In this way, you can analyze the action message for the top-level item that impacts lower level items, such as the need to advance the production order for the top-level item. You can also apply a suggested action as described above.

Guidelines for Effective Use of Action Messages Many companies struggle with effective use of action messages, often because of the sheer volume of messages and the resulting difficulties in taking action. To really be effective, you should consider ways to reduce the number of messages so that you achieve a target "hit rate" of more than 90% for taking action on the messages.

As a starting point, you can reduce the number of messages by reducing the look-ahead window for each type of message, and/or by adjusting the message filters for advance/postpone messages. One guideline involves minimizing the degree to which you create actual supply orders for future periods (in advance of the order date), since this results in additional messages when demands change. In contrast, the use of planned orders will automatically adjust to demand changes. A high volume of messages often stems from poor S&OP game plans and unrealistic promise dates on sales orders, and a subsequent chapter provides guidelines for effective S&OP game plans (Section 10.15).

9.11 Messages about Calculated Delays and Related Policies

Messages about a calculated delay represent one of the tools for coordinating supply chain activities to meet the S&OP game plans. The messages indicate that the projected completion date for a supply order will cause a delay in meeting a requirement. This is especially relevant for a sales order requirement, but it also applies to a requirement stemming from a demand forecast and/or safety stock. A related supply order typically has an associated "advance" action message. However, the messages about calculated delays also represent one of the more complex aspects of master scheduling logic, and they are suppressed in many scenarios. This section summarizes the messages about calculated delays and provides some guidelines for effective usage.

Summary of Messages about Calculated Delays The policy about using calculated delay messages is embedded within the coverage group assigned to an item, and master scheduling logic can generate messages for planned and actual supply orders. As summarized in Figure 9.2, you can specify a look-ahead window to limit the number of messages or simply suppress them. The look-ahead horizon can also be specified as one of the policies for a set of master plan data, which acts as an override to the value within a coverage group.

The messages can be communicated across a multi-level product structure, thereby indicating the impact of delays for key components on the projected completion for end-items. This requires assignment of the message policy to the end-item and to each key component in the end-item's product structure.

Analyzing Messages The messages about calculated delays can be viewed from several different forms for a specified set of master plan data. For example, you can view the messages for a single item on the Net Requirements form.

Guidelines for Effective Use of Messages Many companies struggle with effective use of messages about calculated delays, often because of the sheer volume of messages or because of the complexities associated with using the delayed dates as the basis for requirement dates.

As a starting point, you can reduce the number of messages by reducing the look-ahead window. You can also reduce the number of messages by only assigning the message policy to the key components within the product structure of end-items. A high volume of messages often stems from poor S&OP game plans and unrealistic promise dates on sales orders, and a subsequent chapter provides guidelines for effective S&OP game plans (Section 10.15).

Several policies identify the potential use of delayed dates. As one policy (embedded within the coverage group), you can indicate that the delayed date rather than the requirement date should act as the basis for generating action messages. Other policies (for a set of master plan data) can indicate that the delayed date should be used as the requirement date for planned supply orders. However, these policies assume the calculated delays reflect a perfect model of the supply chain, and most scenarios will not use these policies.

9.12 Negative Days and the Rescheduling Assumption

One of the more confusing aspects of planning data within Dynamics AX involves the significance of negative days and the related policy of dynamic negative days. These policies directly impact the generation of planned orders for an item, and the action messages to advance (or cancel) existing supply orders. A key part of the logic for these "advance" messages is commonly termed the rescheduling assumption.

The rescheduling assumption represents a key aspect of planning calculations in every ERP system. In summary, it is typically easier to expedite an item's existing supply order (to meet demand within the item's lead time) rather than generating a new order. Stated another way, the planning calculations should generate an action message to expedite or "advance" an item's existing supply order to meet demand within the item's lead time, or generate a new planned order if that is not possible. AX provides two basic options for this rescheduling assumption. The first option reflects dominant business practices and the second option represents a special case.

Option #1: Rescheduling Assumption based on Item Lead Time. Most firms employ a companywide policy to indicate rescheduling assumptions should be based on each item's lead time. You define this policy -- labeled Use Dynamic Negative Days – on the Master Planning Parameters form. However, many scenarios will create supply orders for delivery in future periods (beyond the item's lead time), so that the rescheduling assumption should be based on a longer time horizon. In this way, the rescheduling assumption applies to all existing orders. You also avoid the confusion associated with action messages to "cancel" existing orders, while getting new planned orders at the same time. You specify the longer time horizon with a large value (such as 365 days) for the Negative Days field embedded within every coverage group, and this value will be automatically added to the item's lead time.

Several considerations apply to the rescheduling assumption. First, the rescheduling assumption only applies when the item's replenishment reflects a coverage code of Period or Requirement; it does not apply to the coverage codes for Min/Max or Manual. Second, the "advance" action message communicates the need to expedite an existing supply order. The message can be generated for planned and actual supply orders. Third, the combined action message of "Advance and Increase" can also be generated, although my personal preference is to suppress the increase message.

Special Case: Limited Ability to Reschedule Existing Supply Orders. Some scenarios require a different basis for the rescheduling assumption (rather than the item's lead time), such as a purchased item or transfer item with delivery via ocean vessel. In these scenarios, it is impossible to expedite an item's existing supply orders within lead time, so that a new planned order should always be generated. Within AX, you do not employ the policy for dynamic negative days, and you typically specify the item's lead time as the value for negative days. This value serves as the basis for the rescheduling assumption, and you also specify a value for the item's lead time.

9.13 Positive Days and the Assumptions about Current Inventory

With normal netting logic, an item's requirements can be met with current inventory even when the requirement date is in the distant future. Most scenarios will employ this logic, which means that a large value should be used for positive days -- such as 365 days.

Some scenarios prefer to use current inventory only for near-term sales orders, so that sales orders for future shipment dates should be fulfilled by the generation of planned supply orders. This represents an exception to normal netting logic. A classic example involves perishable inventory such as fresh fruits or fish, where current inventory should only be sold for today's sales orders, and sales orders for future shipment dates should be fulfilled by planned supply orders. A time horizon of 1 day (for positive days) might apply in this example. An appropriate time horizon depends on several factors, such as an item's inventory plan, frequency of replenishment, and rate of sales.

9.14 Safety Margins

A safety margin may be employed when you require significant time (such as one or more days) for processing receipts or shipments, or creating supply orders. These correspond to the three possible values for a safety margin labeled receipt, issue and reorder. The value(s) for a safety margin can be defined within the coverage group assigned to an item. Different coverage groups may be needed to reflect differences in the use of a safety margin, as illustrated by the following examples.

◆ *Receipt Safety Margin for a Purchased Item.* A receipt safety margin often applies to purchased material with significant time requirements for receiving inspection or simply processing the incoming material, so that master scheduling logic will schedule a delivery prior to the required date.

◆ *Reorder Safety Margin for a Purchased Item.* A reorder safety margin indicates the number of days to arrange a purchase order, so that master scheduling logic will suggest planned orders with an earlier order date that also reflects the item's lead time and the required date.

◆ *Issue and Receipt Margins related to Transfer Orders.* The issue safety margin reflects the preparation time for picking/shipping a transfer order at the ship-from location, so that the master scheduling logic will generate planned supply orders to arrive prior to the ship date. Master scheduling logic also uses the receipt safety margin to schedule delivery prior to the required date at the ship-to location.

◆ *Issue Safety Margin for a Salable Item.* An issue safety margin reflects the preparation time for picking/shipping a salable item, so that the master scheduling logic will generate planned supply orders to arrive prior to the ship date.

Safety margins may also apply to a manufactured item, such as significant time requirements for issuing components to a production order or the inspection of finished quantities.

As an alternative approach, the number of days for the three safety margins can be defined as part of the policies for a set of master plan data, and these will be added to the values defined within coverage groups (if defined).

9.15 Time Fence Policies

Master scheduling logic uses several time fences that serve different purposes. Most of these time fences are defined as part of the policies for a set of master plan data, since that is the simplest approach and easiest to understand. The time fences reflect the purpose of the master plan data, such as the master plan for day-to-day operations versus a master plan for long-range planning purposes. Some of time fence policies may vary for different items (such as a freeze time fence and its time horizon), so they should be defined as part of a coverage group assigned to these items.

Time Fence Policies for Day-to-Day Operations The significance of time fences can be grouped into several topics, and the following explanation focuses on the master plan data that supports day-to-day operations in a manufacturing operation.

◆ *Planning horizon and related time fence policies.* The planning horizon for manufactured items must extend beyond the cumulative manufacturing lead times in order to provide visibility about requirements for purchased items. This planning horizon should be reflected in the time fences for coverage, explosion, and forecast.

◆ *Capacity time fence and the use of routing data.* The capacity time fence determines when routing data for manufactured items should be ignored by master scheduling logic. For example, routing data may be used for near-term scheduling purposes within the next 30 days, and then ignored after the 30 day time fence so that a fixed lead time applies to manufactured items.

◆ *Freeze time fence and the use of a frozen period.* The concept of a frozen period (termed a *freeze time fence*) is typically employed by the master scheduling role to ensure stability of the near-term schedule, where planned production orders should not be automatically scheduled within the frozen period. When the required date for a planned order falls within the freeze time fence, master scheduling logic will place the due date at the end of the frozen period, and the master scheduler can determine how to handle it.

In order to support selective use of a freeze time fence and its time horizon, it should be defined in the coverage group assigned to those items within the responsibility of the master scheduling role.

◆ *Time Fence Policy for Automatic Firming.* The concept of automatic firming is typically employed in more mature implementations, and it only applies to selected items where the planned orders represent the decision-making logic of the planner or buyer. Automatic firming of planned orders within a specified horizon (for the firming time fence) reduces the need for manual intervention.

Automatic firming of planned purchase orders, for example, will reflect the preferred vendor and result in multi-line purchase orders based on grouping preferences. In order to support selective use of the firming time fence and its time horizon, it should be defined in the coverage group assigned to those items within the responsibility of the purchasing agent.

Automatic firming may also apply to selected manufactured items and transfers, so that selective use should be reflected in the definition and assignment of coverage groups assigned to the relevant items.

◆ *Time fence policies for Action Messages and Calculated Delay Messages.* These time fence policies and their time horizons were described in previous sections (Sections 9.10 and 9.11).

9.16 Additional Case Studies

Case 9.1: Different Coverage Groups to Model SCM Decision Making
A manufacturing company employed several different coverage groups within AX to model the SCM decision making of different roles, such as master schedulers, production planners, buyers and DRP coordinators for transfer orders. As a starting point, they defined several coverage groups to reflect the different values for a coverage code, which included the different period lot sizes (such as daily, weekly, bi-monthly and monthly) and the use of requirements and min-max logic for generating planned orders. Additional coverage groups were needed for several purposes. First, the master scheduler employed additional coverage groups to support differences in forecast consumption logic for salable end-items versus stocked components. Second, buyers and planners employed different groups to support differences in filtering of action message policies, thereby improving the usefulness of action messages. Third, additional groups were needed to identify different safety margins when an item required significant time for picking/shipping or receiving/inspection activities.

Case 9.2 Measuring Improvements in the Models of SCM Decision Making A manufacturing company was using Dynamics AX to coordinate their supply chain activities. They wanted to improve the effectiveness of system usage based on macro-level quality metrics and periodic sampling. They identified several usage characteristics as the basis for the macro-level metrics, and performed sampling on a weekly basis to measure improvements. Examples of the usage characteristics for different roles such as buyers and planners included (1) the percentage of planned orders that reflected the actual SCM decision making, (2) the number of action messages and the percentage that were actually useful, and (3) the number of supply orders and sales order lines with unrealistic or past due dates. These metrics indicated the actual usefulness of the formal system to support SCM decisions, and helped guide incremental efforts to improve system usage.

Case 9.3: Suggested Vendor based on Lowest Price A machine manufacturer purchased several components from the vendor offering the lowest price, whereas other purchased components were always sourced from a single preferred vendor. Each vendor provided price quotes for selected items (with date effectivities), and the quotes were used to update purchase price trade agreement information. Using this information, master scheduling logic generated planned purchase orders for the selected items, where the suggested vendor reflected the one with the lowest price.

Case 9.4: Buy-to-Order Component A manufacturer produced configure-to-order products which included a specialized purchase component requiring delivery that was closely synchronized with the parent item's production order. Due to its size and specialized nature, it was critical for the purchased component to be delivered when actually required, and to identify the related production order at the time of receipt. By designating the item as a buy-to-order component for the parent item, a linked purchase order was automatically created after scheduling the parent item's production order, and also synchronized automatically as the schedule changed.

9.17 Executive Summary

Planned orders communicate the need to replenish an item's inventory, and are generated by master scheduling logic based on an item's coverage planning data and related S&OP game plans. An item's preferred source of supply -- defined on a companywide or site/warehouse-specific basis -- determines whether it reflects a purchase, transfer or production order. This chapter summarized the coverage planning data related to generation of planned orders and the use of action messages and messages about calculated delays. It also provided more detailed explanations of several related topics, such as safety margins and time fence policies.

Chapter

S&OP and Master Scheduling

One of the cornerstones for effective supply chain management in a manufacturing or distribution business consists of effective sales and operations planning (S&OP) game plans. They provide the basis for running the business from the top, and build on the models of the organization's supply chain and decision-making logic. The process typically starts with the definition of all demands for the firm's salable items, and results in S&OP game plans that drive supply chain activities to meet those demands. The nature of an S&OP game plan depends on several factors, such as the need to anticipate demand for an item, the item's primary source of supply, and the need for linkage between a sales order and the item's supply order. Demand forecasts are often used to anticipate demand.

The master scheduling logic within AX plays a critical role in the development and use of S&OP game plans. The term "master scheduling logic" has many different synonyms and the term often varies by ERP software package. Equivalent terms include planning calculations, MRP logic and DRP logic. These planning calculations often reflect one of the more complex aspects of supply chain management and ERP systems.

This chapter reviews common S&OP scenarios and explains the typical business processes to maintain S&OP game plans. It covers key elements of an S&OP game plan, including demand forecasts, sales order promise dates, and the master scheduling task. These considerations are reflected in the following sections within the chapter.

1. Common S&OP Scenarios
2. Typical Process to Maintain S&OP Game Plans for Stocked Products
3. Basics of Demand Forecasts
4. Basics of Demand Forecast Consumption
5. Additional Considerations about Demand Forecasts

6. Calculate Demand Forecasts based on Historical Data
7. Safety Stock Requirements
8. Stocked Components for Make-to-Order Products
9. Common S&OP Scenarios with Link to Sales Orders
10. Sales Order Promise Dates and the Delivery Date Control Policy
11. Typical Process to Run the Master Scheduling Task and Analyze Results
12. Overview of the Master Scheduling Task and Master Plan Data
13. Master Scheduling with Finite versus Infinite Capacity
14. Forecast Scheduling and Forecast Plan Data
15. Simulations for S&OP Purposes
16. Guidelines concerning S&OP Game Plans
17. Typical Process to Maintain S&OP Game Plans for a Stocked Product in a Distribution Operation
18. Workspaces related to Master Planning

Master scheduling logic builds on the supply chain model of a manufacturing or distribution business described in previous chapters. This includes the fundamentals of modeling inventory locations, the definition of material items, the definition of bills of material and routings for manufactured items, and coverage planning data to model SCM decision making. Subsequent chapters cover other aspects of modeling the supply chain, including sales orders and supply orders.

A master scheduler role is typically responsible for entering and maintaining the S&OP game plans in most manufacturing companies. This role is not specifically identified within the standard AX roles -- which do include a production planner role as a rough approximation of a master scheduler. Much of the explanation within this chapter focuses on the master scheduler role with a manufacturing company.

10.1 Common S&OP Scenarios

The nature of an S&OP game plan depends on several factors, such as the need to anticipate demand for an item, the item's primary source of supply, and the need for linkage between a sales order and the item's supply order. When demand needs to be anticipated, for example, min/max quantities or demand forecasts often provide a key element of S&OP game plans for stocked end-items or stocked components. The item's primary source of supply may reflect production orders in traditional manufacturing or kanban orders in lean manufacturing, as well as purchase orders and transfer orders in a distribution operation. The need for linkage becomes important for make-to-order and buy-to-order products in order to provide visibility of the sales order demand and for tracking actual costs of goods sold. A given company typically has several major scenarios where each scenario employs different key elements in the S&OP game plans.

The common S&OP scenarios can be broadly grouped in different ways. For explanatory purposes, we'll consider two different groups reflecting the need for linkage between a sales order and an item's supply order. The first group of S&OP scenarios summarized here do not require linkage, and a subsequent section covers S&OP scenarios with linkage (Section 10.9).

Several common S&OP scenarios are summarized in Figure 10.1 and described below. For each scenario, the figure identifies the key elements of the S&OP game plan and several additional considerations, including the typical basis of sales order delivery promises. The figure identifies an S&OP scenario for a make-to-stock manufactured item that also applies to a stocked product in a distribution operation, where key elements in the S&OP game plan typically include demand forecasts or min-max quantities. Subsequent sections describe a typical process to maintain the S&OP game plans for make-to-stock products (Section 10.2) and for stocked products in a distribution operation (Section 10.17).

Figure 10.1 Common S&OP Scenarios

	Scenario	Key Elements of S&OP Game Plan	Additional Considerations	Basis of Delivery Promises
No Link to Sales Order	Make-to-Stock End-Item or Stocked Product in a Distribution Operation	Min-Max Quantities	Coverage Code = Min-Max Calculation of minimum quantity	ATP
		Demand Forecast	Coverage Code = Period Forecast consumption by sales orders Using an inventory plan (safety stock)	
		Manual Master Schedule	Coverage Code = Manual or Period	
	Completely Make-to-Order	Sales Order	Coverage Code = Period or Requirement	CTP or CTP via Net Change Explosion
	Make-to-Order End-Item	Sales Order for End-Item	Coverage Code = Period or Requirement	
	with Stocked Components	Demand Forecast for stocked components	Coverage Code = Period Forecast consumption by all demands Using an inventory plan (safety stock)	
		or Min-Max Quantities for stocked components	Coverage Code = Min-Max Calculation of minimum quantity	

Stocked End-Item based on Min-Max Quantities   The simplest S&OP approach employs min-max logic to carry inventory in anticipation of actual demand, where an item's coverage planning policies define the minimum and maximum quantities by site/warehouse. The minimum quantity represents an implied demand forecast, where the quantity typically reflects the daily usage rate multiplied by the number of days for the item's lead time.   With min-max logic, when an item's projected inventory falls below its minimum quantity, master scheduling logic will generate a planned order that achieves the item's maximum quantity (subject to an order quantity multiple). The values for an item's minimum and maximum quantities can be fixed, or specified as a pattern (termed the minimum key and maximum key). You can automatically calculate the minimum quantity based on historical average usage over the item's lead time, as described in a subsequent section about calculating safety stock requirements (Section 10.7).   Sales order delivery promises can be based on available-to-promise (ATP) logic.

Stocked End-Item based on a Demand Forecast   Inventory replenishment based on period lot-sizing logic is driven by the combination of demand forecasts and actual sales orders, which typically involves forecast consumption logic. The number of days for period lot-sizing purposes reflect the desired frequency of delivery, with more frequent delivery of A items (such as daily or weekly periods) compared to B and C items (such as monthly periods).

In addition to the demand forecasts, an inventory plan (expressed as safety stock requirements) can be used to anticipate higher-than-expected customer demand, and meet customer service objectives regarding stock outs, partial shipments and delivery lead times.   You can automatically calculate the safety stock requirement based on variations in historical usage and the desired customer service level, as described in a subsequent section about calculating safety stock requirements (Section 10.7).

The planned orders are typically approved (or firmed) in the near term to reflect the desired production schedule and to account for material and capacity constraints. The combination of planned orders and actual production orders represents the item's master schedule, and provides the basis for making delivery promises using ATP logic.

Case 10.1: Demand Forecasts for Office Furniture

An office furniture manufacturer produced and stocked different end-items based on demand forecasts, and sales order delivery promises were based on ATP logic. Entries of the demand forecasts reflected weekly increments (with start-of-week due dates) over a rolling three month time horizon (which reflected the cumulative manufacturing lead time), and monthly increments for the next nine months. The master scheduler translated the monthly forecasts into the weekly increments and relevant due dates over the rolling three month time horizon. The translation considered months containing 4 versus 5 weeks, and also weeks with less than 5 working days. Forecast consumption logic was based on fixed monthly periods defined by a single reduction key assigned to all items. Sales orders with ship dates in a given month consumed the demand forecasts within the month. As time moved forward, the weekly increments of unconsumed forecast became past-due and were ignored by master scheduling logic.

Stocked End-Item based on a Manual Master Schedule The master schedule starts with manually-created planned orders with an approved status, and firming these planned orders results in actual production orders. The item's coverage code can be manual (which does not support net requirement inquiries) or period (where you suppress the action messages). Demand forecasts are not typically entered. This approach avoids the complexities associated with forecast consumption logic, and provides the basis for making delivery promises using ATP logic.

Case 10.2: Manual Master Schedule for Medical Devices

A medical device company produced a line of medical devices that required a manually maintained master schedule to reflect the planner's decision-making logic about production constraints. The medical devices required an expensive outside operation for sterilization, where multiple end-items could be sterilized at the same time. The scheduling considerations included a cost-benefit analysis about amortizing the fixed fee for sterilization over the largest possible number of end-items subject to a weight maximum, while still building the product mix for customer demands and avoiding excess inventory. A manually maintained master schedule proved most effective for this case.

Completely Make-to-Order End-Item The S&OP game plan consists of actual sales orders for a completely make-to-order product, where CTP logic provides the basis for making delivery promises. Alternatively, delivery promises can reflect a quoted lead time that represents the item's cumulative manufacturing time. The master scheduling task generates planned supply orders to meet the sales order demand, where the planned orders reflect the item's planning data (such as coverage codes of period or requirement) as well as the active BOM and route versions for manufactured items. This scenario generally implies a pipeline of sales orders with future delivery dates that exceed the item's cumulative lead time.

Make-to-Order End-Item with Stocked Components The use of stocked components can shorten the delivery lead time for make-to-order products, and provide the basis for delivery promises based on CTP logic. Inventory replenishment of these stocked components can be driven by demand forecasts or min-max quantities, as illustrated by the two options in Figure 10.1.

The use of demand forecasts for stocked components involves forecast consumption by any demand, such as dependent demands stemming from production orders for the make-to-order product. An inventory plan may also apply to stocked components, and a subsequent section explains the calculation of these safety stock requirements to meet demand variability.

Another key element of the S&OP game plan consists of sales orders for the make-to-order product. Master scheduling will generate planned supply orders to meet the sales order demand, where the planned orders reflect the item's planning data (such as a coverage code of period or requirement) as well as the active BOM and route versions for the item.

Case 10.3: Electric Motors built from Stocked Components

A manufacturer of standard electric motors produced end-items based on a pipeline of sales orders, where sales order delivery dates were initially assigned based on CTP logic. The motors were built from stocked components in order to shorten delivery lead times. Replenishment of these long lead-time components was driven by demand forecasts. In this scenario, the demand forecasts were defined for an item allocation key, which identified the stocked components and a mix percentage of their typical usage. The demand forecasts were entered in weekly increments over a 3-month rolling time horizon and monthly increments thereafter.

10.2 Typical Process to Maintain S&OP Game Plans for a Make-to-Stock Product

The S&OP game plans for a make-to-stock product often involve a combination of demand forecasts and actual sales orders that drive the item's master schedule, which consists of planned and actual production orders. The term master schedule generally applies to the highest possible stocking level for manufactured items, which consists of saleable items in this scenario. The master schedule provides the basis for making delivery promises on sales orders using available-to-promise (ATP) logic.

A typical business process to maintain the S&OP game plan consists of multiple steps performed by different roles, as summarized in Figure 10.2 and described below. A key role is often called the master scheduler, but this title is not included with the standard AX roles. The master scheduler role typically maintains the game plans and obtains management agreement. This role requires an in-depth understanding of sales and supply chain capabilities, as well as the political power to achieve agreed-upon game plans.

Figure 10.2 Typical Process to Maintain S&OP Game Plans for a Make-to-Stock Product

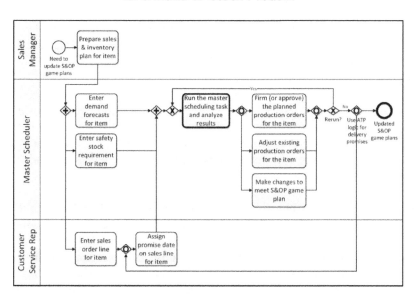

Overview The business process starts with the periodic analysis of historical and projected demands in order to prepare a sales plan and inventory plan for each product, where the sales plan is typically expressed in monthly increments. The inventory plan covers higher-than-anticipated sales order demands to meet desired customer service levels. The master scheduler translates this information into entries for the item's demand forecast and safety stock requirements. After the master scheduling task has been performed, the master scheduler analyzes the results to determine the need for adjustments, and to firm (or approve) planned orders that represent the master schedule. The master schedule provides the basis for realistic promised delivery dates using available-to-promise logic, typically in the context of customer service reps entering sales order lines for the item. In this scenario, actual sales orders consume the item's demand forecast within user-defined forecast periods.

For most scenarios, coverage planning applies to the site/warehouse level, and period lot sizing logic applies to the coverage code assigned to stocked items and their components. The period lot size (expressed in days) represents the frequency of replenishment, and the planned order quantities and dates reflect the time increments and due dates for demand forecasts.

Prepare a sales plan and inventory plan for the item A sales manager role generally has responsibility for analyzing historical and projected demands for the item in order to prepare a sales plan by ship-from location, typically expressed in monthly increments. In many cases the master scheduler must assume this responsibility. The analysis also results in an inventory plan for the item (by ship-from location) to meet the desired customer service levels when actual demands exceed forecast. The analyses may reflect a statistical forecasting technique or some other method.

Enter demand forecast for the item The master scheduler translates the item's sales plan into entries for demand forecasts, typically expressed in weekly increments (or even daily increments) in the near term. In this scenario, actual sales orders for an item will automatically consume the item's demand forecast within the user-defined forecast periods.

Enter safety stock requirement for the item The master scheduler translates the item's inventory plan into entries for a safety stock requirement. The safety stock requirements can be entered as a single value, or the value can be calculated based on historical usage. A subsequent section provides further explanation about calculating safety stock requirements (Section 10.7). The safety stock requirements can also be defined as a pattern of multiple values for different time periods.

Run the master scheduling task and analyze results This activity represents a sub-process with multiple steps and roles. After running the master scheduling task, the master scheduler analyzes the results to identify potential constraints related to material or capacity, and potential problems in meeting demands. The results include planned orders, action messages, and net requirements for material items, and capacity requirements for resources. A subsequent section provides further explanation about running the master scheduling task and analyzing results (Section 10.11).

Firm (or approve) the planned production orders for the item The master schedule consists of the item's production orders, both planned and actual. Planned orders can be approved or firmed, and the suggested quantities and/or dates may be adjusted to ensure a realistic master schedule.

◆ *Approve a planned production order.* By assigning a status of "Approved" to a planned order, master scheduling logic will treat the planned order as if it has been scheduled for the specified quantity and due date. It also locks the

BOM/route information (so that planned changes will not be recognized) and prevents deletion when deleting a set of master plan data (unlike other planned orders). An approved planned order must still be firmed to create an actual production order.

◆ *Firm a planned production order.* Firming a planned order generates an actual production order (typically with a scheduled status) for the specified quantity and due date, and also results in the initial assignment of the order-dependent BOM and route information to the production order.

For example, the master scheduler may firm (or approve) the planned orders to represent a level-loaded schedule, or to account for material or capacity constraints. Alternatively, the master scheduler may simply use planned orders to represent the master schedule, and ultimately firm them just prior to starting production. This alternative approach assumes the planned orders reflect the anticipated master schedule.

Adjust existing production orders for the item   The master scheduler may adjust existing production orders to reflect the master schedule, such as changing the quantity or due dates.

Make changes to meet the S&OP game plan   The master scheduler may need to coordinate several types of changes to meet the master schedule. For example, the changes often involve working with purchasing agents to expedite purchase orders for components, or working with production supervisors to adjust capacity or schedules. The changes may also involve working with customer service representatives to delay the promised delivery date on sales orders. These changes often involve trade-offs between conflicting objectives.

Enter sales order line for item   The customer service rep enters sales orders for the item, where each sales line indicates a quantity, ship-from location, and a requested ship date and delivery date. Based on forecast consumption logic, the actual sales orders for an item will automatically consume the item's demand forecast within the forecast period.

Assign promise date on sales line for the item   When the customer service rep creates a sales order line for the item, the earliest possible dates for shipment and delivery are automatically assigned based on available-to-promise (ATP) logic. The ATP logic reflects the master schedule for the item, which helps align actual sales orders to the S&OP game plans. The customer service rep can view available to promise information to answer questions about availability, or disable the delivery date control logic to assign an unrealistic promise date. A subsequent section provides further explanation of the delivery date control logic, and the assignment of requested and confirmed dates to a sales order line (Section 10.10).

10.3 Basics of Demand Forecasts

Demand forecasts often represent one of several key elements in the business process to maintain S&OP game plans. The basics of demand forecast information include the identifier for a set of forecast data, how to enter a demand forecast for an item, and using the demand forecast entries in the master scheduling task. The basics also include an understanding of the differences between demand forecasts, supply forecasts and safety stock requirements.

Forecast Models and the Identifier for a Set of Forecast Data A set of forecast data has a user-defined identifier termed a forecast model. You specify the forecast model identifier when entering the forecasted quantities and dates for an item. You also specify the relevant forecast model for use in the master scheduling task. Different sets of forecast data can be identified by different forecast model identifiers, but we'll focus on the forecast model containing the current forecast continuously updated as part of the S&OP game plans. A commonly-used identifier for the forecast model is *Current-Forecast* or simply *Forecast*.

An alternative approach to demand forecasts consists of a two-level forecast model, which requires multiple forecast model identifiers. As an example, the forecast model identifier representing the companywide forecast can be associated with several forecast model identifiers representing regional forecasts. Each forecast entry has a forecast model corresponding to a regional forecast. However, you specify the companywide forecast model for use in the master scheduling task, and the regional forecast models will be automatically rolled up into the companywide forecast model.

Project-oriented operations also employ multiple forecast models, as described in a subsequent section that covers other purposes of demand forecasts (Section 10.5).

Demand Forecasts versus Supply Forecasts One confusing aspect of forecast data within Dynamics AX concerns the difference between a demand forecast and a supply forecast. A demand forecast typically applies to stocked products with forecast consumption by actual sales orders. In addition, demand forecasts can also apply to stocked components of make-to-order products, with forecast consumption by any type of demand (such as the dependent demands stemming from production orders for the make-to-order products).

A supply forecast represents an historical approach within AX for driving replenishment of stocked components, where the historical approach has been replaced by the use of demand forecasts. This historical approach involved a completely different conceptual model using different entries and forecast consumption logic (where creation of supply orders consumes the supply forecast), and it provided limited visibility about how supply forecasts impacted master scheduling logic. The supply forecast approach is not generally applicable in most scenarios.

Entering a Demand Forecast for a Saleable Item   A saleable item may represent an end-item or a component, and each forecast entry minimally consists of the forecast model, the item identifier, quantity, date, and ship-from site/warehouse. All of the forecast entries with the same forecast model comprise a set of forecast data.

Other approaches to a demand forecast require additional information. Examples include a demand forecast by customer, a demand forecast for a group of items, and translating monthly or weekly demand forecasts into daily increments. These approaches are described in a subsequent section about additional considerations for demand forecasts (Section 10.5).

Using Demand Forecasts in the Master Scheduling Task   The master scheduling task represents the primary engine for coordinating supply chain activities. It uses several master plan policies to calculate material and capacity requirements. One master plan policy indicates whether to consider demand forecasts in master scheduling logic, and a second policy specifies the relevant forecast model. A third related policy (termed the reduction principle) indicates the primary option for forecast consumption, as described in the next section about the basics of forecast consumption.

Using Demand Forecasts in the Forecast Scheduling Task   While the set of master plan data reflects net requirements and provides coordination for supply chain management, it is sometimes helpful to calculate gross requirements that only reflect forecasted demand. The forecast scheduling task calculates these gross requirements and generates a set of *forecast plan data* based on a specified forecast model. A subsequent section provides further explanation of forecast scheduling and forecast plan data (Section 10.14).

10.4 Basics of Demand Forecast Consumption

The combination of demand forecasts and actual sales orders must be considered to avoid doubled-up requirements for an item. These considerations are commonly termed forecast consumption logic. A basic choice concerns the reduction principle option within the master plan policies for the current master plan. The four major options for the reduction principle are explained below, and an additional subsection describes a Reduction Key (used by two of the options) that defines the forecast periods for forecast consumption purposes.

The four major options of a reduction principle are summarized in Figure 10.2, along with two related policies for an item. The need for these two related policies depends on the selected option for a reduction principle, as indicated by "Yes" versus "N/A" in the figure. You define these additional policies as part of the coverage group assigned to an item. One policy indicates the applicable Reduction Key, and the second "Reduce Forecast By" policy indicates that sales orders (rather than all types of demands) should consume the demand forecasts.

The figure also indicates the estimated usage for each option. As shown by shading for Option #1, the dominant business practices consist of forecast consumption by transactions based on a reduction key with a fixed start date, typically with fixed monthly forecast periods.

Figure 10.3 Summary of Forecast Consumption Policies

Reduction Principle and Description	Related Policies for an Item		Estimated Usage
	Applicable Reduction Key	Reduce Forecast By = Sales Orders	
1 **Transactions – Reduction Key** Sales orders consume demand forecasts within specified forecast periods - Using a Reduction Key with a fixed start date	Yes	Yes	> 70%
- Using a Reduction Key with a floating start date			< 5%
2 **Transactions – Dynamic Period** Sales orders consume demand forecasts within implied forecast periods	N/A	Yes	~ 20%
3 **Percent – Reduction Key** Automatically reduce demand forecasts within specified forecast periods	Yes	N/A	< 1%
4 **None** Manually adjust demand forecasts to reflect forecast consumption	N/A	N/A	< 5%

Legend: ▢ = Dominant Business Practices

Option #1: Sales Orders Consume Demand Forecasts within Specified Forecast Periods   The reduction principle is *Transactions - Reduction Key,* and the option requires the two related policies for an item. One of these policies indicates the applicable reduction key, which defines the forecast periods for forecast reduction purposes. The second "Reduce Forecast By" policy indicates that sales orders (rather than all types of demands) should consume the demand forecasts.

This option is easiest to explain using a reduction key comprised of fixed monthly forecast periods and weekly forecast increments, which also represent dominant business practices. In this example, any sales orders with ship dates within a monthly forecast period will consume the item's demand forecasts within the same monthly bucket, starting with the earliest unconsumed forecast and consuming forward. The demand forecasts within a given month can be over-consumed; there is no carry-forward effect to consume forecasts within a future forecast period. Changing the sales order ship date to another month (especially the confirmed ship date) will consume demand forecasts in the relevant month.

Definition of a Reduction Key   A reduction key defines the forecast periods for forecast consumption purposes. The forecast periods are sometimes called time buckets for forecast consumption. Examples of a reduction key include monthly periods, or a combination of weekly periods for several weeks and monthly periods thereafter.

The two basic approaches for defining a reduction key consist of a fixed start date and floating start date, as shown in Figure 10.3 and described below.

◆ *Reduction Key with a Fixed Start Date.* In a typical example, the fixed start date is specified as January 1st of the current year, and the reduction key defines 12 monthly periods. As time progresses, this approach requires additions to the monthly periods within the reduction key or a change in the fixed start date. This approach is the simplest to understand.

◆ *Reduction Key with a Floating Start Date.* The current date (for running the master scheduling task) acts as the floating start date. This approach is slightly more complex to understand because the forecast periods are relative to the current date, but it provides greater flexibility and granularity in modeling some forecast consumption scenarios.

In order to simplify forecast consumption logic, most scenarios will start with just one reduction key (such as fixed monthly forecast periods), and assign it to every item. The need for additional reduction keys, and the assignment of different reduction keys to different items, reflects increasing sophistication and complexity in modeling forecast consumption logic.

Option #2: Sales Orders Consume Demand Forecasts within Implied Forecast Periods

The reduction principle is *Transactions - Dynamic Period,* and the option requires the "Reduce Forecast By" policy indicating that sales orders (rather than all types of demands) should consume the item's demand forecasts. This option employs implied forecast periods defined by the due dates of forecast entries. It does not employ a reduction key. An implied forecast period ends with the next forecast date for the item and ship-from site/warehouse.

Option #3: Automatically Reduce Demand Forecasts by a Percentage

The reduction principle is *Percent - Reduction Key,* and my research suggest the option is rarely used. This option uses a reduction key but with a specified reduction percentage for near-term time buckets. It does not support forecast consumption by sales orders. As one example, you might define a reduction percentage of 100% for the first monthly forecast period within the reduction key, so that only sales orders should be considered during the month. Otherwise the demand forecast and sales orders will be added together within each forecast period. The reduction key can employ a fixed or floating start date.

This concept is often called a demand fence in other ERP systems, where only sales orders are considered as demand within the demand fence. The concept typically applies to scenarios with a fully-booked sales order backlog over the near-term horizon (defined by the demand fence), where the near-term forecasts can be ignored or factored down. The concept can also be implemented by manual adjustments to the demand forecasts, rather than using reduction percentages within the reduction key.

Option #4: Manually Adjust Demand Forecast to reflect Forecast Consumption

The reduction principle is *None.* With this option, the demands from sales orders and demand forecasts will be added together by master scheduling logic, so that demand forecasts must be manually adjusted to reflect forecast consumption. This option does not involve any related information for an item.

Case 10.4: Demand Forecasts with No Forecast Consumption Logic

---

A manufacturing company produced standard products based on actual sales orders. The limited forward visibility of these sales orders meant that demand forecasts for end-items were used to drive replenishment of long lead time materials. The master scheduler avoided any confusion in forecast consumption logic by using a reduction principle of none. He maintained the demand forecasts so that they represented the incremental demand that will be added to sales order demands.

Forecast Consumption and Sales Orders with Past Due or Invalid Ship Dates A key aspect of forecast consumption involves the requested ship date on a sales order line, or the confirmed ship date if specified. It is assumed that these are realistic dates, and that you maintain the information to avoid past due or invalid ship dates. It is difficult to correctly interpret forecast consumption when sales orders have past-due or invalid ship dates.

10.5 Additional Considerations about Demand Forecasts

Many of the considerations about demand forecasts have been covered in previous sections. Examples include the typical business process to maintain S&OP game plans for a make-to-stock product, the definition of forecast models and forecast consumption logic, and the use of demand forecasts in the master scheduling task. This section provides several additional suggestions, starting with the time horizon, time increments and due dates for demand forecasts. It provides ideas about demand forecasts for a customer or a group of items, and translating monthly or weekly forecasts into daily increments. It also covers the special case of demand forecasts in a multicompany supply chain.

Time Horizon for Demand Forecasts The time horizon for dates assigned to demand forecasts must exceed an item's cumulative manufacturing lead time in order to provide any forward visibility, especially for purchased components. The time horizon should be reflected in several master plan policies -- termed time fences and expressed in calendar days -- for considering forecasts, explosions, and coverage planning.[1] Other time fence policies are typically shorter, such as the time fences for consideration of capacity and action messages.

The time increments for demand forecasts can be different across the time horizon, such as weekly increments over the time horizon reflecting the cumulative manufacturing lead time, and monthly increments thereafter. The next point covers time increments.

---

[1] The use of master plan policies provides the simplest approach to these time fence policies. As an alternative, you can define them as part of the coverage group assigned to each item. This alternative approach applies to scenarios with differing time horizons for different products, but it also involves higher levels of data maintenance and complexity.

Time Increments and Due Dates for Demand Forecasts The time increments and due dates for demand forecasts depend on the situation. One or more of the following suggestions can be considered.

♦ *Granularity of time increments and period lot sizing logic.* This guideline means that the granularity of demand forecasts can support period lot sizing logic for planned orders. Weekly forecasts provide sufficient granularity for many scenarios, although some scenarios can benefit from daily granularity in the near term. As a general rule, monthly forecasts do not provide sufficient granularity. However, monthly forecasts may apply to items produced once a month, and staggered forecast dates could reflect the anticipated production schedule throughout the month.

♦ *Significance of due dates for demand forecasts.* It is important that production planners can consistently interpret the significance of due dates assigned to planned production orders stemming from demand forecasts. For example, the forecast due dates can reflect a Monday date or Friday date in scenarios involving weekly time increments. Other scenarios may stagger the due dates, or use daily time increments in the near term, so that the planned order due dates will be spread throughout the week.

♦ *Time increments for demand forecasts and the time buckets for forecast consumption.* The time increments for demand forecasts can be different than the time buckets for forecast consumption purposes. As a dominant business practice, you might specify weekly demand forecasts and use monthly time buckets for forecast consumption.

♦ *Time increments and reducing the impact of past-due forecasts.* As time progresses, the demand forecasts for today's date or earlier will be ignored by master scheduling logic. This is termed past-due forecast. Past-due forecasts can have a dramatic impact when using an overly-simplified approach to time increments and forecast dates. An example involves monthly forecasts with a due date on the 1st of the month, where the demand forecasts become past due as time progresses. Smaller time increments and staggered dates can lessen the impact of advancing time and the resulting past-due forecasts.

♦ *Reasonable approximation of the item's master schedule.* This guideline means that planned production orders (stemming from the demand forecasts) can be easily firmed with little need for manual adjustments, and that planned orders can provide the basis for making sales order delivery promises based on ATP logic. The guideline does not apply to scenarios with demand seasonality requiring a level-loaded master schedule, as defined by approved planned orders or scheduled production orders.

Demand Forecasts for a Group of Items Some scenarios employ demand forecasts for an item group rather than an individual item.   This approach employs a user-defined template (termed an *Item Allocation Key*) that spreads out a total quantity across several items based on a mix percentage per item.   The synonyms for an item allocation key include a planning bill or planning BOM. With this approach, a forecast entry for the item group would specify the item allocation key and the ship-from site/warehouse.

Each entry within the item allocation key can optionally define the ship-from site/warehouse.   For example, the entries could define the mix percentages for shipping the same item from different sites/warehouses.   With this approach, a forecast entry for the item group would simply specify the item allocation key.

Case 10.5: Aggregate Forecasts by Item Group

A manufacturing company had thousands of stocked end-items, and wanted to minimize the effort to maintain forecasts for individual items.   Items were grouped together for forecasting purposes, with a mix percentage assigned to each item, so that aggregate forecasts could be entered for each group of items. This approach reduced the number of forecasts to be maintained, from thousands of individual items to a few dozen groups.

Demand Forecasts by Customer   Some scenarios involve customer-specific forecasts for salable items, which also involve forecast consumption logic by sales orders from the customer.   The correct logic requires an item-specific policy about forecast consumption – labeled "include customer forecasts in the demand forecast" – embedded in the coverage group assigned to the item. The label is slightly misleading because the policy refers to forecast consumption logic; a master plan policy determines whether demand forecasts will be included.   Customer-specific forecasts are not consumed by sales orders from other customers.

The correct logic involves the previously described basics of forecast consumption, such as the reduction principle with fixed or implied forecast periods, and the item-specific policy to "reduce forecast by" sales orders. Similar to general demand forecasts with forecast consumption within a forecast period, sales orders will consume the earliest customer-specific forecasts within the period prior to consuming forecasts later in the period.

As an alternative, demand forecasts can be entered for a customer group (rather than for a specific customer), so that forecasts are consumed by sales orders from any customer with the same customer group.

Translating a Monthly or Weekly Demand Forecast into Daily Increments Some scenarios employ daily increments in the near-term demand forecast, thereby providing greater granularity for planned order quantities based on period lot sizing logic. The following examples illustrate how to translate monthly or weekly forecasts into daily increments.

◆ *Translate Monthly Forecasts into Daily Increments.* You can enter a monthly demand forecast (for first day of the month) along with a *Period Allocation Key* that will automatically result in daily increments. For example, you would predefine the period allocation key indicating 30 daily increments and a percentage for each daily increment such as 3.33%. This example means that a monthly forecast of 300 would result in daily increments of 10. The assigned percentage may vary to reflect demand patterns within a month, such as higher sales at the end of the month. Other period allocation keys would be needed for months with a different number of days.

◆ *Translate Weekly Forecasts into Daily Increments.* You can enter a weekly demand forecast (for the date corresponding to the first working day of the week) along with a *Period Allocation Key* that will automatically result in daily increments. For example, you would predefine the period allocation key indicating five daily increments and a percentage for each daily increment such as 20%. This example means that a weekly forecast of 100 would result in daily increments of 20. Other period allocation keys would be needed for weeks with a different number of working days.

Demand Forecasts in a Multicompany Supply Chain Some scenarios involve a multicompany supply chain within one AX instance, where demand forecasts must be entered for the relevant company and ship-from location. There are two basic scenarios for using demand forecasts in a multicompany supply chain.

◆ *Enter demand forecasts for the selling company that actually stocks and sells the item.* These requirements will be communicated across company boundaries as planned intercompany demand for the supplying company. Actual sales orders at the selling company can consume these demand forecasts.

◆ *Enter customer-specific demand forecasts for the supplying company that stocks the item.* In this scenario, demand forecasts are entered for the customer that represents the sister company. In addition, the intercompany sales order must consume the customer-specific demand forecast, as defined by policies within the coverage group assigned to the item.

Other Purposes of Demand Forecasts The suggestions for using demand forecasts have focused on using one forecast model and one set of master plan data to support S&OP purposes. These demand forecasts typically involve forecast consumption logic and continuous updates. Different forecast models and different sets of master plan data (or forecast plan data) can serve different purposes, as summarized below.

◆ *Original Annual Forecast.* One forecast model can represent the original annual forecast, thereby supporting comparisons against actual results or other sets of forecast data. The original annual forecast typically reflects one aspect of the budgeting process. For example, the identifier (and description) for the forecast model could refer to "Original Annual Forecast for 201X".

◆ *Long-Range Planning.* An additional forecast model can support long-range planning for material or resources. These demand forecasts can be used by the master scheduling task to generate a separate set of master plan data, or by the forecast scheduling task to generate a set of forecast plan data. For example, the resulting requirements for material can be used in vendor negotiations for purchased items. The requirements for resources, or aggregate requirements for resource groups, can be used to justify equipment investments or anticipate needed head counts.

◆ *S&OP Simulations.* One or more sets of demand forecast data can be used for simulation purposes. One example would be different sets representing the best-case and worst-case scenarios, and the calculation of corresponding requirements. As another example, you can run the master scheduling task using infinite capacity planning to anticipate overloaded periods. After adjusting available capacity and consideration of alternate routings, you run the master scheduling task again using finite capacity to highlight unrealistic delivery dates.

◆ *Project-Oriented Operations.* Project budgets are based on forecasted requirements, where a unique forecast model is often defined for each version of the project's budget. In addition, the forecasted requirements for items and production resources can optionally be included in master scheduling logic. As one example using a two-level forecast model, the sub-models identify the relevant forecast models for various projects.

10.6 Calculate Demand Forecasts based on Historical Data

Some scenarios can benefit from the calculation of demand forecasts based on sales history information. Standard AX functionality supports the calculation of statistical forecasts, and the approach differs between AX 2012 R3 and the New Dynamics AX.

Calculate Demand Forecasts in AX 2012 R3   The calculation of demand forecasts was first introduced in AX 2012 R3, where the forecast models in Microsoft SQL Server Analysis Service are used to create predictions. You can review and adjust these calculated forecasts within an Excel spreadsheet, and upload them automatically into the demand forecast tables within AX.

The calculations require some setup information and involve multiple steps that have been explained elsewhere.[2] In summary, the relevant user must have access to the SQL database. You should identify the relevant set of forecast data to be updated with the newly-generated forecast (aka the forecast model). The items to be forecasted should be assigned to an item allocation key. You also need to define several policies on the Demand Forecasting Parameters form.

The starting point involves the periodic task to Generate Statistical Baseline Forecast, where you specify the start and end dates about historical data. You also specify the start date for the newly-generated forecast and the number of periods to be forecasted. You can optionally forecast a subset of items based on selected item allocation keys.

The newly-generated forecast can then be viewed by opening the Excel file, which displays individual product forecasts and the rollup to item group forecasts. Clicking on the Pivot Table displays the available fields for further analysis. You can then manually adjust the individual product forecasts, or adjust the rolled-up forecast to automatically prorate the change for individual forecasts. When the adjustments have been completed, you can publish the information and then import it into a selected forecast model. You can then view the information within the demand forecast tables, such as the demand forecasts by item group or individual item.

---

[2] A simplified walkthrough of the AX 2012 R3 approach was provided in the blog "Configuring Demand Forecasting" by Murray Fife.

Calculate Demand Forecasts in the New Dynamics AX   Demand forecasts are calculated using the Microsoft Azure Machine Learning cloud service.   The service performs best match model selection and offers key performance indicators for calculating forecast accuracy.[3]

10.7 Safety Stock Requirements

Safety stock represents a key element in S&OP game plans for those scenarios with stocked end-items or stocked components.   Within AX, an item's safety stock requirement is defined by the minimum quantity field.   You can manually enter a value, or calculate a proposed minimum quantity based on an item's historical usage and its lead time.[4]   The significance of the minimum quantity differs between two major approaches for solving S&OP scenarios with stocked items.   One approach employs the minimum quantity as part of min-max logic, and the second approach employs the minimum quantity to represent an inventory plan in combination with demand forecasts.

◆ *Minimum quantity for min-max purposes*.   Min-max quantities provide one approach to S&OP game plans with a stocked item.   When using a min-max coverage code, you specify the item's minimum quantity and maximum quantity for each relevant site/warehouse.   The minimum quantity represents the average daily usage multiplied by the item's lead time.   Alternatively, you can define a pattern (termed a minimum key and a maximum key) to identify different quantities over multiple time periods.

◆ *Minimum quantity for inventory plan purposes*.   A second approach to S&OP game plans with a stocked item involves demand forecasts, where the minimum quantity represents an inventory plan at a relevant site/warehouse. The inventory plan covers demand variability to meet the desired customer service level in order to reduce stock outs, partial shipments, and delivery lead times.   Stated another way, this minimum quantity reflects a percentage of forecast accuracy for a given item; it does not represent a desired inventory position.   The minimum quantity is commonly called an inventory plan or safety stock.   The second approach applies when using a coverage code of period or requirement.

---

[3] A detailed explanation (and the associated testing of different use cases) could not be completed prior to the book publication date.   The topic is included here for completeness sake.
[4] The calculation of a safety stock quantity reflects an item's fixed lead time.   The assignment of these lead times was previously described for purchased items (Section 9.1), manufactured items (Section 9.3) and transfer items (Section 9.5).

The definition of an item's minimum quantity provides the starting point for further explanation calculating proposed minimum quantities to support the two different purposes.

Define an Item's Minimum Quantity You define an item's minimum quantity for a specified site/warehouse on the Item Coverage form, typically with a requirement date reflecting today's date plus the item's lead time. The same form can also be accessed from the Item Coverage Setup form, which identifies items still requiring the setup information. The requirement associated with the item's minimum quantity is identified by pegging information as "Safety Stock" on the Net Requirements inquiry.

Calculate an Item's Minimum Quantity based on Historical Usage Standard AX functionality supports the calculation of a proposed minimum quantity based on an item's historical usage, either for min/max purposes or for inventory plan purposes to cover demand variability. An item's historical usage reflects all issue transactions during a specified time period, including sales order shipments, inventory adjustments and other issue transactions. The calculations also identify the impact of the proposed minimum quantity on inventory value, and the change in inventory value relative to the current minimum quantities. A printed report summarizes the impacts on inventory value for all items included in the calculations.

You perform these calculations using the Item Coverage Journal form and its related form for journal lines (termed the Item Coverage Journal Lines form). These are commonly referred to as the Safety Stock Journal, and the terms Safety Stock Journal and Item Coverage Journal can be used interchangeably. The business process for using the Safety Stock Journal to calculate the proposed minimum quantities is summarized in Figure 10.4 and described below.

Figure 10.4 Typical Process to Calculate Safety Stock Quantities

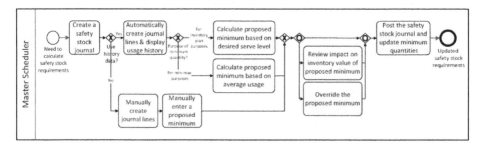

Overview   The master scheduler uses a safety stock journal to calculate proposed minimum quantities for selected items based on historical usage during selected periods.   For a given safety stock journal, the calculation of proposed minimums can reflect either (1) average usage for min/max purposes or (2) demand variability for inventory plan purposes, but not both.   The proposed minimums can be manually overridden if needed, and you can review the potential impact on inventory value of the proposed minimums.   Posting the journal automatically updates the associated minimum quantities.

Create a Safety Stock Journal   The master scheduler starts from the Safety Stock Journal form to create a new journal.   The journal identifier reflects a number sequence defined in the Master Planning Parameters form.   For each new journal, you should enter a meaningful journal name about its purpose.

Automatically Create Journal Lines and Display Usage History   The master scheduler starts from the journal lines form in order to access the dialogue for creating journal lines.   As part of the dialogue, you specify the relevant historical periods (expressed as from and to dates) and the selection criteria for items (such as the buyer group or coverage group).   You also indicate calculation of the standard deviations in order to support calculation of an inventory plan based on a desired customer service level.   This step results in the automatic creation of journal lines, where each line identifies an item and site/warehouse and several calculated quantities about usage history.   The calculated quantities include average issues per the item's lead time, average issues per month, and the monthly standard deviation.   It should be noted that you can only perform the automatic creation of journal lines when no lines exist.

Calculate Proposed Minimum based on Desired Service Level   The master scheduler starts from the journal lines form in order to access the dialogue for calculating proposed minimum quantities.   As part of the dialogue, you select the calculation option for Use Service Levels and the desired percentage (such as 95%), and indicate the proposed minimum should also be displayed in the new minimum field.   This step results in calculation of a proposed minimum for each journal line and also its potential impact on inventory value.

Calculate Proposed Minimum based on Average Usage   The master scheduler starts from the journal lines form in order to access the dialogue for calculating proposed minimum quantities.   As part of the dialogue, you select the calculation option for Use Average Issues During Lead Time, and optionally use a multiplying factor and/or lead time margin.   A multiplying factor (different than 1) can increase or decrease the proposed minimum.   The incremental lead time margin (greater than 0) will be combined with an item's lead time to calculate the proposed minimum.   You can also indicate the proposed minimum should be displayed in the new minimum field. This step results in calculation of a proposed minimum for each journal line and also its potential impact on inventory value.

Review Impact on Inventory Value of Proposed Minimum The master scheduler selects a journal line and views the potential impact on inventory value of the proposed minimum, and also the potential change in inventory value relative to the currently specified minimum. You can view the total potential impact of all journal lines by printing the report for the journal, or by copying the lines to a spreadsheet.

Override the Proposed Minimum The master scheduler selects a line and manually overrides the value for the new minimum quantity field.

Post the Safety Stock Journal and Update Minimum Quantities The master scheduler posts the journal in order to update the minimum quantity associated with each journal line.

Manually Create Journal Lines and Manually Enter Proposed Minimums The master scheduler can manually create journal lines. This approach prevents calculation of a proposed minimum so that it must be manually entered. However, you can still view the potential impact on inventory value of the proposed minimum, and also the potential change in inventory value relative to the currently specified minimum.

10.8 Stocked Components for Make-to-Order Products

Stocked components can support shorter delivery lead times for make-to-order products. The make-to-order product may have a standard BOM and routing, or it may represent a configured item with a BOM/routing defined by a configuration technology. Demand forecasts for these stocked components provide one approach to drive replenishment, but the approach requires the correct forecast consumption logic to avoid doubled-up requirements.

Demand Forecasts for a Stocked Component The entries of demand forecasts for a stocked component are just like demand forecasts for saleable items. The key difference involves forecast consumption logic, so that the demand forecasts will be consumed by any type of demands (also termed issue transactions) within a forecast period. In addition to sales order demand, the demand forecasts for components will be consumed by dependent demands stemming from planned or actual production orders for the make-to-order products. The demand forecasts can also be consumed by transfer requirements to a different warehouse stemming from planned or actual transfer orders. This approach avoids doubled-up requirements when using demand forecasts for stocked components.

To support this forecast consumption logic, the item representing the stocked component must have a "Reduce Forecast By" policy of "All Transactions" rather just "Sales Orders", as defined within the coverage group assigned to the item. This policy works in combination with the selected option for a reduction principle and the use of a reduction key. A previous section described the reduction principle options, and the definition and use of reduction keys (Section 10.4). Cases 10.3 and 10.6 illustrate the use of demand forecasts for stocked components, and Case 10.10 illustrates similar forecast consumption logic for stocked end-items at regional distribution centers.

S&OP Game Plans for Make-to-Order Products with Stocked Components

Demand forecasts for stocked components often represent one of several key elements in the business process to maintain S&OP game plans for a make-to-order product. In a common scenario, the combination of demand forecasts and actual demands for a stocked component drive the item's replenishment. In addition, the stocked components are considered by capable-to-promise logic when making delivery promises on sales orders.

The master scheduler determines which components should be stocked, and works with the sales manager to analyze the projected requirements. These projected requirements must be translated into entries for demand forecasts and safety stock. The master scheduling task generates planned orders for the stocked components, and the master scheduler can approve (or firm) these planned orders as part of the S&OP business process. After entering a sales order line for a make-to-order product, the associated production order can be generated as a planned order by the master scheduling task, or created from the sales order line in order to provide linkage between orders. Figure 10.5 illustrates a typical process to maintain the S&OP game plans for a make-to-order product with stocked components.

Figure 10.5 Typical Process to Maintain S&OP Game Plans
for a Make-to-Order Product with Stocked Components

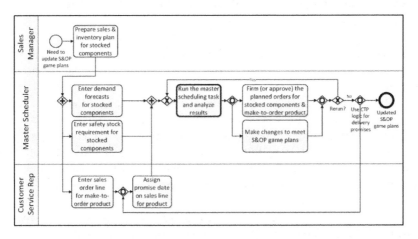

A manufacturing company wanted to forecast a group of stocked components that represented the key components for their make-to-order products. The concept of a planning BOM was implemented with an item allocation key, which identified the stocked components and a mix percentage of their typical usage. A demand forecast for an item group specified the item allocation key and a quantity reflecting expected sales for their make-to-order products. This demand forecast was entered in weekly increments over a 3-month rolling time horizon, and monthly increments thereafter.

10.9 Common S&OP Scenarios with Link to Sales Order

Some S&OP scenarios involve make-to-order or buy-to-order products that require linkage between a sales order and the item's supply order. An additional type of linkage applies to make-to-order components. These scenarios are summarized in Figure 10.6 and described below. For each scenario, the figure identifies the key elements of the S&OP game plan and several additional considerations. These considerations include creation of the supply order, the suggested coverage code, automatic marking, and the typical basis of sales order delivery promises.

Make-to-Order Product with Link between the Sales Order and Production Order A make-to-order production strategy often involves linking a production order to the sales order line, thereby providing visibility of the sales order demand in production. The reference fields for each order display this link. The basis for establishing this linkage builds on AX functionality for marking. The marking functionality simply provides visibility of the linkage for standard cost items. With actual cost items, marking supports additional functionality to override the suggested matching of a receipt (such as the production order) to an issue (such as the sales order).

Figure 10.6 Common S&OP Scenarios with Link to Sales Order

Scenario	Key Elements of S&OP Game Plan	Additional Considerations	Automatic Marking	Basis of Delivery Promises
Make-to-Order or Configure-to-Order Product	Sales Order for the product	Create production order from the sales order line	Yes	CTP or CTP via Net Change Explosion
		Firm the planned production order stemming from sales demand Coverage Code = Requirement	Marking Policy = Yes	
with Stocked Components	Demand Forecast or Min-Max Quantities for stocked components	Coverage Code = Period or Min-Max Calculation of minimum quantity	Marking Policy = No	
with Make-to-Order Components	Reference Orders for pegged supply components	Auto-create the production order Coverage Code = Period or Req	Yes	
Buy-to-Order Item Special Order or Direct Delivery Order	Sales Order & Purchase Order for the Item	Create PO from the SO or Create PO by linking to a SO	Yes	
		Create PO from the SO		

(Row group label on left: With Link to Sales Order)

Two basic approaches can be used to create this linkage. As shown in Figure 10.6, the first approach involves creating the production order from the sales order line, which results in automatic marking. The second approach involves firming the planned production order that stems from the sales order demand, which requires the "update marking" policy as part of the firming dialogue.

The linkage between orders can be considered a soft link, since changes to the sales order quantity or date do not automatically update the production order. When attempting to delete the sales line, a message displays a warning about the linked production order, and a separate step must be taken to delete the production order. Conversely, deleting the production order removes the linkage and does not impact the sales line. If applicable, a new production order can be created for the sales line.

Case 10.7: Configure-to-Order Conversion Vans

A manufacturer of conversion vans used a product configurator to identify the customer requirements, and generate a configuration id and associated BOM/route information. The popular variations of a configured van conversion were predefined, so that a sales order could simply specify the existing configuration id. The production order for a configured van was created from the sales order line. Automatic marking provided linkage between the orders, thereby providing visibility of the sales order demand to production.

Make-to-Order Product with Stocked Components The use of stocked components can shorten the delivery lead time for make-to-order products, as described in the previous section.

Make-to-Order Components with Linkage between Production Orders A make-to-order component may be employed in a make-to-order product, where the production order for the component is tightly linked to the parent item's production order. Within AX, you designate the make-to-order component with a line type of "pegged supply" in the BOM or formula for the parent item. The production order for the parent item automatically generates a linked order (termed a reference order) for each make-to-order component.[5] The linkage is identified by the reference fields for each production order, and also by marking information. This linkage is slightly different then the linkage between a sales order and production order, and reflects much tighter linkage between the production orders.

Case 10.8: Configure-to-Order Farm Trailers

A manufacturer of farm trailers used a product configurator to identify the customer requirements, and generate a configuration id and associated BOM/route information. Several key subassemblies were identified as pegged supply components, so that the production order for final assembly of the farm trailer automatically created the reference orders for the make-to-order components. Changes in the final assembly schedule automatically synchronized these reference orders. The master scheduler would approve the planned production orders for a configured farm trailer, and specify the date reflecting a slot in the final assembly schedule. Two weeks prior to final assembly, the

---

[5] The production order for a make-to-order component is automatically generated when the status of the parent item's production order has been changed from created to estimated, or to a higher status such as scheduled.

master scheduler would firm an approved planned order for a configured trailer (with update marking), which created an actual production order linked to the sales order. This production order also triggered creation of the reference orders.

Buy-to-Order Item Some S&OP scenarios involve selling purchased material as a direct delivery order, or as a special order which must be received and then shipped to the customer. Actual costing typically applies to this purchased material so that the cost of sales can be correctly calculated. Alternatively, the material can be valued with standard costs.

For a given sales order, you can selectively designate which lines should be treated as a special order or direct order, and then automatically create the corresponding purchase order. The linkage is displayed in the reference fields for each order line, and also in the marking and reservation information.

Alternatively, you can start from the Purchase Order form and create a new purchase order by selecting the line items from existing sales orders. As the first step, you use selection criteria to view these existing sales orders, and then select the line items to be included on the purchase order. This alternative approach only works for special orders; it does not work for direct delivery orders.

The linkage between orders has several impacts. Changes to the sales order quantity or date do not automatically update the purchase order. However, master scheduling logic will suggest responses to any changes, such as planned orders, action messages and/or messages about calculated delays. When attempting to delete the sales line, a message displays a warning about the linked purchase order and its status. The sales line can only be deleted prior to purchase order receipt, and a separate step must be taken to delete the purchase order. Conversely, deleting the purchase order removes the linkage and does not impact the sales line. If applicable, a new purchase order can be created for the sales line.

Case 10.9: Direct Delivery of Novelty Items

A distributor of novelty items typically sold and purchased the items for direct delivery to the customer. After identifying the desired items on a sales order, the customer service rep generated the direct delivery purchase orders from the sales order. Automatic marking resulted in linkage between a sales order line and the purchase order line.

Suggestions about Marking The marking functionality within AX provides the basis for establishing linkage between orders. The reference fields in each order display the linked order when one-to-one correspondence exists. You can also view the linkage by accessing the Marking form from each order. Marking also results in reservations. Marking has no impact on the costing for standard cost items; it simply provides visibility of linked orders.

Marking provides additional functionality for items with actual costing, such as LIFO, FIFO and weighted average. In summary, marking happens automatically based on the rules for the item's actual costing method, so that the cost from a receipt is matched to an issue transaction. The Marking form displays this matching and supports manual overrides, although manual overrides are seldom used in practice. Detailed explanations of marking and actual costing methods are provided in the AX user documentation.

Automatic marking applies to most of the S&OP scenarios described here, as indicated in Figure 10.6. For example, automatic marking occurs for a production order created from a sales line, for reference orders stemming from a parent item's production order, and for buy-to-order items.

An additional approach to marking can only be used when firming a planned order, such as firming a planned production order stemming from a sales order demand. It also applies to firming planned purchase orders and planned transfer orders. This approach employs the Update Marking policy. The Update Marking policy has two basic options of "no" and "yes", although the "yes" option has two variations of "standard" and "extended" which do not impact standard cost items.

10.10 Sales Order Promise Dates and the Delivery Date Control Policy

Realistic promise dates for sales order shipments and deliveries can help improve customer satisfaction and supply chain coordination. The initial assignment of the promise dates should align with the item's S&OP game plan, and a sales line with an unrealistic promise date should be highlighted as an exception requiring follow up. After initial assignment, the dates should be changed to reflect changes in the situation, such as changing dates to reflect customer requests or projected delays. Sales orders with unrealistic or past due dates will negatively impact the usefulness of an item's S&OP game plan and the coordination of supply chain activities. The section focuses on promise dates for sales orders in traditional manufacturing scenarios.[6] A similar-yet-different set of policies apply to promise dates for transfer orders, as described in a subsequent chapter about transfer orders (Section 13.2).

The initial assignment of promise dates can be supported using several different approaches that reflect a delivery date control policy. The three major options for a delivery date control policy are labeled *ATP, CTP* and *Sales Lead Time*, and the relevant option depends on the scenario and S&OP approach. All three options enforce basic rules to help ensure realistic promise dates. A fourth option (labeled *None*) will disable enforcement of the basic rules, thereby allowing assignment of unrealistic dates. This fourth option is also referred to as disabling delivery date control.

This section starts with a brief background about the sales order dates for shipment and delivery, and the basic rules for delivery date control, and then summarizes the options for the delivery date control policy.

Sales Order Dates for Shipment and Delivery A sales order header has a requested ship date and a requested delivery date, where the difference represents the transportation time between the ship-from warehouse and the delivery address. It also has a confirmed ship date and confirmed receipt date. A similar set of these four dates applies to each sales order line, and (if applicable) the delivery schedule lines for a sales order line.

The dates on a sales order header can be initially inherited by the sales lines, and changes in the header dates can optionally change the dates on sales lines. You typically employ a prompt to confirm that the change in header dates should change the sales lines. As part of the prompt, you can indicate whether the delivery date control policies on the line items should be disabled, therefore resulting in assignment of the specified header dates to all lines. Alternatively, as part of the prompt, you can indicate that the delivery date control policies should be recognized so that each line item will be rescheduled accordingly. The use of a prompt (after changing header dates) represents a companywide policy, where other values for this policy include automatic changes to line item dates (without a prompt) and preventing the changes.[7]

---

[6] In lean manufacturing scenarios, a slightly different approach for delivery promises (based on CTP logic) applies to sales orders for make-to-order products and the generation of sales event manufacturing kanbans.
[7] The Accounts Receivable Parameters form is used to define companywide policies about updating order lines when making changes to header information, such as changes to the order dates.

Several basic rules can be enforced for the shipment and delivery dates on a sales order header and for each line item, but only when you assign one of major options for delivery date control. The option for a sales order header is inherited from a companywide value, which typically reflects a value of "Sales Lead Time" to enforce basic rules.[8] The option for each sales line is inherited from an item-specific value, where the option should reflect the S&OP approach for the item.[9]

Basic Rules for Delivery Date Control The sales order dates for shipment and delivery should reflect the following basic rules in order to be realistic. These rules apply to the automatic assignment of dates when initially entering a sales order header or line item, and also when manually entering a different date.

◆ *Calendar for the ship-from warehouse.* The calendar assigned to the ship-from warehouse determines the working days when items can be shipped.

◆ *Calendar for the customer receiving point.* The calendar assigned to the customer (or the applicable customer address) determines the working days when items can be received.

◆ *Transportation time to customer.* The number of days for transportation time can be specified for the different combinations of the ship-from warehouse, the delivery address characteristics (such as the country, state, county or ZIP code), and the mode of delivery (such as air or truck).

◆ *Calendar for mode of delivery.* A calendar can be assigned to various modes of delivery for the ship-from warehouse, where the calendar determines the working days when items can be transported. For example, a truck route may only occur on Thursdays.

◆ *Order entry deadlines for taking sales orders.* The concept of an order entry deadline means that orders received after a specified time are treated as if they were received the next day. You define a set of deadlines for each day within a week (termed an order entry deadline group), and then assign the deadline group to each customer and site.

◆ *Sales lead time.* A sales lead time can represent the number of days to prepare a stocked item for shipment (such as a value of 0 or 1 day), or it can represent the quoted lead time for a make-to-order product. It will be

---

[8] You define the companywide option for delivery date control (inherited by the header for a sales order or transfer order) as part of the Accounts Receivable Parameters.

[9] You define the item-specific option for delivery date control (inherited by a sales line) as part of the Default Order Settings or Site-Specific Order Settings for a saleable item.

automatically reflected in the shipment date when using any of the three major options; it is not just for the Sales Lead Time option. The number of days for sales lead time is specified as a companywide value, and it can be defined as item-specific overrides.

As an alternative approach, the number of days for sales lead time can be defined within sales trade agreements, so that an applicable sales line (for the customer and item) inherits the sales lead time as well as the sales price or discount. However, this approach only applies when the trade agreement entry indicates that sales lead time should be considered. A subsequent chapter provides further explanation of sales trade agreements (Section 11.6).

Delivery Date Control Options for a Sales Order Line A delivery date control option applies to a sales order header and to each sales line. At the header level, you typically employ the sales lead time option in order to enforce the basic rules such as considerations of calendars and transportation time. The four options for a delivery date control policy are summarized in Figure 10.7, along with comments about the implications of each option for a sales order line. The bottom row of Figure 10.7 displays an additional approach for the sales lead time option, where you initiate a net change explosion to calculate a shipment date.

Figure 10.7 Delivery Date Control Options for a Sales Order Line

Delivery Date Control Option	Scenario	Comments
Sales Lead Time	Use Basic Rules *or* Quoted Lead Time	Auto-assign requested dates based on basic rules Enforce basic rules for manually entered dates* Analyze supplies using ATP form or Supply Overview form
ATP	Stocked End-Item	Auto-assign requested dates based on basic rules + ATP logic Enforce basic rules + ATP logic for manually entered dates* Analyze supplies using ATP form or Supply Overview form
CTP	MTO/CTO End-Item	Auto-assign requested dates based on basic rules + CTP logic Automatically perform net change explosion Enforce basic rules + CTP logic for manually entered dates*
None	Allow assignment of unrealistic dates	Ignore basic rules for manually entered dates
Sales Lead Time and initiate a Net Change Explosion to determine the promised ship date	MTO/CTO/ETO End-Item	Enforce basic rules for manually entered dates Requires a user-initiated net change explosion, and you can transfer the calculated futures date to the confirmed ship date

* = Display exceptions on *Available Ship and Receipt Dates* form, and transfer a selected set of dates to change confirmed dates (or requested dates)

Using Sales Lead Time as the Delivery Date Control Option This option provides automatic assignment of the requested ship and delivery dates, where the dates reflect the basic rules. It also enforces the basic rules when manually entering dates, and automatically displays exceptions in a separate form labeled Available Ship and Receipt Dates. You can also access this form directly from the delivery tab on the sales line details, and clicking Simulate Delivery Dates. The form displays available dates, and you can optionally transfer a selected set of dates to change either the requested dates or the confirmed dates. You can also analyze available supplies for the item using the ATP form or Supply Overview form.

The "sales lead time" option provides the simplest approach to delivery promises while enforcing the basic rules. The value is typically zero for most scenarios. Specifying a value greater than zero depends on whether it represents a shipment preparation time (for a stocked item) or a quoted lead time (for a make-to-order item).

Using ATP as the Delivery Date Control Option This option typically applies to stocked items, where ATP logic just focuses on the salable item. It provides automatic assignment of the requested ship and delivery dates, where the dates reflect the basic rules and ATP logic. Just like the previous option, it enforces these rules when manually entering a date, and you can view the Available Ship and Receipt Dates form. This form displays available dates, and you can optionally transfer a selected set of dates to change either the requested dates or the confirmed dates. You can also analyze available supplies for the item using the ATP form or Supply Overview form. The ATP form provides an additional capability to specify a different ship-from site and calculate the item's availability.

The ATP option requires several additional policies about underlying assumptions in order to correctly calculate an available-to-promise date, as summarized below.

◆ *ATP time horizon.* The ATP time horizon (expressed in calendar days) often reflects the item's cumulative manufacturing lead time, or a quoted lead time, so that a promise date corresponding to the end of the horizon will be automatically assigned when there is insufficient supply to satisfy the required quantity. In addition, this time horizon constrains the display of ATP information on the associated inquiry for a sales line (termed the ATP form).

◆ *Included planned orders.* An item's planned orders and approved planned orders should be included in ATP logic when you actually follow through on the planned orders.

♦ *Assumptions about the dates for past due orders.* ATP logic requires realistic and up-to-date dates on existing sales orders and supply orders so that promise dates can be correctly calculated. However, some scenarios have orders with past due dates so that you must define several assumptions about how ATP logic should handle these orders. For example, the assumptions (expressed in calendar days) should be defined for considering sales orders with past due dates (termed the backward demand time fence) and supply orders with past due dates (termed the backward supply time fence). The typical values for these time fences depend on the extent to which you update the dates for past due orders. Assumptions also need to made about when the past due orders will actually occur. A value of 0 days indicates that the orders will occur today, or you can specify a different value for these offset days (termed the offset time for delayed demand and the offset time for delayed supply).

♦ *ATP Logic includes the Issue Margin.* An additional option for delivery date control is termed "ATP plus issue margin". An issue margin (expressed in days) should only be used when shipments require significant preparation time, such as 1 or more days. You can define the issue margin as part of the master plan policies for the current master plan, or it can reflect an item-specific value (as defined within the coverage group assigned to an item).

Using CTP as the Delivery Date Control Option This option typically applies to a make-to-order or configure-to-order item. It considers available inventory and receipts for the salable item (if applicable), and automatically results in a net change explosion when needed. It provides automatic assignment of the requested ship and delivery dates, where the dates reflect the basic rules and CTP logic. Just like the previous options, it enforces these rules when manually entering a date, and automatically displays exceptions in a separate dialogue (termed the Available Ship and Receipt Dates form). The dialogue displays available dates, and you can optionally transfer a selected set of dates to change either the requested dates or the confirmed dates. It is not as helpful to analyze available supplies using the ATP form or Supply Overview form, since this information only applies to the salable item.

A special case of CTP logic involves the treatment of existing inventory for the salable item and its components. The availability of this inventory is normally consumed on a first-come-first-served basis. That is, CTP logic will consider existing inventory when entering the first sales order regardless of the delivery date, which can lead to situations where the CTP logic for subsequently-entered sales orders (with an earlier delivery date) will not consider the existing inventory. To correct this issue, the CTP logic should first consider an item's supply orders (within the positive days interval) that meet the required date before considering on-hand inventory. This special case involves the "consume on-hand" policy embedded within the coverage group assigned to a salable item, so that on-hand inventory will be consumed after all other supply orders have been considered.

Implications of No Delivery Date Control Assigning an option of *none* will disable the rules for delivery date control, thereby allowing assignment of unrealistic dates. As a general guideline, any sales line with this option should be highlighted as an exception or alert requiring follow up.

Using a Net Change Explosion to Calculate a Ship Date This approach typically applies to make-to-order products, and only works when the item's coverage code is other than Manual. It typically employs the Sales Lead Time option to enforce basic rules about delivery dates, but it also works for the other options. After entering the sales line, you initiate a net change explosion in order to calculate a projected date, and you can optionally transfer the calculated date to the confirmed ship date.

Continuous Checking of Sales Order Promise Dates The concept of continuously checking the sales order promise dates is embedded in the messages about a calculated delay generated by the master scheduling task. That is, the message indicates when a sales order ship date cannot be met, and identifies the projected ship date.

10.11 Typical Process to Run the Master Scheduling Task and Analyze Results

The master scheduling task represents the primary engine for coordinating supply chain activities. It generates several key outputs that support detailed analysis of the calculations and act as coordination tools. The typical process to run the master scheduling task and analyze results consists of several steps performed by different roles, as summarized in Figure 10.8 and explained below. The explanation includes the role of a coordinator for transfer orders although it is not shown in the figure.

Figure 10.8 Run the Master Scheduling task
and Analyze Results

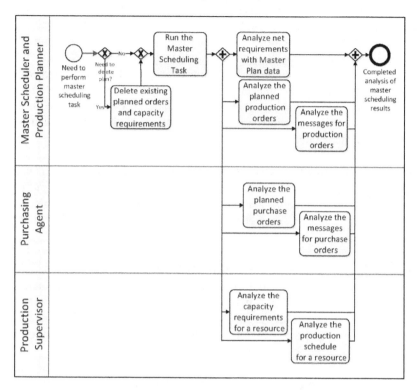

Overview The master scheduler ensures that the master scheduling task is performed on a regular basis. The master scheduler and production planners analyze the results for manufactured items within their responsibility, such as planned orders, messages and net requirements. The purchasing agent similarly analyzes the results for purchased items, and a DRP coordinator similarly analyzes the results for transfers. The production supervisor analyzes resource requirements and the production schedules for resources. These analyses help identify potential material or capacity constraints that require changes to meet the S&OP game plans.

Delete the Existing Planned Orders and Capacity Requirements The master scheduler determines whether to delete an existing plan, which results in the deletion of existing planned orders and capacity requirements. This step provides a clean starting point for the master scheduling task, and it is normally performed automatically by running the master scheduling task for all items.

Run the Master Scheduling Task The master scheduler ensures that the Master Scheduling task is performed on a periodic basis, which represents the primary engine for coordinating supply chain activities. The task generates a set of master plan data based on several master plan policies, such as the identifier for the set of master plan data, the applicable forecast identifier, and several factors affecting the calculations. The resulting set of master plan data provides the basis for further analysis such as analyzing an item's requirements or a resource's capacity requirements. For simulation purposes, the master scheduler can employ multiple sets of master plan data and associated master plan policies, and then select the desired set when viewing material or capacity requirements. A subsequent section provides further explanation of the master plan policies used by the Master Scheduling task (Section 10.12).

Analyze requirements with a set of Master Plan data The master scheduler and other SCM decision makers select the desired set of master plan data when analyzing material and capacity requirements. For example, you can analyze an item's net requirements or gross requirements for a selected set of master plan data.

Analyze the planned production orders The master scheduler and production planners analyze planned production orders to help coordinate supply chain activities for those items within their responsibility. The planned orders are typically firmed to execute the S&OP game plans. A subsequent chapter provides further explanation about coordinating production via planned orders (Section 14.13).

Analyze the messages for production orders The master scheduler and production planners analyze messages about production orders to help coordinate supply chain activities for those items within their responsibility. They employ message filters to eliminate unnecessary messages. A subsequent chapter provides further explanation about coordinating production via messages (Section 14.13).

Analyze the planned purchase orders The purchasing agent analyzes planned purchase orders for those items and vendors within their responsibility, and typically firms the planned orders to execute the S&OP game plans. A subsequent chapter provides further explanation about coordinating procurement via planned orders (Section 12.12).

Analyze the messages for purchase orders The purchasing agent analyzes messages about purchase orders to help coordinate supply chain activities for those items within their responsibility. The purchasing agent employs message filters to eliminate unnecessary messages. A subsequent chapter provides further explanation about coordinating procurement via messages (Section 12.12).

Analyze the planned transfer orders The purchasing agent or other SCM decision maker analyzes planned transfer orders for those items and warehouses within their responsibility, and typically firms the planned orders to execute the S&OP game plans. A subsequent chapter provides further explanation about coordinating transfers via planned transfer orders (Section 13.3).

Analyze the messages for transfer orders The purchasing agent or other SCM decision maker analyzes messages about transfer orders to help coordinate supply chain activities for those items and warehouses within their responsibility. The purchasing agent employs message filters to eliminate unnecessary messages. A subsequent chapter provides further explanation about coordinating transfer orders via messages (Section 13.3).

Analyze the capacity requirements for a resource The production supervisor analyzes the capacity requirements for those resources within their responsibility. The requirements reflect routing data for manufactured items. The analysis typically anticipates overloaded periods for bottleneck resources so that adjustments can be made to capacity or to the load stemming from relevant production orders. The aggregate capacity requirements can also be viewed for a resource group consisting of multiple resources. A subsequent chapter provides further explanation about analyzing capacity requirements for a resource (Section 14.14).

Analyze the production schedule for a resource The production supervisor analyzes the suggested production schedule for those resources within their responsibility. The suggested schedule can be viewed in different formats, such as tabular or Gantt chart. The production supervisor typically coordinates actual production to meet operation due dates and execute the S&OP game plans. A subsequent chapter provides further explanation about coordinating production via production schedules (Section 14.14).

10.12 Overview of the Master Scheduling Task and Master Plan Data

The master scheduling task uses information about demands and supplies, and several master plan policies, to generate a set of master plan data. Each set of master plan data has a user-defined identifier. One set of master plan data typically acts as the primary source for coordinating supply chain activities, and it is commonly labeled *MasterPlan* or *CurrentPlan*. Other sets of master plan data can also be used.

Key Policies for a Set of Master Plan Data Each set of master plan data involves multiple policies that will be used by master scheduling calculations. We'll focus on several key policies for explanatory purposes. The following topics summarize the key policies and indicate the relevant sections containing further explanation.

◆ *Include on-hand inventory and inventory transactions.* The broader AX viewpoint applies to the term "inventory transactions", since they reflect unposted inventory journals as well as supply orders prior to actual receipt.

◆ *Include demand forecasts.* Related policies identify the set of demand forecast data and the basis for forecast consumption logic. Supply forecasts do not apply to most scenarios.

◆ *Basis for scheduling planned production orders.* These considerations include the specified scheduling method and the optional use of finite scheduling

◆ *Selective use of global values for time fences.* You can selectively indicate whether a global value will be used for a given time fence; otherwise the item-specific value will be used for the time fence. Time fences were described in the previous chapter (Section 9.15).

Some of the other policies reflect special cases that do not apply to most scenarios, such as treating the pipeline of sales quotations as a demand (Section 11.12), treating requests for quotes as a supply (Section 12.7), and treating purchase requisitions as a supply. Other polices that rarely apply include the use of calculated delayed dates as the requirement date for planned orders; they assume you have perfectly modeled your supply chain. Production sequencing does not apply to production orders; it only applies to planned batch orders.

Several policies that impact master scheduling calculations are defined as part of the Master Planning Parameters form, as summarized below.

◆ *Basis for the Rescheduling Assumption.* The policy for *Use dynamic negative days* indicates one aspect of the rescheduling assumption about existing supply orders (Section 9.12).

◆ *Calendar for today's date.*

◆ *Receipt time for planned orders.* As a general guideline, this receipt time reflects the middle of the working day such as 10 am.

◆ *Include planned production orders in capacity planning.* The planned production orders should be considered when they reflect the SCM decision making of the production planners. A project-oriented operation may also have capacity requirements for production resources, so that the project-related requirements should also be included in capacity planning.

◆ *Include purchase requisitions as a supply.* This special case only applies when actual purchase orders will be created for all purchase requisitions for trade goods. A related policy involves the time fence for considering approved requisitions as a supply.

◆ *Scheduling start time for production orders.* The scheduling of individual production orders typically reflects the current time, but some scenarios will use the beginning of the calendar work day.

Information within the Master Planning Parameters form also indicates whether you are using a single set of master plan data or two sets of master plan data, as described in the next two subsections.

Master Scheduling with a Single Set of Master Plan Data

Many scenarios can operate with a single set of master plan data, which simplifies its use and understanding. However, those scenarios requiring CTP logic (or net change explosions) for sales order promise dates typically require two sets of master plan data.

Master Scheduling with Two Sets of Master Plan Data

Some scenarios use CTP logic or net change explosions for calculating sales order delivery promises, which generate planned orders when there are insufficient supplies for the end-item or its components. The planned orders immediately communicate the need for replenishment to meet the promised delivery date.

This situation creates difficulties for buyers and planners in determining appropriate actions for planned orders. It becomes even more difficult when using this approach for multiple checks of delivery promise information, or when deleting the sales order because the customer is only asking about delivery promises or finds them unacceptable. The situation results in constant changes to planned orders.

One approach to handling this problem involves two sets of data termed the *static master plan* and *dynamic master plan*. The static master plan contains the results of the previous master scheduling task that generated suggestions about planned orders. The dynamic master plan starts with the same set of data, typically via automatic copy (as defined in the Master Planning Parameters form), but the data is continuously updated by new sales order commitments. This approach insulates buyers and planners from planned orders stemming from delivery promise simulations. However, they can still view the planned orders within the set of data for the dynamic master plan.

Some Options for Running the Master Scheduling Task The Master Scheduling task can be run with a Regeneration or Net Change approach for a selected set of master plan data, either for all items or selected items.

◆ *Regeneration Approach.* The Regeneration approach for all items will automatically delete planned orders (and related planned capacity requirements) within the selected set of master plan data, and then generate new planned orders. When using two sets of master plan data, you run the master scheduling task for a selected master plan that represents the static plan, and the resulting set of master plan data will be automatically copied to the master plan that represents the dynamic plan.

In contrast, the Regeneration approach for selected items will not automatically delete planned orders; they must be deleted beforehand by running the Delete Plan task. In addition, it will not automatically copy the set of master plan data.

◆ *Net Change Approach.* The Net Change approach only applies when running the Master Scheduling task for just the dynamics master plan (which must be identified as such in Master Planning Parameters form). It will generate planned orders that cover only those requirements that were created or changed since the last master scheduling run, and the action dates and delayed dates will be updated for all requirements. A slight variation to this approach – termed the Net Change Minimized approach – means that action dates and delayed dates will only be updated for new or changed requirements.

Master Scheduling Logic within Net Change Explosions A net change explosion reflects the same calculations as the master scheduling task, such as netting logic and the generation of planned orders. It is typically employed when calculating a promised ship date for a sales order line for a make-to-order product. After entering the sales line, you initiate a net change explosion (or explosion for short) in order to calculate a projected date, and you can optionally transfer the calculated date to the confirmed ship date. The net change explosion for an item can also be accessed from other forms, including the Actions and Requirement Profile form. When using two sets of master plan data, the net change explosion only updates the set of master plan data identified as the dynamic plan.

As an additional capability, the net change explosion can provide an explanation of master scheduling logic. You specify the calculation of this "trace" information as part of the dialogue for performing the net change explosion, and then view the results on the "Explanation" tab. The explanation applies to the multi-level product structure for the item. It provides a detailed breakdown of the coverage planning calculations, and the generation of action messages and messages about delayed dates.

10.13 Master Scheduling with Finite versus Infinite Capacity

Considerations about finite versus infinite capacity can be specified as part of the master plan policies so they are reflected in master scheduling logic. They can also be specified when scheduling individual production orders. However, the scheduling logic with finite capacity only applies to designated resources, where finite capacity applies to the resource. The use of master scheduling with finite capacity requires an understanding of available capacity for a resource, the meaning of finite capacity, and the meaning of a bottleneck resource.

Available Capacity for a Resource A resource's available capacity is defined by two basic factors: the calendar defining the hours of operation and the capacity per hour (to handle one or more operations concurrently). A third factor -- termed the *operations scheduling percentage* for a resource -- affects how scheduling logic views the resource's available capacity. A scheduling percentage of 80%, for example, means that the master scheduling logic will only consider 80% of the available capacity when assigning loads to the resource.

Infinite Versus Finite Available Capacity for a Resource A resource's available capacity can be designated as finite or infinite for scheduling purposes. An infinite capacity viewpoint means that scheduling logic ignores existing loads when scheduling a given order, but still considers constraints related to hours of operation and concurrent task capabilities to calculate operation durations. An analysis of resource load versus capacity can be used to identify overloaded periods, so that adjustments can be made to loads or available capacity.

A finite capacity viewpoint means that scheduling logic considers current loads (and the concurrent task capability) for each resource when scheduling a given order.

Designating Bottleneck Resources for Finite Capacity Planning Purposes The optional designation of a bottleneck resource can improve performance of master scheduling calculations. Additional master plan policies must be defined for the use of bottleneck scheduling and for three time fence policies related to bottleneck scheduling (the finite capacity time fence, the backward capacity time fence, and the bottleneck capacity time fence).

10.14 Forecast Scheduling and Forecast Plan Data

The forecast scheduling task calculates demands and supplies within set of forecast plan data based on several policies such as a time horizon and the relevant forecast identifier. Each set of forecast plan data has a user-defined identifier. Multiple sets of forecast plan data can be calculated based on different forecast identifiers, typically to reflect various scenarios for simulation purposes.

A set of forecast plan data represents gross requirements to support planning of materials and capacity, whereas a set of master plan data represents net requirements to support day-to-day supply chain coordination.

10.15 Simulations for S&OP Purposes

A basic simulation approach involves a different set of forecast data with a different forecast identifier. For example, you may define best-case and worst-case scenarios about expected demand with two different forecast identifiers and associated demand forecasts. This forecast identifier is specified as one of the policies for a forecast plan, so that the forecast schedule task can generate a set of forecast plan data. You select the forecast plan data when viewing displayed data about material and resource requirements.

A designated forecast identifier is also a key policy for a master plan, and you typically define a separate master plan for simulation purposes. For example, you may choose to ignore demand forecasts (as a master plan policy) so that the master plan data only reflects demands stemming from actual sales orders. Examples of other master plan policies that support simulations include the following.

◆ Time fences for forecasts, coverage and explosion. The time fences may reflect a long-term time horizon for long range planning.

◆ Capacity Time Fence. The time fence may reflect a long-term horizon for capacity planning purposes. Alternatively, with a capacity time fence of zero, the fixed lead times for manufactured items will be used by master scheduling logic.

◆ Infinite versus finite capacity viewpoint. A master plan with infinite capacity planning can be used to identify overloaded periods, so that available capacity could be adjusted via the calendars assigned to resources.

10.16 Guidelines concerning S&OP Game Plans

Effective game plans lead to improved firm performance and bottom line results. Metrics include reductions in stock-outs, delivery lead time, missed shipments, partial shipments, and expediting efforts. Metrics also include improvements in customer service. The lack of effective game plans is typically cited as a leading cause of poor ERP system implementations. The following guidelines provide suggestions for improving the effectiveness of S&OP game plans.

Minimum Planning Horizon for Each Game Plan A saleable item's cumulative lead time represents the minimum horizon for a game plan, and additional months provide visibility for purchasing and capacity planning purposes. This minimum planning horizon should be reflected in the item's time fences, such as the coverage and forecast time fences.

Reviewing and Updating Game Plans The process for reviewing and updating each game plan should be embedded into the firm's regularly scheduled management meetings focusing on demands and supply chain activities. An agreed-upon game plan reflects a balance of conflicting objectives related to sales, engineering, manufacturing, inventory, purchasing and accounting. Periodic revisions to game plans should be reflected in updated forecasts and promised delivery dates.

Primary Responsibility for Maintaining Game Plans The person(s) acting as a master scheduler typically maintains the game plans and obtains management agreement. This role requires an in-depth understanding of sales and supply chain capabilities, as well as the political power to achieve agreed-upon game plans. The responsibility for providing information about demand forecasts and inventory plans typically belongs to the sales function, with a hand-off to the master scheduler. However, this responsibility is sometimes assigned to the master scheduler. The master scheduler's responsibility for an item's game plans is often identified by the buyer group assigned to the item. .

Formulating Realistic Game Plans Realistic game plans require identification of capacity and material exceptions that would constrain the plans, and then eliminating the constraints or changing the plan. Identification of material-related exceptions typically starts with suggested actions, while capacity exceptions are identified using work center load analysis. In many cases, a realistic game plan must anticipate demands and demand variations via forecasts and inventory plans for stocked material. Finite scheduling can also contribute to a realistic game plan.

Enforcing Near-Term Schedule Stability   Near-term schedule stability provides one solution for resolving many conflicting objectives, such as improving competitive efficiencies in purchasing and production and reducing exceptions requiring expediting. It provides a stable target for coordinating supply chain activities and removes most alibis for missed schedules. Near-term schedule stability can benefit from inventory plans and realistic order promises about shipment dates. It involves a basic trade-off with objectives requiring fast response time and frequent schedule changes.   The critical issue is that management recognizes the trade-offs to minimize near-term changes. An item's freeze time fence represents one approach to support near-term schedule stability, since master scheduling logic will not suggest planned orders during the frozen period.

Making and Maintaining Realistic Sales Order Promises   Realistic delivery promises represent the key link between sales commitments and supply chain activities. You can calculate a realistic promised delivery date during order entry, and also through master scheduling logic and messages that indicate a projected delay in delivery. A key aspect of promised delivery dates is to reduce and isolate the number of exceptions requiring expediting.   When available inventory only partially satisfies the sales order requirement, one solution approach involves splitting delivery across two sales order line items with different shipment dates.

Executing Supply Chain Activities to Plan   Master scheduling logic makes an underlying assumption that everyone works to plan, and provides coordination tools to communicate needed action.   For example, it is assumed that procurement will ensure timely delivery of purchased material so that manufacturing can meet production schedules. It is assumed that distribution will make on-time shipments, and that valid delivery promises were made by sales.   An unmanageable number of exceptions will impact this underlying assumption and the usefulness of coordination tools.

Reducing Exceptions that Require Expediting   The intent of near-term schedule stability, valid delivery promises and shipment dates, realistic game plans, and executing to plan is to reduce the number of exceptions to a manageable level. This improves the usefulness of coordination tools to meet the S&OP game plans.

10.17 Typical Process to Maintain S&OP Game Plans for a Stocked Product in a Distribution Operation

The S&OP game plans for a stocked product in a distribution operation share many similarities to those for a make-to-stock product, such as the use of demand forecasts and safety stock requirement to drive replenishment. However, there are several key differences. First, the primary responsibility for maintaining the S&OP game plans involves a different role (such as a DRP coordinator or inventory manager). Second, the primary focus involves purchase orders and transfer orders rather than production orders. And third, the operation may involve a distribution network with considerations about stocking levels at different locations.

A typical business process to maintain the S&OP game plans for a stocked product in a distribution operation is illustrated in Figure 10.9. It shares many similarities to the typical process for make-to-stock products described in a previous section (Section 10.2) , so that further explanation focuses on the key differences. The figure indicates the common steps with grey shading.

Firm (or approve) the planned transfer orders for the item The use of transfer orders -- both planned and actual - applies to a distribution network. Planned orders can be approved or firmed by a DRP coordinator (or an equivalent role), and the suggested quantities and/or dates may be adjusted.

Firm (or approve) the planned purchase orders for the item A purchasing agent typically firms the planned purchase orders that reflect the S&OP game plans and the model of SCM decision making logic. The suggested quantities and/or dates may be adjusted on planned orders prior to firming.

Make changes to meet the S&OP game plans The DRP coordinator and purchasing agent may need to coordinate several types of changes to meet the S&OP game plans. For example, the changes often involve expediting of existing purchase orders or transfer orders. The changes may also involve working with customer service representatives to delay the promised delivery date on sales orders.

Figure 10.9 Typical Process to Maintain S&OP Game Plans
for a Stocked Product in a Distribution Operation

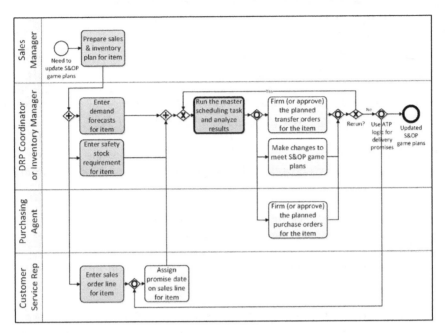

Assign promise date on sales line for the item   When the customer
service rep creates a sales order line for the item, the earliest possible dates for
shipment and delivery can be automatically assigned based on available-to-
promise (ATP) logic.   In scenarios where the item is stocked at multiple
locations, the customer service rep may evaluate the delivery alternatives for
different ship-from locations, and then update the sales line based on the selected
option.

10.18 Workspaces related to Master Planning

The Master Planning workspace summarizes several aspects of information about
a selected set of master plan data, including planned orders, action messages, and
messages about calculated delays.

◆   *Planned Orders.*   You can view existing planned orders, analyze an item's
requirements profile or supply schedule, and firm (or approve) a planned
order. You can also edit a planned order or manually create a planned order.

◆   *Action Messages.*   You can view action messages and the action graph, and
apply the suggested action.

◆ *Messages about Calculated Delays.* Separate sections enable you to identify calculated delays related to sales order lines, and also to the requirement dates for demand forecasts and safety stock.

You can run the master scheduling task from the workspace. The links provide access to information about the master plan(s) and coverage groups, and the master planning parameters. The links also display statistics about item requirements and capacity requirements.

The links about production sequencing only apply to planned batch orders (when using the Formula approach to product structure), and the links about intercompany supply and demand only apply to a multicompany supply chain.

10.19 Additional Case Studies

Case 10.10: Stocked End-Items in a Distribution Network   A manufacturing company had a distribution network consisting of a manufacturing plant, regional distribution centers and selling locations.   An end-item's inventory was stocked at a distribution center, and then transferred to a selling location to meet actual sales order demand. In this scenario, they entered the item's demand forecasts for each distribution center, and the transfer order requirements consumed the demand forecasts. This required the correct forecast consumption logic. That is, the coverage group assigned to the item and the warehouse representing a distribution center had a "Reduce Forecast By" policy of "All Transactions" rather just "Sales Orders".

Case 10.11: S&OP Simulations   A manufacturer employed simulations to assess the impact of changing demands and supplies. Using multiple sets of forecast data to represent various scenarios, and a designated set of forecast data for planning calculation purposes, the management team could analyze the impact of changing demands on material and capacity requirements.   For example, the master scheduling task was first performed using infinite capacity planning to anticipate overloaded periods. After adjusting available capacity and consideration of alternate routings, the master scheduling task was performed again using finite capacity to highlight unrealistic delivery dates.

Case 10.12:   S&OP based on Sales Quote Pipeline A fabricated products company designed, quoted and built hundreds of one-time products to customer specifications. They used configurable items to model one-level and two-level custom products, and to define the unique BOM and routing for each configuration.   This detailed information provided the basis for calculating estimated costs and a suggested sales price for sales quotations. The sales quotation backlog was used as part of the S&OP game plans to anticipate material and capacity requirements.

Case 10.13: Improve Near-Term Stability in the Master Schedule A manufacturing company wanted to enforce near-term stability in the master schedule, thereby gaining production efficiencies and reducing exceptions requiring expediting. They tracked the requested changes to this near-term schedule, and the reasons for each request, and the master scheduler (plus a team of other key people) formally approved or rejected each requested change. An analysis of the requested changes and their reasons provided the basis for improving the near-term stability and the associated benefits.

10.20 Executive Summary

The ability to run the company from the top requires a sales and operations planning process that formulates an S&OP game plan for each saleable product. The nature of an S&OP game plan depends on several factors, such as the need to anticipate demand for the item, the item's primary source of supply, and the need for linkage between a sales order and the supply order. It also depends on the production strategy for manufactured items

The starting point for each game plan typically involves identifying all sources of demand such as sales orders and forecasts, and forecast consumption logic determines how the combination of these demands will drive supply chain activities. Master scheduling logic helps formulate and analyze S&OP game plans, especially in using multiple sets of data for simulation purposes. Realistic promises for sales order delivery can be based on the S&OP game plans and delivery date control policies that enforce basic rules such as calendars and transport time. Unrealistic promises can be highlighted by disabling the delivery date control logic, and the exceptions should require follow-up.

Several scenarios illustrated how to maintain S&OP game plans.   Guidelines were suggested to improve S&OP game plans, such as how to formulate realistic game plans, enforce near-term schedule stability, and make realistic delivery promises. The case studies highlighted variations in the use of S&OP game plans, such as a manually maintained master schedule, demand forecasts for stocked components, and S&OP simulations.

Chapter 11

Sales Order Processing

Sales orders capture demands for a firm's products and services. They comprise a key element in two larger contexts: the sales and operations (S&OP) game plans driving supply chain activities, and customer service across the customer relationship life cycle. Sales orders may originate from one or more order streams, such as direct customer communication with sales representatives or customer service reps, customer self service via web-based applications, and electronically transmitted customer schedules.

Sales order processing involves a wide spectrum of considerations and many variations in business practices. As an explanatory approach, it is easiest to start with a basic model of sales order processing embedded within AX. The basic model provides a foundation for explaining key considerations and major variations. Examples of major variations include the approach to sales pricing, the use of sales quotations, customer returns and commissions. These considerations are reflected in the following sections within the chapter.

1. Basic Model of Sales Order Processing
2. Typical Process for Entering a Sales Order
3. Key Considerations in Sales Order Processing
4. Warehouse Management Considerations
5. Major Variations in Sales Order Processing
6. Sales Prices and Trade Agreements
7. Sales Agreements
8. Direct Delivery Orders
9. Special Orders
10. Customer Returns and RMAs
11. Sales Orders for Configurable Items
12. Sales Quotations
13. Commissions for Sales Orders
14. Customer Information

15. Sales Analysis
16. Performance Metrics related to Sales Orders
17. Workspaces related to Sales Orders

11.1 Basic Model of Sales Order Processing

The typical steps in sales order processing can vary based on several factors, such as different approaches for creating an order and different approaches for sales order picking/shipping. This section summarizes a basic model of sales order processing, and identifies the different options for creating a sales order and the different types of sales orders.

Overview of the Basic Model The basic model of sales order processing starts with the role of a customer service rep, and the manual entry of a sales order for standard products. A warehouse worker and shipping clerk perform subsequent steps for sales order picking/shipping, which differ when using the basic versus advanced approach to warehouse management. Both approaches support order-based picking described in the basic model. An accounts receivable clerk completes the process by generating an invoice reflecting actual shipments. These roles and steps are summarized in Figure 11.1 and described below.

Figure 11.1 Basic Model of Sales Order Processing

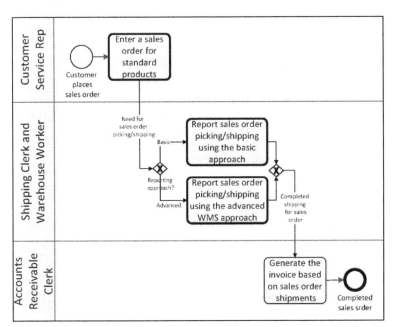

Enter a Sales Order for Standard Products The customer service rep creates a new sales order by starting from the Customer form or the Sales Order form (and using the Create Sales Order dialogue), which results in a sales order header. If needed, the rep maintains aspects of the sales order header information, such as designating (or adding) the desired address or delivery mode, or overriding information inherited from the customer master. The customer service rep also creates sales order line items, where each line item identifies a product, quantity, sales price, ship-from location and the requested dates for shipment and delivery. When a line item's requested date cannot be met for a sales line, the system can suggest a date based on the delivery date control policy assigned to the line item. The item's inventory may also be reserved for a sales line in some scenarios. When all line items have been defined, the customer service rep generates a sales order confirmation and sends it to the customer.

Report Sales Order Picking/Shipping using the Basic Approach to Warehouse Management The shipping clerk typically uses the Release Sales Order Picking form to review and select open sales order lines that require picking/shipping, and then generate the picking lists for selected orders. This represents an order-based picking approach. The generation of a picking list will reserve the item's inventory for the sales line (if not already reserved). The warehouse worker reports actual picking against a sales order picking list. The shipping clerk reports actual shipment by posting the sales order packing slip for picked items.

Report Sales Order Picking/Shipping using the Advanced WMS Approach to Warehouse Management The shipping clerk typically uses the Release to Warehouse form to review and select open sales order lines that require picking/shipping, and then releases selected orders to the warehouse (which updates the release status for each order). With an order-based picking approach, the release-to-warehouse step can automatically create a shipment and load (with a waved status) and a shipment wave (with a released status) for each sales order. In addition, the released shipment wave automatically creates a picking work order consisting of work lines that identify the pick and put instructions.

The warehouse worker uses the mobile device to report completion of picking work orders with delivery to an outbound dock, which results in a *ready to ship* status for the related shipment and load. The shipping clerk reports actual shipment by confirming the outbound shipments and posting the sales order packing slips for picked items.

Report Sales Order Picking/Shipping using a Simple Inventory Transaction The shipping clerk reports actual picking when posting the packing slip for a sales order. This simple inventory transaction applies to both the basic and advanced approaches to warehouse management, and it avoids the use of picking lists or picking work orders respectively. This step is not shown in Figure 11.1 because it applies to both approaches.

Generate the Invoice based on Sales Order Shipment The accounts receivable clerk periodically generates the sales order invoices based on information about which sales lines have been picked and shipped.

Enforce Steps in the Basic Model Several steps in the business process for sales order picking/shipping can be mandated by two item-specific policies. The first policy can mandate that picking must be reported before posting the packing slip for a sales order, and the second policy can mandate that the packing slip must posted before you generate the invoice for a sales order. These two policies -- termed the *Picking Requirements* policy and the *Deduction Requirements* policy -- are embedded in the Item Model Group assigned to the item.

Life Cycles related to Sales Order Processing The life cycles related to a sales order include a status for the header and each line item, a document status, and an inventory status for the item on a sales lin. Steps in the business process automatically update the status. These steps are summarized in Figure 11.2, along with the status of related life cycles. The steps represent the minimum number of touch points for updating status.

Figure 11.2 Life Cycles related to Sales Order Processing

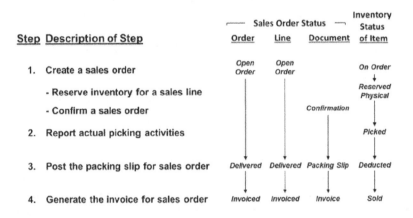

An order status indicates the following steps in the life cycle of a sales order.

♦ *Open Order.* The status indicates the order has been created.

♦ *Delivered.* The status indicates all order lines have been shipped.

♦ *Invoiced.* The status indicates all order lines have been invoiced.[1]

A line status indicates the following steps in the life cycle of a sales order line

♦ *Open.* The status indicates the line has been created, and partial shipment or invoicing may have occurred.

♦ *Delivered.* The status indicates the delivered quantity equals the order quantity. When using delivery tolerances, the delivered quantity can exceed the order quantity or a sales line with an under-delivery can be flagged as closed.

♦ *Invoiced.* The status indicates the line item quantity has been completely invoiced, taking into account the over- or under-delivery considerations.

A document status indicates the last document printed (aka posted) for the sales order, which includes the following documents.

♦ *Confirmation.* The status indicates the confirmation has been posted. Each time a sales order confirmation has been posted, a separate version of the confirmation is automatically created with a numerical suffix. You can view and print/reprint a selected version of a sales order confirmation.

♦ *Picking List.* The status indicates a picking list has been created, which represents the release for picking/shipping. A picking list only applies to the basic approach to warehouse management.

♦ *Packing Slip.* The status indicates the packing skip has been posted, which automatically creates a packing slip journal about the transactions. Each time a packing slip has been posted for a sales order, a separate version of the packing slip journal is automatically created with a numerical suffix. You can view and print/reprint a selected version of a packing slip journal. The packing slip journal also provides an option to cancel the associated transaction(s) or make corrections.

♦ *Invoice.* The status indicates the invoice has been posted.

---

[1] Information about a sales order and/or line item with an invoiced status can be deleted immediately (by the system), or subsequently deleted (by a user-initiated process) based on companywide policies. Another policy determines whether the system retains manually deleted sales orders as voided orders.

The inventory status for the item on a sales line is shown on the right side of Figure 11.2. The steps in sales order processing will change this status from *on order* to *reserved physical, picked, deducted* and *sold.*

An additional status -- termed the Released Status -- applies when using the advanced approach to warehouse management, and it reflects the release to warehouse step. It is not included in the figure. The released status of a sales order has the following significance.

◆ *Open.* The status indicates the sales order has not yet been released to warehouse for picking/shipping.
◆ *Released.* The status indicates that all sales order line items have been released to the warehouse for picking/shipping.
◆ *Partially Released.* The status indicates that some of the sales order lines items have been released to warehouse for picking/shipping.

The advanced approach to warehouse management also involves several additional constructs for managing sales order picking/shipping. These include a shipment, load, wave and work orders, where each construct has a life cycle with different values for a status.

Different Approaches for Creating a Sales Order A manually entered sales order represents one of the common approaches for creating an order. The different approaches for creating a sales order are listed below along with the relevant book section providing further explanation. Steps within the basic model also apply to these other sources of creating a sales order.

◆ Enter a sales order for standard products (Section 11.2)
◆ Enter a sales order for configurable products (Sections 11.11 and 19.5)
◆ Create a sales order via release from a blanket sales order (Section 11.7)
◆ Create a sales order from a sales quotation (Section 11.12)
◆ Create a sales order for a replacement item related to an RMA (Section 11.10)
◆ Automatically create an intercompany sales order from an intercompany purchase order (Section 18.2)

Additional approaches to creating a sales order apply to retail-oriented operations and project-oriented operations, but these fall outside the book's scope. For example, you can enter a sales order using the call center capabilities, or you can enter sales orders and item requirements related to a project.

Other Types of Sales Orders   You indicate the sales order type when initially creating a sales order. In addition to a normal sales order, the order types include a returned order, journal and subscription.

◆   *Returned Order.* A sales order with a type of returned order is automatically created for an RMA (returned material authorization), and it handles the arrival, receipt and credit note for the returned goods (via a negative quantity line item). It also supports sending the returned item back to the customer. A subsequent section provides further explanation of customer returns and RMAs (Section 11.10).

◆   *Journal (or Draft).* A journal sales order does not represent a demand. It is typically used to capture information early in the sales cycle, and you change the order type to sales order upon placement by the customer.

◆   *Subscription.* A subscription sales order represents a demand, and the system automatically recreates it after the order has been shipped and invoiced.

Sales quotations reflect a separate construct and not a different type of sales order. A sales quotation can be confirmed, thereby generating a sales order with linkage back to the sales quotation.   A subsequent section describes sales quotations (Section 11.12).

11.2 Typical Process for Entering a Sales Order

The manual entry of a sales order represents a common approach to creating an order, and the first step in the basic model described in the previous section. It consists of multiple steps typically performed by a customer service rep, as summarized in Figure 11.3 and described below.

Initially create the sales order header information   The customer service rep initially creates a sales order for a specified customer, which results in a sales order header.   The header information is automatically inherited when starting from a selected customer; it can be modified on the Create Sales Order dialogue when starting from the Sales Order form.   If applicable, the dialogue enables the customer service rep to identify the related blanket sales order with the customer, or to identify a one-time customer (which automatically creates a customer master record).

Figure 11.3 Typical Process to Enter a Sales Order

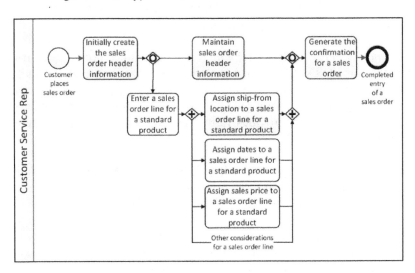

Maintain the sales order header information   The customer service rep optionally maintains or views the header information after initial creation. For example, the rep can view sales trade agreements with the customer or view totals for the sales order. The rep can also make changes that optionally update sales lines, such as changing the delivery date, delivery mode or ship-from location. You typically employ a prompt to confirm that changes in header information should change the sales lines. The use of a prompt (after changing selected fields in the header information) represents a companywide policy, where other values for this policy include automatic changes (without a prompt) and preventing the changes to line items.

Enter a sales order line for a stocked product   The customer service rep identifies the item number, order quantity and UM for each sales line. Other key information includes the ship-from site/warehouse, mode of delivery, shipment/delivery dates and sales price. Each sales line can optionally include a delivery schedule, where each delivery line specifies a quantity and the shipment/delivery dates.

Assign a ship-from location to a sales order line for a standard product   When entering a sales order line, the ship-from site/warehouse can default from the item or from the sales order header (which can default from the selected customer).   The first approach represents a preferred (or mandated) ship-from location for an item; the second approach represents the preferred ship-from location for a customer. The ship-from warehouse (and ship date) can also reflect an analysis of delivery alternatives from different warehouses, where the selected alternative updates the sales line.

Assign dates to a sales order line for a standard product The dates include the requested ship date and delivery date, where the difference represents the transportation time between the ship-from warehouse and the delivery address. The transportation time can differ for different modes of delivery. The dates also include a confirmed ship date and receipt date. The assignment of realistic dates reflects a delivery date control policy for the sales line, which is initially inherited from an item-specific policy that should reflect the S&OP game plans for the item. A previous chapter explained the significance of a delivery date control policy (Section 10.10). The dates can also affect sales pricing, and forecast consumption logic when applicable.

The ship date and delivery date can reflect an analysis of delivery alternatives from different warehouses and different modes of delivery, where the selected alternative updates the sales line.

Assign sales price to a sales order line for a standard product The sales price (or discount) often reflects the sales price trade agreements with the customer, or the related blanket sales order. The rep can optionally override the sales price.

Other considerations for a sales order line The simple figure does not include all considerations, and they are covered in the next section.

Generate the confirmation for a sales order The customer service rep generates the confirmation for a sales order and sends it to the customer. Generating the confirmation results in automatic assignment of a version number consisting of the sales order number and a numeric suffix (such as -1 and -2). A sales order may be changed and the confirmation reposted in order to track versions of a sales order and communicate the changes to customers.

Delete or Cancel a Sales Order The customer service rep can optionally delete or cancel a sales order line (or the entire order) prior to reporting picking activities. These steps are not included in the figure.

11.3 Key Considerations for Sales Order Processing

Many of the variations in sales order processing can be supported by standard AX capabilities. Some of these can be viewed as major variations while others can be viewed as key considerations. This section summarizes a number of key considerations and a subsequent section summarizes the major variations. A subset of these topics will apply to a given company.

The following list of key considerations and their extended explanations represent a compendium of topics about AX capabilities. The list has been broadly segmented into three groups consisting of common and special considerations (covered in this section) and warehouse management considerations (covered in the next section). Each topic has been assigned an identifier for ease of reference, as shown below.

List of Common Considerations

◆ A1: Assign a ship-from location to a sales order
◆ A2: Assign sales order dates for shipment and delivery
◆ A3: Delivery schedule for a sales order line
◆ A4: Assign a sales price to a sales order line
◆ A5: Analyze supply options for making delivery promises
◆ A6: Delivery address by sales order line
◆ A7: Totals for a sales order
◆ A8: Versions of a sales order
◆ A9: Reserve material for a sales order line
◆ A10: Effective use of notes for sales orders
◆ A11: Identify sales-related backorders
◆ A12: Analyze delivery alternatives for a sales order line

List of Special Considerations

◆ B1: Place a sales order on hold
◆ B2: Impact of a customer hold and other types of stop flags and restrictions
◆ B3: Create sales order lines via the copy function
◆ B4: Create sales order lines via copy from Item Lists
◆ B5: Create sales lines via selection from a sales hierarchy of product categories
◆ B6: Identify changes to sales orders via order events
◆ B7: Relevance of order entry deadlines

- B8: Start and end dates for selling an item
- B9: Automatically assign an alternate item
- B10: Significance of Inventory Status for sales order processing
- B11: Month-end revenue recognition of sales order shipments not yet invoiced

A1: Assign a Ship-From Location to a Sales Order A ship-from location consists of a site and warehouse, and it applies to the sales order header and line items. The default values for a sales order header can be inherited from the customer, where they typically reflect the nearest ship-from location. These values will be inherited by the line items unless item-specific defaults have been defined. The item-specific defaults for sales order shipments can be defined as a companywide or site-specific policy, where they typically reflect the preferred source or the sole source for the item. As an alternative approach, you can define a default ship-from warehouse for a site (aka the fallback warehouse for a site) which will be inherited when you simply enter a site.

The ship-from warehouse (and ship date) can reflect an analysis of delivery alternatives from different warehouses, where the selected alternative updates the sales line.

The ship-from site and warehouse can have several impacts. The warehouse calendar can be considered when assigning ship dates, and the warehouse can be used for determining the transportation time to the customer address. They can also affect sales order pricing and discounts, and also master scheduling logic about replenishment.

The default values also apply to coordination of a multicompany supply chain, such as the assignment of ship-from locations to an intercompany sales order (Section 18.2) and planned intercompany demand (Section 18.3).

A2: Assign Sales Order Dates for Shipment and Delivery A sales order header has a requested ship date and a requested delivery date, where the difference represents the transportation time (termed transport days) between the ship-from warehouse and the delivery address. It also has a confirmed ship date and confirmed receipt date. The assignment of these dates are affected by the delivery date control policy assigned to the sales order header, which can enforce basic rules about applicable calendars (for the ship-from warehouse, the customer, and the mode of delivery), the expected transportation time to the customer address, and order entry deadlines.

A sales order line also has a requested ship date and delivery date as well as confirmed dates. These dates can be inherited from the sales order header, and changes in the header dates can optionally update information for the sales lines. However, the ability to assign a ship date and delivery date are impacted by the delivery date control policy for a line item, which is initially inherited from the specified item. A previous chapter provided further explanation about the delivery date control policy (Section 10.10).

The ship date and delivery date can reflect an analysis of delivery alternatives from different warehouses and different modes of delivery, where the selected alternative updates the sales line.

The confirmed dates can be manually assigned, or automatically assigned using the "Calculate confirmed delivery dates" function. As part of the dialogue, you indicate the confirmed dates should be automatically updated, and optionally indicate whether to change the delivery date control policy (in order to meet the confirmed dates).

A3: Delivery Schedule for a Sales Order Line A sales order line item normally consists of a single quantity and its associated ship and delivery dates. You can optionally specify a delivery schedule for a sales line, where each schedule line consists of a quantity and its associated dates. The total quantities within the delivery schedule lines must equal the quantity for the sales line, or the sales line quantity will be automatically adjusted.

A4: Assign a Sales Price to a Sales Order Line An item's sales price on a sales line be assigned by several different approaches. The common approaches include a sales price trade agreement (Section 11.6) and a sales agreement (Section 11.7), where sales prices can reflect company-wide or site/warehouse-specific prices. Other approaches include the inherited sales price from a sales quotation or from copying a source document.

A5: Analyzing Supply Options for Making Delivery Promises You can view alternative supply options (using the Supply Overview form) for a sales order line item. These options include inventory and scheduled receipts at different sites and warehouses, quarantined inventory, an alternative item (if specified on the item master), and lead times to obtain the item from various sources.

A6: Delivery Address by Sales Order Line Each line item inherits the delivery address from the sales order header, and it can be overridden. When printing a document such as a picking list or packing list, a separate document can be printed for each delivery address. The separate documents correctly communicate which line items are being sent to the delivery address.

A7: Totals for a Sales Order The system calculates several order totals, including revenue, cost and margin, discounts and taxes, and total weight and volume. Order totals can be displayed for order quantities, picked quantities, or shipped quantities.

A8: Versions of a Sales Order Posting a sales order confirmation results in automatic assignment of a version number. Each version is identified by the sales order number and a numeric suffix (such as -1 and -2). A sales order may be changed and the confirmation reposted in order to track versions of a sales order and communicate the changes to customers. The version number is displayed on a printed sales order confirmation. These historical versions can be viewed as part of inquiries about posted confirmations for a sales order. The system uses the existing sales order data (regardless of the assigned version number) for picking purposes and the related packing slip and invoice.

You can revert the existing sales order data to a previous version by using the *Copy from Journal* function. You select from the displayed list of versions, and specify to delete lines from the existing order, so that the existing sales order data gets updated. You can optionally repost the sales order confirmation to assign a new version number.

A9: Reserve Material for a Sales Order Line Most scenarios employ reservations at the time you release a sales line for picking, and the picking list (or picking work) communicates these reservations. Some scenarios require reservations at the time of order entry, or reservations against an item's scheduled receipts.[2] Other scenarios sometimes require reservations of specific batches.

The reservation policy assigned to a sales order line item indicates whether inventory will be reserved automatically or manually. The options for this reservation policy include *Automatic* and *Manual*. A third option is termed *Explosion* and it supports automatic reservations of the components for a make-to-order product. When initially adding a line item, its reservation policy can be inherited from the item or from the sales order header.

---

[2] The policy concerning reservations defaults from the sales order header, which defaults from a companywide policy embedded in the A/R parameters. An additional companywide policy determines whether reservations can be made against scheduled receipts.

◆ *Inherit reservation policy from the item.* The item's reservation policy is embedded in the Item Model Group assigned to the item, with a value of *Automatic, Manual* or *Explosion* (but not *Default*).

◆ *Inherit reservation policy from the sales order header.* The option for the item's reservation policy (embedded in the Item Model Group) should be *Default.* The reservation policy for a sales order header can be inherited from the companywide policy (embedded in the A/R Parameters), and this acts as a default value when adding sales order line items. A change to the reservation policy in the sales order header can update the policy for every line item.

The reservation logic differs between the basic and advanced approaches to warehouse management. The advanced approach requires assignment of an additional item policy for the reservation hierarchy.

A10: Effective Use of Notes for Sales Orders Many situations require textual explanations about the sales order and/or line items, where the information can be defined as a note and its associated note type. The notes can be inherited from the customer and/or item.[3] The inherited notes can be optionally overridden, and notes can also be manually entered. The various considerations about notes are summarized below.

◆ *Inherit an Item-Related Note on the Sales Line Item.* The note(s) associated with an item can be automatically inherited by a sales line for the item.

◆ *Inherit a Customer-Related Note on the Sales Order Header.* The note(s) associated with a customer can be automatically inherited by the sales order header.

◆ *Printing Notes on Sales Documents.* The setup policies for A/R forms determine whether printed documents include a specified note type. These documents include the confirmation, picking list, packing slip, and invoice for a sales order; they also include sales quotations and sales agreements. The specified note type can be different for each document.

◆ *Displaying Notes on Mobile Device Transactions for Sales Order Picking.* When using the advanced approach to warehouse management, the note(s) associated with the sales order header and its related shipment can be displayed on the mobile device transactions for sales order picking. The

---

[3] A companywide policy determines whether the notes for customers and items will be inherited by a sales order. The "copy notes" policy is embedded in the A/R Parameters form.

applicable note type for mobile device transactions is defined by a companywide policy (on the Warehouse Management Parameters form).

♦ *Displaying Notes on Other Documents and Screens.* The concept of an applicable note type also applies to several other printed documents and screens related to the advanced approach to warehouse management. This includes the bill of lading, a load report, a shipment picking list and the packing screen. The applicable note type for each of these is defined by companywide policies (as part of the Warehouse Management Parameters).

A11: Identify Sales-Related Backorders
A sales-related backorder within AX simply refers to any sales line with a ship date prior to a specified date (aka the backorder date).[4] This simple definition also applies to a sales line with an unshipped or partially shipped quantity, where the line has not been closed short when reporting actual shipment. This represents the more common interpretation of a sales-related backorder. Some scenarios need to identify the quantity for an unshipped or partially shipped line as "backordered" on sales order documents.[5] A standard inquiry provides information about sales-related backorders (labeled Backorder Lines, within Sales and Marketing).

The customer service rep typically reviews sales-related backorders and takes action for a selected backorder. The actions include updating the promise date or reducing the quantity for the sales order line. The rep can also request expediting of a supply order for the item.

A12: Analyze Delivery Alternatives for a Sales Order Line
The delivery alternatives for meeting a customer's requested delivery date and quantity can reflect product availability at different ship-from warehouses and different modes of delivery. It may also reflect different product variants (such as size or color) in some scenarios. You can evaluate these options for a sales line using the Delivery Alternatives information, and select the desired option for updating the promised dates, ship-from warehouse and mode of delivery on the sales line. You can also choose to ship a smaller quantity than ordered (based on availability) and ship the remainder at a later date, which results in a delivery schedule for the sales line. Case 11.1 illustrates the use of the Delivery Alternatives information.

B1: Place a Sales Order on Hold
Assigning a "hold code" to a sales order will prevent any further processing -- such as a confirmation, picking/shipping or

---

[4] This simple definition is critical for understanding "backordered lines" with a future ship date when compared to a specified backorder date in the future.

[5] The treatment of unshipped and partially shipped line items is defined by the Backorder Tracking policy for printing packing slips and invoices (within the Forms Setup form in Accounts Receivable).

invoicing -- while still allowing changes to the order. An additional policy for a hold code determines whether the reservations for a sales order (if any) should be removed after placing it on hold. In either case, the sales order demand will still be recognized by master scheduling logic. You create user-defined codes that represent variations of an order hold, and then select the relevant code when identifying a hold order. The hold for a sales order is identified by a "do not process" checkbox, by a hold icon in a list of sales orders, and by optional color coding when editing the order.[6]

In the simplest scenario, you simply access the Order Hold screen from the selected sales order, and assign an order hold code. One or more hold codes can be assigned to a sales order. You can then clear the code after the hold has been resolved. The system automatically tracks the user and the date/time related to creation and clearing of a hold code. A hold code cannot be manually deleted; it must be cleared.

Some scenarios require an authorized user for clearing a hold code, such as the sales manager role for a hold code related to sales. You designate the authorized user as part of the setup information for a hold code, so that the hold code can be checked out and then cleared by the authorized user. If needed, you can override the designated user (when viewing the Order Hold screen) so that an authorized user can quickly clear the hold.

The Order Hold screen displays additional information about the sales order, such as the order total, payments to-date, and different types of notes. These notes may have been defined for the customer or the sales order header, or directly entered as a hold note.

A hold code can also be assigned to an RMA to prevent further processing, such as receipts or creation of a replacement order.

B2: Impact of a Customer Hold and other Types of Stop Flags and Restrictions
The assignment of a customer hold for "all" transactions (as the policy for Invoicing and Delivery on Hold) will prevent new sales orders as well as transactions for existing orders, and result in a corresponding message. Other types of stop flags and restrictions include the following.

◆ *Impact of Stopped Transactions for an Item.* The sales order transactions for an item can be stopped, either as a companywide or site-specific policy. The stopped flag prevents new sales orders and further transactions for an item's

---

[6] You can optionally define the color coding for a hold order as part of the setup information for an order hold code, or as part of a company-wide policy for hold orders (on the A/R Parameters form).

existing sales orders, and results in a corresponding message. A similar stopped flag can be specified for an item's inventory transactions, which only prevents further transactions for an item's existing sales orders.

◆ *Impact of Stopped Flag for a Sales Order Line* The stopped flag will prevent updates to the sales line. It also prevents the next steps in the business process for the line item such as the sales order confirmation or picking/shipping.

◆ *Restricted Sales from a Single Site/Warehouse.* Sales orders for an item can be limited to a single site or warehouse, as defined by the mandatory flag within the Default Order Settings and Site-Specific Order Settings forms.

B3: Create Sales Order Lines via the Copy Function A copy function (termed Copy from All) can be used to create line items from an existing sales order and other sources such as quotes and invoices. For example, you can select the desired sales order and the desired line item(s) from a displayed list of all existing orders. You can also select from versions of sales orders, or from sales quotations, packing slips and invoices. You indicate how to update the existing order, such as appending information to the existing line items and recalculating prices for the new line items.

B4: Create Sales Order Lines via Copy from Item Lists The concept of a sales order template can be implemented using the Item List capabilities within AX, so that you can easily create sales order line items by copying selected items from a user-defined list. As setup information, you initially create an Item List with an identifier and name. An Item List can be applicable to a single customer or all customers, and you can define multiple Item Lists to support different purposes. The items within a customer-specific Item List can be initially generated based on previous sales orders to the customer. For example, the previous sales orders can reflect a time period such as the last 100 days. You can also manually maintain the items within an Item List. When using the Sales Order form to enter a sales line, you can access the function "Copy From Item List" to display the applicable Item List(s) and select items within a list to automatically create sales lines. When Item Lists are commonly used, you can assign a companywide policy (within the A/R Parameters) so that the Item Lists are always displayed after initially creating a sales order.

B5: Create Sales Order Lines via selection from a Sales Hierarchy When entering line items on the Sale Order form, the "Add Products" function can be used to select an applicable sales hierarchy and a node within the hierarchy, and then select the product(s) to be automatically added to the sales order.

B6: Identify Changes to Sales Orders via Order Events An order event provides one approach for identifying changes to sales orders. As part of setup, you use the Order Event Setup form to indicate which sales-related transactions will generate an order event. Examples include changes to a sales order (such as creating an order or adding an order hold) and changes to sales lines (such as cancelling a line). Other types of order events can be tracked for customer returns, sales quotations and direct delivery sales orders. The order events can be viewed for a sales order, and all order events can be viewed on the Order Events form.

B7: Relevance of Order Entry Deadlines Some scenarios involve same day shipments for sales orders that have been entered by a specified deadline. This order entry deadline frequently represents a prerequisite for meeting the departure time of a shipping vehicle, so that adequate time is available for picking/shipping activities. An order entry deadline also means that an order entered after the specified time will be treated as if it were entered the next day, thereby affecting the assignment of a promised ship date. You define a set of deadlines for each day within a week (termed an order entry deadline group), and then assign the deadline group to each customer and site.

B8: Start and End Dates for Selling an Item As part of the item master information, you can assign a start date and/or an end date for selling an item, thereby limiting the ability to enter a sales order line for the item. An additional "shipping start date" will limit the ability to enter a ship date. These policies can be used for new product introductions, seasonal availability, and other purposes.

B9: Automatically Assign an Alternate Item When an alternate item has been defined for an item, the alternate can automatically replace the originally entered item number. An item-specific policy determines whether the system always suggests replacement or only when available inventory is insufficient to cover the ordered quantity.

B10: Significance of Inventory Status for Sales Order Processing The use of Inventory Status only applies to WMS-enabled items, as described in a subsequent chapter about warehouse management (Section 16.2). A value for Inventory Status must be assigned to each sales order line, typically with a value of *Available* or its equivalent in most scenarios. In some scenarios, the value for Inventory Status may indicate the grade or condition of the inventory being sold, which may or may not affect sales prices. Examples include *Off-Spec, Refurbished* or *Used.* The value may also indicate the need for cross-docking of a special order receipt, as described in a subsequent section about special orders (Section 11.9).

B11: Month End Revenue Recognition of Sales Order Shipments not yet Invoiced Certain month-end situations require revenue recognition based on shipments prior to actual invoicing. In this case, the shipment (recorded via the packing slip update transaction) can update a revenue account that will be cleared upon invoice generation. The *post physical revenue* policy (embedded in the Item Model Group assigned to the item) indicates that shipments should update the *packing slip revenue* account and the *packing slip revenue offset* account (defined in the Item Group assigned to the item).

11.4 Warehouse Management Considerations

Several warehouse management considerations impact sales order processing, especially the activities for sales order picking/shipping. Some of these have already been mentioned in the previous section, such as order entry deadlines, reservations and effective use of notes. This section highlights some additional considerations related to warehouse management, and starts with a list of the considerations. Each topic has been assigned an identifier for ease of reference.

◆ C1: Indicate expediting for sales order picking/shipping
◆ C2: Customer pickup for a sales order
◆ C3: Sales order charges for freight
◆ C4: Release to warehouse for sales orders
◆ C5: Significance of the fulfillment rate on the release to warehouse step
◆ C6: Significance of prevent partial delivery policy
◆ C7: Quality orders for sales order picking/shipping

C1: Indicate Expediting for Sales Order Picking/Shipping Several different approaches can be used to identify the need for expediting or prioritizing the sales order picking/shipping activities. The ship date provides the primary basis for scheduling the picking/shipping activities. It is frequently used in conjunction with other policies assigned to a sales order header or line item that indicate a priority or need for expediting, as summarized in Figure 11.4 and described below. The relevant fields can then be used as selection criteria when generating picking lists (or creating picking work) for sales orders.

◆ *Mode of delivery.* The mode of delivery often provides an organizing focus for picking/shipping activities, especially when preparing shipments for a scheduled pickup time. A delivery mode may reflect faster or expedited delivery, and can be associated with an Expedite Code.

Figure 11.4 Indicate a Priority or Expediting
for Sales Order Picking/Shipping

Field Name	Applicable Construct		
	SO Line	SO Header	Customer
Ship date	Yes	Yes	N/A
Mode of delivery	Yes	Yes	N/A
Expedite code *	Yes	Yes	N/A
Sales order priority for fulfillment *	N/A	Yes	N/A
Customer classification group	N/A	N/A	Yes
Shipping carrier/service	Yes	Yes	N/A

★ = Not available as standard selection criteria within the advanced approach to warehouse management.

◆ *Expedite code.* A user-defined Expedite code can be assigned to a sales order header and/or line item to indicate the need for expediting. In addition, you can associate an Expedite code with a mode of delivery, so that selecting the expedited mode of delivery also updates the Expedite code on a sales order.

◆ *Sales order priority for fulfillment.* A predefined priority can only be assigned to a sales order header, and it provides an additional basis for expediting. The ten predefined values reflect different priorities, ranging from "High-1" to "Low-10."

◆ *Customer classification group.* A user-defined customer classification group can be assigned to a customer, and it can act as one of the criteria for selecting sales lines to be picked. For example, it can be used for selecting lines when using the Release Sales Order Picking form (in the basic approach to warehouse management) or when using the Automatic Release to Warehouse task (in the advanced approach).

◆ *Shipping carrier and carrier service.* The shipping carrier and carrier service can be used as an organizing focus of picking/shipping activities, especially when preparing shipments for a scheduled pickup time by the carrier.

C2: Customer Pickup for a Sales Order A customer pickup must be designated as a policy for a user-defined delivery mode, and you assign this delivery mode to a sales order. A typical name for the delivery mode would be

Customer-Pickup. The Sales Pickup form displays sales orders having one or more line items with a delivery mode for customer pickup, and provides a short-cut approach for reporting shipment and invoicing transactions.

C3: Sales Order Charges for Freight The charges related to freight can be manually assigned to a sales order, either as order-level charges or line item charges or both. A user-defined Charges Code identifies each type of charge and its related ledger account. The charges can be expressed as a fixed amount, an amount per piece, or a percentage of value. A fixed amount (for an order-level charge) needs to be allocated to the lines.

Some scenarios involve predefined agreements about charges, such as freight or handling charges for selected items or customers. An agreement about charges can be embedded in the sales price trade agreement information, or they can be specified separately as *auto charges*. These auto charges can be applied to an entire sales order or to individual line items, and expressed as a fixed amount, an amount per piece, or a percentage of value.

◆ *Order-Level Charges.* Charge agreements related to the entire sales order can be defined for a single customer, all customers or a group of customers (identified by the *Customer Charges Group* assigned to relevant customers). Examples of an order-level charge include order preparation costs for selected customers.

◆ *Line item charges.* Charge agreements related to the sales order line item can be defined by customer and item, such as charges for a single item, all items, or a group of items (identified by the Item Charges Group assigned to relevant salable items).[7] Examples of a line item charge include a setup fee for producing selected items for a customer.

When using the advanced approach to transportation management, the relevant charges can reflect the transportation costs associated with the sales order load (or the shipment or container) containing the sales order lines. These charges are automatically assigned to sales lines after confirming the outbound shipment.

C4: Release to Warehouse for Sales Orders The release-to-warehouse step represents a key part of any business process for sales order picking/shipping when using the advanced approach to warehouse management. It automatically updates the Release Status for a sales order. There are four options for the release-to-warehouse step. A sales order can be released to the warehouse as part

---

[7] Two policies (embedded within the A/R parameters) indicate whether the system recognizes auto charges for the entire order and for line items.

of order entry, or you can use the Release to Warehouse form for releasing selected sales order lines. Both options require reservations before the release-to-warehouse step, whereas the next two options can defer reservations until the time of release. A third option employs a periodic task to support automatic release to warehouse for sales order lines meeting the selection criteria. A fourth option employs the Load Planning Workbench to support the release to warehouse for all sales orders within a load.

C5: Significance of the Fulfillment Rate on the Release to Warehouse Step   When using the advanced approach to warehouse management, a set of rules about a fulfillment rate allows a sales order to be released to the warehouse with partial reservations of the ordered quantities rather than being fully reserved. The rules apply to all four options of the release to warehouse step. For example, a fulfillment rate of 90% means that the total of reserved quantities for all sales lines must be 90% or greater that the total of the ordered quantities. The fulfillment rate can apply to the total quantity or total value (quantity times price) of a sales order's lines. In either case, it is possible that the reservations for a given line on a multiline sales order may not meet the fulfillment rate but the overall sales order does.

A related policy (labeled the "fulfillment violations message") determines whether an exception for the fulfillment rate will prevent the release to warehouse for a sales order, or simply provide a warning (or no message) while still allowing the release. When prevented, an example message would be "A fulfillment rate of 90 was not met for sales order 12345," which is displayed after attempting to release to warehouse.

The set of rules about a fulfillment rate can be defined as a companywide policy (as part of the Accounts Receivable Parameters), and optionally overridden as a customer-specific set of rules. The set of rules do not apply when using a fulfillment rate of 0% and/or a fulfillment violation message policy of "none."

C6: Significance of the Prevent Partial Delivery Policy A sales order line can be flagged as "prevent partial delivery" so that you will receive an error unless you ship the entire quantity when posting the sales order packing slip.[8] As an alternative approach, the same concept can be enforced using the delivery tolerance functionality, since delivery tolerances of zero percent for a sales line mean that the shipped quantity must equal the ordered quantity.

---

[8] The policy of "prevent partial delivery" for a sales order line was called "ship complete" in previous AX versions such as AX 2012 R3.

An additional "ship complete" flag for the entire sales order has a slightly different significance, since it prevents the generation of the picking list (or the picking work) until all lines have sufficient inventory to be reserved for the ordered quantity. Hence, using both policies will help ensure that all lines will be picked and that order quantities for individual lines will be shipped complete.

C7: Quality Orders for Sales Order Picking/Shipping A quality order can be automatically generated when you create a picking list (or a picking work order), or post the packing slip for a sales order, as defined by Quality Associations related to sales orders for an item. For example, the validation of test results may be required before you can report actual picking. A subsequent chapter provides further explanation of quality orders (Section 17.4).

11.5 Major Variations in Sales Order Processing

The basic model of sales order processing provides a foundation for covering several major variations. The basic model included one major variation about sales order picking/shipping using the basic versus advanced approach to warehouse management. The explanation of the basic model also identified different ways to create a sales order.

Several other major variations merit a separate section, such as sales prices and trade agreements (Section 11.6), sales agreements (Section 11.7), direct delivery orders (Section 11.8), special orders (Section 11.9), customer returns and RMAs (Section 11.10), sales orders for configurable items (Section 11.11), sales quotations (Section 11.12) and commissions for sales orders (Section 11.13). This section summarizes several additional variations.

Generating a Production Order from a Sales Order You can immediately generate a production order when the sales order line item represents a make-to-order product requiring a link to the sales order. This approach was previously described for the S&OP scenarios requiring a link to sales orders (Section 10.9). The dialogue for creating the production order identifies the item's BOM version and route version. These versions may have been specified on the sales line and inherited by the dialogue. As part of the dialogue, you can also assign a different version that has been approved for the item.

After creating the production order, you can view and maintain information on the Production Order form, such as immediately scheduling the order. The sales order line item is linked to the associated production order (and vice versa), as indicated by the reference fields on each order. A subsequent chapter provides further explanation of production order processing (Chapter 14).

Selling a Kit of Material Items The BOM version for a manufactured item can represent a kit of components, and the kit can be sold as individual components. When entering a sales order line for the item, you can view and select the components using the function *Explode BOM*. A sales line will be automatically added for each selected component, with pricing based on the component item and quantity. The original line item is displayed on the form but not on printed documents.

11.6 Sales Prices and Trade Agreements

A sales trade agreement represents predefined information for selling products to customers, such as published list prices, customer-specific prices, and/or discount schemes. There are four types of sales trade agreements -- about the sales price, line discount, multi-line discount and total discount -- and further explanation focuses on the sales price aspects. The different types can be used in combination with each other, such as defining the sales price and a discount.

Sales Price Trade Agreement Sales price trade agreements provide the primary approach for defining a named price list for different groups of customers. Synonyms of a price list include a price book. A key construct -- termed the Price Group -- typically represents a named price list, such as a named price list for those customers representing Direct Sales or Distributors. Price groups are user-defined, and you assign a price group to relevant customers so that it is automatically inherited by sales orders for the customers.

Price trade agreements are expressed as multiple entries that identify the price group, the applicable items and their prices, and the effectivity dates. Other factors may include a different sales price based on the item's sales UM or for a quantity breakpoint on a sales order line. These factors affecting sales price trade agreement entries are summarized in Figure 11.5 and described below.[9] The following description focuses on the column labeled Sales Prices and the use of the Price Group to represent a named price list.

---

[9] A set of companywide policies (embedded in the *Activate Price/Discount* form within A/R setup) determines whether the system recognizes these factors.

Figure 11.5 Sales Trade Agreements

Factor		Sales Price	Types of Discounts		
			Line Discount	Multi-line Discount	Total Discount
Item	Item and UM	X	X	N/A	See item policy about including item value
	Group of Items	N/A	X Line Discount Group	X Multi-line Discount Group	N/A
	All Items		X	X	
Sold-To Customer	Customer	X	X	X	X
	Group of Customers	X Price Group	X Line Discount Group	X Multi-line Discount Group	X Total Discount Group
	All Customers	X	X	X	X
Other Factors	Validity Period	X	X	X	X
	Currency Code	X	X	X	X
	Order Quantity Breakpoints	X	X	X	Order Value Breakpoint
	Delivery Days Price Charge	X X	N/A	N/A	N/A
Policies		Price Group Policy: Price includes sales tax			Item Policy: Include item value for total discount purposes

(Warehouse-Specific Information / Companywide Information — N/A, N/A)

◆ Pricing for a named price list as identified by the Price Group field. The price group typically reflects a group of similar customers.

◆ Pricing for a specific customer. The sales pricing can be for a specific customer, but a Price Group is still typically used to identify the named price list

◆ Pricing with validity period, for supporting periodic price updates or seasonal price promotions. A companywide policy determines whether the sales price assignment reflects the order entry date on a sales order, or the requested ship date or receipt date for sales order lines.[10]

◆ Pricing by item and unit of measure, such as different prices per piece and per case.

◆ Pricing by currency type, such as separate pricing for foreign sales.

◆ Pricing with quantity breakpoints for the sales line quantity.

◆ Pricing based on delivery days. A higher price may apply for faster delivery, or the delivery lead time could vary by ship-from site/warehouse. However, the number of delivery days are normally defined as part of transport time between a warehouse and the customer's address, so that you normally the designate the "disregard lead time" policy as part of the entry.

◆ Pricing involves an additional charge, such as a charge for fast delivery, small order quantity or freight.

---

[10] You define this companywide policy as part of the A/R parameters about sales prices.

As noted earlier, price trade agreements are expressed as one or more entries that identify the applicable factors. A simple pricing scheme that represents this year's price list for Distributors, for example, would be expressed as one entry for each saleable item. Every entry would also identify the price group (representing the Distributor price list) and the effectivity dates. Additional entries would be required for each site/warehouse when using site- or warehouse-specific pricing. Figure 11.5 illustrates the site/warehouse factor as a third dimension, since pricing for an item can be companywide or site/warehouse-specific (as defined by policies within the Storage Dimension Group assigned to the item).

During order entry, the price group assigned to the sales order determines the applicable trade agreement entries. This price group represents the named price list, and is initially inherited from the sold-to customer but can be overridden. The system uses the trade agreement information to automatically assign an item's price using the lowest price of applicable trade agreement entries.[11] The system also assigns the charge associated with the price if applicable. You can view available prices during order entry, such as viewing quantity breakpoints or future pricing to guide customer decisions.

Types of Sales Discounts in Trade Agreements The types of sales discounts can be related to a single line item, multiple lines, the order total value, or a combination of these approaches.

♦ *Line Discount.* The line discount is expressed as a fixed amount or a percentage or both. In particular, the percentage discount can be expressed as a single value or as two values (e.g., using a 10% discount for both values results in a 19% discount). In the case where both a fixed amount and a percentage discount are applied, the system applies the discount percentage after reducing the price by the fixed discount amount. Line discounts often reflect one or more of the factors shown in Figure 11.5, and a line discount can be companywide or site/warehouse-specific.

♦ *Multi-Line Discount based on Total Quantity.* The multi-line discount reflects a discount based on total quantity for multiple line items. It is expressed the same way as a single line discount -- as a fixed amount or a percentage or both. The trade agreement entries can reflect the factors shown in Figure 11.5, such as a discount that applies to a group of customers or a group of items. Two different group codes (both termed the *Multi-line Discount Group*) can be predefined – one for items and one for customers –

---

[11] The logic for finding the lowest applicable price requires an additional policy for each trade agreement record – termed the *find next* checkbox – otherwise the search will stop at the first applicable record.

and then assigned to relevant items and customers. A multi-line discount only reflects companywide information, and can only be defined for a group of items or all items. You must initiate calculation of multiline discounts on a sales order after all line items have been entered.

The combination of a line discount and multi-line discount can be handled different ways, as defined by a companywide policy (embedded in the A/R Parameters). A typical approach views the two values as additive. An alternative approach views the two percentages as multiplicative, or indicates use of the lowest value or highest value, or indicates use of only one of the values.

◆ *Discount (or Surcharge) based on Total Order Value.* The total discount reflects a discount based on total order value. It is expressed the same way as a single line discount -- as a fixed amount or a percentage or both. Expressing the fixed amount as a negative value represents a surcharge based on total order value. The trade agreement entries can reflect the factors shown in Figure 11.5, such as a discount with order value breakpoints that apply to a group of customers. Note that a different group code – the *Total Discount Group* – can be assigned to relevant customers. An item-related policy determines whether the system includes or excludes the item in calculating total order value. You must initiate the calculation of the total discount on a sales order after all line items have been entered.[12]

Maintaining and Viewing Sales Trade Agreement Information

Information about sales trade agreements must be prepared beforehand and then used to update the database containing trade agreement information. Preparing data beforehand (using the Price/Discount Agreement Journal and its associated line items) offers several advantages in data maintenance. For example, you can create a new journal for preparing next year's sales price trade agreements, and then initially populate the entries with information about existing sales price agreements for selected items or customers. The information can then be manually maintained prior to posting the journal. In addition, you can perform mass changes to the entries (such as increasing the sales price a specified percentage or amount), or copy the entries in order to prepare price agreements for another item, customer, validity period or currency.

Use the Sales Prices report to view sales price trade agreement information, or a subset of information based on the report's selection criteria (such as the selected items, customers or currency). Use the Price/Discount List report to view all

---

[12] Alternatively, the total discount can be automatically calculated (based on a companywide policy embedded in the A/R parameters).

types of price and discount trade agreement information. Use the Price List report to view a comprehensive list of item sales prices, or the Customer Price List report to view the comprehensive list for each customer. Each report has selection criteria to view a subset of information.

Agreements about Supplementary Items   Some sales environments involve predefined agreements about supplementary items such as "buy one and get an additional item free" which result in additional line items on a sales order. Supplementary items can also represent related items that should be sold together, or opportunities for up-selling or cross-selling. The definition of supplementary items can be tied to a customer or item or both, so that information about the relevant supplementary items can be viewed during order entry. The definition of each supplementary item includes an item number and quantity which can be designated as mandatory or optional, and chargeable or free-of-charge. The rules may also include date effectivities, a minimum order quantity and/or a one-time-only offer.

11.7 Sales Agreements

Sales agreements define a commitment to sell products to a customer over a time period in exchange for special prices or discounts. Synonyms include a blanket sales order. The various types of a commitment include a total quantity for a specific product (with a specified sales price and/or discount percent), or a total value for a specific product, a category of products, or all products and categories (with a specified discount percent). After defining the sales agreement, you change its status from *on-hold* to *effective* in order to allow usage, such as creating sales orders linked to the sales agreement.

Types of Commitment for a Sales Agreement The type of commitment is defined in the header information for a sales agreement, which then affects the information for each line item, as summarized below.

◆ *Create a line item for a product quantity commitment.* You define the total commitment quantity and the sales price and/or discount percent for a specified item. An optional minimum or maximum release quantity may also be defined.

◆ *Create a line item for a product value commitment.* You define the total commitment value and discount percent for a specified item. An optional minimum or maximum release amount may also be defined.

◆ *Create a line item for a product category value commitment.* You define the total commitment value and discount percent for a specified category of items. Section 3.1 (and Figure 3.3) previously explained categories and a category hierarchy for sales purposes. An optional minimum or maximum release amount may also be defined.

◆ *Create a line item for a value commitment.* You define the total commitment value and discount percent that will be applicable to all items or categories sold to the customer. An optional minimum or maximum release amount may also be defined.

As part of the header information, you indicate whether the maximum should be enforced on related sales orders. Additional terms and conditions may also be specified -- such as the payment terms and mode of delivery -- which will be inherited by related sales orders.

Linkage between Sales Orders and a Sales Agreement Several different approaches are used to link a sales order to a sales agreement, as summarized below. As a result of these approaches, you can view the sales orders linked to a selected sales agreement or generate the equivalent report.

◆ *Release a sales order from a sales agreement.* You create the sales order by starting from a selected sales agreement, and specify the item and quantity for a sales order line item. The sales order header inherits the terms and conditions from the sales agreement, and a line item inherits the applicable sales price or discount percent from the sales agreement.

◆ *Manually create a sales order linked to a sales agreement.* You specify the identifier of the applicable sales agreement when manually creating a sales order. The sales order header inherits the terms and conditions from the sales agreement, and a line item inherits the applicable sales price or discount percent from the sales agreement.

You can also unlink a sales order currently linked to a sales agreement, which means the sales price or discount percent for the line item will no longer reflect the sales agreement.

11.8 Direct Delivery Orders

Some companies sell purchased items as a direct delivery order in addition to selling stocked products. One or more lines on a sales order can be designated as a direct delivery order, where each line requires creation of a corresponding purchase order (aka direct PO for short) for shipping to the customer address.

Hence, a direct delivery order requires close coordination of sales order and purchase order processing.

A purchased item primarily sold as a direct delivery order can be designated on the item master so that the sales order line inherits the designation. You can also specify the default warehouse that applies to direct delivery orders for the item; it typically reflects a non-WMS warehouse. The items never physically arrive at a warehouse, but a warehouse must still be defined for sales lines and purchase lines. A preferred vendor should also be assigned to items that will be directly delivered.

A typical process for direct delivery orders involves several steps for the sales order and the corresponding purchase order, as illustrated in Figure 11.6 and described below. Several steps can be performed from the Direct Delivery form, which acts as a workbench for coordinating both the sales order and purchase order involved in a direct delivery.

Figure 11.6 Typical Process for Direct Delivery Orders

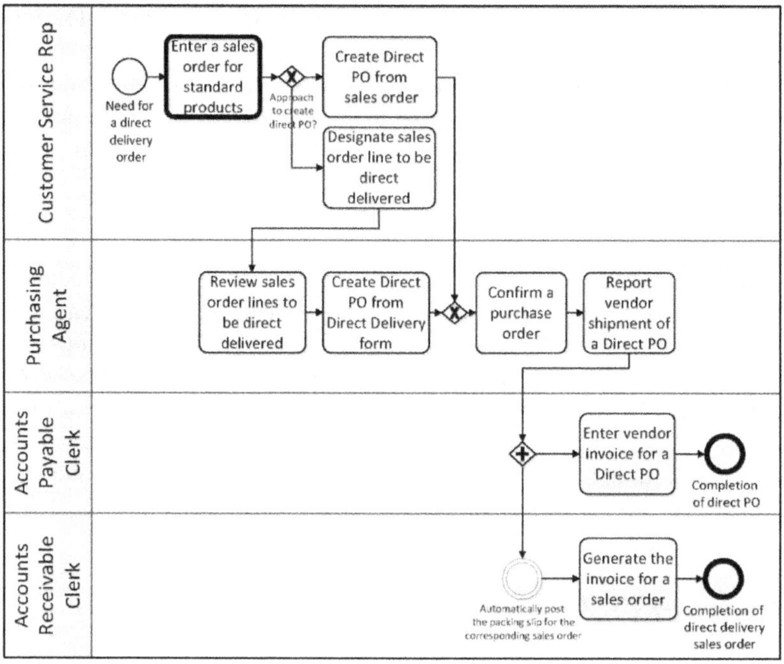

Overview   One or more lines on a sales order can be designated for direct delivery, which results in a corresponding direct purchase order (aka direct PO for short). There are two basic approaches for designating direct delivery for a sales order line. The first approach is typically performed by the customer service rep, where you create the direct PO from the sales order. In the second approach, the customer service rep manually designates a line item for direct delivery (or the designation can be inherited from the item), and the purchasing agent subsequently reviews these designated lines in order to create and confirm the corresponding purchase orders. The purchasing agent also reports vendor shipment of a direct PO, which automatically posts the packing slip for the corresponding sales order.

The accounts receivable clerk generates the invoice for direct delivery sales orders, and the accounts payable clerk enters the vendor's invoice for a Direct PO.

Enter a sales order for standard products (requiring direct delivery)
The customer service rep initially creates a sales order for a specified customer and enters sales order line items. Each line item identifies a product, quantity, sales price, ship-from location and the requested dates for shipment and delivery. These dates can be automatically assigned based on the delivery date control option for the sales line. For a direct delivery, the option typically reflects the item's quoted lead time, or CTP logic that will consider the item's purchasing lead time. Each line item can also identify the customer address which will be inherited by a corresponding Direct PO. When information has been completely entered, the customer service rep generates a sales order confirmation and sends it to the customer.

The customer service rep can immediately create a corresponding purchase order for a direct delivery line item, or it can be subsequently created by the purchasing agent for sales lines that have been designated for direct delivery.

Create Direct PO from sales order After completing the sales order information, the customer service rep accesses a separate form (labeled Create Direct Delivery) to indicate which sales lines should create a corresponding Direct PO. The selected lines inherit the sales order quantity and the item's preferred vendor and purchase price, and these values can be overridden. You can optionally indicate that the quantity on the corresponding purchase order should reflect the item's order quantity modifiers for a minimum, multiple and maximum related to purchases. Indicating completion will automatically create the corresponding Direct PO, and the PO number will be identified as reference information for the sales line. A Direct PO may contain multiple line items sourced from the same vendor. As a result of the linkage between orders, any changes to the dates or addresses in one order can automatically update the corresponding order.

Designate a sales order line to be direct delivered The customer service rep can manually designate a line item for direct delivery or the designation can be inherited from the item. A related direct delivery status for the sales line indicates "to be direct delivered."[13] This approach allows a purchasing agent to review sales lines with "to be direct delivered" status using a separate form (the Direct Delivery form), and create the corresponding Direct PO.

Review sales order lines to be direct delivered Using the Direct Delivery form, the purchasing agent reviews the sales order lines to be direct delivered.

Create Direct PO from Direct Delivery form Using the Direct Delivery form, the purchasing agent creates direct delivery purchase orders for selected sales order lines that have been designated for direct delivery. As a result of the linkage between orders, any changes to the dates or addresses in one order can automatically update the corresponding order.

Report vendor shipment of a Direct PO The purchasing agent reports the vendor's shipment of a Direct PO, which automatically posts the packing slip for the corresponding sales order. The vendor's shipment is actually recorded as a product receipt for the purchase order. The product receipt can be reported two different ways, using either a simple inventory transaction or the Direct Delivery form.

◆ *Use Direct Delivery form.* You can report a full or partial receipt of the item using the Direct Delivery form, but only when the item does not require a batch or serial number. The product receipt number will be automatically assigned based on a number sequence.

◆ *Use a simple inventory transaction.* You can register the item when posting the product receipt for a purchase order, and also specify the vendor's packing list as the product receipt number.

Automatically post the packing slip for the corresponding sales order As a result of reporting the vendor's shipment of a Direct PO, the packing slip for the corresponding sales order will be automatically posted. In some scenarios, the vendor's invoice will be reported without reporting the vendor's shipment beforehand, and this also results in automatic posting of the packing slip for the corresponding sales order.

---

[13] The values for the direct delivery status include *to be direct delivered, purchase order created, purchase order released* (after it has been confirmed) and *purchase order shipped* (after reporting the product receipt).

Generate the invoice for a direct delivery sales order The accounts receivable clerk periodically generates invoices that reflect the automatic posting of packing slips for direct delivery sales orders.

Enter vendor invoice for a direct delivery purchase order The accounts payable clerk records the vendor's invoice against a purchase order, and typically populates the invoice lines based on the vendor's shipments that have been recorded.

Additional Steps in the Basic Model The basic model of a direct delivery order often includes additional steps not shown in Figure 11.6 so that the diagram does not become too complex. These steps include changes to dates, cancelling a Direct PO, and deleting a sales order line with a Direct PO.

♦ *Changes to Dates.* When you change the requested receipt date on a sales order line, it automatically changes the delivery date on the corresponding purchase order line. In a similar fashion, changing the confirmed date on the purchase order line will automatically change the confirmed ship date and delivery date on the corresponding sales order line.

♦ *Cancel a Direct PO for a selected sales line.* The customer service rep can cancel a Direct PO by starting from the sales order line item, but only prior to reporting vendor shipments for the purchase order. This step deletes the Direct PO and removes the direct delivery designation on the sales line.

♦ *Delete a sales line with a Direct PO.* The customer service rep can delete a sales line with a Direct PO, but only prior to reporting vendor shipments for the purchase order. A warning message is displayed about the corresponding purchase order. This step deletes the Direct PO and the sales order line.

11.9 Special Orders

Some companies sell purchased items as a special order in addition to selling stocked products. The material for a special order must be received and then shipped to the customer. One or more lines on a sales order can be designated as a special order, where each line requires creation of a corresponding purchase order (aka Special PO for short). Alternatively, you can start from an existing purchase order and then create linkage by selecting the applicable sales order. In either case, a special order requires coordination of sales order and purchase order processing, especially in warehouse activities to receive and immediately ship the material. This coordination of warehouse activities is commonly termed cross-docking.

With current AX capabilities, you typically place the received material in a bin location that represents the need for cross-docking; the bin location is often labeled "Cross-Dock." The suggested placement in the "Cross-Dock" bin location can be identified on the sales order line -- by specifying the bin location and/or an equivalent value for Inventory Status -- so that the information will be inherited by the corresponding Special PO and communicated to receiving clerks.

A typical process for special orders involves several steps and roles for the sales order and the corresponding purchase order, as illustrated in Figure 11.7 and described below.

Figure 11.7 Typical Process for Special Orders

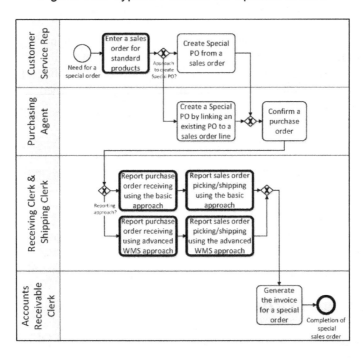

Overview   One or more lines on a sales order can be designated as a special order, where each line requires creation of a corresponding purchase order (aka Special PO for short).   Alternatively, you can start from an existing purchase order and then create linkage by selecting the applicable sales order.   In either case, the receiving and shipping processes differ when using the basic versus advanced approaches to warehouse management.

Enter a sales order for standard products (requiring a special order)

The customer service rep initially creates a sales order for a specified customer, and also enters sales order line items. Each line item identifies a product, quantity, sales price, ship-from location and the requested dates for shipment and delivery. In order to communicate the need for cross-docking, the suggested placement in a "Cross-Dock" bin location can be identified on the sales order line by specifying the bin location and/or an equivalent value for Inventory Status -- so that the information will be inherited by the corresponding Special PO and communicated to receiving clerks.

The customer service rep can immediately create a corresponding special PO, or the purchasing agent can subsequently link an existing purchase order to the sales order line.

Create Special PO from sales order After completing the sales order information, the customer service rep accesses a separate form (labeled Create Purchase Order) to indicate which sales lines should create a corresponding Special PO. The selected lines inherit the sales order quantity and the item's preferred vendor and purchase price, and these values can be overridden. You can optionally indicate that the quantity on the corresponding purchase order should reflect the item's order quantity modifiers for a minimum, multiple and maximum related to purchases. Indicating completion will automatically create the corresponding Special PO, and the PO number will be identified as reference information for the sales line. A Special PO may contain multiple line items sourced from the same vendor. As a result of the linkage between orders, any changes to the dates or quantities in one order can automatically update the corresponding order.

Create a Special PO by linking an existing PO to a sales order line

The purchasing agent can start from an existing purchase order for the item, and then select the applicable sales order line for creating a special order.

Confirm a Purchase Order The purchasing agent confirms a purchase order when information has been completely entered and confirmed with the vendor. The confirmation enables subsequent steps in purchase order processing such as reporting receipts. The purchase order must be confirmed again after updating information. Each confirmation creates a history record so that the purchasing agent can track historical versions.

Report Purchase Order Receiving using the Basic Approach to Warehouse Management The receiving clerk typically uses the Arrival Overview form to review and select open purchase order line items that require receiving, and then generate an arrival journal containing the selected lines.

Alternatively, the receiving clerk can manually create an arrival journal, typically to handle an unplanned receipt. The arrival journal indicates the need for cross-docking of a Special PO based on the specified "Cross-Dock" bin location and/or an equivalent value for Inventory Status, so that the received material can be placed in the correct location. The receiving clerk registers the actual receipts against each journal line item and then posts the journal to update inventory balances.

Report Purchase Order Receiving using the Advanced WMS Approach to Warehouse Management The receiving clerk typically uses the mobile device to register the purchase order arrival of a Special PO and putaway into the "Cross-Dock" bin location, as defined by a location directive for purchase order putaway.

Report Sales Order Picking/Shipping using the Basic Approach to Warehouse Management The shipping clerk typically uses the Release Sales Order Picking form to review and select open sales order lines that require picking/shipping, and then generate the picking lists for selected orders. The filter criteria may include a bin location of "Cross-Dock" and/or an equivalent value for Inventory Status in order to identify line items that involve cross-docking. The warehouse worker reports actual picking against a sales order picking list, and the shipping clerk reports actual shipment by posting the sales order packing slip for picked items.

Report Sales Order Picking/Shipping using the Advanced WMS Approach to Warehouse Management The shipping clerk typically uses the Release to Warehouse form to review and select open sales order lines that require picking/shipping, and then releases selected orders to the warehouse (which updates the release status for each order). The filter criteria may include a bin location of "Cross-Dock" and/or an equivalent value for Inventory Status in order to identify line items that involve cross-docking. With an order-based picking approach, the release-to-warehouse step can automatically create a shipment and load (with a waved status) and a shipment wave (with a released status) for each sales order. In addition, the released shipment wave automatically creates a picking work order consisting of work lines that identify the pick and put instructions.

The warehouse worker uses the mobile device to report completion of picking work orders with delivery to an outbound dock, which results in a *ready to ship* status for the related shipment and load. The shipping clerk reports actual shipment by confirming the outbound shipments and posting the sales order packing slips for picked items.

11.10 Customer Returns and RMAs

Customer returns generally require an authorization, termed a returned material authorization (RMA) number. In a simple situation, for example, the customer wants to return a defective product and obtain a credit. The company creates an RMA and provides the RMA number to the customer, who returns the item. The company subsequently records receipt of the returned item and creates a credit note for the customer. RMA situations can become more complex with variations in handling a returned item, its replacement, and the related financial transactions. Each variation involves different steps and considerations.

RMA processing builds on sales order functionality. Each RMA has an associated sales order (termed the *return order*) for handling returns, and an optional second sales order (termed the *replacement order*) for handling replacements. Both sales orders have the same order number (but a different order type) with linkage to the originating RMA number.

◆ *Return Order.* Every RMA has an associated sales order (with a sales order type of return order) to only handle the arrival, receipt and credit note for the returned item. Creation of an RMA automatically creates the associated return order, which represents a mirror image of the RMA. Changes to the RMA information automatically change information on the return order; you cannot directly maintain data on the returned order.

◆ *Replacement Order.* An RMA can have a second associated sales order when a replacement must be shipped to the customer. This replacement order can be created from the RMA to support immediate shipment, or created after a reporting arrival of an RMA line item (with a disposition code indicating replacement). This replacement order has all the functionality previously described for sales orders.

A simple-yet-typical process for a customer return is illustrated in Figure 11.8 and described below.

Create an RMA for a customer return The customer service rep initially creates a return order for a specified customer, which results in a return order header identified by a sales order number and a system-assigned RMA number. The return order provides the means to handle actual customer returns and credit notes. As part of the dialogue for creating the return order, the customer service rep can specify the return reason code, the return deadline, and the return-to location.

Figure 11.8 Typical Process for a Customer Return (RMA)

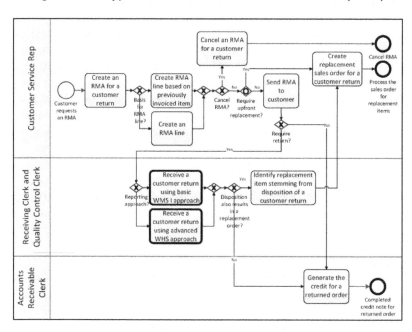

Create an RMA line based on previously invoiced item The customer service rep creates an RMA line by finding a previously invoiced sales order for the bill-to customer, and selecting the line item(s) and quantity being returned. The search can be based on the item number or sales order number. Each selected line item creates a line item on the return order, along with the original cost and the sales price (which acts as the credit amount). For each RMA line, the customer service rep can optionally specify a return reason code and unlimited text, such as a description of damaged goods. The customer service rep can also assign a disposition code indicating that the material does not require actual return.

Create an RMA line for a customer return The customer service rep creates an RMA line item by specifying the item number, quantity, cost and credit amount. The cost defaults to the item's inventory cost, and the credit amount defaults to the item's current sales price. The credit amount may be adjusted to reflect partial credit.

Send RMA to customer After completing the RMA information, the customer service rep can optionally print a return order and send it to the customer.

Create replacement sales order for a customer return (RMA) When the customer requires upfront replacement, the customer service rep creates a separate replacement order identified by a sales order number (with a reference to the RMA number). Only one replacement order is created for a return order. The line items on the replacement order initially reflect the RMA information, and further processing of the replacement order is just like a sales order. For example, the customer service rep can maintain information or add lines to the replacement order. The replacement order can also be created (or added to) after reporting the disposition of a returned item, and identifying the desired replacement item(s).

Cancel an RMA for a customer return The customer service rep can cancel a return order at any time prior to receipt of returned items or invoicing. A cancelled returned order does not affect the related replacement order (if applicable), so that the replacement order may require deletion.

Receive a returned order using the basic approach to warehouse management The receiving clerk typically uses the Arrival Overview form to review and select open return order lines that require receiving, and then generate an arrival journal containing the selected lines. The receiving clerk registers the actual receipts against each journal line item and then posts the journal to update inventory balances. A return acknowledgement can be optionally sent to the customer. When receiving has been completed, the receiving clerk posts the packing slip for the return order in order to update financial information.

As part of the arrival journal information, the receiving clerk can report the disposition code assigned to the returned material. The disposition code indicates whether the material is placed in inventory or scrapped. It can also indicate whether a replacement should be sent, and an additional step can identify the desired replacement item in order to create (or add to) the related replacement order. A subsequent chapter about quality management provides further explanation of RMS disposition codes (Section 17.5).

Receive a returned order using the advanced approach to warehouse management The receiving clerk uses the mobile device to register arrival of a customer return into a receiving location, and indicate the disposition code. The disposition code indicates whether the material is placed in inventory or scrapped. It can also indicate whether a replacement should be sent, and an additional step can identify the desired replacement item in order to create (or add to) the related replacement order. A subsequent chapter about quality management provides further explanation of RMS disposition codes, and the use of combined disposition codes (Section 17.5). A combined disposition code is mapped to a combination of an RMA disposition code and a value for Inventory Status.

When the disposition code indicates placement in inventory, the registered arrival automatically creates a work order for putaway, and the warehouse worker uses the mobile device to report putaway from the receiving location to a stocking location. Alternatively, the receiving clerk registers the arrival and disposition code, and also reports putaway as part of a single mobile device transaction. In either case, the receiving clerk subsequently posts the product receipt for the return order.

Identify replacement item stemming from disposition of a customer return After reporting the disposition of a returned item that involves "replace," you can identify the desired replacement item in order to create (or add to) the replacement order.

Create a return to vendor for the returned material When the customer return reflects a purchased item, you can create a return to vendor as part of RMA processing. A purchasing agent can subsequently enter the vendor's RMA number and confirm the purchase order. The figure does not include this step.

Generate the credit for a returned order The accounts receivable clerk generates a credit note for the customer return, where the RMA may not require actual return of the material. The credit note reflects the credit amount specified on the return order.

11.11 Sales Orders for Configurable Items

A configurable item provides the starting point for configuring a custom product, typically in the context of a line item on a sales order or sales quotation. Dynamics AX provides two different configuration technologies to support configurable items, as described in a subsequent chapter (Section 19.1). With each approach, the configuration process results in a configuration id, and the combination of item number and configuration id provides a unique identifier.

The configuration process varies based on the configuration technology. With the constraint-based configuration technology, for example, the process reflects a product configuration model assigned to the configurable item. The item may have multiple models reflecting different versions with different validity dates, so that the order date determines the relevant version. The configuration process results in creation of a configuration id and its associated BOM and route versions. The configuration process can also calculate a sales price and delivery date, which can automatically populate the information on the sales line. A subsequent chapter describes a typical process for entering a sales order using the constraint-based configuration technology (Section 19.5).

11.12 Sales Quotations

A key step in many scenarios involves a sales quotation for the prospect or customer, where the sales quote can be converted into a sales order or identified as lost or cancelled. There are different variations of using sales quotations. As a foundation, the explanation starts with the structure and life cycle of a sales quotation, and a typical business process. The variations include the use of price simulations, the relationship between multiple quotations, and the consideration of demands by master scheduling logic.

Structure and Life Cycle of a Sales Quotation   The basic structure consists of a header and line item information. The header identifies the prospect or customer, and each line item identifies an item, quantity, price and other information. The life cycle of a sales quotation consists of three basic steps (create, send, and disposition), with three possible dispositions (confirmed, lost or cancelled), that are represented by five statuses.

◆ *Created.* The quotation has been created. It can be sent to or confirmed with the business relation contact.

◆ *Sent.* The quotation has been sent to the business account (via the *Send Quotation* update). The specified business relation cannot be changed. The quotation can be updated to a disposition of confirmed, lost or cancelled.

◆ *Confirmed.* The quotation has been converted into a sales order (via the *Confirmation* update), and all quote line items are converted into line items on the new sales order. The system identifies the link between the quotation and sales order.

◆ *Lost.* The quotation has been identified as lost (via the *Quotation Lost* update).

◆ *Cancelled.* The quotation has been identified as cancelled (via the *Quotation Cancelled* update).

Typical Process for a Sales Quotation   A typical process for a sales quotation consists of multiple steps performed by a customer service rep, as illustrated in Figure 11.9 and summarized below. Several steps involve more detailed explanations that are covered in subsequent subsections.

Figure 11.9 Typical Process for a Sales Quotation

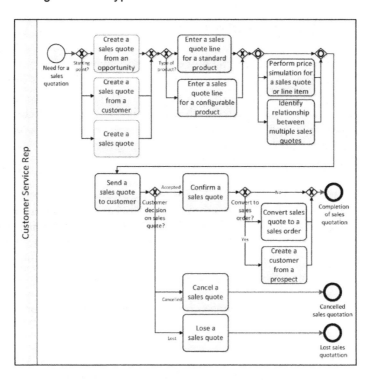

As a starting point, the rep often creates the sales quote from an opportunity. It can also be created directly or from a selected customer, with an optional prompt to automatically create an associated opportunity.[14] Each quote line for a standard product identifies a quantity, sales price, ship-from location and the requested dates for shipment and delivery. The sales price (and discount) can be automatically inherited from sales trade agreements. A quote line for a configurable product requires additional steps for using a product configurator to define a new configuration ID and calculate a suggested sales price.

The customer service rep can perform price simulations as part of the process, and (if needed) identify the relationship between multiple related quotes. When information has been completely entered, the customer service rep sends the sales quote to the customer. The sales quote can be revised and resent, and the

---

[14] An opportunity can be automatically created for a sale quotation based on a companywide policy (on the Sales and Marketing Parameters form).

different versions of sent quotations are tracked. Based on the customer decision, the customer service rep indicates whether the sales quote has been accepted, cancelled or lost. An accepted sales quote can then be converted to a sales order, and (if needed) a customer can be created from a prospect.

Perform price simulations for a sales quote or line item The customer service rep can optionally perform price simulations for a sales quote in order to support price negotiations while still retaining visibility of the desired margins and contribution ratio. For example, the impact of a discount percentage, a discount amount, or a specified price can be evaluated. A price simulation can be performed for individual line items or for the entire quotation, and then saved as a scenario with a user-defined description. Multiple scenarios can be saved, and you can optionally apply a saved scenario to the quotation.

◆ *Perform Price Simulation for a Sales Quote Line Item.* The customer service rep can enter a discount percent, a discount amount, and/or a specified price, and the price simulation displays the impact on margin and contribution ratio. Alternatively, you can enter a specified margin (or contribution ratio) and the price simulation displays the impact on price. Applying a saved scenario updates the price, discount percent and amount on the quotation line item.

◆ *Perform Price Simulation for an Entire Sales Quote.* The customer service rep can enter a discount percent, and the price simulation displays the impact on margin and contribution ratio. Alternatively, you can enter a margin (or contribution ratio) to view the impact on discount percentage. Applying a saved scenario updates the discount percent in the quotation header.

Identify Relationship between Multiple Sales Quotes The customer service rep may employ multiple sales quotes in certain situations, such as quotes for different quantity breakpoints. Other examples would be quotes for multiple phases or for different groups of items such as basic versus optional. You establish the relationship by starting with a parent quotation, and then assigning the child quotation(s) using the Alternative Quotations function. The same function displays alternative quotations that have already been defined.

Confirm a sales quote The customer service rep confirms the sales quote, thereby indicating that it has been accepted by the customer/prospect. A win/loss reason code can be entered. After confirming a sales quote, the customer service rep can convert it to a sales order. All quote line items are converted into line items on the new sales order, and the system identifies the linkage between the sales quote and sales order. If the sales quote applies to a prospect, the customer service rep must first create the customer from a prospect and then enter additional information about the customer.

Alternatively, the customer service rep can indicate a sales quote was cancelled or lost, and identify a win/loss reason code.

Sales Quotation Follow-up Date and Expiration Date   Each sales quotation has a follow-up date and an expiration date.   The dates provide reference information and the basis for selectively viewing sales quotations.

Mass Creation of Sales Quotations using a Template Certain situations may require the mass creation of sales quotations, such as providing the same quote to several different contacts or customers. An initial quote must be created and then designated as an active template (with a user-defined template name). The periodic task for *Mass Create Quotations* can then be used with the specified template and a user-defined selection of business relations. The system creates a sales quotation for each business relation.

Deleting Sales Quotations Quotations are not automatically deleted by the system since win/loss analysis requires historical data. Periodic deletion of quotations should reflect the desired data retention policies. Use the Delete Quotations task to select quotations to be deleted based on criteria such as the status, creation date, and/or expiration date.

Master Scheduling Logic and the Sales Quotation Win Probability A win probability associated with an opportunity applies to its related sales quotations and line items. Master scheduling logic can optionally include demands stemming from sales quotation line items with a win probability greater than a specified percentage. Sales quotations do not consume a demand forecast.

11.13 Commissions for Sales Orders

Sales commissions often involve a complex business process in many companies. The many variations in sales rep assignments and commission plans contribute to this complexity. This section provides an overview of the sales commission capabilities within AX.

A commission sales group (or sales group for short) identifies one or more sales reps. The sales group assigned to a customer acts as a default for a sales order, which then acts as a default for line items. The sales group represents a primary factor in calculating commission amounts for the sales order, along with the customer and products being sold. The calculated commission amount reflects a specified commission percentage times the sales order value (such as the gross revenue or net margin). Figure 11.10 illustrates these factors affecting commission calculations along with two scenarios. The first scenario can be defined by a single entry in the commission setup. It represents a single rep obtaining a 10% commission on all product sales to a given customer based on gross revenue value and this year's commission plan. An additional entry could define next year's commission plan. The second scenario represents a 10% commission split between two sales reps based on the type of product and customer. Multiple entries in the commission setup would be needed to define the various combinations of item groups and customer groups.

Figure 11.10 Examples of Sales Commission Calculations

			Scenario #1	Scenario #2
			Single rep obtains 10% commission for all sales to customer	Split commission of 10% based on type of product and customer
Factor	Item	Item		
		Group of Items (Commission Item Group)		X
		All Items	X	
	Sold-To Customer	Customer	X	
		Group of Customers (Commission Customer Group)		X
		All Customers		
	Sales Group*	Sales Group With One Rep	100% for Rep #1	
		Sales Group With Multiple Reps		60% for Rep #1 40% for Rep #2
Commission Percentage			10%	10%
Commission Rules		Value basis: Revenue vs Margin	Revenue	Revenue
		Value basis: Net vs Gross	Gross	Gross
		Date Effectivity	Current year's Commission plan	Current year's Commission plan
		Applicability Search	One Entry	Multiple Entries

* = The sales group indicates the applicable sales reps and split commission information.

Commission calculations are normally based on the most specific entry related to a commission percentage, such as an entry for a specific item and customer rather than groups. With searching enabled, the system uses all of the applicable entries (when multiple entries exist) for calculating commissions. Commissions are calculated (with associated G/L entries) after posting a sales order invoice.

11.14 Customer Information

A subset of customer information directly relates to sales order processing. Each customer is defined in a customer master file by a unique identifier. Sold-to and bill-to customers require unique identifiers.[15] The following data elements have particular significance to sales order processing.

Preferred Ship-From Site/Warehouse   Each sold-to customer can have a preferred ship-from site/warehouse which acts as the default value in sales order header information.   The preferred ship-from location typically reflects the nearest location.

Ship-to Addresses   A sold-to customer can have one or more addresses for delivery purposes, and a delivery address can be assigned to each sales order line item. When defining additional addresses, you can designate one as the default delivery address and others as alternates. During sales order entry, the system displays the default delivery address but you can select (transfer) an alternate to the order or create an order-specific delivery address. You can optionally designate (move) the order-specific delivery address as customer master information.

Bill-To Customer and Invoicing Considerations   Each customer can optionally have a designated bill-to customer (termed the *invoice account customer*) that acts as a default on sales orders. The system supports a customer-specific numbering sequence for invoices. An invoice can be generated for each sales order or for multiple orders (e.g., with the same bill-to customer and currency) as a summary invoice.

Attributes Related to Pricing and Discounts   The sold-to customer determines applicable pricing and discounts for a sales order. Sales prices in trade agreements can be based on the price group assigned to the sold-to customer. Discounts in trade agreements can be based on three other groups assigned to the sold-to customer -- the line discount group, the multi-line discount group, and the total discount group. A previous section described sales trade agreements (Section 11.6).

---

[15] The concepts of a sold-to and bill-to customer represent a basic viewpoint representative of many situations. The sold-to customer determines the applicable sales trade agreements, whereas the bill-to customer determines the applicable credit management policies. Each sold-to customer can have multiple delivery address (ship-to) locations which determine the applicable sales taxes. More complex situations often require additional information, such as the corporate entity associated with various sold-to customers, or the end-user associated with a delivery address.

Attributes Related to G/L Account Number Assignment General ledger account number assignments (such as revenue and cost of sales) can be based on a combination of customer and item characteristics. For example, the revenue account can reflect sales based on customer group and item group.

Financial Dimensions for a Customer The financial dimension(s) assigned to a customer provide a means to analyze sales by customer type. It can be used in conjunction with financial dimensions assigned to other entities -- such as items, sales campaigns and sales persons -- to provide multi-dimensional sales analyses.

One-Time Customers and Creating Customers during Order Entry When initially entering a sales order, the sold-to customer can be created on the fly by indicating a one-time customer. You enters the customer name and address information as part of creating the sales order, and the system automatically creates a new customer that is flagged as a one-time customer. Additional information defaults from an existing customer designated as the source of one-time customer information. The customer information can then be manually maintained, including the removal of the one-time customer flag.

Customer Hold Status A customer hold status (termed the *Invoicing and Delivery On Hold* policy) can prevent all transactions from being recorded, or just prevent shipments and invoicing to the customer.

Language for a Customer The language assigned to each customer determines which language version should be displayed on printed documents and other customer interactions. For example, the assigned language determines the language version for an item description on a printed packing slip or invoice.

Intercompany Trading Partner Some enterprises have multiple companies defined within a single Dynamics AX instance, and trading between the companies. A sister company can act as a vendor (or customer) for intercompany trading purposes. A vendor (or customer) must be defined that represents the sister company. A subsequent chapter explains a multicompany supply chain (Chapter 18).

Customer Calendar of Work Days Assigning a calendar to a customer and related delivery addresses enables delivery dates to reflect the available hours of operation (when using the delivery date control capabilities). The delivery dates are based on the companywide calendar when a customer calendar is not specified.

Credit Management Policies The bill-to customer can have no requirement for a credit check, or a mandatory credit limit check with an associated credit limit amount. A companywide policy (embedded in the A/R Parameters) defines the basis for credit limit comparisons, such as the customer's current balance, shipments not yet invoiced, and open sales orders. You can check credit limit information during order entry, and the system prevents further transactions such as confirmations and shipments when the credit limit has been exceeded. A periodic task must be performed to enforce a credit limit consistency check on open orders when you change the basis for credit limit comparisons.

Summarized Information Summarized information about a customer can viewed, and transaction detail can be viewed by type of sales document such as outstanding quotes, sales orders, and return orders.

11.15 Sales Analysis

Requirements for sales analysis information vary significantly between firms and decision makers within a firm. Dynamics AX includes a number of standard sales analysis inquiries and reports, as illustrated below. Each company tends to develop customized reports to meet their unique requirements.

Sales Analysis for Individual Sales Quotations and Orders The summarized data for a sales order or quote include calculated totals for revenue, cost, margin and contribution ratio.

Sales Analysis for Individual Customers The Customer Turnover report displays the total value of sales orders or invoices by customer. The Top Customers report displays total revenue, margin and quantity for each customer, with optional sequencing based on any of the three totals. A pivot table inquiry provides multi-dimensional sales analysis, such as sales by item group and customer group.

Data Warehouse and Sales Analysis Sales analysis often requires summarized data for large volumes of detailed transaction data. This data summarization requires periodic data extractions into a data warehouse. Dynamics AX includes an installation wizard and population tools to support out-of-the-box data warehouse functionality with minimal technical expertise and implementation effort. The cubes within the data warehouse reflect several business areas, including customers, sales, inventory, vendors, purchasing and general ledger information. They also reflect the financial dimensions employed within Dynamics AX. A number of predefined reports are based on an analysis of best practices, and end-users can easily develop ad hoc customized reports -- presented as graphs, maps, charts and objects.

11.16 Performance Metrics related to Sales Orders

Sales analysis can provide many of the performance metrics related to sales orders. Additional performance metrics include on time delivery and full quantity delivery, typically measured over a specified time interval. Each performance metric reflects several underlying assumptions, as described below.

◆ *On Time Delivery.* On-time delivery for a sales line reflects a comparison between the actual and promised ship date. The basis of the promised date can be the requested or confirmed date for the sales line, and either option should reflect consistent assignment of the promised date. In addition, achievement of on-time delivery typically reflects an exact match between dates or early delivery, so that only late shipments indicate a performance problem.

◆ *Full Quantity Delivery.* Full quantity delivery for a sales line reflects a comparison between the ordered quantity and the actual shipped quantity. The achievement of full delivery typically requires an exact match between quantities, so that quantity differences indicate a performance problem. Some would argue that delivery tolerances for over- and under-shipment quantities on a sales line (expressed as a percentage) should be considered in the performance metric.

You can identify these two performance metrics and their underlying assumptions using a standard report (labeled Top Sales Order Lines Not Shipped in Full or Not Shipped on Time, within Inventory Management), where the report dialogue also specifies the applicable time interval and warehouses(s). The standard report does not account for delivery tolerances.

A standard inquiry provides a similar performance metric for on-time delivery (labeled Deviations Between Actual and Expected Shipments, within Sales and Marketing). The displayed information identifies sales lines with late shipments, and reflects a selected basis for the promised ship date and time interval (expressed as a number of look-back days).

11.17 Workspaces related to Sales Orders

Several predefined workspaces are related to sales orders, as described in the following summary of each workspace and its applicable functionality.

Sales Order Processing & Inquiry Workspace This workspace summarizes several aspects of information about sales orders, and provides information for answering sales price inquiries. It identifies unconfirmed sales orders, orders on hold, delayed order lines, and partially shipped orders. You can create a new sales order, sales quotation or a return order, and create a new customer. For price inquiries, you can find the best sales price for a product (for a specified customer, date and quantity) and the associated discount if applicable. The links provide access to related information such as order events.

Sales Return Processing Workspace This workspace summarizes several aspects of information about return orders. It identifies expired orders and those that will expire within a week. It identifies the returns that have been registered as arrived. It also identifies open replacement orders. The links provide access to related setup information such as RMA disposition codes and return reason codes.

Master Planning Workspace This workspace identifies the sales order lines with a calculated delay so that you can respond appropriately, such as notifying the customer of the delayed delivery date or expediting the supply.

Prices and Discounts Workspace This workspace focuses on sales prices and discounts for retail purposes. However, it does cover the use of sales trade agreements and identifies those expiring within the next seven days.

11.18 Additional Case Studies

Case 11.1: Analyze Delivery Alternatives for a Sales Order Line The customer service reps at a manufacturing/distribution company frequently encountered situations where the customer's requested delivery date could not be met. They needed to quickly assess product availability at different ship-from warehouses, for different product variants (if applicable), and for different modes of delivery in order to identify the options with the earliest delivery dates. They accessed the Delivery Alternatives information to support these order promising tasks. This approach allowed them to review the available options and select one as the basis for updating the promised ship date and delivery date on the sales line. In some cases, they opted to ship a smaller quantity than ordered (based on availability) and ship the remainder at a later date, which resulted in a delivery schedule for the sales line.

Case 11.2: Sales Prices based on Total Order Weight A manufacturer employed the standard AX functionality for sales price trade agreements as the foundation for supporting their price lists based on total order weight. Each item had a lower sales price when total order weight exceeded a breakpoint. For example, the Distributor price list had two different prices for an item based on the weight brackets of less than and greater than 10,000 pounds. Within AX, this involved two different price groups labeled "Distributor-LT10k" and "Distributor-GT10k." Each trade agreement record identified the price group, item number and sales price, so that a given item had two trade agreement records reflecting the different sales prices for the two brackets. During order entry, the customer service rep (CSR) might initially specify the price group corresponding to the lower weight bracket as the basis for assigning sales prices. In those cases where total order weight exceeded 10,000 pounds, the CSR changed the Price Group in order to automatically re-price the sales order line items for the higher weight bracket.

Case 11.3: Commission Calculations A manufacturing company defined the commission plans (termed a commission sales group) for each sales rep, and tracked commissions based on sales order invoices. The commission plan identified the sales rep, the applicable items and customers, the effectivity dates, and the basis for commission calculations such as net versus gross and revenue versus margin. The commission plan could also define split commissions when there are multiple sales reps, brokers or managers involved in the sale. Commissions were calculated (with associated G/L entries) after posting a sales order invoice.[16]

Case 11.4: Sales Quotations A manufacturing company typically created and sent a sales quotation to customers and prospects (aka business relations) when initially conducting business with them. Each line item minimally specified an item, quantity, ship date, price, ship-from site/warehouse, and a win probability. The pipeline of sales quotations with a high win probability (above 90%) was used by planning calculations to drive supply chain activities. When the quote was accepted by the customer, it was converted to a sales order, which sometimes required prior conversion of the prospect information to a customer master record. When not accepted, the sales quotation was identified as lost or cancelled along with a reason code. Each sales quotation had a follow-up date and an expiration date to support these follow-up activities.

Sales quotations often involved negotiated prices. In these situations, the sales person employed price simulations (for individual lines or all lines) to evaluate the impact of a specified price, a discount percentage or a discount amount on the desired margins and contribution ratio. A price simulation could be saved with a user-defined description, and multiple scenarios could be saved, so that the sales person could optionally apply a saved scenario to the quotation.

---

[16] The variations in commission calculations often require customizations or an add-on module, such as the add-on functionality from www.RedMaple.com.

Case 11.5: EDI for Sales Order Processing A supplier to retail chains needed to communicate details of their product lines, and process the subsequent sales orders for fulfillment from various locations around the world. The price/sales catalogs were produced as EDI 832 documents and used to update a customer-accessible global product catalog. Customers could place sales orders for delivery to a single store, multiple stores, or a regional distribution center, and the product could be marked with the customer's retail information including pricing. The fulfillment locations were based on the ship-to locations and product availability. An add-on module provided integration and crucial business process mapping for each type of business transaction, and easily supported additional trading partners while leveraging the value of standardized procedures and systems.

Case 11.6: Automotive Tire Outlets A firm specializing in automotive tires required customized sales order processing to match the business processes at their outlets. The typical customer contact starts with a telephone inquiry about the options, pricing and availability about a given tire type, and proceeds through several steps including a quotation, sales order, work order and invoice. As part of the customizations for the quotation process, the system displayed alternative items with availability, pricing, and profitability along with highlighting to steer the customer's decision toward corporate promotions and higher margins. The system also suggested additional sales order line items about related services (such as tire installation and balancing) and indicated prior business with the customer. The quotation could be converted to a sales order and a work order with scheduling based on tire availability. When inventory was unavailable at the local outlet, the system checked availability across all outlets and recommended an inventory transfer, or generated a purchase order to the tire manufacturer. Many of the customizations represented work simplification and advanced decision support, with extensive prototyping to ensure ease-of-use, user acceptance and security considerations.

Case 11.7: Mobile Order Entry via Hand-Held Devices A manufacturing company had field sales representatives that wrote orders on paper forms that were faxed to the home office for manual re-keying. This manual system was replaced with hand-held devices (with a built-in bar-code scanner) that allowed sales reps to enter quotes, orders and invoices, and print them via a portable printer. At headquarters, the sales documents were seamlessly and automatically posted into Dynamics AX during each user's synchronization. The solution increased order efficiency and reduced errors, and allowed the average order size to grow significantly.

Case 11.8: Rules-Based Pricing A distribution company employed several types of rules-based pricing when selling their products to retailers. The approaches included a surcharge for a small order and discounts for a large order (based on total order value), as well as discount percentages and supplementary items based on total quantity ordered for different items within a product line. A miscellaneous charge was added to items requiring faster-than-normal delivery lead time.

Case 11.9: Tiered Sales Prices based on YTD Sales A manufacturing company required tiered sales pricing based on year-to-date quantities specified in a contract. For example, the contract price was $10 for a YTD quantity up to 999, $9.50 for 1000-1999, and $9.00 for a YTD quantity of 2000 or greater. A contract consisted of multiple line items, specifying the item, the contract period (expressed as from- and to-validity dates), and the price for each quantity breakpoint. The cumulative sales were tracked for sales orders linked to the contract, with a complete transaction history for each sales order line.

11.19 Executive Summary

Sales orders capture demands for the firm's products and service, and comprise a key element in the larger contexts of customer relationship management and the S&OP process. This chapter described a basic model of sales order processing, which provided the foundation for explaining key considerations and major variations. The variations included sales pricing approaches, direct delivery orders, customer returns, and sales quotations. The chapter also covered sales analysis and performance metrics related to sales orders. The case studies highlighted several aspects of sales order processing, such as quotations, commission calculations and EDI.

Chapter 12

Purchase Order Processing

A primary responsibility of procurement is to coordinate and execute the supply chain activities driven by the firm's S&OP game plans. Procurement activities can significantly impact the firm's bottom-line performance in terms of reduced material costs and inventories, improved quality and lead time agility, and fewer disruptions stemming from stock-outs or delivery problems.

Purchase order processing for material represents a key business process within procurement, and involves a wide spectrum of considerations and variations. As an explanatory approach, it is easiest to start with a basic model of purchase order processing. The basic model provides a foundation for explaining key considerations and major variations. Examples of major variations include the approach to purchase order pricing, the use of purchasing RFQs (request for quote), workflow approvals, returns to vendor, and coordination of procurement activities. These considerations are reflected in the following sections within the chapter.

1. Basic model of purchase order processing
2. Approved vendors for a purchased item
3. Key considerations for purchase order processing
4. Major variations in purchase order processing
5. Purchase prices and trade agreements
6. Purchase agreements
7. Purchasing RFQs
8. Workflows and purchase order approval
9. Receiving inspection
10. Purchase order returns
11. Vendor information
12. Coordinate procurement activities
13. Metrics related to vendor performance
14. Workspaces related to purchase orders

12.1 Basic Model of Purchase Order Processing

The typical steps in purchase order processing can vary based on several factors, such as different approaches for creating an order and different approaches for purchase order receiving. This section summarizes a basic model of purchase order processing and the related life cycles. It also identifies the different options for creating a purchase order and the different types of purchase orders.

Overview of the Basic Model The basic model of purchase order processing starts with the role of a purchasing agent and a requirement for purchased material. The requirement is typically identified by a planned order stemming from S&OP game plans and the item's planning data, and the planned order can be analyzed and firmed to create an actual purchase order. The purchasing agent can also manually enter a purchase order, typically as a result of an unplanned requirement. The purchasing agent can optionally generate a purchase inquiry for external review by the vendor. The purchasing agent confirms a purchase order when information has been completely entered.

A receiving clerk and warehouse worker perform subsequent steps for purchase order receiving, which differ when using the basic versus advanced approach to warehouse management.[1] An accounts payable clerk completes the process by entering the vendor invoice that typically reflects actual receipts. These roles and steps are summarized in Figure 12.1 and described below.

Firm a Planned Purchase Order The purchasing agent typically uses the Planned Purchase Orders form to analyze and firm planned orders, which creates actual purchase orders with one or more purchase order lines based on grouping preferences.

Enter a Purchase Order The purchasing agent creates a new purchase order by starting from the Vendor form or the Purchase Order form (and using the Create Purchase Order dialogue), which results in a purchase order header. If needed, the rep maintains aspects of the header information, such as overriding information inherited from the vendor master. The purchasing agent also enters purchase order line items, where each line item identifies a product, quantity, purchase price, ship-to location and the delivery date.

---

[1] Several steps in the business process for purchase order receiving can be mandated by two item-specific policies. The first policy can mandate that item arrival must be registered before you can post product receipt, and the second policy can mandate that the actual receipt must reported before you can post the vendor invoice. These two policies – termed the *Registration Requirements* policy and the *Receiving Requirements* policy – are embedded in the Item Model Group assigned to the item.

Figure 12.1 Basic Model of Purchase Order Processing

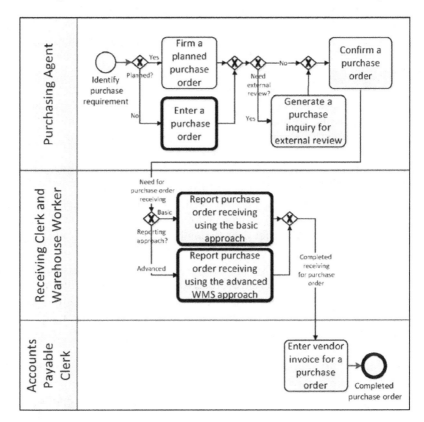

Generate a Purchase Inquiry for External Review   The purchasing agent generates a Purchase Inquiry in order to communicate the contents of a purchase order to the vendor, thereby providing the basis for external review before confirming the purchase order.   Each generation of a Purchase Inquiry creates a history record so that you can view historical versions.

Confirm a Purchase Order   The purchasing agent confirms a purchase order after completing the information, using either the Purchase Order form (for a selected order) or the Confirm Purchase Order form (for multiple orders satisfying the query criteria).   The confirmed order can be sent to the vendor, and the confirmation enables subsequent processing steps such as receipts.   Changes to a confirmed purchase order require an additional confirmation.   Each confirmation creates a history record so that you can view historical versions of a purchase order.

Report Purchase Order Receiving using the Basic Approach to Warehouse Management The receiving clerk typically uses the Arrival Overview form to review and select open purchase order line items that require receiving, and then generate an arrival journal containing the selected lines. Alternatively, the receiving clerk can manually create an arrival journal, typically to handle an unplanned receipt. The receiving clerk registers the actual receipts against each journal line item and then posts the journal to update inventory balances. The receiving clerk also identifies the vendor's packing list number when posting the product receipt for a purchase order. For received material with putaway requirements, the warehouse worker uses the Transfer Journal form to report transfers from the receiving location to the putaway location.

Report Purchase Order Receiving using the Advanced WMS Approach to Warehouse Management The receiving clerk typically uses the mobile device to register a purchase order arrival into a receiving location (and assign license plate IDs), which automatically creates a work order for putaway. The warehouse worker uses the mobile device to report putaway from the receiving location to a stocking location. A suggested stocking location can reflect location directives, or the warehouse worker can determine and report the stocking location. Alternatively, the receiving clerk registers the arrival and reports putaway as part of a single mobile device transaction. In either case, the receiving clerk subsequently identifies the vendor's packing list number when posting the product receipt for the purchase order.

Report Purchase Order Receiving using a Simple Inventory Transaction The receiving clerk registers the item when posting the product receipt for a purchase order. This simple inventory transaction applies to both the basic or advanced approach to warehouse management, and it avoids the use of arrival journals and mobile devices respectively. This step is not shown in the figure.

Enter Vendor Invoice for a Purchase Order The accounts payable clerk uses the Posting Invoice form to record the vendor's invoice number and invoice information. The form can be accessed from the Purchase Order form, thereby inheriting information from the selected purchase order. It can also be accessed directly, which means that you must identify the applicable purchase order(s) for the vendor invoice. As part of the step, you indicate the quantity basis for initially populating the invoice information (such as the product receipt quantities) and whether to print the invoice.

Life Cycles related to Purchase Order Processing   The life cycles related to a purchase order include a status for the header and each line item, and an inventory status for the item on a purchase line, where steps in the business process automatically update the status. These steps are summarized in Figure 12.2 along with the status of related life cycles. The figure also identifies the approval status and document status for a purchase order.

Figure 12.2 Life Cycles related to Purchase Order Processing

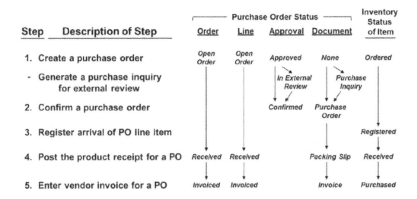

An order status indicates the following steps in the life cycle of a purchase order.

◆ *Open Order*. The status indicates the order has been created.
◆ *Delivered*. The status indicates all order lines have a delivered status.
◆ *Invoiced*. The status indicates all order lines have an invoiced status.
◆ *Cancelled*. The status indicates the purchase order has been cancelled.

A line status indicates the following steps in the life cycle of a purchase order line, or a line within the delivery schedule for a purchase order line.

◆ *Open Order*.   The status indicates the line has been created, and partial receipts or invoices may have been entered.
◆ *Delivered*. The status indicates that the delivered quantity equals the order quantity. When using delivery tolerances, the delivered quantity can exceed the order quantity or the under-delivery can be flagged as closed when posting the product receipt.
◆ *Invoiced*. The status indicates the line item quantity has been completely invoiced, taking into account the over- or under-delivery considerations mentioned above.

◆ *Cancelled.* The status indicates the purchase order has been cancelled, and the quantity not yet registered or received will be cancelled.

A document status indicates the last document posted for the purchase order, as described below.

◆ *None.* The status indicates that a confirmation or purchase inquiry has not been posted for the purchase order.
◆ *Purchase Inquiry.* The status indicates a purchase inquiry has been posted.
◆ *Purchase Order.* The status indicates a purchase order confirmation has been posted.
◆ *Packing Slip.* The status indicates a product receipt has been posted for all lines.
◆ *Invoiced.* The status indicates the vendor's invoice has been posted.

The purchase order approval status indicates whether a purchase inquiry and/or a confirmation have been posted for the order, as described below.

◆ *Approved.* The status indicates the purchase order needs to be confirmed.
◆ *In External Review.* The status indicates a purchase inquiry has been posted for the order.
◆ *Confirmed.* The status indicates the purchase order confirmation has been posted, so that subsequent steps (such as receiving) can be reported.

Note: Other statuses (for *Draft* and *In Review*) pertain to purchase orders requiring an approval process, as described below.

◆ *Draft.* The status indicates creation of a purchase order that must go through an approval process, where the purchase order has not yet been submitted for approval.
◆ *In Review.* The status indicates a purchase order going through an approval process, where the order has been submitted but not yet approved.

The inventory status for the item on a purchase line is shown on the right side of Figure 12.2, and the steps in purchase order processing will change this status from *ordered* to *registered, received* and *purchased.*

Different Approaches for Creating a Purchase Order The basic model identifies two common approaches for creating a purchase order -- by firming a planned order and by manual entry. The different approaches for creating a purchase order are listed below along with the relevant book section providing further explanation. The steps within the basic model also apply to these other sources of creating a purchase order.

◆ Firm a planned purchase order (Section 12.12)

◆ Create a purchase order via release from a blanket purchase order (Section 12.6)

◆ Automatically create a purchase order from an accepted reply to a request for quote (Section 12.7)

◆ Automatically create a direct delivery purchase order for a sales order, aka Direct PO (Section 11.8)

◆ Automatically create a purchase order from a sales order, aka a Special PO (Section 11.9)

◆ Automatically create a purchase order for a buy-to-order component of a production order (Section 9.4)

◆ Automatically create an intercompany purchase order from an intercompany sales order (Section 18.2)

◆ Automatically create a purchase order from an approved requisition

Other approaches to creating a purchase order only apply to a project-oriented operation, such as entering a purchase order related to a project.

Other Types of Purchase Orders   You indicate the purchase order type when initially creating a purchase order. In addition to a normal purchase order, the order types include a returned order and journal.

◆ *Returned Order.* A purchase order with a type of returned order is used for returns to vendor, and a subsequent section provides further explanation (Section 12.10).

◆ *Journal (or Draft).* A purchase order with a type of journal is typically used to define information about a possible purchase, and you change the order type to purchase order when ready.

12.2 Approved Vendors for a Purchased Item

A purchased item can have one or more approved vendors, as defined on the Approved Vendor List for the selected item. You also define the start and expiration dates for an item's approved vendor. You can anticipate upcoming expiration dates using the Approved Vendor List Expiration form. The expiration date indicates when a vendor is no longer approved. An item's approved vendor represents a companywide policy.

Most companies will enforce the use of an item's approved vendor, as defined by an item-specific policy labeled the *approved vendor check method*. This policy designates whether the approved vendor information will (1) be ignored, (2) prevent entry or (3) provide a warning. The policy is initially inherited from the Item Model Group assigned to the item. Enforcement of the approved vendor policy applies to several situations, as summarized in the following list. The list includes the relevant book sections providing further explanation.

♦ Specify the item's preferred vendor in coverage planning data (Section 9.3)
♦ Create a purchase order line for the item (Section 12.1)
♦ Firm a planned purchase order for the item (Sections 12.1 and 12.11)
♦ Define a purchase trade agreement for the item (Section 12.5)
♦ Define a purchase agreement for the vendor and item (Section 12.6)
♦ Create a purchase order from a sales order line for the item (Section 11.8 and 11.9)
♦ Create a purchase order from an accepted RFQ reply (Section 12.7)
♦ Specify the preferred vendor for a buy-to-order component in a BOM line or in an order-dependent BOM (Sections 5.4.and 5.6)
♦ Specify the preferred vendor for a subcontracted service in a BOM line (Section 15.4)

As noted in the above list, the approved vendors for an item should include those vendors identified as the preferred source, and also those with purchase trade agreements or purchase agreements.

12.3 Key Considerations for Purchase Order Processing

Many of the variations in purchase order processing can be supported by standard AX capabilities. Some of these can be viewed as major variations while others can be viewed as key considerations. This section summarizes a number of key considerations and the next section summarizes the major variations. A subset of these topics will apply to a given company.

The following list of key considerations and their extended explanations represent a compendium of topics about AX capabilities. The list has been broadly segmented into three groups consisting of common considerations, special considerations, and warehouse management considerations. Each topic has been assigned an identifier for ease of reference, as shown below.

List of Common Considerations

- ◆ A1: Purchase order quantity and UM
- ◆ A2: Alternative sources of an item's purchase price
- ◆ A3: Significance of a confirmed delivery date
- ◆ A4: Delivery schedule for a purchase order line
- ◆ A5: Totals for a purchase order
- ◆ A6: Versions of a purchase order
- ◆ A7: Effective use of notes for purchase orders
- ◆ A8: Identify potential problems in purchase order delivery dates
- ◆ A9: Identify purchase-related backorders

List of Special Considerations

- ◆ B1: Impact of a vendor hold and other types of stop flags or restrictions
- ◆ B2: Create purchase order lines via the copy function
- ◆ B3: Create purchase order lines via selection from a procurement hierarchy of product categories
- ◆ B4: Generate a credit note from a purchase order
- ◆ B5: Change the buy-from or pay-to vendor on a purchase order

List of Warehouse Management Considerations

- ◆ C1: Purchase order charges for freight
- ◆ C2: Significance of Inventory Status for purchase order processing
- ◆ C3: Quality orders for purchase order receiving
- ◆ C4: Significance of the prevent partial delivery policy

A1: Purchase Order Quantity and UM An item's purchase order quantity often reflects order quantity modifiers consisting of a minimum, maximum and multiple. They are expressed in the item's default purchase UM (if specified) otherwise they reflect the item's inventory UM. The order quantity modifiers impact planned purchase order quantities. They are also considered when manually creating or maintaining a purchase line for the item, where a soft warning will be displayed when you enter a quantity that does not meet these criteria. The item's standard purchase order quantity also reflects considerations about order quantity modifiers, and it acts as a default value when manually entering a purchase line for the item.

An item's purchase order quantity can reflect any authorized UM for the item. In many cases, the different values for an item's authorized UM will also be reflected in purchase price trade agreements and/or purchase agreements.

A2: Alternative Approaches to an Item's Purchase Price An item's purchase price can be defined several different ways. As summarized in Figure 12.3, the four major approaches include a purchase agreement, purchase price trade agreements, the inherited purchase price from a source document, and a companywide standard purchase price.

Figure 12.3 Alternative Sources of an Item's Purchase Price

Source of Purchase Price on a Purchase Order		Factors	Significance of the Item's Purchase Price
Purchase Agreement	Purchase Agreement for a product quantity commitment	Committed quantity Minimum release quantity Validity period	Companywide or Site/Warehouse-specific Purchase Price
Trade Agreement	Purchase Price Trade Agreement	Vendor Unit of measure Quantity breakpoints Validity period	Companywide or Site/Warehouse-specific Purchase Price
Source Document	Purchase Requisition	N/A	Inherit Purchase Price From Source Document
	Accepted RFQ Reply		
	Copy a Purchase Order		
Standard Purchase Price	Manually Entered Standard Purchase Price	N/A	Companywide Purchase Price
	Updated by Last Purchase Invoice		

As the simplest approach, an item's standard purchase price can be defined on the item master along with its default purchase UM. It represents a companywide purchase price that acts as the default on a purchase line when other sources of pricing information do not exist. This standard purchase price can be manually specified or automatically updated by the last purchase invoice.

As the second major approach, the purchase price can be inherited from a source document used to create the purchase order. Examples of a source document include an approved requisition, an accepted RFQ reply, and copying information into a purchase order.

The third major approach involves purchase price trade agreements, which can represent companywide or site/warehouse-specific purchase prices for an item. They can reflect different purchase UM, validity dates, and quantity breakpoints. A subsequent section provides further explanation of purchase trade agreements (Section 12.5).

The fourth major approach involves a purchase agreement, which specifies the item's purchase price based on a commitment quantity over a validity period. Releases against the purchase agreement create a purchase order, and the item inherits the specified price. Purchase agreements can also define a discount percent (rather than a purchase price), and a subsequent section provides further explanation (Section 12.6).

A3: Significance of a Confirmed Delivery Date Each purchase order line has a delivery date and a confirmed delivery date. The confirmed delivery date is initially blank, and should be updated to reflect actual conditions, such as a delayed delivery. Master scheduling logic employs the confirmed delivery date as the basis for suggested action messages and messages about calculated delays.

A4: Delivery Schedule for a Purchase Order Line A purchase order line item normally consists of a single quantity and its associated delivery dates. You can optionally specify a delivery schedule for a purchase line, where each schedule line consists of a quantity and its associated dates. The total quantities within the delivery schedule lines must equal the quantity for the purchase line, or the system will automatically adjust the purchase line quantity.

A5: Totals for a Purchase Order The system calculates several order totals, including a total amount, weight and volume. Order totals can be displayed for order quantities or received quantities. For example, the volume and weight of order quantities can be used for truckload planning purposes.

A6: Versions of a Purchase Order Different versions of a purchase order can identify the history of changes. The system assigns a version number each time you confirm a purchase order, where the version reflects a numeric suffix to the purchase order number (such as -1 and -2). Hence, each confirmation provides a history of changes. The version appears on a printed purchase order confirmation, and the historical versions can be viewed and compared. The most recent version is used for master scheduling and the reporting of arrivals/receipts and vendor invoices. Two versions of a purchase order confirmation can be compared in order to identify differences.

A7: Effective Use of Notes for Purchase Orders Many situations require textual explanations about the purchase order and/or line items, where the information can be defined as a note and its associated note type. The notes associated with a specified note type can be inherited from the vendor and/or item. The inherited notes can be optionally overridden, and notes can also be manually entered. The various considerations about notes are summarized below.

◆ *Inherit an Item-Related Note on the Purchase Line Item.* The note(s) associated with an item can be automatically inherited by a purchase line for the item.

◆ *Inherit a Vendor-Related Note on the Purchase Order Header.* The note(s) associated with a vendor can be automatically inherited by the purchase order header.

◆ *Printing Notes on Purchase Documents.* The setup policies for procurement determine whether printed documents include a specified note type. These documents include the confirmation and purchase inquiry for a purchase order; they also include purchase agreements, purchase requisitions, and requests for quotes. The specified note type can be different for each document.

◆ *Displaying Notes on Mobile Device Transactions for Purchase Order Arrivals* When using the advanced approach to warehouse management, the note(s) associated with the purchase order header can be displayed on the mobile device transactions for reporting purchase order arrivals. The applicable note type for mobile device transactions is defined by a companywide policy (on the Warehouse Management Parameters form).

A8: Identify Potential Problems in Purchase Order Delivery Dates
The delivery date for a purchase order line provides the basis for expected receiving in the warehouse. In particular, the confirmed delivery date for a purchase line (or a line within a delivery schedule) typically indicates the most realistic up-to-date information from the vendor. Several standard inquiries identify potential problems about deliveries. You can identify purchase order lines without confirmed delivery dates or with past due delivery dates. You can also identify purchase-related backorders. These problems typically require action by the purchasing agent and coordination with the vendor, but they are also relevant for expected receiving activities in the warehouse.

A9: Identify Purchase-Related Backorders A purchase-related backorder within AX simply refers to any purchase line with a delivery date prior to a specified date (aka the backorder date). [2] This simple definition includes purchase lines with a partially delivered quantity, where the line has not been closed short when posting the product receipt. A partially delivered quantity is the normal interpretation of a purchase backorder. Standardized inquiries can be used to identify all purchase-related backorders or just those related to a vendor. The purchasing agent typically reviews purchase-related backorders and takes action for a selected backorder. The actions include expediting delivery from the vendor, updating the confirmed delivery date, and/or reducing the quantity for the purchase line.

B1: Impact of a Vendor Hold and other Types of Stop Flags and Restrictions The assignment of a vendor hold for "all" transactions will prevent posting of confirmations and product receipts and result in a corresponding message. As part of assigning a vendor hold (aka vendor status), you can optionally select a reason code and/or specify a release date. The vendor hold does not prevent purchase order entry or registration of purchase order arrivals for the vendor. Other types of stop flags and restrictions include the following.

◆ *Impact of Stopped Transactions for an Item.* The purchase order transactions for an item can be stopped, either as a companywide or site-specific policy. The stopped flag prevents new purchase orders and further transactions for an item's existing purchase orders, and results in a corresponding message. A similar stopped flag can be specified for an item's inventory transactions, which only prevents further transactions for an item's existing purchase orders.

◆ *Impact of a Stopped Flag on a Purchase Order Line.* The assignment of a Stopped flag for a purchase order line prevents further transactions until it has been removed, and results in a corresponding message.

◆ *Restricted Purchases to a Single Site/Warehouse.* Purchase order transactions can be limited to a single site (or site/warehouse) that actually purchases the item, as defined by the mandatory flag within the Default Order Settings and Site-Specific Order Settings forms.

---

[2] This simple definition is critical for understanding "backordered lines" with a future delivery date when compared to a specified backorder date in the future.

B2: Create Purchase Order Lines via the Copy Function A copy function (labeled Copy from All) can be used to create line items from a previously-entered purchase order. For example, you can select the desired purchase order and the desired line item(s) from a displayed list of all previous orders. You can also select from versions of purchase orders, or packing lists and invoices. You indicate how to handle updates, such as appending line items and recalculating prices for the new line items.

B3: Create Purchase Order Lines via selection from a Procurement Hierarchy When entering line items on the Purchase Order form, the "Add Products" function can be used to select an applicable procurement hierarchy and a node within the hierarchy, and then select the product(s) to be automatically added to the purchase order.

B4: Generating a Credit Note from a Purchase Order Some situations require creation of a credit note while in the midst of purchase order entry. One approach employs a negative quantity for the purchase order line item. When posting the receipt or vendor invoice, the system will subtract the value from the invoice and record an issue rather than a receipt.

A second approach (termed the create credit note function) acts like the copy order function, since you must select the applicable order from the displayed list of the vendor's previously invoiced purchase orders. This requires historical information but supports access to the original information such as purchase price. Just like the copy function, the selected line item can then be added to the purchase order (with a negative quantity).

B5: Changing the Buy-From or Pay-To Vendor on a Purchase Order Changes to the buy-from or pay-to vendor can be made prior to posting receipts, but the changes have several impacts. For example, changing the buy-from vendor may result in a new pay-to vendor. After changing the buy-from vendor, you can respond to prompts about updating information impacted by the change, such as prices and discounts that reflect purchase trade agreements with the new vendor.

C1: Purchase Order Charges for Freight The charges related to freight can be manually assigned to a purchase order, either as order-level charges or line item charges or both. A user-defined Charges Code identifies each type of charge and its related ledger account. The charges can be expressed as a fixed amount, an amount per piece, or a percentage of value. A fixed amount (for an order-level charge) needs to be allocated to the lines.

Some scenarios involve predefined agreements about charges, such as freight or handling charges for selected items or vendors. An agreement about charges can be embedded in the purchase price trade agreement information, or they can be specified separately as *auto charges*. These auto charges can be applied to an entire purchase order or to individual line items, and expressed as a fixed amount, an amount per piece, or a percentage of value.

◆ *Order-Level Charges.* Charge agreements related to the entire purchase order can be defined for a single vendor, all vendors, or a group of vendors (identified by the *Vendor Charges Group* assigned to relevant vendors).

◆ *Line item charges.* Charge agreements related to the purchase order line item can be defined by vendor and item, such as charges for a single item, all items, or a group of items (identified by the *Item Charges Group* assigned to relevant purchased items).[3] Examples of a line item charge include a setup fee for purchasing selected items from a vendor.

When using the advanced approach to transportation management, the relevant charges can reflect the transportation costs associated with the purchase load (or the shipment) containing the purchase order lines. These charges are automatically assigned to purchase lines after confirming the inbound shipment.

C2: Significance of Inventory Status for Purchase Order Processing

The use of Inventory Status only applies to WMS-enabled items, as described in a subsequent chapter about warehouse management (Section 16.2). A value for Inventory Status must be assigned to each purchase order line, typically with a value of *Available* or its equivalent in most scenarios. In some scenarios, the value for Inventory Status may indicate the grade or condition of the inventory being purchased (which may or may not affect purchase prices), or the need for receiving inspection. Case 12.1 illustrates the use of Inventory Status to indicate the need for inspection.

Case 12.1: Indicate Inspection Requirements using Inventory Status

The Inventory Status value of *Needs-Inspection* was assigned to purchase lines for items requiring inspection, thereby communicating the need for inspection when reporting purchase order arrival. A given item that always requires inspection was assigned a default value of *Needs-Inspection* for each supplying vendor (using the Default Item Status form). In this way, the value will be

---

[3] Two policies (embedded within the Procurement and Sourcing Parameters form) indicate whether the system recognizes auto charges for the entire order and for line items.

inherited when creating a purchase order line or firming a planned order. The quality control clerk changed the value of Inventory Status after inspecting the received material, such as changing the value to *Available* or *Damaged*.

C3: Quality Orders for Purchase Order Receipts A quality order can be automatically generated when you report purchase order arrival for an item, or when posting the product receipt, as defined by Quality Associations related to purchase orders for an item. A subsequent chapter provides further explanation of quality orders (Section 17.4).

C4: Significance of the Prevent Partial Delivery Policy A purchase order line can be flagged as "prevent partial delivery", so that you will receive an error unless you receive the entire quantity when posting the product receipt for the purchase line.[4] As an alternative approach, the same concept can be enforced using the delivery tolerance functionality, since delivery tolerances of zero percent for a purchase line mean that the received quantity must equal the ordered quantity.

12.4 Major Variations in Purchase Order Processing

The basic model of purchase order processing provides a foundation for covering several major variations. The basic model included one major variation about the receiving process using the basic versus advanced approach to warehouse management. The explanation of the basic model also identified different ways to create a purchase order.

Several other variations merit a separate section, such purchase prices and trade agreements (Section 12.5), purchase agreements (Section 12.6), purchasing RFQs (Section 12.7), purchase order approvals (Section 12.8), receiving inspection (Section 12.9), and purchase order returns (Section 12.10). This section summarizes several additional variations, including direct delivery orders, special orders, buy-to-order components, subcontracted services and purchase requisitions.

Direct Delivery Orders A direct delivery order reflects a purchase order directly linked to a sales order, with material directly shipped to the customer. The previous chapter described the typical process for direct delivery orders (Section 11.8).

---

[4] The policy of "prevent partial delivery" for a purchase order line was called "receive complete" in previous AX versions such as AX 2012 R3.

Special Orders A special order reflects a purchase order directly linked to a sales order, with cross-dock receipts shipped to the customer. The previous chapter described the typical process for special orders (Section 11.9).

Purchase Orders for a Buy-to-Order Component When the BOM for a manufactured item contains a buy-to-order component (identified by a component type of *Vendor*), a scheduled production order for the manufactured item automatically generates a linked purchase order for the component. The purchase order is automatically created for the component's preferred vendor (if defined) or the item's preferred vendor. The reference field information identifies the linkage in each order and the system reserves the scheduled receipt for the production order. Changes to the scheduled date for the production order can automatically update the schedule date for the linked purchase order (aka the reference order).

Purchase Orders for a Subcontracted Service A subcontracted service represents one example of a buy-to-order component and a key aspect of subcontracted production. A subsequent chapter provides further explanation of subcontracted production and the purchase of subcontracted services (Chapter 15).

Purchase Requisition Purchase requisitions generally apply to many types of indirect materials, where procurement is triggered by a user request and involves an approval process before items can be purchased. However, a purchase requisition approval process sometimes applies to direct material items with requirements driven by S&OP game plans, such as sourcing a new item from a new vendor. The approval process employs the workflow management capabilities within AX, where you define one or more workflows for purchase requisition approval. A purchase order can be automatically created for an approved requisition.

12.5 Purchase Prices and Trade Agreements

A purchase trade agreement represents predefined information for buying material from suppliers, such as published list prices, negotiated purchase prices, and/or discount schemes. There are four types of purchase trade agreements -- about the purchase price, line discount, multi-line discount and/or total discount -- and further explanation focuses on the purchase price aspects. The different types can be used in combination with each other, such as defining the purchase price and a discount.

Purchase Price Trade Agreements   A purchase price trade agreement indicates the purchase price for an item. The purchase price typically reflects one or more of the factors shown in Figure 12.4 and illustrated below.[5]

Figure 12.4 Purchase Trade Agreements

	Site or Warehouse-Specific Information			N/A	N/A
	Companywide Information				
Factor	**Purchase Price**	**Types of Discounts**			
		Line Discount	**Multi-line Discount**	**Total Discount**	
Item — Item and UM	X	X	N/A	See policy about including item value	
Item — Group of Items	N/A	X Line Discount Group	X Multi-line Discount Group	N/A	
Item — All Items		X	X		
Buy-From Vendor — Vendor	X	X	X	X	
Buy-From Vendor — Group of Vendors	X Price Group	X Line Discount Group	X Multi-line Discount Group	X Total Discount Group	
Buy-From Vendor — All Vendors	X	X	X	X	
Other Factors — Date Effectivity	X	X	X	X	
Other Factors — Currency Code	X	X	X	X	
Other Factors — Quantity Breakpoints	X	X	X	Order Value Breakpoint	
Other Factors — Delivery Days / Price Charge	X X	N/A	N/A	N/A	
Policies	Price Group Policy: Price Includes Sales Tax			Item Policy: Include item value for total discount purposes	

- ◆ Pricing by item and unit of measure, such as different prices per piece and per carton.
- ◆ Pricing by currency type, such as separate pricing for foreign purchases.
- ◆ Pricing with validity period, for supporting annual price updates or seasonal price promotions. The applicable validity period for assigning a price reflects the order date on a purchase order.
- ◆ Pricing with quantity breakpoints for the purchase line quantity.
- ◆ Pricing based on delivery days. A higher price may apply for faster delivery, pr the delivery lead time could vary by ship-to site/warehouse. However, the number of delivery days are normally embedded in the item's lead time for purchasing, so that you designate the "disregard lead time" policy as part of the entry.
- ◆ Pricing that involves an additional charge, such as a charge for fast delivery, small order quantity or freight.

---

[5] A set of companywide policies (embedded in the Activate Price/Discount form) determines whether the system recognizes these factors.

Price trade agreements are expressed as one or more entries that identify the applicable factors. A simple pricing scheme that represents a single purchase price, for example, would require one entry for each item purchased from the vendor. Additional entries would be required for defining next year's price, quantity breakpoints, and variations in the items' purchase UM. Additional entries are also required for each site and warehouse when using site- and warehouse-specific pricing. Figure 12.4 illustrates the site/warehouse factor as a third dimension, since pricing can be companywide or site/warehouse-specific.

When manually creating a purchase order, or firming a planned purchase order, the trade agreement information will be used to automatically assign an item's price using the lowest price of applicable trade agreement entries. The system also assigns the charge associated with the price if applicable. You can view available prices during purchase order entry, such as viewing quantity breakpoints or future pricing to guide purchase decisions.

There are several considerations with respect to purchase price trade agreements:

◆ Trade agreements for an item's purchase price and line discounts can represent either companywide or site/warehouse-specific information, based on an item-specific policy (embedded in the Storage Dimension Group assigned to the item).

◆ Master scheduling logic can suggest a vendor for planned purchase orders based on lowest price or delivery lead time.[6]

◆ The price trade agreement information for purchased components can be used for calculating the planned cost of a manufactured item (described in Section 7.9).

An additional consideration involves the system logic when there are multiple trade agreement entries that apply to a situation. Each trade agreement entry typically indicates searching for other applicable entries, so that the search will find the most specific entry possible rather than stopping at the first entry.

Types of Purchase Discounts in Trade Agreements Purchase discounts are calculated after the line item prices have been identified on a purchase order. The discounts can be related to a single line, multiple lines, the order total value, or a combination of these approaches.

---

[6] A companywide policy (embedded in the Master Planning Parameters form) determines whether master scheduling logic considers trade agreement information for planned purchases and whether the criterion should be lowest price or lead time.

◆ *Line Discount.* The line discount is expressed as a fixed amount or a percentage or both. In particular, the percentage discount can be expressed as a single value or as two values (e.g., using a 10% discount for both values results in a 19% discount), and the system applies the discount percentage after reducing the price by the fixed discount amount. Line discounts often reflect one or more of the factors shown in Figure 13.5 and illustrated below.

   – Discounts for a single item, all items, or a group of items (based on the *Line Discount Group* assigned to relevant items). For example, the groups could represent different product lines. Two different group codes (both called the *Line Discount Group*) can be predefined -- one for items and one for vendors -- and then assigned to relevant items and vendors.

   – Discounts based on date effectivities, quantity breakpoints, and currency code for foreign purchases.

   A simple discount scheme involving a discount percent by group of items, for example, would require one trade agreement entry for each group. Note that a line discount can be companywide or site/warehouse-specific, as illustrated in Figure 13.5.

◆ *Multi-Line Discount based on Total Quantity.* The multi-line discount reflects a discount based on the total quantity for multiple line items. It is expressed the same way as a single line discount (as a fixed amount or a percentage or both). The trade agreement entries can reflect the factors shown in Figure 13.5, such as a discount that applies to a group of items. Two different group codes (both called the *Multi-line Discount Group*) can be predefined -- one for items and one for vendors -- and then assigned to relevant items and vendors. You must initiate calculation of multiline discounts on a purchase order after all line items have been entered.

   The combination of a line discount and multi-line discount can be handled different ways, as defined by a companywide policy (embedded in the A/P Parameters). A typical approach views the two values as additive. However, you could specify the policy as use the lowest value or highest value, use only one of the values, or treat them as multiplicative.

◆ *Discount (or Surcharge) based on Total Order Value.* The total discount applies to the total order value. It is expressed the same way as a single line discount -- as a fixed amount or a percentage or both. Expressing the fixed amount as a negative value represents a surcharge. The trade agreement entries can reflect the factors shown in Figure 13.5, such as a discount with order value breakpoints. An item-related policy determines whether the system includes or excludes the item in calculating total order value for the purpose of a total discount. You must initiate calculation of the total discount on a purchase order after all line items have been entered, or the total discount can be automatically calculated (based on a companywide policy embedded in the A/P Parameters).

Maintaining and Viewing Purchase Trade Agreement Information
Information about purchase trade agreements must be prepared beforehand and then used to update the database containing trade agreement information. Preparing data beforehand (using the Price/Discount Agreement Journal and its associated line items) offers several advantages in data maintenance. For example, you can create a new journal for preparing next year's purchase price trade agreements, and then initially populate the entries with information about existing purchase price agreements for selected items or vendors. The information can then be manually updated prior to posting the journal. In addition, you can perform mass changes to the entries (such as increasing the price a specified percentage or amount), or copy the entries in order to prepare price agreements for another item, vendor, validity period or currency. The concept of preparing data beforehand is employed within the request for quotes (RFQ) business process, so that a vendor reply can be used to prepare purchase trade agreement information.

Use the Purchase Price report to view purchase price trade agreement information, or a subset of information based on the report's selection criteria (such as the selected items, vendors or currency). Use the Price/Discount List report to view all types of price and discount trade agreement information, or a subset based on the report's selection criteria.

Agreements about Supplementary Items Some purchase environments involve supplementary items, such as "buy one and get an additional item free," which result in additional line items on a purchase order. Supplementary items can also represent related items that should be purchased together, thereby providing a reminder to the purchasing agent. A supplementary purchase item and quantity can be designated as mandatory or optional, and chargeable or free-of-charge. The rules may also include validity dates, a minimum order quantity and/or a one-time-only offer. The supplementary item information can be associated with a specific item or vendor, where you define a group code (termed the *Supplementary Item Group*) and assign it to relevant items and vendors.

During the process of entering purchase order line items, you initiate a calculation that displays the applicable supplementary items. The items are segmented into mandatory and optional (with user selection of the optional items), and acceptance results in additional purchase order line items.

12.6 Purchase Agreements

Purchase agreements define a commitment to buy products from a vendor over a time period in exchange for special prices or discounts. Synonyms include a blanket purchase order. The various types of a commitment include a total quantity for a specific product (with a specified purchase price and/or discount percent), or a total value for a specific product, a category of products, or all products/categories (with a specified discount percent). After defining the purchase agreement, you change its status from *on-hold* to *effective* in order to allow usage, such as creating purchase orders linked to the purchase agreement.

Type of Commitment for a Purchase Agreement The type of commitment is defined in the header information for a purchase agreement, which then affects the information for each line item, as summarized below.

◆ *Create a line item for a product quantity commitment.* You define the total commitment quantity and the purchase price and/or discount percent for a specified item. An optional minimum or maximum release quantity may also be defined.

◆ *Create a line item for a product value commitment.* You define the total commitment value and discount percent for a specified item. An optional minimum or maximum release amount may also be defined.

◆ *Create a line item for a product category value commitment.* You define the total commitment value and discount percent for a specified category of items. The concept of product categories and a category hierarchy for purchasing purposes was previously explained in Section 3.1. An optional minimum or maximum release amount may also be defined.

◆ *Create a line item for a value commitment.* You define the total commitment value and discount percent that will be applicable to all items or categories purchased from the vendor. An optional minimum or maximum release amount may also be defined.

As part of the header information, you indicate whether the maximum should be enforced on related purchase orders. Additional terms and conditions may also be specified -- such as the payment terms and mode of delivery -- which will be inherited by related purchase orders.

Linkage between Purchase Orders and a Purchase Agreement

Several different approaches are used to link a purchase order to a purchase agreement, as summarized below. As a result of these approaches, you can view the purchase orders linked to a selected purchase agreement or generate the equivalent report.

◆ *Release a purchase order from a purchase agreement.* You create the purchase order by starting from a selected purchase agreement, and specify the item and quantity for a purchase order line item. The purchase order header inherits the terms and conditions from the purchase agreement, and a line item inherits the applicable purchase price or discount percent from the purchase agreement.

◆ *Firm planned purchase orders with grouping by purchase agreement.* You firm the planned purchase orders with grouping by purchase agreements, which results in a purchase order with multiple line items. Regardless of the grouping preference when firming planned orders, each resulting purchase order will inherit information from the applicable purchase agreement.

◆ *Manually create a purchase order linked to a purchase agreement.* You specify the identifier of the applicable purchase agreement when manually creating a purchase order. The purchase order header inherits the terms and conditions from the purchase agreement, and a line item inherits the applicable purchase price or discount percent from the purchase agreement.

You can also unlink a purchase order currently linked to a purchase agreement, which means the purchase price or discount percent for the line item will no longer reflect the purchase agreement.

12.7 Purchasing RFQs (Request for Quote)

A request for quote (RFQ) provides a structured approach for soliciting and using purchase quotations for material items. The creation of an RFQ oftentimes starts with planned purchase orders and the intent of using a vendor reply to create a purchase order. A vendor reply can also be used to create purchase trade agreement entries. Other variations of an RFQ process involve different starting points and different intentions for using vendor replies. For example, an RFQ can be manually created with the intent of using a vendor reply to create a purchase order or a purchase agreement. An RFQ can also be created for a purchase requisition with the intent of updating the requisition status from *pending RFQ* to *pending completion*.

This section focuses on a basic RFQ process from the starting point of a planned purchase order, and illustrates key aspects of the AX conceptual model. The key aspects apply to other variations of an RFQ process. As one key aspect, the terms *RFQ* and *vendor-specific RFQ* represent two different yet related constructs within AX. An RFQ has a unique identifier, and you create an RFQ to identify the items to be purchased and the applicable vendors that should be sent RFQ information. By sending the RFQ information, you create a vendor-specific RFQ (with its unique identifier) for each applicable vendor, and the vendor can reply to the vendor-specific RFQ.

Basic RFQ Process starting from Planned Purchase Orders The basic RFQ process consists of several steps performed by a purchasing agent, where the RFQ is created from planned purchase orders.[7] The purchasing agent sends the RFQ to selected vendors to obtain reply information, and then enters and analyzes the received replies in order to make decisions about accepting or rejecting a reply. A reply can also be entered by the vendor. These steps are reflected in the status of a vendor-specific RFQ, which consists of *created, sent, received, accepted* and *rejected*. Accepting a reply will automatically create a corresponding purchase order, and a reply can also be used to create purchase trade agreement entries. These steps are illustrated in Figure 12.5 and described below.

◆ *Create RFQ from planned purchase orders.* The purchasing agent creates an RFQ by selecting and converting one or more planned purchase orders, which populates the RFQ lines with the planned order information -- such as the item, quantity, UM, ship-to location and delivery date. The RFQ can also inherit the items' preferred vendor.

◆ *Add a vendor to reply to RFQ.* The purchasing agent adds a vendor to the RFQ in order to send a vendor-specific RFQ and receive their reply.

---

[7] Converting a planned purchase order to an RFQ will delete the planned order, and master scheduling logic will generate another planned purchase order unless RFQs are treated as a scheduled receipt (as specified by a policy for a set of Master Plan data). This policy should only be employed if there is a 100% probability that all RFQs for direct material will result in an accepted reply that generates a purchase order.

Figure 12.5 Basic RFQ Process starting from Planned PO

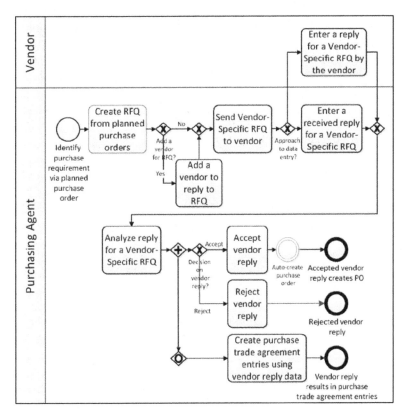

◆ *Send vendor-specific RFQ to vendor.* The purchasing agent sends an RFQ to the selected vendors, which automatically creates the vendor-specific RFQs. When sending the information, you can optionally print an RFQ Reply document that specifies the desired information to be supplied by the vendor. If you subsequently add a vendor to the RFQ, then sending the RFQ a second time will create a vendor-specific RFQ for the additional vendor.

◆ *Enter a received reply for a vendor-specific RFQ.* The purchasing agent can manually enter the reply information for a vendor-specific RFQ, or automatically populate the reply (with information from the RFQ) and manually override values as needed.

◆ *Enter reply for a vendor-specific RFQ by the vendor.* The vendor can view their vendor-specific RFQs and indicate whether they will decline or submit a bid for a new RFQ.[8] Prior to submitting a bid, the vendor completes the required information such as the purchase price, quantity and delivery date. The vendor can also review the status of all vendor-specific RFQs, such as new, submitted and expired RFQs as well as accepted and rejected RFQs.

◆ *Analyze reply for a vendor-specific RFQ.* The purchasing agent can compare replies from different vendors, and also request an updated reply by indicating a decision to return the RFQ.

◆ *Create trade purchase agreement entries using vendor reply information.* The purchasing agent can optionally create a trade agreement journal with entries that reflect a selected vendor reply. The information may be reviewed and updated prior to posting the journal.

◆ *Accept vendor reply.* The purchasing agent indicates that a vendor reply is accepted, which automatically creates a purchase order. An RFQ Acceptance document can be printed and sent to the vendor.

◆ *Reject vendor reply.* The purchasing agent indicates that a vendor reply is rejected, and an RFQ rejection document can be printed and sent to the vendor.

Manually Create an RFQ A manually created RFQ must be assigned an RFQ type of Purchase Order or Purchase Agreement. The RFQ type determines the needed information and the impact of an accepted reply. Other steps in the above-described RFQ process are basically the same for a manually created RFQ.

Additional Considerations about the Basic RFQ Process Several considerations apply to the basic RFQ process, such as manually creating an RFQ without an item number, coordinating follow-up, measuring vendor performance, and creating RFQs for components of a manufactured item.

◆ *RFQs for Items without an Item Number.* An RFQ is sometimes required for something that does not yet have an item number, where the item number will be assigned prior to completing the RFQ process. A line item on an RFQ normally identifies an item number, but a line type of *none* enables you to indicate the desired purchase (without an item number) by entering

---

[8] Previous AX versions such as AX 2012 R3 supported a vendor portal so that a vendor could view and reply to a vendor-specific RFQ. These capabilities are reflected in the descriptive text. However, these capabilities were built on the deprecated Enterprise Portal application which has been replaced by the new web client platform. A replacement for these vendor portal capabilities is not yet available.

information in the name, unit of measure, external item number, and text fields. The line item can be changed from none to an actual item number (on the RFQ or the vendor-specific RFQ) at any time prior to accepting the vendor reply. You cannot accept a vendor reply unless an item number has been assigned.

◆ *Coordinating Follow-up on RFQs.* Vendor-specific RFQs frequently require follow-up to ensure the vendor reply has been received prior to the expiration date. Use the Request for Quote Follow-up form to view all vendor-specific RFQs, and selectively filter the information based on the expiration date, vendor, item, or other attribute.

The Alert functionality within AX provides another approach for coordinating follow-up efforts. For example, the alert notification can be generated when the RFQ expiry date has been reached, so that you can verify whether all of the replies have been received.

◆ *Viewing Transaction History related to an RFQ.* The RFQ transaction history (viewed on the Request for Quote Journal form) contains a record for each vendor-specific RFQ that has been sent, received, accepted or rejected. It also displays the reason for an acceptance or rejection if a reason was entered by the user.

◆ *RFQ Reports and Vendor Performance.* A vendor performance report indicates the ratio of accepted RFQs (and line items) versus the number sent, and also provides a frequency analysis of reason codes for acceptance and rejection. A report of previous RFQs (and their vendor-specific RFQs) can be viewed by item or by vendor.

◆ *RFQs for Components of a Manufactured Item.* When RFQs are required for the components of a manufactured item, you can enter the manufactured item on the RFQ and then use the Explode BOM function to view and select the components.

Vendor Performance Metrics on RFQs The primary metric involves a comparison between the number of RFQs sent to the vendor versus the number of accepted replies (and rejected replies), where the numbers reflect a specified time interval. A higher ratio between the numbers of accepted replies versus sent RFQs indicates better performance. An analysis of the reason codes for accepted and rejected replies provides an additional measure.

12.8 Workflows and Purchase Order Approval

Some scenarios require a purchase order approval process when buying trade goods. An approval process is not typically required when purchasing trade goods based on requirements driven by S&OP game plans, as indicated by planned purchase orders. Within AX, an approval process does not apply to purchase orders that have been created by firming a planned order. Hence, an approval process only applies to a manually-created purchase order.

The term *change management* refers to use of an approval process for purchase orders. The associated policy -- termed *activate change management* -- can be companywide, vendor-specific or order-specific. Use of change management requires the definition of a purchase order approval process, which identifies the steps and responsibilities for approval. A detailed explanation of this setup information falls outside the book's scope because of book length considerations.

When an approval process applies to a manually-created purchase order, an approval status of *draft* is initially assigned to the order. This approval status automatically changes to *in review* after you submit the order for approval, and it subsequently changes to *approved* after successful completion of the approval steps. The status can then be changed to *confirmed*, as previously described in the basic model of purchase order processing (Section 12.1).

12.9 Receiving Inspection

There are several variations of receiving inspection for a purchase order. For example, the inspection may be performed by receiving clerks at the time of reporting arrival, where the clerk can immediately assign an Inventory Status such as *Needs-Inspection* or *Damaged*. Alternatively, inspection may be performed after reporting arrival, where a quality control clerk reports test results against an automatically-created quality order. The test results may be reported while the material remains in a receiving location, or the material may be placed in a separate QC area until test results have been reported. Validation of the quality order can automatically update the Inventory Status of the received material.

The use of quality orders and Inventory Status were mentioned as part of the warehouse management considerations for purchase orders (Section 12.3), and a subsequent chapter about quality management provides further explanation about inspection approaches and quality orders (Sections 17.3 and 17.4).

12.10 Purchase Order Returns

Returning material to a vendor typically involves a different type of purchase order (termed a returned order), but it can also be handled via a purchase order line item with a negative quantity. These two approaches are summarized below, along with a typical business process for returns to vendor.

♦ *Purchase Order Type of Returned Order.* When creating a purchase order, you designate the order type as returned order and enter the vendor RMA (Return Material Authorization) number. The line items for a returned order are expressed with a negative quantity. Line items can be manually entered, or the original purchase order information can be copied precisely (via the *Copy from All* function or the *Create Credit Note* function) with an inverted quantity. A user-defined reason code (termed the *Return Action* code) can be specified for each line item. You can also indicate a line item does not warrant an actual return to vendor (via a scrap flag). After returning the item, the printed invoice reflects a credit note.

A returned order for a purchased item can also be created as part of the process for handling customer returns (Section 11.10).

♦ *Negative Quantity for Purchase Order Line Item.* A line item with a negative quantity can indicate a return to vendor, rather than using a separate purchase order type of returned order. The additional line item typically reflects situations where quality or delivery problems require an immediate return, or an incorrect receipt quantity must be reversed.

Typical Process for a Purchase Order Return   When using returned orders, the typical process consists of several steps performed by different roles, as illustrated in Figure 12.5 and summarized below. The process starts with a request for a return to vendor, and ends with a completed purchase order return.

Overview   The purchasing agent creates a returned order for a specified vendor and identifies the vendor's RMA number. The purchasing agent also creates a line item for each returned item, where the line item identifies an item, a negative quantity, purchase price, ship-from location and the requested ship date. The line item information can also be created by selecting lines from a previously invoiced purchase order, which helps identify the original purchase price. The purchasing agent confirms a purchase order when information has been completely entered. In some scenarios, these steps are performed by an accounts payable clerk.

Figure 12.6 Typical Process for a Purchase Order Return

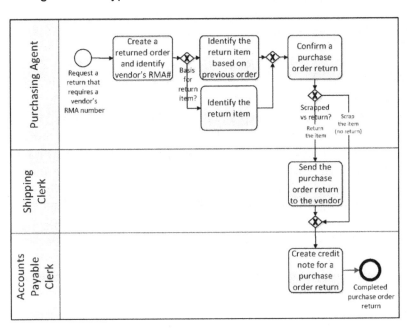

The shipping clerk typically reports the item(s) being sent back for a returned order. The accounts payable clerk creates the vendor's credit note based on the quantity of each item returned, or based on the returned order quantity (when there is no return).

Create a purchase order return and identify the vendor's RMA number The purchasing agent manually creates a returned order for a specified vendor, and identifies the vendor's RMA number. If applicable, the purchasing agent identifies the related blanket purchase order with the vendor. The purchasing agent also creates a line item for each returned item, where the line item identifies an item, a negative quantity, a purchase price, ship-from location and the requested ship date.

Identify the return item based on previously invoiced purchase order The purchasing agent creates a line item on a returned order by finding a previously invoiced purchase order for the pay-to vendor, and selecting the line item(s) and quantity being returned. The search can be based on the item number or purchase order number. Each selected line item creates a line item on the returned order, along with the original purchase price (which acts as the credit amount).

Identify the return item for a return to vendor The purchasing agent creates a line item on the returned order, which specifies the item number, a negative quantity, and a purchase price representing the credit amount. The credit amount defaults to the item's current purchase price with the vendor, and it may be adjusted to reflect partial credit.

Confirm a purchase order return The purchasing agent confirms a purchase order return when information has been completely entered. The confirmation enables subsequent steps in purchase order processing such as sending the return. The purchase order must be confirmed again after updating information. Each confirmation creates a history record so that the purchasing agent can track historical versions.

Send the purchase order return to the vendor The shipping clerk reports the item(s) being sent back for a purchase order return. More specifically, the shipping clerk uses the Posting Product Receipt form to select a line representing a return, and then identifies the "pick" information about the inventory being

returned. The posting can print the packing slip to accompany the items being sent, and it automatically creates a Product Receipt Journal that identifies the financial impact.

12.11 Vendor Information

A subset of vendor information directly relates to purchase order processing. Each vendor is defined in a vendor master file by a unique identifier. Buy-from and pay-to vendors require unique identifiers, and a buy-from vendor can optionally have one or more ship-from addresses. The following data elements have particular significance to purchase order processing.

Vendor Calendar of Work Days When purchase lead times are expressed in working days, the calculation of a purchase order start date and/or delivery date can be based on a specified calendar of the vendor's working days. The calculations use the companywide calendar as the default when a vendor calendar is not specified.

Language for a Vendor The language assigned to each vendor determines which language version should be displayed on printed documents and other vendor interactions. For example, the assigned language determines the language version for an item description on a purchase order confirmation.

Attributes Related to G/L Account Number Assignment General ledger (G/L) account number assignments (such as trade payables and purchase price variances) are based on a combination of vendor and item characteristics. For example, the trade payables account updated by a purchase order receipt can be based on the vendor group and item group assigned to the vendor and item respectively.

Financial Dimensions for a Vendor The financial dimension(s) assigned to a vendor provide a means to analyze purchases by vendor type. They can be used in conjunction with financial dimensions assigned to other entities such as items to provide multi-dimensional purchase analyses.

One-Time Vendors and Creating Vendors during Purchase Order Entry When initially entering a purchase order, the buy-from vendor can be created on the fly by indicating a one-time vendor. You enter the vendor name and address information as part of creating the purchase order, and the system automatically creates a new vendor that is flagged as a one-time vendor. Additional information defaults from an existing vendor designated as the source of one-time vendor information. The vendor information can then be manually maintained, including the removal of the one-time vendor flag.

Vendor Hold Status A vendor hold status can prevent all transactions from being recorded, or only prevent invoices or payments from being entered for the vendor. You assign the vendor hold status by explicitly accessing the *change vendor status* function from the vendor master. Optional information about the hold status includes a hold release date and the assignment of a user-defined reason code. An additional policy only applies to a multi-company scenario (in which the same vendor has been defined in multiple AX companies within one AX instance), so that you can optionally assign the vendor's hold status to all companies.

Same Vendor defined for Multiple Companies Some multi-company scenarios involve the same vendor serving multiple companies. In this case, you can define the vendor in one company, and then add the vendor to another company along with an applicable vendor group and vendor hold status. However, you must define all other aspects of vendor information in each additional company.

Intercompany Trading Partner Some enterprises have multiple companies defined within a single Dynamics AX instance, and trading between the companies. A sister company can act as a vendor (or customer) for intercompany trading purposes. A vendor (or customer) must be defined that represents the sister company. A subsequent chapter explains intercompany orders (Chapter 18).

Summarized Information by Vendor Summarized information about a vendor can be viewed, and transaction detail can be viewed by type of purchase document, such as outstanding purchase orders, receipts, invoices, and backorder purchase lines.

12.12 Coordinate Purchase Orders

A firm's S&OP game plans provide the primary driver of purchasing activities for material items. The key tools for coordinating these activities include planned purchase orders and action messages, which reflect the model of SCM decision-making embedded in coverage planning data for purchased items (Section 9.3). Several other coordination tools can also be employed, such as vendor schedules and the inquiries/reports about problems in delivery dates.

Planned Purchase Orders The planned orders can be viewed on the Planned Purchase Orders form or the Planned Orders form, where the displayed information typically represents the current master plan.[9] Planned orders can be viewed based on selection criteria such as the buyer group and order date, so that the responsible buyer can mark and firm the planned orders accordingly.

Actual purchase orders can be created from planned orders via a function termed *firming planned orders.* You typically mark (via a check box) the planned orders needing to be firmed. The firming function creates single-line purchase orders unless you indicate grouping preferences via the firming dialogue.[10] For example, the grouping preferences can reflect the vendor, a period size (such as daily or weekly) and purchase agreements, resulting in a multi-line purchase order with all lines related to the same purchase agreement. Execution of the firming function automatically deletes the selected planned orders, and creates a log for tracking which planned orders have been firmed and by whom.

---

[9] You can view information based on a selected set of master plan data or forecast plan data. For simplicity's sake the explanation focuses on the set of data representing the current master plan.
[10] The default values for grouping preferences (when firming planned purchase orders) are defined as part of the Master Planning parameters.

In many cases, you may need to analyze the rationale for a planned purchase order prior to firming. You can view the net requirements and related action messages for a selected planned order. In addition, the analysis may lead to one or more of the following actions prior to firming.

◆ Approve a planned order. Approving a planned order will lock the scheduled date and quantity, and prevent it from being deleted by master scheduling logic or the Delete Plan task.

◆ View and select an alternative vendor. The selection list for the vendor field identifies the alternative vendors based on the item's approved vendor list, purchase price trade agreement information, or vendor item information. The trade agreement information provides the basis for selecting a vendor based on purchase price, quantity breakpoints, and validity dates.

◆ Change quantity and/or delivery date for the planned purchase order.

◆ Split the planned purchase order using a specified quantity and date.

◆ Group together several selected planned orders for the same item, where the delivery date of the firmed order reflects the currently selected planned order.

◆ Assign the planned order to an existing purchase order so that the firming process adds a line item to the existing order.

◆ Convert the planned order to a request for quote, as described in a previous section (Section 12.7).

◆ Identify a different source of supply (such a transfer or production) by changing the planned purchase order to a planned transfer order or production order.

Some scenarios have correctly modeled their SCM decision making for selected items so that the planned purchase orders can be automatically firmed (within the time period defined by a firming fence). Other scenarios employ the freeze time fence to indicate the shortest possible lead time for a purchase item, so that master scheduling logic will place planned orders at the end of the frozen period. These time fence policies are embedded in the coverage group assigned to an item.

Action Messages Action messages represent one of the key tools for coordinating procurement activities to meet the S&OP game plans. Master scheduling logic can generate action messages for planned and actual purchase orders. The logic reflects the action message policies embedded within the coverage group assigned to an item, as described in a previous chapter (Section 9.10). The action messages can be viewed and acted upon in several different ways:

◆ View action messages for a selected item as part of the Net Requirements inquiry.

◆ View action messages for all items on the Actions form, and optionally apply the suggested action for a selected message or access the Action Graph.

◆ View related action messages (for a selected message) by accessing the Action Graph, and optionally apply a suggested action.

◆ View the action messages for just actual purchase orders using the Actions for Purchase Orders form or the Actions for Purchase Orders to Advance form, and optionally apply the suggested action for a selected message or access the Action Graph.

As a general guideline, you should view related action messages using the Action Graph in order to understand the context of production orders or transfer orders that are causing an action message for a purchase order.

Messages about Calculated Delays This message indicates that a purchase order delivery date will cause a delay in meeting a requirement date, and the purchase order typically has an associated "advance" action message. The messages can be viewed from several different starting points (such as the Net Requirements inquiry) and you the relevant purchase order to indicate a change. A previous chapter provided guidelines for effective use of messages about calculated delays (Section 9.11).

Vendor Schedules A vendor schedule provides visibility of actual and planned purchase orders to the vendor. However, standard AX does not currently provide a vendor schedule, so that a customized report must be developed.

Identify Potential Problems in Delivery Dates The confirmed delivery date for a purchase line (or a line within a delivery schedule) typically indicates the most realistic up-to-date information from the vendor. A standard inquiry identifies confirmed purchase orders without confirmed delivery dates, and a second inquiry identifies purchase lines with past due delivery dates. You can also identify purchase-related backorders. These problems typically require action by the purchasing agent and coordination with the vendor.

12.13 Metrics related to Vendor Performance

Several different metrics indicate vendor performance. Example metrics include on-time delivery of purchase orders, returns to vendor, and purchase price variances for standard cost items. Other metrics reflect a quality perspective, such as failed quality orders (and related test results) for purchase receipts, and purchasing-related cases. Another source of metrics involves user-definable evaluation criteria, and the manual assignment of a rating for a vendor. These various types of performance metrics are described below.

◆ *Review on-time delivery of purchase orders.* The purchasing manager can review several metrics of on-time delivery for a vendor. Example metrics include the percent of on-time receipts (and the percent late and percent early), and the average days late (and average days early).

◆ *Review returns to vendor.* The purchasing manager can review purchase order returns to a vendor, expressed in units or value.

◆ *Review purchase price variances for standard cost items.* With a standard cost item, the purchasing manager can review purchase price variances related to purchase receipts and vendor invoices.

◆ *Review failed quality orders related to purchase receipts.* When using quality orders, the quality manager can review the purchasing-related quality orders that have failed the validation of test results.

◆ *Review cases related to purchase orders or vendors.* When using cases, the quality manager can review the cases related to purchase orders or vendors.

◆ *Review the ratings assigned to user-definable vendor evaluation criteria.* The user-definable criteria can reflect any metric, and you manually assign the vendor's rating for each metric. The rating consists of a 5-point scale ranging from 1 (very poor) to 5 (very good).

◆ Review vendor replies to RFQs. The primary metric involves a comparison between the number of RFQs sent to the vendor versus the number of accepted replies (and rejected replies), where the numbers reflect a specified time interval. A higher ratio between the numbers of accepted replies versus sent RFQs indicates better performance.

Additional examples of vendor performance metrics are illustrated in Case 12.4 and Case 12.5.

12.14 Workspaces related to Purchase Orders

Several predefined workspaces are related to purchase orders, as described in the following summary of each workspace and its applicable functionality.

Purchase Order Preparation Workspace   This workspace identifies purchase orders with a status of "In External Review" or "Approved", and the order lines without a confirmed delivery date. You can confirm orders and create new purchase orders. The displayed information can be filtered for a selected buyer group. The links provide access to information about planned purchase orders and the RFQ replies from vendors.

Purchase Order Receipt and Follow-up Workspace This workspace identifies purchase lines with delayed receipts and with pending receipts, and registered arrivals that still need posting of the product receipt. It also identifies order receipts where the vendor invoice has not yet been entered. The links provide access to information about open purchase order lines, the product receipt journal, and the Direct Delivery form (for coordinating direct delivery orders).

12.15 Additional Case Studies

Case 12.2: Purchase Requisitions for Indirect Material A manufacturer used purchase requisitions for many types of indirect materials, where various types and amounts of purchases required an approval process. They wanted to use the workflow management capabilities within AX. A typical approval process involved the following steps.

1.   Create a purchase requisition for one or more items. The identity of the person acting as the requisitioner (and their position within the organizational hierarchy) can limit the items being requested, and impact an approval process based on the organizational hierarchy.

2.   Submit the purchase requisition. After submission, the workflow should define additional steps related to task completion and approval.

3.   Report a task as completed. A typical task involves an RFQ, and an accepted RFQ reply represents completion of the task.

4. Approve or reject the purchase requisition. The approval process can contain one or more approval steps. A simple approval process might contain a single approval step and a specified user as the assigned approver. Alternatively, the assigned approver for an approval step can reflect the organization hierarchy or a group of users.

5. Create the purchase order for an approved purchase requisition.

Case 12.3: Supplier Coordination via E-Commerce A manufacturer wanted to improve coordination via several e-commerce initiatives with their suppliers. The e-commerce initiatives included Biztalk and electronic marketplace capabilities. They communicated purchase order releases and changes to their suppliers, and received confirmations and changes from the suppliers. Automating these basic business processes improved coordination and reduced data entry errors and time. Additional capabilities included a common baseline of vendor performance metrics (such as delivery quantities/dates and tolerances), tracking of in-transit materials, and replenishment of vendor-managed inventory.

Case 12.4: Vendor Performance A manufacturing company wanted to enhance vendor performance analysis beyond the standard reports for quantity and cost variances. They wanted an overall score for each vendor based on the metrics described below, where the metrics reflected receipts during a specified time period.

◆ *Delivery Timeliness.* The scoring percentage reflected the number of on-time receipts divided by the total number of receipt transactions. On-time receipts reflected the line item's confirmed date and delivery tolerances expressed in days.

◆ *Delivery Quantity.* The scoring percentage reflected the number of correct quantity receipts divided by the total number of receipt transactions. The correct quantity receipts reflected the line item's order quantity and delivery tolerances in percentages. This metric required the ability to accept receipts outside of tolerances.

◆ *Quality.* The scoring percentage reflected the total good quantity divided by the total received quantity. This metric required linkage between the reporting of good and scrapped material to the originating purchase order receipt.

◆ *Price.* The scoring percentage reflected a standard costing approach, with the total value of purchase price variances divided by the total value of received items.

Case 12.5:   Vendor Performance Metrics   A manufacturing company wanted to customize the vendor performance metrics within standard AX. One metric involved complete delivery quantity for purchase lines during a specified time period, where the metric reflected a comparison of actual quantity received versus the ordered quantity. The metric consisted of three categories for (1) exact quantity, (2) under-delivery within delivery tolerance, and (3) over-delivery within tolerance. Another metric involved purchase receipts of items requiring a certificate of analysis from the vendor, where the metric indicated whether the COA was included with the receipt.

Case 12.6: Invoice Matching using Quality Results   The accounts payable function at a manufacturer performed invoice matching against the purchase order, receipts, and actual quality of the received material. The actual values for several batch attributes of an item were recorded upon receipt, and then compared to the allowable ranges, in order to use the quality results as the basis for invoice matching.

12.16 Executive Summary

Purchase order processing for direct material often involves a wide spectrum of business practices. This chapter described a basic model for purchase order processing, which provided the foundation for explaining key considerations and major variations. It covered sourcing and agreement information for purchased items, including the preferred vendor and agreements about purchase prices. Master scheduling logic can help coordinate procurement activities by communicating the need for planned orders and suggested changes to existing orders. The case studies highlighted variations in purchase order processing, including vendor coordination via e-commerce initiatives.

Chapter 13

Transfer Order Processing

Many businesses involved in manufacturing and distribution have inventory at multiple physical sites, and require transfers between these sites. Transfers between sites can be managed using transfers orders or intercompany orders, depending on the grouping of physical sites into companies. This chapter focuses on transfer orders for coordinating transfers between inventory locations in a single company, and a subsequent chapter focuses on transfers in a multicompany supply chain.

As an explanatory approach, it is easiest to start with a basic model of transfer order processing. The basic model provides a foundation for explaining key considerations and coordination of transfer orders. These considerations are reflected in the following sections within the chapter.

1. Basic Model of Transfer Order Processing
2. Key Considerations about Transfer Order Processing
3. Coordinate Transfer Order Activities

Previous chapters have covered the fundamentals of modeling inventory locations (Chapter 3), and the use of coverage planning data to model SCM decision-making about transfers between inventory locations (Section 9.7). A subsequent chapter explains the use of transfer orders in scenarios with subcontracted production, such as transferring supplied material or a finished quantity.

13.1 Basic Model of Transfer Order Processing

The typical steps in transfer order processing can vary based on several factors, such as different approaches to warehouse management at the ship-from and ship-to warehouses. This section summarizes a basic model of transfer order processing and the related life cycles.

Overview of the Basic Model   The basic model of transfer order processing starts with a requirement to transfer material, and the role of a purchasing agent or DRP coordinator.[1] This explanation primarily employs a role title of DRP coordinator. The requirement is typically identified by a planned order stemming from S&OP game plans and the item's planning data, and the planned order can be analyzed and firmed to create an actual transfer order. A planned transfer order can also be manually entered (and optionally approved) and then firmed, or an actual transfer order can be manually entered. These manual entries often stem from unplanned requirements. At the ship-from warehouse, a warehouse worker and shipping clerk perform subsequent steps for transfer order picking/shipping, which differ when using the basic versus advanced approach to warehouse management. Both approaches support order-based picking described in this basic model. After actual shipment, an item's inventory is moved to the in-transit warehouse associated with the ship-from warehouse, and receipts reduce the in-transit inventory.

At the ship-to warehouse, a receiving clerk and warehouse worker perform subsequent steps for transfer order receiving, which differ when using the basic versus advanced approach to warehouse management. These roles and steps are summarized in Figure 13.1 and described below.

Firm a Planned Transfer Order   The purchasing agent or DRP coordinator typically uses the Planned Transfer Orders form to analyze and firm planned orders, which creates actual transfer orders with one or more transfer order lines based on grouping preferences.

Enter a Transfer Order   The purchasing agent or DRP coordinator creates a new transfer order by starting from the Transfer Order form and specifying the ship-from and ship-to warehouses (and the dates for shipment and receipt) as part of the transfer order header. The DRP coordinator also enters transfer order line items, where each line item identifies a product, a quantity, and the shipment and receipt dates.

---

[1] The role title of a DRP coordinator is not specifically identified within the standard AX roles. Similar titles within the standard AX roles include the logistics manager, transportation coordinator and warehouse planner.

Figure 13.1 Basic Model of Transfer Order Processing

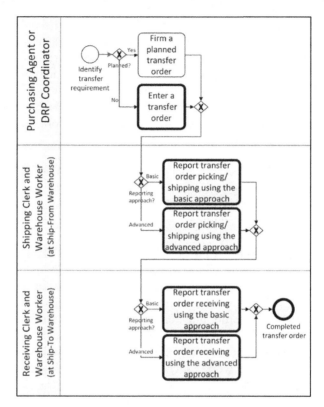

Report Transfer Order Picking/Shipping using the Basic Approach to Warehouse Management   The shipping clerk typically uses the Release Transfer Order Picking form to review and select open transfer order lines that require picking/shipping, and then generate the picking lists for selected orders. The generation of a picking list will reserve the item's inventory for the transfer line (if not already reserved).   As alternative approaches, a picking list can be generated from a transfer order, or the picking lists can be generated from a periodic task.

The warehouse worker reports actual picking against a transfer order picking list and then posts it.   The shipping clerk reports actual shipment by posting the transfer order shipment for picked items.

Report Transfer Order Picking/Shipping using the Advanced Approach to Warehouse Management In a typical scenario, the shipping clerk uses the Release To Warehouse form to review and select open transfer order lines that require picking/shipping, and then releases selected orders to the warehouse (which updates the release status for each order). With an order-based picking approach, the release-to-warehouse step can automatically create a shipment and load (with a waved status) and a shipment wave (with a released status) for each transfer order. In addition, the released shipment wave automatically creates a picking work order consisting of work lines that identify the pick and put instructions.

The warehouse worker reports actual picking by using the mobile device to report completion of picking work orders. Completion of the picking work to an outbound dock results in shipments and loads that are ready to ship. The shipping clerk reports actual shipment by confirming the outbound shipments.

Report Transfer Order Picking/Shipping using a Simple Inventory Transaction The shipping clerk can use the Transfer Order form to simply report actual shipment of the transfer order, where the relevant details about the picked inventory (such as bin location and possibly the license plate ID) must be identified for each transfer order line item prior to posting. This simple inventory transaction works for both the basic and advanced approach to warehouse management. It avoids the use of picking lists in the basic approach, and it avoids the use of picking work orders (and the use of loads, shipments and waves) in the advanced approach. This option is not shown in Figure 13.1 in order to simplify the diagram.

Review In-Transit Inventory for an Item You can view an item's in-transit inventory on various on-hand inquiries, or view the on-hand inquiries for the in-transit warehouse.

Report Transfer Order Receiving using the Basic Approach to Warehouse Management The receiving clerk typically uses the Arrival Overview form to review and select shipped transfer order lines, and then create an arrival journal containing the selected lines. The receiving clerk registers the actual receipts against each journal line item and posts the journal to update inventory balances. As a final step, the receiving clerk posts the receipt for a transfer order. For received material with putaway requirements, the warehouse worker uses the Transfer Journal form to report transfers from the receiving location to the putaway location.

Report Transfer Order Receiving using the Advanced Approach to Warehouse Management The nature of transfer order receiving depends on whether the shipped material has been identified with a license plate ID. In a typical process, the receiving clerk uses the mobile device to receive a license plate ID for a transfer order shipment, which updates inventory balances and automatically creates putaway work. The warehouse worker uses the mobile device to report putaway from the receiving location to a stocking location. A suggested stocking location can reflect location directives, or the warehouse worker can determine and report the stocking location. As an alternative reporting approach, the receiving clerk can report receipt and putaway as part of a single mobile device transaction.

When the shipped material is not identified with a license plate ID, the receiving clerk uses the mobile device to receive a transfer order number, and subsequent receiving steps are the same.

Report Transfer Order Receiving using a Simple Inventory Transaction A simple inventory transaction applies when using the basic approach to warehouse management. The receiving clerk can use the Transfer Order form to simply post the transfer order receipt, and avoid the use of arrival journals. When using the advanced approach to warehouse management, this simple inventory transaction becomes quite complicated so that it does not represent a useful alternative. The option for a simple inventory transaction is not shown in Figure 13.1 in order to simplify the diagram.

Life Cycles Related to Transfer Order Processing The life cycles related to the basic model of transfer order processing include a status for the transfer order, and an inventory status for the item on a transfer order line, where steps in the business process automatically update the status. These steps are summarized in Figure 13.2, along with the status of related life cycles. The steps represent the minimum number of touch points for updating status.

An order status indicates the following steps in the life cycle of a transfer order.

- *Created.* A created status means that line items can be added and data maintained on a transfer order.
- *Shipped.* All lines have been shipped.
- *Received.* All lines have been received. Information cannot be changed for transfer orders with a shipped or received status.

Figure 13.2 Life Cycles Related to Transfer Order Processing

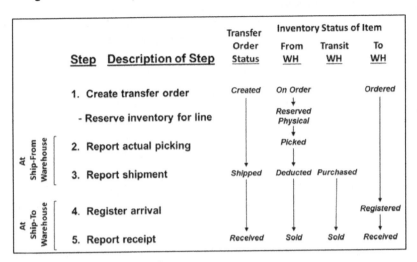

Each line item on a transfer order has a remaining status, as described below. This status is not shown in Figure 13.2 in order to keep the diagram simple.

- *Shipping Updates.* The line has only been created or the line has not been completely shipped.
- *Receive Updates.* The line has been completely shipped but not yet completely received.
- *Nothing.* The line has been completely shipped and received.

The inventory status for the item on a transfer order line is shown on the right side of Figure 13.2, where the inventory status varies for the different warehouses involved in the transfer. With respect to the ship-from warehouse, for example, the steps in transfer order processing will change the status from *On Order* to *Reserved Physical, Picked, Deducted* and *Sold.*

13.2 Key Considerations for Transfer Order Processing

Several aspects of AX functionality represent key considerations for transfer order processing. The following list of key considerations and their extended explanations build on the basic model of transfer order processing.

- Significance of a Single Transfer Order
- Shipment and Delivery Dates for a Transfer Order
- Transportation Time between Warehouses
- Tracking Number for a Transfer Order
- One-Step Shipment for a Transfer Order
- Reserving Material for a Transfer Order Line
- Cost Change Variances on Transfers between AX Sites

Significance of a Single Transfer Order A single transfer order usually represents a single shipment and the line items reflect the shipment contents. It sometimes represents a container with a unique identifier, and the transfer order number can be manually assigned to reflect the container identifier.

Shipment and Delivery Dates for a Transfer Order The transfer order header specifies a shipment date and receipt date, along with the ship-from and ship-to site/warehouses and a mode of delivery such as air or truck. The difference between the two dates reflects the expected transportation time (expressed in days) between the two locations.

The assignment of these dates is affected by the delivery date control policy assigned to the transfer order header, which can enforce basic rules such as the working calendar for both warehouses, the calendar for the delivery mode, and the expected transportation time between a pair of warehouses.

A delivery date control policy is also assigned to each transfer order line. It is inherited from the item based on its companywide or site-specific order settings (for transfer orders), much like an item's delivery date control policy (for sales orders) is inherited by a sales line. Figure 13.3 summarizes the delivery date control options for a transfer order line, and the significance of each option.

Transportation Time between Warehouses The transportation time between a pair of warehouses can be defined. The transportation time is expressed in days, and you can optionally specify a different number of days for different modes of delivery.

In certain special cases, the transportation time between warehouses will vary by item, such as a very large item that requires special transportation arrangements and a longer time for moving the item via large trucks. You can define this transfer time as part of the item's site/warehouse-specific coverage planning data.

Figure 13.3 Delivery Date Control Options
for a Transfer Order Line

Delivery Date Control Option	Scenario	Comments
Sales Lead Time	Use Basic Rules	Auto-assign requested dates based on basic rules Enforce basic rules for manually entered dates*
ATP	Stocked Item	Auto-assign requested dates based on basic rules + ATP logic Enforce basic rules + ATP logic for manually entered dates*
None	Allow assignment of unrealistic dates	Ignore basic rules for manually entered dates

Legend: * = Display exceptions on *Available Ship and Receipt Dates* form, and transfer
a selected date to change the ship date

Tracking Number for a Transfer Order You can optionally specify a tracking number for a transfer order and print an associated document (titled the Transfer Order Shipment) to accompany the transferred material.

One-Step Shipment for a Transfer Order Some scenarios employ a one-step shipment process for a transfer order, which means there is no tracking of in-transit inventory and no receipt transaction. You indicate this policy (termed the auto-receive policy) when posting a transfer order shipment. The one-step approach can be used with short transportation times.

Reserving Material for a Transfer Order Line Most scenarios employ reservations at the time you release a transfer order for picking, and the picking list (or picking work) communicates these reservations. Some scenarios require reservations at the time of creating a transfer order, and the reservation policy assigned to a transfer order line item indicates whether inventory will be reserved automatically or manually. When initially adding a line item, this policy – labeled Reserve Items Automatically -- is inherited from the transfer order header, and it can be overridden. The policy for the transfer order header can be inherited from a companywide policy (embedded in the Inventory and Warehouse Management parameters).

The reservation logic differs between the basic and advanced approaches to warehouse management. The advanced approach requires assignment of an additional item policy termed the reservation hierarchy.

Cost Change Variances on Transfers between AX Sites   With a standard cost item, the item's site-specific standard costs can differ between two AX sites. The difference frequently reflects a higher standard cost at the ship-to site because of freight or other landed costs. Transferring the item will result in a cost change variance when the costs differ between two AX sites, where the variance is generated upon receipt at the ship-to site.

13.3 Coordinate Transfer Order Activities

A firm's S&OP game plans provide the primary driver of transfers for material items. The key tools for coordinating these activities include planned transfer orders and action messages, which reflect the model of SCM decision-making embedded in coverage planning data for transfers (Section 9.5). Other coordination tools include the visibility of needed picking/shipping and expected receiving for transfer orders.

Planned Transfer Orders   The planned orders can be viewed on the Planned Transfer Orders form or the Planned Orders form, where the displayed information typically represents the current master plan.[2] A planned transfer order identifies the item's preferred refilling warehouse. You can also manually add a planned transfer order.

Actual transfer orders can be created from planned orders via a function termed *firming planned orders*. You typically mark (via a check box) the planned orders needing to be firmed. The firming function creates single-line transfer orders unless you indicate grouping preferences via the firming dialogue, such as grouping by a daily or weekly period size. Execution of the firming function automatically deletes the selected planned orders, and creates a log for tracking which planned orders have been firmed and by whom.

In many cases, you may need to analyze the rationale for a planned transfer order prior to firming. You can view the net requirements and related action messages for a selected planned order. In addition, the analysis may lead to one or more of the following actions prior to firming.

-   Approve a planned order. Approving a planned order will lock the scheduled date and quantity, and prevent it from being deleted by master scheduling logic or the Delete Plan task.
-   Change quantity and/or delivery date for the planned transfer order.
-   Split the planned transfer order using a specified quantity and date.

---

[2] You can view information based on a selected set of master plan data or forecast plan data. For simplicity's sake the explanation focuses on the set of data representing the current master plan.

- Group together several selected planned orders for the same item.
- Assign the planned order to an existing transfer order so that the firming process adds a line item to the existing order.
- Change the ship-from warehouse, thereby indicating an alternate source of supply. You can view inventory availability at other sites to support decisions about changing the source of supply.
- Identify a different source of supply (such as a purchase or production) by changing the planned transfer order to a planned purchase order or production order.

Some scenarios have correctly modeled their SCM decision making for selected items so that the planned transfer orders can be automatically firmed (within the time period defined by a firming fence). These time fence policies are embedded in the coverage group assigned to an item as part of the site/warehouse-specific policies at the ship-to location.

Action Messages   Action messages represent one of the key tools for coordinating transfer order activities to meet the S&OP game plans. Master scheduling logic can generate action messages for planned and actual transfer orders. The logic reflects the action message policies embedded within the coverage group assigned to an item, as described in a previous chapter (Section 9.9). The action messages can be viewed and acted upon in several different ways:

- View action messages for a selected item as part of the Net Requirements inquiry.
- View action messages for all items on the Actions form, and optionally apply the suggested action for a selected message or access the Action Graph.
- View related action messages (for a selected message) by accessing the Action Graph, and optionally apply a suggested action.

As a general guideline, you should view related action messages (using the Action Graph) in order to understand the context of production orders, purchase orders or other transfer orders that are causing an action message for a transfer order. Additional guidelines were described in a previous chapter (Section 9.10).

Messages about Calculated Delays   This message indicates that a transfer order delivery date will cause a delay in meeting a requirement date, and the transfer order typically has an associated "advance" action message. The messages can be viewed from several starting points (such as the Net Requirements inquiry) and you can access the relevant order to indicate a change.

A previous chapter provided guidelines for effective use of messages about calculated delays (Section 9.11).

Special Case for Suggested Transfers between AX Warehouses at an AX Site   Warehouses within a given AX site often reflect close proximity, so that actual transfers between warehouses are generally handled through a transfer journal rather than a transfer order. In this case, planned transfer orders can be used to communicate requirements, but firming the planned orders will generate a transfer journal which can be subsequently posted after physically moving the material. This approach requires a site-specific policy termed "Use transfer journals for movements within site" otherwise firming a planned order results in a transfer order.

Other Coordination Tools for Transfer Orders   Other coordination tools provide visibility of picking and receiving activities, and the tools vary when using the basic versus advanced approach to warehouse management. With the basic approach, for example, you can anticipate picking activities using the Release Transfer Order Picking form, and anticipate arrivals using the Arrival Overview form. With the advanced approach, you can anticipate picking activities using the Release to Warehouse form or the Load Planning Workbench.

13.4 Additional Case Studies

Case 13.1: Transfer Orders in a Distribution Network   A manufacturing company had a distribution network consisting of smaller manufacturing plants that supplied products to two regional distribution centers. The transfers between plants and the distribution centers were coordinated by transfer orders. The smaller plants employed the basic approach to warehouse management for reporting transfer order picking/receiving, while each distribution center employed the advanced WMS approach for reporting transfer order receipts.

Case 13.2: Transfers between Adjacent Warehouses   The warehouse manager at a manufacturing company with two adjacent warehouses (within the same AX site) employed transfer journals for moving inventory between the warehouses. A Transfer Journal was initially created and populated with the items and quantities to be moved. The printed version provided a picking list (and turnaround document) for warehouse workers at the originating warehouse, and they entered the actual results for the "from warehouse" on the journal lines. After the material was received, warehouse workers entered the results for the "to warehouse" and posted the transfer journal.

In this scenario, the transfer journals were created by firming planned transfer orders. This reflects a site-specific policy to "use transfer journals for movements within the site" since both warehouses are within the same AX site. It also reflects the item's coverage planning policies about the warehouse source for planned transfer orders.

Case 13.3: Transfer Orders to/from a Subcontractor Warehouse As part of supporting subcontracted production, a manufacturer used transfer orders to send the supplied material to the subcontractor warehouse and also transfer the finished quantities back to their internal warehouse. The actual receipt of a transfer order at the subcontractor was entered into AX (by a coordinator role) as a simple inventory transaction. A simple inventory transaction was also entered for actual shipment of a transfer order from the subcontractor.

13.5 Executive Summary

This chapter focused on transfer orders for coordinating transfers between inventory locations in a single company. It started with a basic model of transfer order processing and related life cycles, and the basic model provided a foundation for explaining key considerations and coordination of transfer orders. Several case studies illustrated the use of transfer orders, such as transfers between adjacent warehouses, transfers in a distribution network, and transfers for subcontracted production.

Chapter 14

Production Order Processing

Production orders provide a key coordination tool for scheduling and reporting production activities in most discrete manufacturers. Some mixed mode scenarios also use batch orders and/or kanban orders to coordinate production, but this chapter focuses on the terminology and use of production orders.

A basic model of production order processing provides the starting point for further explanation, such as the order life cycle, the significance of the picking list journal, and other key considerations. It also provides a baseline for explaining variations, such as different approaches to report picking, labor, and finished quantities, and different approaches to coordination of production activities. These topics are reflected in the following sections within the chapter.

1. Basic Model of Production Order Processing
2. Life Cycle of a Production Order
3. Significance of a Single Order and the Picking List Journal
4. Key Considerations about Production Order Processing
5. Production Order Picking using the Advanced WMS Approach
6. Labor Reporting using Route Cards and Job Cards
7. Labor Reporting using the MES Capabilities
8. Report the Finished Quantity of a Production Order
9. Rework Order for a Finished Quantity
10. Production Inspection for a Production Order
11. Schedule an Individual Order
12. Costing for a Production Order
13. Coordinate Production Activities
14. Production Schedules and Capacity Analysis
15. Performance Metrics for Production
16. Workspaces related to Production Orders

14.1 Basic Model of Production Order Processing

The typical steps in production order processing can vary based on several factors, such as different approaches to creation, picking, receiving and inspection.   This section summarizes a basic model of production order processing with several characteristics that simplify the model and explanations. First, the basic model focuses on internal production of a standard product, where a single production order represents one production run and the picking list reflects the entire order quantity.   Second, firming a planned production order typically provides the basis for creating the production order.   Third, the manufactured item and its components do not require batch or serial tracking. And fourth, the basic model does not include production inspection steps. The basic model provides a foundation for explaining variations in subsequent sections.

Overview of the Basic Model   The basic model of production order processing starts with the role of a production planner and a requirement for a manufactured item.   The requirement is typically identified by a planned order stemming from S&OP game plans and the item's planning data, and the planned order can be analyzed and firmed to create an actual production order. Alternatively, the planner manually creates and then schedules a production order, typically to meet an unplanned requirement.   If needed, the planner reviews and updates the production order prior to reporting the order as released or started.

A machine operator and warehouse worker perform subsequent steps for production order picking and receiving, and the steps differ when using the basic versus advanced approach to warehouse management.   The machine operator also reports actual labor and resources against the production order, and updates the order status to Ended when all activities have been reported. These roles and steps are summarized in Figure 14.1 and described below.

Firm a Planned Production order   The production planner analyzes and firms a planned production order that reflects requirements stemming from the S&OP game plans and the item's coverage planning data.   The production planner can analyze the source of requirements and action messages for the planned order, and optionally edit the planned order -- such as changing the suggested quantity or date -- prior to firming. Firming a planned order results in an actual production order; the actual order is typically assigned an order status of *Scheduled.*[1]

---

[1] The status assigned to a production order generated by the firming process reflects an item-specific policy embedded in the coverage group assigned to the item. A *Scheduled* status reflects a commonly used policy.

Figure 14.1 Basic Model of Production Order Processing

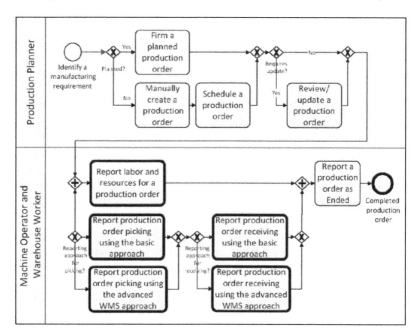

Manually Create a Production order   The production planner manually creates a production order, typically to meet an unplanned requirement or as part of a manually-maintained master schedule. When creating the order (using the Create Production Order dialogue), the planner specifies the item, quantity, site/warehouse and delivery date.   Based on this information, the dialogue displays the active BOM version and route version, and these can be optionally overridden prior to order creation. Completion of the dialogue results in the creation of a production order (with a *Created* status) and an order-dependent BOM and routing.

Schedule a Production Order   The production planner schedules a manually-created production order so that the requirements for components and resources will be recognized. The scheduling logic assigns the start/end dates to the production order, and also the operation start/end times when using routing data. This step changes the order status to *Scheduled,* and it may also be taken for a production order that has already been scheduled. The two choices for scheduling an order – termed operations scheduling and job scheduling -- were discussed in a previous chapter about routing information (Section 6.10).

Review/Update the Production Order The production planner may need to review and update the production order. For example, the production planner may change the order quantity or the order-dependent BOM, schedule the production order on different dates, or lock the order to prevent rescheduling. When using routing data and job scheduling of production orders, the production planner can review the detailed schedule of operation start/stop times in tabular or Gantt chart format, and optionally assign an operation to a different resource.

Report Labor and Resources for a Production Order The need for reporting labor and resources depends on the use of routing data, and the reporting approach can vary. When actual time must be reported, the machine operator can report actual operation time and unit completions against a Route Card Journal (or a Job Card Journal) and then post the journal. Reporting unit completions at the last operation can optionally update the finished quantity of the parent item. A Route Card Journal can be manually created, and also automatically created as part of starting an order. Alternatively, the machine operator can use the Manufacturing Execution System (MES) capabilities to report time. The reporting of labor and resource usage provides the basis for calculating remaining work for the production order.

Some scenarios will backflush the use of labor and resources, which can be triggered by reporting a production order as started or by reporting a finished quantity. The started quantity or finished quantity automatically generates and posts a Route Card Journal.

Report Production Order Picking using the Basic Approach to Warehouse Management The basic approach supports an order-based picking approach for production orders. In a typical process, the machine operator reports a production order as Started which acts as the trigger for creating a picking list journal based on the Start dialogue policies. The warehouse worker reviews the printed version of the picking list journal, reports actual picking against the picking list journal, and then posts it. The picked material is charged to work in process for the production order, and deducted from inventory. The picked material is typically delivered physically to production but not to a specific location.

In some cases, the machine operator may need to revise actual usage relative to the picked material. The machine operator manually creates a picking list journal containing the adjustments and then posts it.

Report Production Order Picking using the Advanced WMS Approach to Warehouse Management In a typical process with order-based picking, the machine operator reports a production order as Released, which acts as the trigger for several automatic actions to support actual production. This includes creating and releasing a production wave for the order, which triggers creation of picking work for delivering components to a production input location when it has insufficient component inventory.

The warehouse worker reviews the released production waves and the associated picking work for raw material. Using the mobile device, the warehouse worker reports completion of the raw material picking work for delivering components to the designated production input location.

When ready, the machine operator reports a production order as Started, which automatically generates a picking list journal based on the Start dialogue policies. The machine operator reports actual material usage on the picking list journal and posts it. In some cases, the machine operator will manually generate a picking list as an alternative to automatic generation, or to identify unexpected component requirements. In either case, the machine operator posts the picking list journal after reporting actual material usage.

An alternative process employs wave picking, where the contents of a production wave consist of raw material picking work orders that have been created for multiple released production orders. The contents of the production wave are defined by a wave planning process, where some of the steps can be performed automatically to reflect normal decision making logic, as modeled by policies within a wave template. For example, a production wave template might be defined so that the raw material picking work created by releases of different production orders at different times will be automatically added to an existing wave. If needed, the planner can manually update the wave contents (such as adding or deleting wave lines) prior to processing and releasing the production wave. At that point in time, the warehouse worker uses the mobile device to report completion of the raw material picking work for delivering components to the designated production input location.

Report Production Order Receiving using the Basic Approach to Warehouse Management The finished quantity of a production order can be reported using different approaches and delivered to different locations. For example, the finished quantity may be reported multiple times for a given order, or reported once when it represents the entire order quantity. The finished quantity can be reported using the Report as Finished form or the Report as Finished Journal, or by using the Route Card Journal for reporting unit completions at the last operation. In addition, the finished quantity may be reported into a production location by the machine operator, or it may be reported into a stocking location by a warehouse worker. The machine operator updates the order status to *Reported as Finished* after all production output has been reported.

Report Production Order Receiving using the Advanced WMS Approach to Warehouse Management   The finished quantity of a production order can be reported using different approaches. For example, the finished quantity may be reported multiple times for a given order, or reported once when it represents the entire order quantity. The finished quantity can be reported using a mobile device transaction, or using the same client transactions employed by the basic approach. These include the Report as Finished form or the Report as Finished Journal, and the Route Card Journal for reporting unit completions at the last operation. The machine operator updates the order status to *Reported as Finished* after all production output has been reported.

The finished quantity of a production order can also be placed in different locations. For example, the finished quantity may be reported into a production output location by the machine operator, and a work order for putaway can be created automatically. A warehouse worker can then use the mobile device for reporting completion of the putaway work order. A single mobile device transaction can also be used to report both the finished quantity and its associated putaway to a location.

Report a Production order as Ended   The machine operator reports the end of a production order, indicating that no additional transactions need to be reported. When there are missing transactions, the system provides warning messages and does not change the order status to *Ended*, although specifying an override will force an Ended status. After ending the production order, the variances are automatically calculated for a standard cost item, and actual costs are calculated for an actual cost item.

Enforce Steps in Production Order Processing   Some scenarios need to limit the ability to change production order status, such as preventing a jump to a started status so that orders must be reported as released before they can be started. The ability to enforce or skip steps is determined by companywide or site-specific policies, which consist of a matrix about the allowed changes from one status to another.[2]

---

[2] The ability to skip steps can be defined as a companywide policy (on the Status Tab of the Production Control Parameters form) or as a site-specific policy (on the Status Tab of the Production Control Parameters by Site form).

Different Approaches to Create a Production Order The basic model identifies two common approaches for creating a production order – by firming a planned order and by manual entry. Several approaches for creating a production order are listed below along with the relevant book section providing further explanation. The steps within the basic model also apply to these other sources of creating a production order.

◆ Firm a planned production order (Section 14.13)
◆ Create a production order from a sales order line (Section 11.5)
◆ Automatically create a production order for a make-to-order component of a production order (Sections 5.4 and 9.6). This is also termed a reference order.

Other approaches to creating a production order apply to project-oriented operations, such as entering a production order related to a project.

Terminology about Order Status and the Life Cycle of a Production Order

Those readers familiar with the concept of a production order life cycle and order status in other ERP packages often ask for clarification about the differences with AX. In Dynamics AX, for example, a planned production order represents a separate construct so there is no order status called planned. Planned production orders are typically generated by master scheduling logic, but you can also manually enter a planned production order.

You can assign an approved status to a planned production order in order to "lock down" the scheduled date and quantity, typically in the context of the master scheduling role. However, it also locks down the BOM and route versions, so that planned changes to the BOM/route versions are not recognized. The approved status also prevents automatic deletion of the planned production order.

The process of firming a planned production order -- or an approved planned order -- generates a production order, typically with a designated order status such as Scheduled. There is no order status called firmed. A production order can be rescheduled (even at subsequent steps in the order status), and its schedule can be optionally locked.

Changing the order status to Released indicates the order is ready to be worked on. Material availability is typically checked prior to order release, and the release step can generate picking work orders for delivering components to a production location. Production supervisors can sequence the jobs associated with the routing operations of released orders.

Changing the order status to Started indicates an authorization to report actual production activities, such as reporting actual labor time, material consumption and finished quantities.

Changing the order status to Reported as Finished means that master scheduling logic will ignore the remaining requirements (for time or material) and any expected parent receipts, but additional transactions can still be reported.

Changing the order status to Ended prevents any further transactions, and results in the calculation of actual costs (for an actual cost item) or production variances (for a standard cost item). The order status can be reset at any time prior to ended status, and the system will automatically reverse all associated transactions.

14.2 Life Cycle of a Production Order

The life cycle of a production order consists of several steps that update an order status. The order status represents a linear progression that affects order behavior, such as the ability to report actual production activities. The actual reporting of steps in the linear progression can be skipped. However, the unreported steps will still be performed automatically in most cases. Steps can also be reversed by resetting order status.

Each step involves a user-initiated update task (and an associated dialogue) and the update task can change the order status. For example, changing order status to *Started* involves a start task and an associated start dialogue, and default values can be defined for many of the dialogue fields. The order status requires an understanding of these update tasks. The types of update tasks and their significance are summarized in Figure 14.2 and explained below. The figure also indicates the ability to define dialogue default values, and the option to include reference orders linked to the production order.

Create Order Task The critical information in the create order dialogue includes the item, quantity, delivery date, and the deliver-to site/warehouse. Based on this information, the dialogue displays the active BOM version and routing version, but these can be optionally overridden. Once the order has been created, the order-dependent BOM and routing initially reflect the specified versions, and they can be manually maintained.

Figure 14.2 Update Tasks for Production Orders

	Significance of Update Task	Dialogue Default Values	Option to Include Reference Orders
Create	Initially create a new production order	N/A	N/A
Estimate	Initially perform (if needed) to calculate material requirements and order costs Perform (if needed) cost-plus-markup calculation of a sales price Perform again (if needed) to recalculate order costs based on updated information	Yes	Yes
Schedule	Initially schedule material and capacity requirements Perform again (if needed) to reschedule order based on updated information	Yes	Yes
Release	Perform (if needed) to print shop traveler of routing operations Perform (if needed) to support order scheduling via MES approach Create work orders for raw material picking (when using Advanced WMS approach)	Yes	Yes
Start	Indicate started quantity (and selected operations) Generate picking list journal for the started quantity (and selected operations) Generate route card journal for the started quantity (and selected operations) Perform again (if needed) to define additional started quantity (and selected operations) Perform again (if needed) to indicate completion of all picking and/or all operations	Yes	Yes
Report as Finished	Report receipts, and optionally indicate completed order, picking, or all operations Perform again (if needed) to report additional receipts or indicate completed order Perform again (if needed) to indicate completion of all picking and/or all operations	Yes	N/A
End	Change status to ended, thereby preventing further transactions Calculate variances for standard cost items, and actual costs for actual cost items	Yes	
Reset Status	Change order status to created, thereby allowing deletion of order Change order status, thereby reversing all associated transactions	Yes	Yes

Row label (rotated, left side): Type of Update Task

Create Order Task   The critical information in the create order dialogue includes the item, quantity, delivery date, and the deliver-to site/warehouse. Based on this information, the dialogue displays the active BOM version and routing version, but these can be optionally overridden. Once the order has been created, the order-dependent BOM and routing initially reflect the specified versions, and they can be manually maintained.

Estimate Order Task   The estimate order task calculates the order costs based on the order-dependent BOM and routing, the related cost information, and the order quantity. A price calculation inquiry displays the order's per-unit costs. The estimate order task represents an optional step when you need to calculate estimated costs prior to scheduling or starting an order. It is typically performed automatically as a result of updating order status to a higher status such as scheduled or started.

Schedule Order Task   There are two scheduling methods -- termed operation scheduling and job scheduling -- to choose from. The scheduling method is only relevant when using routing data, and the choice depends on how you assign resource requirements to an operation (described in Section 6.10). Job scheduling must be used when resource requirements are defined in terms of resource capabilities or employee competencies, or when you perform detailed scheduling of production resources (e.g., via Gantt charts).

When scheduling an order using either method, you specify the critical information in a schedule order dialogue, such as the scheduling direction and several scheduling policies. The scheduling direction, for example, could be forward from today's date or backward from a specified scheduling date. The scheduling policies can optionally include consideration of finite capacity and material. A subsequent section provides further explanation about scheduling individual orders (Section 14.11). The schedule order task must be repeated after changing the order quantity or the order-dependent BOM and routing.

You can optionally specify that an order is locked, thereby preventing rescheduling by master scheduling logic or by the schedule order task.

Release Order Task The release order task has three major purposes. First, the release dialogue can be used to optionally print shop traveler paperwork (related to routing information) prior to starting production activities. Second, the information about released orders can be used for adjusting daily schedules when using the MES capabilities (Section 14.7). And third, the release order task can generate work orders for raw material picking when using the advanced approach to warehouse management (Section 14.5).

Start Task Starting an order quantity (via a start order dialogue) represents an authorization for reporting actual production activities. The relevant information depends on the significance of a single order, as described in the next section. In some scenarios, you will start the entire order quantity and all operations. In other scenarios, you will start a partial order quantity or selected operations. You can also indicate completion of all picking activities or routing operations so that master scheduling logic will ignore remaining requirements.

The reporting of actual production activities includes component material usage, time and unit completions by operation, and finished quantities. Unit completions at the last operation can optionally update the finished quantity for the parent item.

Report as Finished Task The report-as-finished task provides one approach for reporting finished quantities, expressed in terms of the good quantity and an optional scrap quantity. The scrap quantity is also termed the error quantity or trashed quantity. As part of the report-as-finished dialogue, you can optionally indicate completion of all picking activities or routing operations, so that master scheduling logic will ignore remaining requirements. The order status changes to *Reported as Finished* after flagging the order as complete using the End Job flag.

The reported-as-finished status means that the system ignores remaining component/routing requirements and expected parent receipts, but additional transactions can be reported. The Report as Finished Journal contains these transactions for parent receipts.

Order status will not change to *Reported as Finished* when transactions are missing unless you indicate that errors will be accepted (as part of the report-as-finished dialogue). Missing transactions may include expected parent receipts or remaining requirements for components and operations.

End Task The end task changes the order status to ended. The end dialogue also indicates how to handle costs associated with a scrap quantity, either by allocating scrap costs to actual parent receipts or by charging them to a specified G/L account. Charging scrap costs to a specified G/L account only works when actual costing applies to the parent item.

Under certain conditions the end task can be performed instead of the report-as-finished task (via the reported-as-finished flag in the end task dialogue), where the system assumes the entire order quantity will be reported as finished.

Reset Status Task A production order can be reset to a previous status, and you indicate the desired order status on the reset order dialogue. For example, order status may be changed to created to allow deletion, or changed to released from started so that the system automatically reverses all transactions about actual production activities.

Update Tasks and the Option to Include Reference Orders Several update tasks for a production order have an option to include reference orders, as indicated in the right-hand column of Figure 14.2. A reference order reflects a buy-to-order or make-to-order component. The reference orders can be included in cost calculations, scheduling, releasing, and the authorization to start production activities. For example, the estimate task will always generate reference orders, and the schedule order task can optionally include reference orders and even synchronize them. Resetting order status can apply to reference orders. Deleting an order can optionally delete the reference orders. The update tasks can also be performed for a production order that represents a reference order.

The nature of reference orders has been covered in a previous chapter about common S&OP scenarios requiring linkage between orders (Section 10.9). Previous chapters have also covered the definition of buy-to-order and make-to-order components in bill of material information (Section 5.4), and the impact on coverage planning data for purchasing (Section 9.4) and production (Section 9.6).

Significance of Production Order Status The update tasks provide a context for understanding the order status of a production order. The update tasks allow you to skip steps in the order status, since the system automatically performs the intervening update tasks based on default values for each dialogue. For example, you could manually create an order and then change status to started, and it would be automatically estimated and scheduled. As another example, the firming process can generate a production order with a scheduled status or started status. The order status also affects several aspects of system behavior, as illustrated in Figure 14.3 and summarized below.

Figure 14.3 Significance of Production Order Status

Significance of the Current Status	Created	Estimated	Scheduled	Released	Started	Reported as Finished	Ended
Logic in Master Scheduling — Recognize Expected Parent Receipt			Yes			No	
Recognize Expected Co-Product Receipt			Yes			No	
Recognize Component Requirements	No		Yes		Yes*	No	
Recognize Operation Requirements	No		Yes		Yes*	No	
Status Option for Firming a Planned Order	No		Yes			No	
Modify Order-Dependent BOM or Routing			Yes			No	
Timing Option for Automatic Reservations	No		Yes			No	
Copy BOM or Routing to Order	Yes		No				
Generate Shop Paperwork for Routing Operations		No		Yes			No
Create work orders for raw material picking		No			Yes	No	
Generate Picking List Journal			No			Yes	No
Report Actual Production Activities			No			Yes	No
Change or Split Order Quantity			Yes			No	
Register the Batch Numbers for Finished Item			Yes			No	
Reset Order Status	N/A		Yes			No	
Ability to Delete Order	Yes		No				Yes

* = Remaining component requirements are ignored after reporting a picking list as completed, and remaining operation requirements are ignored after reporting an operation as completed

The order status determines whether master scheduling logic recognizes expected parent receipts, and the expected requirements for components and operations. It also affects the ability to modify the order-dependent BOM and routing, generate a picking list, report actual production activities, split an order quantity, reset order status, and delete an order.

When firming a planned order, an item-specific policy (embedded in the coverage group assigned to the item) determines the order status of the resulting production order. In most cases, you should employ the option for a scheduled status.

When using automatic reservations for the components of a production order, an order-related policy determines when the reservations will be performed. In most cases, you should employ the option for a released status or a started status.

Life Cycles Related to a Production Order   The life cycle of a production order consists of several steps represented by an order status automatically updated by the system, as illustrated in Figure 14.4. The figure also shows the impact of various steps on the inventory status for the parent and component items, and the figure includes the related construct of a picking list journal. It does not include all related constructs and their life cycles in order to keep the diagram simple. For example, it does not include the route card journal (when using routing data) or quality orders (during and after production). Nor does it include several constructs related to the advanced approach to warehouse management, such as the production wave and work orders for raw material picking, and the work orders for putaway of a finished quantity.

Figure 14.4 Life Cycles related to a Production Order

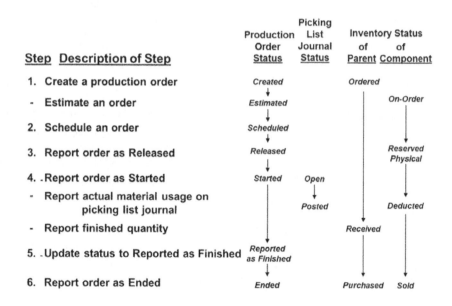

14.3 Significance of a Single Order and the Picking List Journal

The production order and its related picking list journal(s) represent critical tools for coordination and reporting of production and warehouse activities. Their significance can differ widely depending on the scenario. In a simple scenario, for example, the production order represents a single production run and the picking list journal contains all components and reflects the entire order quantity.

The picking list journal can be used in different ways. For example, it may be used by a warehouse worker for reporting actual picked quantities, or by a production worker for reporting actual material usage. This section summarizes several factors impacting the use of picking list journals. These factors include the significance of a single production order, the production BOM, the warehouse source of components, reservations for components, the significance of the flushing principle for components, and the variations for generating and posting a picking list journal.

Significance of a Single Production Order The significance of a single production order can vary in different scenarios, especially those involving manufactured items with batch tracking. It may represent a single production run (aka physical batch) in some scenarios, or the order quantity may represent multiple production runs within a day or week in other scenarios. Depending on the significance of a single order, it impacts the reporting of the started quantity for an order, the automatic generation of picking list journals for the started quantity, the reporting of finished quantities for the order, and the assignment of batch numbers to finished quantities.

Production BOM A production order can be created in different ways, such as firming a planned order or manually creating the order. A key aspect involves the item's BOM version at the time you create the production order; it is typically inherited from the item's active BOM version. This provides the basis for initially creating the order-dependent BOM (aka the Production BOM), and you can optionally modify the Production BOM.

The Production BOM provides the basis for line items in a picking list journal. Multiple aspects of this BOM information impact the generation and use of the picking list journal. For example, one aspect involves the BOM line type (such as phantom) for a manufactured component, and the resulting impact on required components. Other aspects involve the impact of planned scrap factors on component quantities, and the operation number assigned to components. Finally, the suggested locations on the picking list journal reflect the approach for defining the components' warehouse source.

Warehouse Source of Components A component's warehouse source indicates where to pick the item for a production order. You define a component's warehouse source as part of the BOM and routing information for its parent item, and this information will be inherited by the Production BOM and ultimately by the picking list journal. A previous chapter explained the four major options for defining the warehouse source of components (Section 5.5).

Reservations for Production Order Components The reservation policy assigned to a production order determines when components will be reserved relative to order status. The reservation policy for an order is initially inherited as a companywide or site-specific policy and it can be overridden. In most scenarios, you select a reservation policy so that components will be automatically reserved at the time of releasing or starting the production order. Some scenarios employ a reservation policy of Manual. You can view and update reservations for components in the Production BOM or the Picking List Journal by accessing the Reservations form.

A related reservation policy only applies to the Advanced WMS approach to warehouse management, and it determines whether components must be fully reserved or partially reserved in order to release a production order.

Significance of the Flushing Principle for Populating Picking Lists
The flushing principle assigned to a component item provides the basis for populating a picking list journal. For example, a flushing principle of *Start* provides the basis for populating a picking list when you report an order as Started. A flushing principle of *Finish* provides the basis for populating a picking list when reporting finished quantities for an order. A flushing principle of *Manual* typically applies to items that should not be included when generating a picking list.

In order to effectively use the flushing principle, it must be considered in the Start dialogue when reporting an order as Started, and in the Report as Finished dialogue when reporting a finished quantity. As part of the Start dialogue, you can optionally populate the picking list with all components (regardless of flushing policy), or immediately post the picking list (which provides auto-deduction of components).

Variations in Generating and Posting a Picking List Journal Material usage can only be reported through a picking list journal. There are multiple variations for generating a picking list, where the variations reflect differences in modeling the business process. In the basic model, for example, starting a production order generated a single picking list journal for all components, and a manually-created picking list was used for reporting adjustments and corrections. The following examples illustrate some of the variations.

◆ *Generate a single picking list based on starting the entire order quantity.* This represents the simplest scenario, where the picking list would be populated by all components with a flushing principle of Start.

◆ *Generate multiple picking lists based on different start quantities.* A typical scenario involves a production order quantity that represents multiple physical batches. You report a started quantity for each physical batch so that the picking list journal identifies component quantities for just one batch. Another scenario involves a production order quantity that represents a week's worth of production, but picking occurs in daily increments. You report a started quantity for each daily increment.

◆ *Generate multiple picking lists based on different operation numbers.* A typical scenario involves a production order with multiple operations and differing component requirements at each operation. For example, you can report the entire order quantity as started but segment the picking lists by operation. Another scenario involves an extended time between operations, so that you only report the started quantity for a specified operation.

◆ *Generate and immediately post a picking list based on the started quantity.* This approach is commonly termed forward flushing because the picking list is generated and then automatically posted. The approach reflects a policy in the Start dialogue.

◆ *Generate and immediately post a picking list based on the finished quantity.* A typical scenario would populate the picking list with components assigned a flushing principle of Finish. This approach is commonly termed back flushing because the picking list is automatically posted. The approach reflects the policies in the Report As Finished dialogue.

◆ *Manually generate a picking list.* This approach starts from the Picking List Journal where you specify the basis for automatically populating a picking list via a Create Lines dialogue. For example, you can automatically create lines based on a specified quantity or the order's started quantity. You post the picking list after reporting actual material usage. The approach ignores the flushing principle assigned to component items.

◆ *Generate a picking list when reporting labor.* You can optionally generate a picking list when reporting labor via route card journals or the MES capabilities.

◆ *Reverse the entries for a previously posted picking list.* When manually generating a picking list (described above), the basis for automatically populating the picking list can reflect reversing entries for a previously posted picking list. The resulting line items have a negative quantity, and line items can be deleted and modified. This approach is typically employed to record adjustments or corrections.

◆ *Issue unexpected components to an order.* This approach starts from the Picking List Journal where you manually add a line item for issuing the component.   A manually-created line item represents an unexpected component which will be added to the Production BOM with a required quantity of zero. It will also result in a material substitution variance for a standard cost item.   It does not represent an additional quantity for an existing component.

14.4 Key Considerations about Production Order Processing

The basic model of production order processing provides the foundation for explaining key considerations that reflect different ways of doing business. Many of these considerations have been covered in previous sections, such as the differences in production order picking and receiving based on the warehouse management approach, the different approaches for creating a production order, the significance of the production order status, and the significance of a single order and the picking list journal.

This section summarizes additional considerations, some of which merit a separate section.   The following list of considerations identifies the relevant section when applicable, and is followed by extended explanations for the other topics.

◆ Production Order Quantity
◆ Splitting the Quantity for a Production Order
◆ Production Lead Time
◆ Lock a Production Order to Prevent Rescheduling

◆ Assign a Stop Flag to a Production Order
◆ Identify Material Shortages for a Production Order
◆ Report Production Order Picking via Auto-Detection
◆ Production Order Picking using the Advanced WMS Approach (Section 14.5)
◆ Labor Reporting using Route Cards and Job Cards (Section 14.6)
◆ Labor Reporting using the MES Capabilities (Section 14.7)
◆ Report the Finished Quantity of a Production Order (Section 14.8)
◆ Rework Order for a Finished Quantity (Section 14.9)
◆ Production Inspection for a Production Order (Section 14.10)
◆ Scheduling an Individual Order(Section 14.11)
◆ Costing for a Production Order (Section 14.12)

Production Order Quantity The production order quantity can reflect order quantity modifiers consisting of a minimum, multiple and maximum. For example, these modifiers are considered when manually creating an order, or overriding the quantity for a planned order or actual order. In addition, when creating an order, the order quantity can impact the suggested route version when you have defined quantity breaks for different route versions.

Splitting the Quantity for a Production Order Splitting a production order results in a new order for the specified quantity and delivery date. The split order quantity must be less than the originating order quantity, and you normally split an order prior to a started status. A started production order can be split, but only for a quantity that has not yet been reported as started. This approach avoids the complications associated with allocations of issued components and reported operation times to the split orders.

Production Lead Time Scheduling logic can calculate a variable production lead time for planned and actual production orders based on routing data, or use a fixed lead time when no routing data applies. Several factors apply to the calculation of a variable lead time, such as the order quantity, the resource requirements for routing operations, and the available capacity of resources. The uses of a fixed lead time were described in a previous chapter about the coverage planning data for a manufactured item (Section 9.5).

Lock a Production Order to Prevent Rescheduling A production order can be flagged as locked to prevent rescheduling, and then unlocked when desired.

Assign (and Remove) a Stop flag for a Production Order The Stop flag primarily serves warehouse management purposes and prevents changes in order status prior to starting a production order. For example, assigning the Stop flag to a scheduled order prevents a change in order status to Released (which prevents creation of raw material picking work) or Started (which prevents reporting of actual material usage). The Stop flag also prevents resetting order status. You assign and remove the Stop flag as an explicit step on the Production Orders form, and a Stop flag is also displayed as part of the warehouse management information for the order. The Stop flag has no impact when raw material picking work already exists, or when assigned after a production order has been started.[3]

Identify Material Shortages for a Production Order A material shortage represents the remaining requirements for a component in the Production BOM for a started production order. The system ignores the components' remaining required quantity under several conditions: when a specific component has been flagged as completely picked; when picking for all components has been flagged as complete; when an operation linked to the material has been flagged as complete; or when the production order status becomes *Reported as Finished*. Shortages can be viewed on the Material Stock-out List inquiry.

Report Production Order Picking via Auto-Deduction Reporting a production order as Started can trigger automatic deduction of components based on policies in the Start dialogue. For example, as a result of starting an order, the picking list journal can be generated and posted immediately for components with a flushing principle of *Start*.[4]

Reporting the finished quantity for a production order can also trigger automatic deduction of components based on policies in the Report as Finished dialogue. For example, as a result of reporting a finished quantity, the picking list journal can be generated and posted immediately for components with a flushing principle of *Finish*.

---

[3] An additional option (within the new AX release) enables you to assign the Step flag and unpick the components, which reverses the raw material picking work when using the Advanced WMS approach to production order picking.
[4] When using the advanced approach to warehouse management, reporting a production order as Started via the mobile device will automatically create and post the picking list journal. The transaction ignores the Start dialogue policies, and all components in the Production BOM (regardless of flushing principle) will be deducted from inventory.

14.5 Production Order Picking using the Advanced WMS Approach

When using the Advanced WMS approach to warehouse management, production order picking involves two additional constructs in comparison to the basic approach. The two additional constructs consist of a production wave and the associated work orders for raw material picking. These work orders identify the need for picking components from warehouse locations and delivering them to a production input location. The assignment of production input locations reflect BOM/routing information described in a previous chapter about the warehouse source of components (Section 5.5).

Production order picking still uses the picking list journal, but its primary purpose is different. It is used to report actual material usage after raw material picking work has delivered material to a production input location; it is not used to report picking from the warehouse locations.

A typical process for production order picking illustrates the use of these new constructs of a production wave and work orders for raw material picking. To simplify the scenario, the typical process reflects order-based picking and normal material (rather than serialized or batch-controlled material). The typical process shown in Figure 14.5 consists of several steps typically performed by a machine operator and warehouse worker, but there are many variations about the role responsibilities. It highlights the mobile device transaction for raw material picking, and identifies several automatic actions within the system. The process starts with the need to issue goods to production and ends with the completed issues to production.

Overview The machine operator reports a production order as Released, which acts as the trigger for several automatic actions to support actual production. This includes creating and releasing a production wave for the order, which triggers creation of picking work for delivering components to a production input location when it has insufficient component inventory.

The warehouse worker reviews the released production waves and the associated work orders for raw material picking. Using the mobile device, the warehouse worker reports the picking work for delivering components to the designated production input location.

Figure 14.5 Typical Process for Production Order Picking using the Advanced WMS Approach

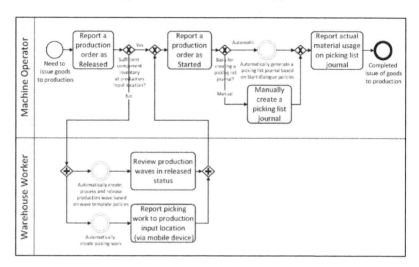

When ready, the machine operator reports a production order as Started, which automatically generates a picking list journal (based on the Start dialogue policies). The machine operator reports actual material usage on the picking list journal. In some cases, the machine operator will manually generate a picking list journal as an alternative to automatic generation, or to identify unexpected component requirements. In either case, the machine operator posts the picking list journal after reporting actual material usage.

Report a production order as Released   The machine operator reports a production order as Released, which acts as the trigger for several automatic actions to support actual production. The release step can automatically reserve the component inventory (based on the reservation policy for the production order). It will automatically create and process and release a production wave for the production order (based on policies within the applicable production wave template). The "process" step for a production wave also triggers creation of raw material picking work for delivering components to a production input location. This includes all components in the Production BOM regardless of flushing principle.

Review production waves in released status   The warehouse worker reviews released production waves to identify which production orders require delivery of components to production input locations, and optionally prints a picking list for a production wave..

Report picking work to the production input location (via mobile device) Using the mobile device, the warehouse worker reports work for picking components from stocking locations and delivering them to production input locations. The warehouse worker can optionally print the work order with bar-coded information to simplify recording of the work.

Report a production order as Started The machine operator reports a production order as Started, which automatically generates a picking list journal based on the Start dialogue policies. As part of the Start dialogue, for example, the machine operator will start the entire order quantity and generate the picking list journal for components with a forward flushing principle.

Based on the reservation policy for the production order, the component inventory can be automatically reserved (at the time of releasing or starting the order), so that the picking list journal indicates the reserved quantity for each component.

Manually create a picking list journal In some cases, the machine operator will manually generate a picking list as an alternative to automatic generation, or to identify reversing transactions for previously reported material usage. It may serve other purposes, such as identifying unexpected requirements so that the warehouse worker can use the printed picking list to pick and deliver additional material.

Report actual material usage on picking list journal The machine operator reports actual material usage on the picking list journal. For a given component, the machine operator can indicate when material usage has been completely reported so that remaining requirements (if any) will be ignored. The machine operator posts the picking list journal when completed.

Additional Steps in the Typical Process The typical process often includes several additional steps or slight variations which are not shown in Figure 14.5 so that the diagram does not become too complex. For example, you can assign a stop flag to prevent changes in order status; report an order as started or report component scrap using the mobile device; or move unused raw material at the production input location back to a stocking location.

Wave Picking for Production Orders A wave picking approach commonly refers to a grouping of released production orders with the same start date, so that a single wave contains the raw material picking work for multiple orders. The grouping is termed a production wave or wave for short. There are many variations of a wave picking approach. At its simplest, a production wave reflects the raw material picking work for a single production order, so that the wave picking approach is frequently termed order-based picking. This variation was employed in the typical process described above, where each wave was automatically created and released by reporting a production order as Released.

Other wave picking variations involve a grouping of released production orders. The planning aspects of wave picking consist of several steps typically performed by a warehouse planner. Some of the steps can be performed automatically to reflect the planner's normal decision making about wave planning, as modeled by policies within a wave template. For example, a production wave template might be defined so that releases of different production orders at different times will be automatically added to an existing wave.

14.6 Labor Reporting using Route Cards and Job Cards

The internal operations within the routing for a started production order provide the basis for reporting actual operation time and unit completions via a route card journal or job card journal. The primary difference between the two involves the approach to time reporting. You specify the elapsed time on the route card, whereas you specify start and end times (with automatic calculation of the elapsed time) on the job card. In addition, the job card journal only applies when orders have been scheduled via the job scheduling method, which identifies a job for each time element such as setup and process time. Further explanation focuses on using the route card journal for simplicity's sake.

Report Operation Time and Unit Completions by Operation A route card journal is used to report operation time and unit completions by operation. It consists of header information and one or more journal lines.

♦ *Report Operation Time by Operation.* Each journal line indicates the operation number, the resource and the actual hours expended. The route card journal provides several user options, such as overriding the basis for costing and indicating the employee performing the work.

♦ *Report Unit Completions by Operation.* Each journal line can also be used to report the units completed for an operation, and unit completions can be reported without a time entry. Unit completions are reported as a good quantity, with an optional incremental quantity for scrapped units and a reason code.

Reporting unit completions for the last operation has special significance. The good unit completions can optionally update parent receipts by designating the report-as-finished flag. This represents one option for reporting a finished quantity, as described in a subsequent section (Section 14.8).

As part of a journal line, you can indicate the operation is completed so that remaining requirements are ignored.

The unit completions and processing hours provide measures of progress against the routing operation. The system automatically calculates a completion percentage based on actual versus expected process hours as one indicator of remaining work. The completion percentage can be manually overridden. The completion percentage for each operation can be used to schedule the remaining work for a production order.

Order-Dependent Routing The order-dependent routing provides the foundation for generating a route card. Creation and maintenance of this information was previously described (Section 6.11). Several aspects have particular relevance to route cards.

- Operation number assigned to the operation
- Resource assigned to the operation
- Warehouse location assigned to components based on the resource
- Automatic consumption policy assigned to an operation
- Significance of the operation's time elements (defined in the Route Group)
- Impact of a phantom component on the order-dependent routing

Automatic Consumption Policy for an Operation Time expended for an operation's run time and setup time can be manually reported or auto-deducted; likewise for unit completions. These represent different aspects of a routing operation. A routing operation has several policies (embedded in the Route Group assigned to the operation) indicating whether each aspect should be manually reported or auto-deducted.

The auto-deduction policies for routing operations are slightly different than the ones for material, since they do not differentiate between a flushing principle of forward or finish. Hence, a fundamental decision is typically made about using either forward or backward flushing, so that auto-deduction does not result in doubled-up reporting.[5] The same triggers for automatically generating picking lists also apply to generating route cards, as described below.

♦ *Start Trigger.* The start quantity and specified operation(s) determine how a route card journal will be created, where journal lines identify the auto-deducted routing operation transactions. Policies embedded in the start order dialogue determine whether it is posted immediately. Reviewing the route card journal prior to posting allows you to make corrections.

♦ *Finish Trigger.* The quantity of good plus scrapped items determines how many auto-deducted hours will be in the route card journal, and the journal is posted immediately without an option to be reviewed.

Remaining Time Requirements for an Operation   The remaining time requirements for a routing operation can be ignored under several conditions: when the operation has been flagged as complete, when the entire routing has been flagged as complete; or when the order status becomes reported-as-finished.

14.7 Labor Reporting using the MES Capabilities

The Manufacturing Execution System (MES) module supports data collection for reporting unit completions and operation time via clock-in and clock-out registrations for specific production orders and operations. Based on this registration information, the system automatically accumulates the times and unit completions by operation, which can then be used to create line items in route card (or job card) journals. This functionality builds on the time and attendance capabilities within the module, and also supports preparation of payroll data from a single source of labor data. The typical process to report labor for production orders using the MES approach is summarized in Figure 14.6 and described below.

As the first step, the production planner indicates the production orders that are released or started, which triggers the generation of route cards that reflect routing operations. A started status represents an authorization to report actual production activities, and the step can also generate a picking list journal based on the Start dialogue policies.

---

[5] The decision about forward- versus backward-flushing is embedded in the *automatic route consumption* policy associated with the start order and report-as-finished tasks (and associated dialogues), where the policy is specified as *never* for one task. When using a backward-flushing approach, for example, the policy would be *never* for the start task and *routing group dependent* for the report-as-finished task. Conversely, the policy would be *never* for the report-as-finished task when using a forward-flushing approach.

Figure 14.6 Labor Reporting using the MES Capabilities

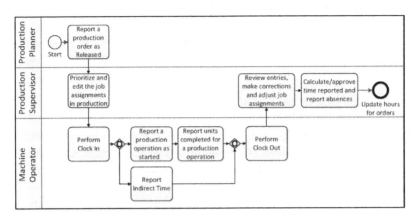

Prioritize and Edit the Job Assignments in Production Prior to reporting production, the production supervisor uses a key form (termed the Edit Job List) to fine-tune the daily schedule, such as re-sequencing or moving jobs, assigning available resources, and designating high priority jobs. This form provides information about each production order, the material availability, and capacity loads to support decision making about efficiency and on-time completions. The resulting job list provides the machine operators the sequence to perform their daily tasks.

Perform Clock In and Clock Out, and Report Actual Production When reporting production, a machine operator or production worker can "clock in" to a resource group or a specific resource. The operator is presented up-to-date job information and related documents such as drawings and process specifications. The operator can start a specific job or start a bundle of multiple jobs, or indicate indirect time such as meetings. The operator provides feedback about units completed (including the scrap quantity) and updates the status of the operation, such as completed or stopped. The operator can "clock out" when done working at a resource, or done for the day.

Review Entries, Make Corrections and Adjust Job Assignments The production supervisor reviews and analyzes the reported time throughout the day, such as reviewing who has clocked in, correcting time entries, or shifting jobs to different machines or operators.

Calculate/Approve Time Reported At the end of the day, the supervisor performs a calculation to determine elapsed hours from the clock in/clock out transactions. The production supervisor may enter adjustments or identify absences, and then approve the information in order to update the hours reported for the production order. The approved information can also be transferred to a payroll or time-and-attendance system.

The MES capabilities require setup information, and a detailed explanation of this setup information falls outside the book's scope because of book length considerations.

14.8 Report the Finished Quantity of a Production Order

The finished quantity of a production order can be reported in different ways. This section summarizes the major options. It also summarizes the related approaches for updating order status to Reported as Finished, and the conditions which prevent a change to order status.[6]

Options for Reporting a Finished Quantity Several different options can be used to report a finished quantity for a production order. In the following four options, the first three represent client transactions applicable to both the basic and advanced approaches to warehouse management. The fourth option only applies to the advanced approach, and it employs a mobile device transaction.

♦ *Option #1: Report as Finished form.* The Report as Finished form can be accessed by starting from the Production Order form, or accessed directly, in order to report a finished quantity. Completing the transaction will automatically create and post an inventory journal for the finished quantity (labeled the Report as Finished Journal). The transaction can also change order status to *Reported as Finished* by selecting the End Job flag.

♦ *Option #2: Report as Finished Journal.* The Report as Finished Journal form can be accessed by starting from the Production Order form, or accessed directly, in order to manually create a new journal for reporting a finished quantity. The journal consists of header information (identifying the production order) and one or more line items, where each line identifies an item and its finished quantity. The transaction can also change order status to *Reported as Finished* by selecting the Report as Finished flag for a journal line.

---

[6] The term "report as finished" has several contexts that can lead to confusion. The primary context involves the order status of Reported as Finished. Other contexts include the Report as Finished form and the Report as Finished Journal form; the latter can optionally update order status by selecting the Report as Finished flag. A similar flag termed Production Report as Finished applies to the use of a Route Card Journal (or Job Card Journal) for reporting unit completions at the last operation within a routing.

♦ *Option #3: Route Card Journal (or Job Card Journal) for Reporting Unit Completions at the Last Operation.* When using routing information, the Route Card Journal (or Job Card Journal) can be accessed by starting from the Production Order form, or accessed directly, in order to report unit completions and operation time. When reporting for the last operation in the Production route, the good quantity can update the finished quantity by selecting the Production Report as Finished flag for a journal line. The transaction can change order status to *Reported as Finished* by also selecting the Operation Complete flag.

♦ *Option #4: Mobile Device Transaction for Reporting a Finished Quantity.* When using the advanced approach to warehouse management, a mobile device transaction can be used to report a finished quantity, or to report both a finished quantity and putaway. Completing the transaction will automatically create and post an inventory journal for the finished quantity (labeled the Report as Finished Journal). The transaction cannot change order status to *Reported as Finished;* the order status can only be updated via the options for client transactions.

Update the Order Status to Reported as Finished As described above, the first three options for reporting a finished quantity can update order status to *Reported as Finished.* You can also report a zero quantity in order to update the order status. After updating order status, it is assumed no more transactions need to be reported, so that any remaining component requirements or expected receipts will be ignored, although transactions can still be reported until order status has been updated to Ended. However, several conditions can prevent a change to the order status.

Conditions Preventing updates to Order Status Missing feedback or errors can prevent an order status update to *Reported as Finished*, and a warning message identifies the conditions. You can override these warnings by using the Accept Errors flag when reporting the finished quantity. Examples of missing feedback or errors include the following.

♦ Each component must be completely issued, or flagged as completed in the picking list journal.
♦ Each operation must be flagged as completed.

Report a Trashed Quantity for a Production Order Some scenarios will identify scrap when reporting a finished quantity rather than receiving the inventory for subsequent reporting of scrap. This scrapped quantity is also termed the error quantity or trashed quantity. The trashed quantity represents an incremental output in addition to good quantity. The trashed quantity is not tracked in inventory and does not result in an inventory transaction. The value of the trashed quantity can be charged to a specific G/L account but only for actual cost items, and it is identified as a substitution variance for standard cost items. The ability to report a trashed quantity only applies to the first three options described above; it does not apply to the option for using a mobile device transaction.

14.9 Rework Order for a Finished Quantity

Rework may be necessary for the finished quantity of a production order that has not been reported as scrapped. A separate production order can be used to formally manage the rework for an item, where you identify the same item as the parent and a component. More specifically, you manually create a new production order for the item but with an unspecified BOM version, and you add the same item as a component in the Production BOM. The component should also be reserved after updating the order status to Estimated, especially when it represents a batch-controlled or serialized item. The rework activities may involve usage of other component materials, which can be simply issued to the production order, or added to the Production BOM and then issued.

Some scenarios also track the labor and resources for rework activities. When creating the order, you typically indicate an unspecified route version, and manually add at least one operation so that time can be reported against the operation number. The operation typically identifies a master operation that represents rework.

After a production order has been created for rework purposes, the remaining steps are exactly the same as the basic model of production order processing described earlier (Section 14.1). For example, the production order picking and receiving can reflect the basic or advanced approach to warehouse management.

The nature of a rework order is slightly different for the finished quantity of a Formula item, and for rework of a purchased item.

◆ *Rework order for a Formula item.* When creating a batch order for rework purposes, you can explicitly flag it as a rework order so that the item will be automatically added to the order-dependent formula.

◆ *Rework order for a purchased item.* A production order for rework purposes can only be created for a purchased item with a Production Type of BOM.

14.10 Production Inspection for a Production Order

There are several variations of production inspection for the finished quantity of a production order. For example, the inspection may be performed by machine operators at the time of reporting a finished quantity, so that the operator can immediately identify a trashed quantity or assign an Inventory Status such as *To-be-Scrapped* or *Needs-Rework*. Alternatively, inspection may be performed after reporting a finished quantity, where a quality control clerk reports test results against an automatically-created quality order. The test results may be reported while the material remains in a production location, or the material may be placed in a separate QC area until test results have been reported. Validation of the quality order can automatically update the Inventory Status of the finished quantity.

There are also several variations of production inspection at one or more steps in the routing for a production order. For example, a routing operation can identify the resource requirements for an inspector, or a quality order can be automatically created by reporting completion of a routing operation.

A subsequent chapter about quality management provides further explanation about quality orders and inspection approaches (Chapter 18).

Case 14.1: Production Inspection by Machine Operators The production manager at a manufacturing company wanted the machine operators to report inspection of finished quantities for production orders. A machine operator could immediately report a trashed quantity (aka the error quantity) when reporting a good quantity on the Reported as Finished form, thereby bypassing the need for additional steps. Alternatively, the machine operator could assign an inventory status of *To-Be-Scrapped*, *Needs-Rework* or *Needs-Inspection* to a received quantity, thereby indicating the need for an additional step. The additional step involved an inventory adjustment, a rework order, or a quality order.

Case 14.2: Production Inspection using Quality Orders and Inventory Status The quality control manager at a manufacturing company enforced quality procedures using automatically-generated quality orders for finished quantities of production orders. The list of open quality orders provided a coordination tool for the quality control clerks. As part of reporting test results for a quality order, a quality control clerk indicated the expected value of Inventory Status upon validation. For example, passing the validation would change the value to *Good*. Failing the validation would change the value to *To-*

Be-Scrapped or *Needs-Rework*. In addition, the quality control clerk can create a nonconformance related to problems with the item or production order, and/or create a case about the problem. .

Case 14.3: Quality Orders during the Production Process The quality manager at a manufacturing company wanted to obtain test results during the production process for a manufactured item. The item's routing information identified multiple operations with operation numbers (such as 10, 20, 30 and 40), and the test results were needed at selected operation numbers (such as 20 and 30). These testing requirements were defined as part of a Quality Association for the item and each selected operation number, which would trigger automatic creation of a quality order after the operation was reported as finished.

Case 14.4: Production Inspection at a Separate QC Area For certain electronic items at a manufacturing company, the entire finished quantity of a production order was placed in a separate QC location for so that each unit could go through a burn in process. Several test results were monitored for the burn in process. The quality control clerk reported these test results for the associated quality order with a sample size of one unit. After the units passed validation, a warehouse worker would report putaway from the QC location to a stocking location.

14.11 Schedule an Individual Order

Scheduling an individual production order has several considerations. It can change order status to scheduled, or update an already scheduled order, so that requirements for resources and materials will be correctly recognized and scheduled. The resource requirements and related scheduling logic only apply when using routing data. The considerations include the scheduling method, the scheduling direction and several scheduling options.

Choose a Scheduling Method You choose one of the scheduling methods - termed operation scheduling and job scheduling – in order to schedule an individual production order. Job scheduling supports several additional capabilities, as described in a previous chapter about routing data (Section 6.10).

Scheduling Direction Both scheduling methods support different scheduling directions. The basic scheduling directions are forward and backward as of a given date, such as the requirement date. Figure 14.7 summarizes the variations in scheduling directions for both scheduling methods. Fewer options are available for rescheduling a planned order.

Figure 14.7 Variations in Scheduling Direction

		Other Parameter	Applicability		
			Operations Scheduling	Job Scheduling	Reschedule Planned Order*
Variations in Scheduling Direction	Forward from today		Yes	Yes	No
	Forward from tomorrow				No
	Forward from the planned start date				
	Forward from a specified schedule date & time	Specify a Schedule Date & Time			Yes
	Backward from a specified schedule date & time				
	Backward from the delivery date				No
	Backward from the planned end date				
	Backward from the calculated action date				Yes
	Backward from the calculated futures date				
	Use information from last scheduling				
	Forward from a specified job	Specify a Job Identifier			No
	Backward from a specified job				
	Backward from requirement date		No		Yes
	Forward from order date				

* = Planned orders are initially scheduled using backward scheduling from the requirement date.

Scheduling Options Scheduling logic for individual orders can optionally include finite capacity and finite material, the use of properties (for block scheduling purposes), and reference orders. Selected time elements can be excluded, such as queue and transit time, to calculate the fastest possible production throughput. Another option limits the consideration of resources based on existing assignments of warehouses.

◆ *Finite Capacity.* When a bottleneck resource has finite capacity, the scheduling logic ensures the scheduled loads do not exceed the available capacity. The consideration of available capacity can be factored down by an operations schedule percentage assigned to the resource, so that the resource is not loaded to 100% of available capacity.

◆ *Finite Material.* Scheduling logic requires on-hand inventory on the start date of the production order or the relevant operation (if applicable). When there is insufficient inventory of the component item, the scheduling logic uses the item's lead time to determine when it will be available. The components' availability date determines when the order can be started.

◆ *Finite Property and Block Scheduling.* The finite property approach represents a form of block scheduling for grouping similar operations to minimize setup time, and performing them during a predefined block of time in the calendar assigned to a resource. The option only applies when using job scheduling.

◆ *Reference Orders.* You can optionally schedule and synchronize reference orders related to the selected order, thereby synchronizing downstream (and upstream) orders via forward (and backward) scheduling.

◆ *Limit the consideration of resources based on existing assignments of input warehouses.* The existing assignment of an input warehouse for a resource should be considered by scheduling logic in order to avoid the problem of scheduling on a resource with a different input warehouse. This problem impacts the calculation of component requirements by warehouse, and may create unnecessary complexities. The limitation is normally identified by the "Keep input warehouse from resource" flag. It can also be identified by the "Keep production unit" flag, since a production unit has a specified input warehouse.

14.12 Costing for a Production Order

The estimated costs for a production order can be initially calculated by performing the Estimate task, where the calculated costs reflect the order quantity and the order-dependent BOM and routing. The Estimate task may be used to recalculate estimated costs after changes, such as changes to components or operations, or changes to the active cost records for items, labor rates, or overhead formulas.

The actual costs (termed realized costs) for a production order are automatically calculated based on reported production activities, such as actual material usage and operation times. You can view detailed transactions about reported activities on the Production Posting inquiry for a production order. Several reports summarize the activities for all current orders, including the raw materials in process report, the work in process report (for routing transactions), and the indirect costs in process report (for overheads incurred).

You can analyze estimated and actual costs using the price calculation inquiry for the order. Cost information is shown for each component, operation, and applicable overhead formula.

Updating an Item's Actual Cost Actual costs are calculated after ending a production order for an actual cost item.

Calculated Variances for a Standard Cost Item Variances are calculated after ending a production order for a standard cost item. The variances reflect a comparison between the reported production activities and the item's standard cost calculation (not to the order's estimated costs).[7] Four types of variances are calculated: lot size variance, production quantity variance, production price variance, and production substitution variance. Figure 14.8 identifies these four variances for a manufactured item. The figure also identifies similar variances related to co/by-products of a batch order.

Figure 14.8 Order Variances for Production Orders

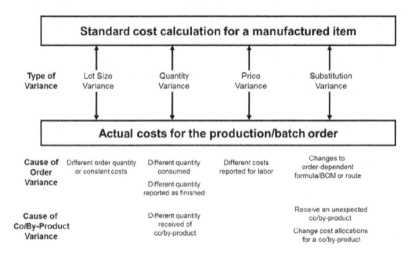

The common sources of order variances are shown in the bottom half of Figure 14.8, such as a different quantity issued or received.

You can analyze the order variances for a selected production order. The variances can also be viewed on the Variance Analysis Statement report and the Cost Estimating and Costing report. The Standard Cost Transactions inquiry provides another approach to analyzing order variances. For example, you can identify the variances associated with every production order for an item. In

---

[7] The calculated standard cost for a manufactured item reflects the specified BOM version, route version, quantity, calculation date, and active cost records as of the calculation date. Calculation of a manufactured item's cost was previously explained in Chapter 7.

order to anticipate variances prior to ending a production order, you can analyze the realized costs for a selected order or by using the Cost Estimates and Costing report.

14.13 Coordinate Production Activities

A firm's S&OP game plans provide the primary driver of production activities. The key tools for coordinating these activities include planned production orders and action messages, which reflect the model of SCM decision-making embedded in coverage planning data for manufactured items (Section 9.5). The next section covers additional coordination tools when using routing data, such as production schedules and capacity analysis.

Planned Production Orders   The planned orders can be viewed on the Planned Production Orders form or the Planned Orders form, where the displayed information typically represents the current master plan.[8] Planned orders can be viewed based on selection criteria such as the buyer group and order date, so that the responsible planner can mark and firm the planned orders accordingly.

Actual production orders can be created from planned orders via a function termed *firming planned orders*. You typically mark (via a check box) the planned orders needing to be firmed. The generated orders have an assigned order status based on an item-related policy (embedded in the Coverage Group assigned to the item). A status of scheduled is a typical policy Execution of the firming function automatically deletes the selected planned orders, and creates a log for tracking which planned orders have been firmed and by whom.

The Planned Orders form can also be accessed in the context of making sales order delivery promises by using a Net Change Explosion, since this approach also creates planned orders.

In many cases, you may need to analyze the rationale for a planned production order prior to firming. You can view the net requirements and related action messages for a selected planned order. You can also view requirements associated with components and routing operations. The analysis may lead to one or more of the following actions prior to firming.

♦ Approve a planned order. Approving a planned production order will lock the scheduled date and quantity, and prevent it from being deleted by master

---

[8] You can view information based on a selected set of master plan data or forecast plan data. For simplicity's sake the explanation focuses on the set of data representing the current master plan.

scheduling logic or the Delete Plan task. In addition, it will also lock the BOM and routing information, so that planned changes will not be recognized.

◆ Change quantity and/or delivery date for the planned order.

◆ Re-schedule the planned order using a specified scheduling method and scheduling direction, with optional consideration of finite material and capacity.

◆ Split the planned order using a specified quantity and date.

◆ Group together several selected planned orders for the same item, with a total quantity for a single production order. The delivery date reflects the currently selected planned order.

◆ Identify a different source of supply (such as a purchase or transfer) by changing the planned production order to a planned purchase order or transfer order.

Some scenarios have correctly modeled their SCM decision making for selected items so that the planned production orders can be automatically firmed (within the time period defined by a firming fence). Other scenarios employ the freeze time fence to support near-term schedule stability in production, since master scheduling logic will place planned orders at the end of the frozen period. These time fence policies are embedded in the coverage group assigned to an item.

Action Messages   Action messages represent one of the key tools for coordinating production activities to meet the S&OP game plans. Master scheduling logic can generate action messages for planned and actual production orders. The logic reflects the action message policies embedded within the coverage group assigned to an item, as described in a previous chapter (Section 9.9). The action messages can be viewed and acted upon in several different ways:

◆ View action messages for a selected item as part of the Net Requirements inquiry.

◆ View action messages for all items on the Actions form, and optionally apply the suggested action for a selected message or access the Action Graph.

◆ View related action messages (for a selected message) by accessing the Action Graph, and optionally apply a suggested action.

As a general guideline, you should view related action messages using the Action Graph in order to understand the context of other orders. Additional guidelines were described in a previous chapter (Section 9.10).

Messages about Calculated Delays   This message indicates that a production order delivery date will cause a delay in meeting a requirement date, and the production order typically has an associated "advance" action message. The messages can viewed from several different starting points (such as the Net Requirements inquiry), and you access the referenced order to indicate a change. A previous chapter provided guidelines for effective use of messages about calculated delays (Section 9.11).

14.14 Production Schedules and Capacity Analysis

When using routing data, master scheduling logic can calculate capacity requirements and generate suggested production schedules for each resource. The visibility of these calculations is constrained by a capacity time fence expressed in days, which is normally defined as part of the policies assigned to a master plan. For example, the capacity time fence may reflect several weeks for near-term scheduling purposes in the current master plan, or it may reflect one year or longer for long-term capacity analysis in a set of master plan data for long range planning purposes.

Capacity Analysis   Capacity analysis reflects a comparison between a resource's available capacity and the requirements stemming from production orders. The nature of capacity analysis depends on the consideration of finite capacity limits, the set of master plan data, and the definition of resource requirements in routing operations.

♦ *Consideration of finite capacity.*   A resource's available capacity can be viewed as infinite or finite. An infinite capacity viewpoint means that scheduling of each operation's duration considers the available working hours at a resource, but an unlimited number of orders can be scheduled concurrently. This means capacity analysis can identify overloaded periods.

A finite capacity viewpoint typically means that only one order can be scheduled concurrently during working hours, and that scheduling logic considers existing loads. Scheduling logic only considers a finite capacity limit for resources designated as having finite capacity.

♦ *Set of Master Plan data.*   Capacity analysis can be viewed for a specified set of master plan data or forecast plan data. Several policies for a set of master plan determine whether finite capacity applies to planned production orders and the applicable time horizon (aka the finite capacity time fence).

◆ *Definition of an operation's resource requirements.* The resource requirements for an operation can be defined in several ways, as previously described in Chapter 6. For example, they may be specified for a single resource, a resource group, or a resource capability, and an operation may have requirements for a primary resource and secondary resources.

With these factors in mind, capacity analysis can be viewed for a resource (or a resource group) using a tabular or graphic format.

◆ *Tabular Format for Capacity Analysis.* The Capacity Load Inquiry provides a tabular format for load analysis of one resource or a resource group. It displays total load hours in daily increments and highlights overloaded days. You can view detailed reference information about routing operations comprising a daily load. A separate form (termed Capacity Reservations) provides a tabular format about all routing operations for the resource.

◆ *Graphical Format for Capacity Analysis.* The Capacity Load Graphical Inquiry provides a setup dialogue that determines how to display the information. For example, the information can be displayed in hours or percentages, and in specified increments (such as daily, weekly or monthly) for a specified range of dates. These time increments represent the continuum of aggregate to detailed capacity analysis, and the percentage viewpoint can highlight overloaded periods.

Additional variations include displaying loads for a range of resources, either as multiple graphics or as a single graphic with an accumulated load. Selected sources of loads can be excluded, such as loads stemming from planned orders. You cannot access detailed reference information about the operations comprising a resource load.

Production Schedules The nature of a production schedule depends on the three major factors mentioned above -- the definition of an operation's resource requirements, the consideration of capacity limits, and the set of master plan data. A production schedule identifies each routing operation performed in the resource. It consists of the same detailed reference information as the load analysis drill-down, but is presented in a format more appropriate for communicating the needed action. In particular, it provides visibility of production orders at various order statuses so that production personnel can finish those already started as well as anticipate those that need to be started.

Production schedules can be displayed in different formats, such as tabular or Gantt chart. Each firm tends to customize their production schedule to fit their operations, but a typical tabular format can be described. A production schedule in tabular format identifies operations in a priority sequence with the hottest operations listed first. The simplest sequencing rule is based on operation start (or ending) date and time. Operation information includes the remaining units and time and also the units completed to-date. It may include other information that proves useful to the planner or production personnel, such as the prior and next operation, the expected operation scrap percentage, and the operation description. Much of the information may be identified by the shop paperwork for each order, thereby minimizing the need for including it in the production schedule. The Operations List Inquiry provides one example of a production schedule.

Basic Sequencing Capabilities for a Production Schedule Some basic capabilities can be used to sequence the operations for a selected resource by accessing the Dispatching form. For example, you can view the current sequence of selected operations for the next day or two, manually change the sequence, and then perform scheduling to re-schedule the operations based on their assigned sequence.

An alternative approach to basic sequencing is included in the MES capabilities described earlier (Section 14.7). You can use the Edit Job List form to adjust the daily schedules, such as re-sequencing or moving jobs, assigning available resources, and designating high priority jobs. This form provides information about each production order, the material availability, and capacity loads to support decision making about efficiency and on-time completions. The resulting job list provides the machine operators the sequence to perform their daily tasks.

14.15 Performance Metrics for Production

Production performance can be assessed by several different metrics. One metric involves a comparison of actual costs against planned costs for production orders. Another metric involves on-time completion. One or more metrics of quality can also be used, such as failed test results on quality orders, production-related cases about quality, or production orders with a trashed quantity.

Review actual vs planned costs for a production order The production supervisor can review the actual versus planned costs for a production order, either during or after execution of the production activities.

Review actual vs standard costs for a production order For a standard cost item, the production supervisor can review the actual versus standard costs for a production order, either during or after execution of the production activities. The production variances are only calculated after reporting the production order as Ended.

Review on-time completion of production orders The production supervisor can compare the actual reported-as-finished date of a production order against the scheduled completion date.

Review failed production-related quality orders When using quality orders, the quality manager can review the production-related quality orders that have failed the validation of test results. The quality orders and related test results can be reported during production operations or after reporting the finished quantity.

Review open production-related cases When using cases, the quality manager can review the production-related cases for production orders.

Review production orders with a trashed quantity The quality manager can review production orders with a trashed quantity (aka error quantity) and the associated reason codes.

14.16 Workspaces related to Production Orders

Several predefined workspaces are related to production orders, as described in the following summary of each workspace and its applicable functionality.

Production Floor Management Workspace This workspace primarily supports the production supervisor role. It summarizes several aspects of information about production orders and their related operations (as of a selected date). For example, it identifies the production orders to release and the component availability for each order, and it supports the release of selected orders. It helps prioritize the sequence of jobs for released orders. It identifies the jobs that need to be completed and the jobs with reported deviations (such as a scrap quantity). In addition, it summarizes the number of jobs that are not yet started, stopped, and in progress. By configuring the workspace, you can filter the displayed information for a selected resource, resource group and/or production unit.

The links provide access to information about production orders, resources, and the various production journals (such as the picking list journal or job card journal). They also provide access to the calculation and approval of time and attendance information reported through the MES capabilities. The labor reporting aspects of these MES capabilities also provide the basis for viewing staff attendance.

Production Worker Reporting via the Job Card Device Page The Job Card Device page provides an alternative reporting approach for production workers when using the MES capabilities within the New Dynamics AX. It works on mobile devices (such as tablets and phones) and supports touch-enabled reporting. For example, the production worker can report the start (and started quantity) of a production order as well as the finished quantity, identify the operation being worked on, and view attachments about the operation.

Cost Administration Workspace This workspace identifies production orders with high variances, and the links provide access to reports/inquiries about production variances and postings. Menu items provide access to production orders and batch orders.

Master Planning Workspace This workspace identifies the planned production orders, and also the action messages and calculated delay messages about production orders.

14.17 Additional Case Studies

Case 14.5: Advanced Planning and Scheduling (APS) Integration A fabricated products company required APS capabilities to minimize setups and avoid additional equipment purchases for its line of extruded plastic products. Multiple extrusion machines produced plastic pipes of varying diameters and colors. Scheduling considerations included sequence-dependent setup time (based on pipe diameter and color), and machine capabilities for handling different products. Scheduling considerations also included machine-specific run rates, and secondary resources for tooling and skilled operators. To integrate an APS application, additional attributes were required for resources (e.g., machine capabilities), routing operations (e.g., setup attributes) and calendars (e.g. available crew size by shift).[9]

Case 14.6: Graphical Schedule Board for Production Orders The production planners at a manufacturing company employed a graphical schedule board to coordinate production orders by viewing the related routing operations at selected work centers, and adjusting them accordingly.[10] The graphical display could include both actual and planned production orders, and it reflected current information within AX as well as the standard scheduling logic. It did not involve additional APS functionality. Changing the displayed information via drag-and-drop techniques -- such as changing an operation duration, or

---

[9] See www.Preactor.com for additional information about their Advanced Scheduler module.
[10] See www.DynamicsSoftware.com for additional information about their Graphical Schedule Board.

assigning the operation to a different work center -- automatically updated the current information within AX. Alternatively, the information could be adjusted in simulation mode to achieve the desired schedule, and then used to update the current information. Using the graphical schedule board, the planners could perform every function related to a production order, such as firming a planned order, scheduling/releasing/starting an order, or viewing the BOM and route information.

14.18 Executive Summary

Production represents the distinctive competency of many manufacturers. Production activities can be coordinated and reported using production orders, and the significance of a single order affects these activities. Several considerations apply to production orders, such as the order status within the order life cycle, the order-dependent BOM and routing, and the production order lead time. Production activities can be reported against started orders, such as picking material, reporting operation time, and receiving finished quantities. Coordination of production activities is based on suggestions for planned orders, action messages and production schedules by resource. The chapter reviewed several variations of production inspection and the use of rework orders.

Chapter 15

Subcontracted Production

Subcontracted production and internal production share many similarities in the use of basic constructs like production orders and picking list journals. They both employ BOM and routing information. However, subcontracted production involves significant differences and several variations that merit a separate explanation. One key difference stems from the AX approach to modeling subcontracted production, which requires a unique item representing the subcontracted service, and a BOM line specifying it as a buy-to-order component for the manufactured item. As a result, a production order for the manufactured item automatically creates the associated purchase order for the subcontracted service. The dual constructs of a production order and its associated purchase order involve additional complexity in setup information and business processes in comparison to internal production.

Subcontracted production can have many possible scenarios. The different scenarios typically reflect variations of the supplied material and handling of finished quantities, and how these are modeled and reported within AX. A basic model of production order processing for subcontracted production provides a baseline for explaining these variations. A key issue concerns the visibility of inventory at the subcontractor site and in transit. These considerations are reflected in the following sections within the chapter.

1. Variations of Subcontracted Production
2. Basic Model of Production Order Processing for Subcontracted Production
3. Define an Item representing a Subcontracted Service
4. BOM Information for Subcontracted Production
5. Routing Information for Subcontracted Production
6. Single Receipt Transaction for Subcontracted Production
7. Additional Considerations for Subcontracted Production
8. Additional Case Studies

15.1 Variations of Subcontracted Production

There are many possible scenarios of subcontracted production. The different scenarios typically reflect variations of (1) the routing information with an external operation, (2) the supplied material, (3) the handling of finished quantities and (4) modeling the inventory locations involved in subcontracted production. These four major factors provide an organizing focus for further explanation. A key issue concerns the visibility of inventory at the subcontractor site and the in-transit inventory.

Variations of Routing Information with an External Operation   The simplest scenario involves just a single operation within the routing for the manufactured item, where the item's BOM identifies the supplied material for the external operation. More complex scenarios involve a multi-step routing, where each additional step may reflect an internal operation or another external operation.   Further explanation focuses on the simplest scenario, and a subsequent section summarizes the definition of routing information for an external operation (Section 15.5).

Variations of Supplied Material for Subcontracted Production
Subcontracted production involves supplied material and the use of production orders.[1] There are two major delivery options for the supplied material. The two options include issuing the supplied material to the production order, and stocking the supplied material at the subcontractor site.

◆ *Supplied Material issued to Production Order.* The picked material for a subcontracted production order reflects delivery to the subcontractor. The approach to picking material varies slightly for the basic versus advanced approaches to warehouse management, as described in the previous chapter. This option provides no visibility of component inventory at the subcontractor or in transit.

◆ *Supplied Material stocked at Subcontractor Site.* A stocked component at the subcontractor site typically reflects purchase order receipts or transfer order receipts. This option provides visibility of the component inventory.

---

[1] Subcontracted production of a "turnkey" item does not require supplied material, and is typically coordinated via a purchase order rather than a subcontracted production order.

Actual usage of the supplied material can be reported in different ways. You can report actual usage (or adjustments to actual usage) on a picking list journal for the production order. Alternatively, usage may reflect automatic deduction where the started quantity or finished quantity for the production order can trigger automatic creation and posting of a picking list journal.

The applicable delivery option determines how you define the warehouse source of components in BOM/routing information (Section 5.5). For example, you can specify the warehouse source on the BOM line for a supplied component.

Variations of Receiving a Finished Quantity for Subcontracted Production There are two major variations for receiving a finished quantity for subcontracted production. As summarized in Figure 15.1, you can (1) receive the purchase order for the subcontracted service or (2) receive the subcontracted production order, either at an internal site or at the subcontractor site. The figure also identifies the two delivery options, and highlights the option for reporting usage of supplied material at the subcontractor site.

Figure 15.1 Major Variations of Subcontracted Production

Options for Supplied Material	Options for Receiving Finished Quantities for Subcontracted Production		
	1 Receive Purchase Order for the Subcontracted Service		
	2 Receive Subcontracted Production Order		
	At Internal Site	At Subcontractor Site	
Supplied Material issued to Production Order	No Visibility of Subcontractor Inventory	Partial Visibility of Finished Inventory at Subcontractor	Support Sales Order Shipments or Transfer Order Shipments from the Subcontractor Site
Supplied Material Stocked at Subcontractor	Option for Reporting Usage of Supplied Material		
	Partial Visibility of Component Inventory at Subcontractor	Full Visibility of Component and Finished Inventory at Subcontractor	

◆ *Receive the Purchase Order for the Subcontracted Service.* A purchase order receipt of the subcontracted service can automatically update the finished quantity of the associated production order, thereby supporting a single receipt transaction for both constructs. A subsequent section provides further explanation of the single receipt transaction (Section 15.6).

◆ *Receive the Subcontracted Production Order.* The finished quantity of the production order can be reported using several different approaches, as described in the previous chapter (Section 14.8). For example, you can report the finished quantity using the Report as Finished form. This approach requires a separate transaction to report the purchase order receipt or invoice for the subcontracted service.

The finished quantity can optionally trigger backflushing of supplied components. A finished quantity received at the subcontractor can be subsequently used for sales order shipments or transfer order shipments.

Visibility of Inventory at Subcontractor Site A key issue in subcontracted production concerns the visibility of inventory at the subcontractor site and the in-transit inventory. Figure 15.1 summarizes the three major variations consisting of no visibility, partial visibility and full visibility. The use of a transfer order for supplied material and/or finished quantities provides additional visibility of in-transit inventory.

Modeling the Inventory Location for a Subcontractor Site The ability to track inventory of supplied components and/or finished quantities means that subcontractors must be identified by an AX site and warehouse (in addition to identification as a vendor and resource). The fundamentals of modeling inventory locations were described at the beginning of the book (Chapter 3), but a key limitation merits repeating for subcontracted production.

As a key limitation, the components' warehouse source and the destination warehouse for a production order must be within the same AX site. For some scenarios, this means that the subcontractor locations are modeled as different AX warehouses within a single AX site, where the AX site also includes AX warehouses representing the related internal warehouses. This approach simplifies the definition of item cost records for the single AX site when using standard costing.

Other scenarios employ a unique AX site and related AX warehouse to model each subcontractor location. This approach typically applies when a manufactured item can be produced by different subcontractors, so that the item's BOM version, route version and costs are site-specific. The approach sometimes mandates the use of transfer orders for supplied components and/or finished quantities because of the key limitation mentioned above. The approach also means that item cost records must be maintained for each AX site when using standard costing. As a side effect, this approach means that a unique resource group must be defined for each resource representing a subcontractor.

15.2 Basic Model of Production Order Processing for Subcontracted Production

The typical steps in production order processing for subcontracted production can vary based on many different factors, as illustrated in the previous section. However, each variation involves the dual constructs of a production order and its associated purchase order for the subcontracted service. This section summarizes a basic model that provides a baseline for explaining variations.

The basic model focuses on a standard product, where its BOM identifies the supplied material and its routing identifies a single external operation. For each production order, all of the supplied materials are picked and sent to the subcontractor from an internal warehouse. The internal warehouse receives the finished quantity by reporting a purchase order receipt for the subcontracted service. This approach provides no visibility of inventory at the subcontractor, whereas other variations can provide visibility.

Overview of the Basic Model The basic model starts with a requirement for subcontracted production, typically identified by a planned production order stemming from S&OP game plans and the item's planning data. The production planner firms the planned order, which automatically creates an associated purchase order for the subcontracted service that can be confirmed by a purchasing agent. A warehouse worker and shipping clerk perform subsequent steps for picking the supplied material and sending it to the subcontractor, and the steps differ when using the basic versus advanced approach to warehouse management.

After the subcontractor sends the finished item back, a receiving clerk reports the purchase order receipt for the subcontracted service (which also results in automatic updating of the associated production order). The production planner updates the production order status to Ended when all activities have been reported. These roles and steps are summarized in Figure 15.2 and described below.

Figure 15.2 Basic Model of Production Order Processing
for Subcontracted Production

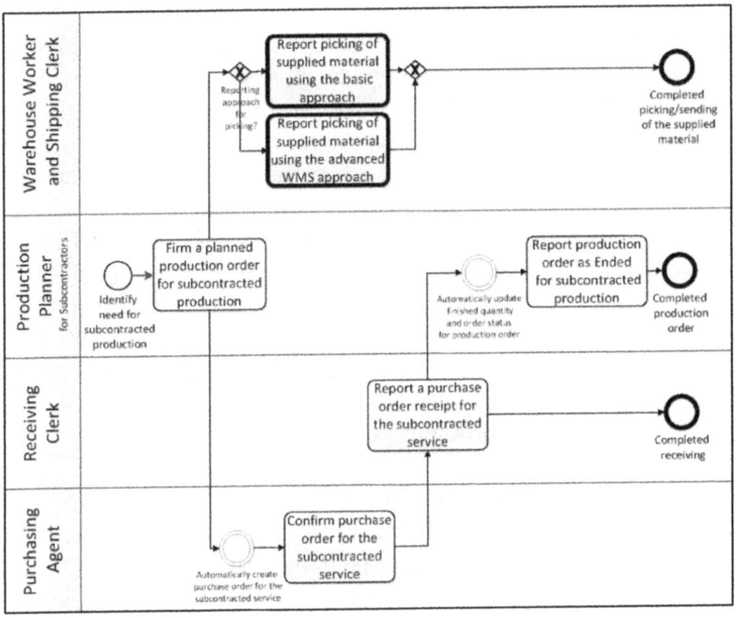

Confirm a Purchase Order for the Subcontracted Service The purchasing agent confirms a purchase order for the subcontracted service, using either the Purchase Order form (for a selected order) or the Confirm Purchase Order form (for multiple orders satisfying the query criteria). The purchasing agent can use the Subcontracted Work form to view all current purchase orders for a subcontracted service and their associated production order. The confirmed order can be sent to the vendor, and the confirmation enables subsequent processing steps such as receipts. Changes to a confirmed purchase order require an additional confirmation. Each confirmation creates a history record so that you can view historical versions of a purchase order.

Report Picking of Supplied Material using the Basic Approach to Warehouse Management In a typical process, the production planner reports a production order for subcontracted production as Started, which acts as the trigger for creating a picking list journal based on the Start dialogue policies.

The warehouse worker reviews the printed version of the picking list journal, reports actual picking against the picking list journal, and then posts it. The printed version reflects a delivery note layout indicating where to send the picked material. The warehouse worker works with the shipping clerk to physically send the supplied material to the subcontractor.

Report Picking of Supplied Material using the Advanced WMS Approach to Warehouse Management In a typical process, the production planner reports a production order as Released, which acts as the trigger for several automatic actions to support actual production. This includes creating and releasing a production wave for the order, which triggers creation of picking work for delivering components to a production input location. This location typically represents an outbound dock, and its identifier typically reflects the subcontractor.

The warehouse worker reviews the released production waves and the associated picking work for raw material. Using the mobile device, the warehouse worker reports completion of the raw material picking work for delivering components to the designated production input location.

The warehouse worker also reports the start of a production order for subcontracted production, which automatically generates a picking list journal based on the Start dialogue policies. The printed version of the picking list journal reflects a delivery note layout indicating where to send the picked material. Posting the journal reflects actual material usage at the production input location.

An alternative process employs the wave picking concept, where the contents of a production wave consist of raw material picking work orders that have been created for multiple released production orders for a given subcontractor.

Report a Purchase Order Receipt for a Subcontracted Service The receiving clerk reports a purchase order receipt for a subcontracted service, typically using the Purchase Order form to report product receipt. The receiving clerk also identifies the vendors' packing list number when reporting the receipt. The receipt transaction automatically updates the finished quantity for the related production order and places the inventory in a receiving location for the warehouse. It can also update the order status to *Reported as Finished.*

Report a Production order as Ended for Subcontracted Production
The production planner reports the end of a production order for subcontracted production, indicating that no additional transactions need to be reported. When there are missing transactions, the system provides warning messages and does not change the order status to *Ended*, although specifying an override will force

an Ended status. After ending the production order, the variances are automatically calculated for a standard cost item, and actual costs are calculated for an actual cost item.

15.3 Define an Item representing a Subcontracted Service

You define a unique item number to represent a subcontracted service. As a rule of thumb, each parent item produced by a subcontractor typically requires an associated service item. The name and UM for the service item typically match the parent item being produced by the subcontractor, and are shown on purchase orders for the subcontracted service. The item defines the value-added costs for calculating a manufactured item's cost, and you can define approved vendors and purchase agreements for the item. The typical business process for defining a subcontracted service is very similar to the process for defining a material item, which was described in a previous chapter (Section 4.1). However, several aspects of item information merit special consideration.

Product Type of Service The item number representing a subcontracted service should be defined with a product type of *Service*. As a result, the item must be assigned an Item Model Group with several key policies, as described in the next point.[2]

Item Model Group A unique Item Model Group should be defined and assigned to items representing a subcontracted service. The key policies include actual costing for an inventory valuation method (since standard costing does not apply to a service) and a "stocked product" designation (so that the item can be identified as a BOM component).

Storage Dimension Group You typically assign a storage dimension group that just reflects a site and warehouse, since locations do not apply to an item representing a subcontracted service.

Tracking Dimension Group The tracking of batch and/or serial numbers does not apply to an item representing a subcontracted service, and these requirements are specified for the parent item.

---

[2] Some scenarios have identified the item representing a subcontract service with a Product Type of Item rather than Service. This approach can support standard costing for the item (and the calculation of purchase price variances), but it does not support the use of a single receipt transaction. When using this approach, the cost group assigned to the item should have a cost group type of Undefined rather than Direct Outsourcing.

Purchase Information The purchase information for an item representing a subcontracted service includes the approved vendors, the preferred vendor, and agreements about purchase prices.

◆ *Approved Vendors.* You define the approved vendors for a subcontracted service just like any other purchased item (Section 12.2).

◆ *Preferred Vendor.* The item's preferred vendor will be assigned when the system automatically creates a purchase order as a result of updating the related production order. The preferred vendor can be defined as a companywide or site/warehouse policy, or it can be defined within the component information in a BOM line. A third option only applies when using routing data for the parent item, where you specify the preferred vendor as part of the resource representing the subcontractor. [3] The system prevents automatic purchase order creation when a preferred vendor does not exist in any of the three options.

◆ *Agreements about Purchase Prices.* You define agreements about purchase prices just like any other item (Sections 12.5 and 12.6).

Accounting Information The accounting information for an item representing a subcontracted service includes the item group, cost group, and the optional assignment of standard costs.

◆ *Item Group.* You define a unique item group for subcontracted service items, which defines the relevant G/L account numbers (Section 4.13). A typical name for the item group would be Subcontracted Service.

◆ *Cost Group.* You define a unique cost group for subcontracted service items to support cost segmentation in the calculated cost the parent item. A typical name for the item group would be Subcontracted Service. The designated cost group type for this cost group should be Direct Outsourcing.

◆ *Assigning a Standard Cost to a Subcontracted Service* You can optionally assign a standard cost to the item representing a subcontracted service in order to support cost roll-up calculations for the parent item. The standard cost is site-specific, so that multiple item cost records are required when the subcontracted service is performed at different sites representing different subcontractors.

---

[3] These three options represent increasing levels of specificity, so that the suggested vendor on a purchase order reflects the highest level specified.

Planning Data Planning data does not apply to an item representing a subcontracted service, since its purchase order will be automatically created for the production order that coordinates subcontracted production. Planning data should be defined for the parent item produced by the subcontractor, such as the coverage code, order quantity modifiers and production lead time. It should be noted that master scheduling logic will generate planned purchase orders for the service item, thereby providing visibility of planned purchases, but they cannot be firmed.

Flushing Principle You typically assign a flushing principle of Finish to the item, so that reporting the finished quantity of a production order will trigger back flushing of the subcontracted service item.

Item Template An item template should be defined for items representing a subcontracted service, so that the template can be used for partially populating information about new items.

15.4 BOM Information for Subcontracted Production

The BOM version for a subcontract manufactured item contains one line item for the subcontracted service item, and other line items identify the supplied components. The typical business process for defining BOM information for subcontracted production is exactly the same process used for an internally produced item, which was described in a previous chapter (Section 5.1). However, several aspects merit special consideration.

Define BOM Version Policies The BOM version is typically site-specific so that you can identify the warehouse source of a supplied component on the BOM line. A site-specific BOM version should also be used when the same item is produced by different subcontractors.

Define BOM Line for the Subcontracted Service The BOM line defines the subcontracted service item and a line type of Vendor indicating a buy-to-order service. The required quantity is typically one. When using routing data, you also specify the related operation number and flag the line as due at the end of the operation. This will align the due date for the item's purchase order with the due date of the related production order.[4] You typically assign a flushing policy of Finish.

---

[4] The current AX design requires routing data to correctly align due dates of the purchase order and production order for subcontracted production, and to support a single receipt transaction for updating the purchase order

The example BOM shown in Figure 15.3 illustrates the definition of BOM lines for the subcontracted service and the supplied material, and the external operation to produce the parent item. The left side of the figure also highlights the dual constructs of a production order and its associated purchase order (for the subcontracted service item) in order to support coordination of subcontracted production.

Figure 15.3 Example BOM for Subcontracted Production

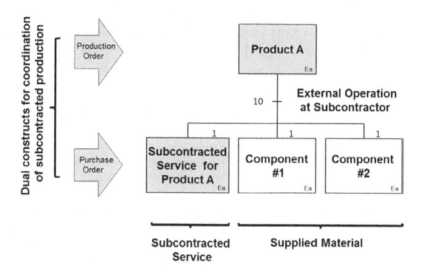

Define BOM Line for a Supplied Component A separate BOM line defines each supplied component and its required quantity. The warehouse source of components is typically specified as part of the BOM line, or it can reflect one of the other options described in the chapter about BOM information (Section 5.5). The applicable option and the component's flushing policy should reflect the desired variation of supplied components.

Some scenarios also identify the material provided by the subcontractor. These are often termed reference components. A separate BOM line can define each reference component and its required quantity. In addition, you indicate the BOM

---

and associated production order. A customization can support the alignment of due dates without the need for routing data, as illustrated in Case XX.

line should not be included in cost rollup calculations. An item representing a reference component is typically assigned a manual flushing policy and a manual coverage planning code (so that planned supply orders will not be generated).

15.5 Routing Information for Subcontracted Production

The fundamental design of AX requires routing information to support subcontracted production, especially in calculating the turnaround time at the subcontractor, aligning the purchase order due date for the subcontracted service, and supporting a single receipt transaction. However, the definition and use of this routing information involves additional complexity compared to routings for internal production.

For simplicity's sake, this explanation focuses on routings with a single external operation that represents processing by the subcontractor. The typical business process for defining an item's routing for subcontracted production is exactly the same process used for an internally produced item, which was described in a previous chapter (Section 6.6). However, several aspects merit special consideration.

Define a Production Resource representing a Subcontractor Each subcontractor must be identified as a separate production resource so that the relevant subcontractor can be specified as the resource for an external operation. You indicate a resource type of *Vendor* when initially defining the resource. You can optionally specify the vendor's identifier, which represents one option for indicating the preferred vendor for purchasing a subcontracted service. These resources can be assigned to a single resource group that represents all subcontractors for a given AX site.

Define Route Version Policies The route version for a manufactured item must be site-specific. Multiple route versions may be needed when the same parent item can be produced at different subcontractors.

Define an External Operation in a Routing An external operation serves two primary purposes: it identifies the required resource that represents the applicable subcontractor, and it provides the basis for calculating the turnaround time for the subcontracted service. The turnaround time is typically specified as a fixed amount (using either the time element for setup or queue after) because a variable amount of run time does not apply. The fixed amount of hours must reflect the calendar of working hours for the resource. For example, a turnaround time of four days can be expressed as 32 hours when the calendar consists of 8-

hour days. However, the operation must also include a run time in order to support a single receipt transaction, as described in a subsequent section (Section 15.6). The run time is typically expressed as a very small amount so that it does materially impact the calculated turnaround time.

Each external operation can have its own master operation, or just a single master operation can be defined (with different applicability rules), so that you can specify the master operation as part of the routing information for the parent item.
An external operation does not typically have any costs.   You can optionally designate an operation's route type as Vendor (rather than Standard), but this only provides reference information and does not affect functionality.

15.6 Single Receipt Transaction for Subcontracted Production

The dual constructs of a production order and its related purchase order can be received separately, or a single purchase order receipt for the subcontracted service can update both orders.   The single receipt transaction triggers several automatic steps and involves some additional aspects of setup information.

The single receipt transaction triggers several automatic steps that require an understanding of the AX capabilities for reporting unit completions at the last routing operation in order to update the finished quantity of a production order. In addition to updating the purchase order receipt, it automatically generates and posts a route card journal for the outside operation.   The journal line inherits a "good quantity" (from the receipt) and the reported-as-finished flag.   This acts as a trigger to automatically update the finished quantity for the related production order, which also acts as a trigger to automatically create and post a picking list journal identifying the component representing the subcontracted service, and possibly backflush the supplied components stocked at the subcontractor site. These components have a flushing principle of finish.

Many aspects of relevant information for a single receipt transaction have been covered in previous sections, such as the definition of an item representing the subcontracted service, the BOM and routing information for subcontracted production of a manufactured item, and the warehouse source of components. The additional aspects include the desired impact of a purchase order receipt for a subcontracted service, and the need for a run time element in the external operation.

Impact of a Purchase Order Receipt for a Subcontracted Service The desired impact is identified by two policies about automatic updates within the production control parameters. These policies can be defined as part of the site-specific or companywide parameters. One policy about automatic BOM consumption typically indicates use of the *flushing principle* for components. The second policy about automatic route consumption must indicate *always* or use of the *route group* policy for an operation, otherwise the single receipt transaction cannot trigger the automatic creation and posting of the route card journal.

When the second policy reflects the route group, the route group must include automatic route consumption policies for run time and quantity. This enables the purchase order receipt quantity to be inherited by the good quantity on the automatically-created route card journal, and a good quantity only applies to the run time element.

Run time for the External Operation A run time must be specified for the external operation (even if it is a very small amount of time), otherwise the single receipt transaction does not create a route card journal with a good quantity for the run time element.

15.7 Additional Considerations about Subcontracted Production

Many of the considerations about subcontracted production have been covered in the previous chapter about production order processing. These include the significance of a single production order, the variations in generating and posting a picking list journal, the significance of production order status, the options for defining the warehouse source of components in BOM/route Information, the options for reporting production order receipts, the inspections related to production orders, and rework orders. This section covers some additional considerations.

Purchasing Considerations for the Subcontracted Service Many of the purchasing considerations have already been mentioned, such as approved vendors, the preferred vendor and the agreements about purchase prices. Other considerations include the definition of vendor information (Section 12.11), miscellaneous charges for a purchase order, and the impact of a vendor hold and other stop flags (Section 12.3).

Coverage Planning Data for a Subcontract Manufactured Item The coverage planning data for a manufactured item was covered in a previous chapter (Section 9.5), such as the coverage group, production lead time, order quantity modifiers, and the planner responsibility. For a subcontract manufactured item, the production lead time represents the turnaround time at the subcontractor. The turnaround time should reflect the approach to supplied materials and finished quantities such as transportation time considerations.

Using the Subcontracted Work form   The Subcontractor Work form displays any production order with a linked purchase order for a buy-to-order component. The buy-to-order component represents a subcontracted service in scenarios with subcontracted production. The form displays information about purchase order status, and enables you to update the production order status via the start task and report-as-finished task.

15.8 Additional Case Studies

Case studies can be used to illustrate the variations of subcontracted production. The basic model described at the beginning of the chapter provided a baseline for explaining these variations. It represented one scenario involving production order picking and receiving with no visibility of inventory at the subcontractor.

Case 15.1: Subcontracted Production with Full Visibility   A manufacturing company produced several products at subcontractors located in other states and countries. The supplied material was transferred and stocked at each subcontractor, and the finished quantities were reported prior to transferring the goods to an internal warehouse. This approach provided full visibility of inventory at the subcontractor site and in transit, and also modeled the associated transportation time. Figure 15.4 illustrates the bill of material information, and the shaded arrows identify the inventory-related transactions. In particular, the purchase order receipt for the subcontracted service resulted in a finished quantity of the subcontracted production order, which triggered backflushing of the supplied components at the subcontractor warehouse. In this case study, the subcontractor site was identified as a non-WMS warehouse, and the manufacturing plant consisted of WMS-enabled warehouses which involved use of the advanced approach to warehouse management.

Case 15.2: Subcontracted Production without Routing Data   A manufacturing company employed subcontractors to produce several different products, and wanted to model subcontracted production without routing data. The solution approach involved a proposed customization so that the purchase order due date for the subcontracted service automatically aligned with the due date of the production order for the parent item. The lead time for the parent item defined the turnaround time at the subcontractor. In addition, the proposed customization supported a single purchase order receipt transaction that automatically updated the finished quantity for the production order.

Figure 15.4 Subcontracted Production with Full Visibility

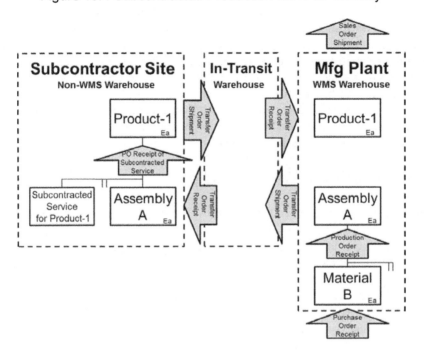

Case 15.3: Separate Receipt Transactions for Reporting Subcontracted Production A manufacturing company employed subcontractors to produce several different products, which involved the dual constructs of a production order and its associated purchase order (for the subcontracted service). The dual constructs required two separate receipt transactions. One transaction identified the production order receipt quantity (to indicate the good and trashed quantity, and to trigger backflushing of supplied components). The second transaction identified the purchase order receipt quantity (to indicate the quantity they would pay for). The two quantities were frequently different.

Case 15.4: Multiple Subcontractors build same Item A manufacturing company employed multiple subcontractors to produce the same item, where the supplied components were stocked at each subcontractor. Each subcontractor's location was identified as a unique AX site, and site-specific BOM versions for a parent item defined the supplied components for each subcontractor. A subcontracted service item was defined for each parent item. Since the company was using standard costs, different site-specific standard costs were assigned to the subcontracted service item and to the supplied components. This approach also entailed the calculation of site-specific standard costs for the parent item.

Case 15.5: Purchase Orders for Supplied Material Delivered to a Subcontractor Warehouse As part of supporting subcontracted production, a manufacturer had vendors deliver the purchased items (representing the supplied material) to the subcontractor warehouse. The actual receipt of a purchase order at the subcontractor was entered into AX as a simple inventory transaction.

Case 15.6: Sales Order Shipments from a Subcontractor Warehouse A manufacturing company stocked an item's finished quantity at the subcontractor warehouse, and entered sales orders for shipment from the subcontractor warehouse. In order to communicate the need for sales order shipments from the subcontractor warehouses, the DRP coordinator generated the sales order picking lists and e-mailed a copy to the relevant contact person. The contact person sent a return e-mail after completing the requested shipments, and the DRP coordinator simply posted each completed sales order picking list and packing slip.

Case 15.7: Identify BOM Components provided by the Subcontractor A food products manufacturer found it helpful to define formula information that included material provided by the co-packer. These are sometimes called reference ingredients. In this way, the food engineers could specify the exact recipe information with all ingredients. The theoretical usage (of reference ingredients) could be calculated for each production order, which helped reconcile a co-packer's claims about actual usage. Other benefits included a comparative cost calculation with all ingredients included, and the calculated requirements (for the reference ingredients) helped in negotiating agreements with suppliers.

15.9 Executive Summary

Subcontracted production and internal production share many similarities. However, there are many variations of subcontracted production scenarios which involve significant differences about inventory visibility and supply chain coordination via the dual constructs of a production order and a corresponding purchase order for the subcontracted service. The chapter explained the major variations associated with supplied material and finished quantities, and the key constructs such as service items, BOMs and routings to support subcontracted production.

Several case studies illustrated the variations in subcontracted production. These included subcontracted production with full visibility of inventory (Case 15.1), the need for routing data (Case 15.2), reporting subcontracted production with separate receipt transactions (Case 15.3), multiple subcontractors building the same item (Case 15.4), purchase orders delivered to a subcontractor warehouse (Case 15.5), sales order shipments from a subcontractor warehouse (Case 15.6), and BOM components provided by the subcontractor (Case 15.7).

Chapter 16

Inventory and Warehouse Management

Inventory and warehouse management involve the physical storage and movement of products within and between physical sites, as well as handling outbound and inbound shipments with trading partners. Various terms refer to these activities, and the responsibilities may be assigned to different roles within one or several functional areas. This book primarily uses the term warehouse management, and the typical roles include the warehouse manager, warehouse planner and warehouse worker. Other roles include receiving clerks, shipping clerks and transportation coordinators.

Many aspects of inventory and warehouse management have already been covered in previous chapters. For example, several fundamentals for modeling inventory locations were introduced at the beginning of the book, which explained the use of AX sites and AX warehouses to identify inventory locations. Subsequent chapters identified the applicability of these inventory locations in the definition of items, bills of material, resources and routings, product costing, coverage planning data and S&OP game plans.

One of the fundamentals for modeling inventory locations involves the choice of a warehouse management option, where the choice can be warehouse-specific. The two major options consist of a basic approach and an advanced approach to warehouse management, and they represent two different conceptual models for managing inventory and related business processes. The impact on business processes were covered in previous chapters about sales orders, purchase orders, transfer orders and production orders. This chapter summarizes the two options, starting with an explanation of the strategic options for warehouse management and the significance of Inventory Status. It also explains the AX viewpoint of inventory transactions. These considerations are reflected in the following sections within the chapter.

1. Strategic Options for Warehouse Management
2. Significance of Inventory Status
3. Basic Approach to Warehouse Management
4. Advanced Approach to Warehouse Management
5. AX Viewpoint of Inventory Transactions
6. Workspaces related to Inventory and Warehouse Management
7. Additional Case Studies

A separate book provides comprehensive explanations about the warehouse management capabilities within AX.[1] The comprehensive explanations are summarized here because of book length considerations. A page count comparison about the explanation of the basic and advanced approaches to warehouse management (covered here in Sections 16.3 and 16.4) indicates that 300+ pages have been summarized here into 20+ pages. The summarized version simply covers a basic process and illustrative BPM diagram for each type of transaction, and a brief description of their major variations. Hence, almost all of the graphics and detailed insights -- about the key constructs and related life cycles, reversing transactions, major variations and key considerations -- are not included here. The separate book represents a companion volume to this book, and it is recommended for those needing more comprehensive explanations.

16.1 Strategic Options for Warehouse Management

Dynamics AX supports a range of options for warehouse management capabilities, but the options can be broadly grouped into a basic approach and an advanced approach. The choice of an approach can be warehouse-specific, so that a company may use the advanced approach at some warehouses and the basic approach at other warehouses. The two approaches share a high degree of common functionality, but the advanced approach has a much broader amount of functionality and supports out-of-the-box mobile device transactions. Both approaches can optionally take advantage of capabilities related to Inventory Status.

For some firms, the key question involves "which option is best for my operation". A related question often involves "what are the strategic options for starting with basic capabilities and evolving into more advanced capabilities." The flexibility to evolve can be considered within each of the two major approaches, and from one approach to the other. Multiple case studies will be

---

[1] The separate book is titled "Warehouse Management using Microsoft Dynamics AX", and it represents a companion book to this book.

used to illustrate evolving strategies about starting simple and growing in sophistication. These considerations are reflected in the following topics within the section.

◆ Major Options for Warehouse Management
◆ Applicability of Inventory Status
◆ Guidelines for choosing the Basic vs Advanced Approach
◆ Strategic Options and Summary of Case Studies
◆ Evolving Strategies for Strategic Options
◆ Details of Case Studies
◆ Comparing Approaches

Major Options for Warehouse Management The various warehouse management options have been called many different names, but they boil down to two major options.[2] For simplicity's sake, one major option can be termed the "Basic Inventory approach" or the "basic approach" for short. The second major option can be termed the "Advanced WMS approach" or the "advanced approach" for short. The two options have also been called "WMS I" and "WHS" to reflect Microsoft acronyms.

The two major options are differentiated by a warehouse policy and an item-related policy about "use warehouse management processes." The advanced approach only applies to warehouse transactions for a WMS-enabled item at a WMS-enabled warehouse, whereas the basic approach applies to the other combinations of these two policies. Figure 16.1 summarizes these key policies and the two major options for warehouse management, identified as Option #1 and #2. It also identifies the terminology about items and warehouses, such as a WMS-enabled item, a WMS-enabled warehouse and a non-WMS warehouse.

The two major options are also reflected in the AX user documentation, which differentiates various topics as applicable to "features in the warehouse management module" versus "features in the inventory management module." Each option has some unique constructs and functionality, but the two major options also share a high degree of common functionality. For those already familiar with previous AX versions, you already know most of the functionality associated with the basic approach based on your experience with the historical "WMS I" capabilities.

---

[2] The two major options reflect the license key for the "Warehouse and Transportation Management" capabilities. When using AX 2012 R3, you must disable an alternative but mutually exclusive approach. That is, you disable the feature set for the old "Warehouse Management II" functionality.

Figure 16.1 Major Options for Warehouse Management

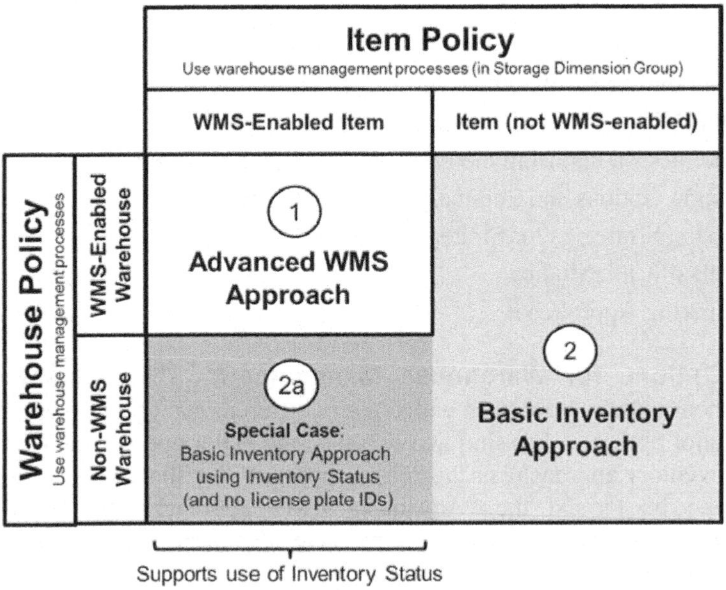

Applicability of Inventory Status   The capabilities related to Inventory Status only apply to WMS-enabled items.   It always applies to the advanced approach, and it represents a special case for the basic approach -- identified as Option #2a in Figure 16.1.   The significance of Inventory Status is largely determined by user-defined values, and most scenarios employ at least two values.   One value typically indicates good inventory, such as a value of *Available* or *Good*. One or more values can be designated as blocked in order to prevent usage of inventory with the assigned value, and master scheduling logic treats inventory with a blocked value as non-nettable. Examples of these blocked values include *Damaged* or *To-Be-Scrapped*. The next section provides further explanation about the significance of Inventory Status.

Guidelines for choosing the Basic vs Advanced Approach   As a general guideline, the advanced approach typically applies to those warehouses that require tracking of palletized inventory (identified by license plate IDs), more sophisticated capabilities to support warehouse/transportation requirements, and out-of-the-box functionality for mobile devices, especially when warehouse users need guidance about finding or placing inventory. However, the advanced approach also supports scenarios that do not employ license plate tracking in their inventory locations, and the use of license plate IDs is largely hidden from end-users. The more sophisticated capabilities to support warehouse and transportation requirements are sometimes a leading indicator for choosing the advanced approach.

The basic approach typically applies to a warehouse (or company) that does not have sophisticated requirements for sales order picking/shipping, and does not require tracking of palletized inventory. Inventory within the warehouse is typically tracked by piece rather than by pallet. In addition, the basic approach does not support out-of-the box mobile device transactions, although third-party applications can be used. The basic approach supports simple order-based picking for sales orders and transfer orders, and also supports the wave picking concept for these orders.

As an additional consideration, the amount of functionality within the advanced approach is approximately twice as much as the basic approach, and often requires a longer and more costly implementation. A subsequent point provides some metrics about the comparative amount of functionality and complexity for each approach.

Strategic Options and Illustrative Case Studies The strategic options for warehouse management go beyond the choice of one approach or the other. For example, the choice of an approach can be warehouse specific. In addition, a key question often involves "what are the strategic options for starting with basic capabilities and evolving into more advanced capabilities." The flexibility to evolve can be considered within each of the two major approaches, and from one approach to the other.

As an explanatory approach, it is easiest to consider the various strategic options in terms of illustrative case studies. Illustrative case studies are summarized in Figure 16.2, and the details of each case will be described shortly. The numbered case studies are superimposed on the previous diagram about major options, and the arrows indicate the applicable option. These do not necessarily reflect an exhaustive list of strategic options.

Evolving Strategies for Strategic Options An evolving strategy can help reduce the complexity and cost of the initial phase of an ERP implementation. The flexibility to evolve can be considered within each of the two major approaches, and from one approach to the other. As one example of an evolving strategy within the Advanced WMS approach, a given warehouse may start with the simplest use of mobile device transactions and the advanced functionality (Case 16.1) and then evolve to fully utilize them (Case 16.2) and to fully use the advanced transportation management capabilities (Case 16.3).

Figure 16.2 Strategic Options for Warehouse Management

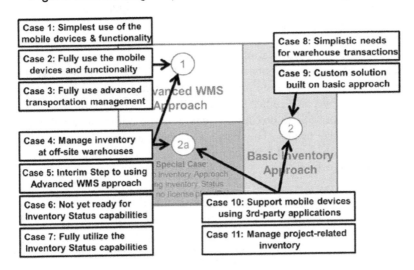

As an example for the Basic Inventory approach, a given warehouse may start without using the Inventory Status capabilities (Case 16.6) and then evolve to fully utilize the capabilities (Case 16.7). A given warehouse may also start with the basic approach as an interim step to the advanced approach (Case 16.5). Even when the primary warehouses employ the advanced approach, the basic approach is typically required for managing inventory at off-site warehouses such as subcontractors or smaller locations (Case 16.4).

A firm with simplistic needs for warehouse management can start with out-of-the-box functionality in the basic approach (Case 16.8), and then selectively develop custom solutions built on the basic approach (Case 16.9) and implement mobile device transactions via third party applications (Case 16.10).

Details of Case Studies Illustrative case studies about the strategic options for warehouse management were summarized in Figure 16.2. Each case study can be described in more detail.

Case 16.1: Simplest use of the Mobile Device Transactions and Advanced WMS functionality
The implementation project team at a manufacturer/distributor wanted to implement the Advanced WMS approach as simply as possible, and then evolve into more sophisticated usage as needed. They considered several options for simplified usage at their main warehouses, including the following.

◆ *Minimum scope for advanced functionality.* The minimum scope can start with just the basic inventory transactions and the basic processes for handling purchase receipts and the order-based picking for sales orders and transfer orders. It does not need to include the many aspects of more advanced functionality, such as load planning, manual packing or replenishment of picking locations.

◆ *Minimum scope for using mobile device transactions.* The minimum scope can start with just the mobile device transactions for the above-mentioned basic inventory transactions and basic business processes. The related putaway transactions for receipts of purchases and transfers can be user-directed. The logic for suggested putaway locations can be added later. The detailed design of interacting with the mobile devices can reflect simplistic out-of-the-box capabilities.

◆ *Minimal tracking of inventory by License Plate IDs.* The minimum scope can start with minimal tracking and use of license plate IDs. Minimal tracking reflects the use of inventory locations designated as "not license plate controlled," and the related use of putaway transactions into these locations. The minimal tracking can apply to selected locations (such as production floorstock) or to almost every location.

◆ *Minimum scope for advanced transportation capabilities.* The minimum scope can start without using the incremental capabilities for advanced transportation management. These capabilities can be phased in at a later date.

◆ *Single value for Inventory Status.* The minimum scope can start with a single value of *Available* as the default value for all possible transactions, or with just two values of *Available* and *Blocked*. Additional values and their impact on business processes can be phased in at a later date.

Case 16.2: Fully use the Mobile Device Transactions and Advanced WMS functionality A manufacturing/distribution company fully utilized the mobile device transactions and the functionality within the Advanced WMS approach. The mobile device transactions were used at every possible step in each business process, and the detailed design of interacting with the mobile device was tailored to their operation and warehouse personnel. They were not yet ready for any of the advanced transportation management capabilities.

Case 16.3: Fully use the Advanced Transportation Management capabilities A manufacturing/distribution company used the Advanced WMS approach at their key warehouses to identify and manage outbound loads (for sales orders and transfer orders) and inbound loads (for purchase orders), and used this load information for transportation management purposes. This included the assignment of rates and routes to inbound and outbound loads, the scheduling and reporting of transportation appointments for inbound and outbound docks, and performing freight entry and reconciliation.

Case 16.4: Manage Inventory at Off-site Warehouses A manufacturer/distributor employed the Advanced WMS functionality and mobile device transactions at their main warehouse. However, they also needed to track inventory and report transactions at their off-site warehouses that represented subcontractors and remote locations. They used simple inventory transactions for many situations, such as reporting purchase order receipts of supplied material at a subcontractor, or transfer order receipts at a remote warehouse. In some situations, they selectively employed capabilities within the Basic Inventory approach, such as generating picking lists for all sales order shipments from a subcontractor or remote warehouse.

Case 16.5: Interim Step to using Advanced WMS approach A manufacturing and distribution company was implementing AX with a two-phased approach for warehouse management. For Phase 1, they employed the simpler Basic Inventory approach, which would serve as an interim step before implementing the Advanced WMS approach. More specifically, they defined items as WMS-enabled and initially defined non-WMS warehouses and their locations. For Phase 2, they would define another set of WMS-enabled warehouses with the exact same location identifiers. When cutting over to Phase 2, the inventory in their previous warehouses will be transferred to the corresponding WMS-enabled warehouse and location, and also assigned the relevant license plate ID. In addition, the demands and supply orders would be updated to reflect the change to WMS-enabled warehouses.

Case 16.6: Not yet ready for Inventory Status capabilities A manufacturing and distribution company was implementing AX in a short time frame, and did not want any additional complexities that would delay the cutover. In terms of using different values of an Inventory Status, they simply used the two values of *Available* and *Blocked*, since they were not quite ready to think through the potential impacts of other possible values. They assigned the value of *Available* as the default for all possible transactions. They planned to revisit the use of Inventory Status after the initial cutover.

Case 16.7: Fully Utilize the Inventory Status capabilities   A manufacturing and distribution company identified multiple values for the Inventory Status in order to support requirements for quality, warehousing and sales.   The use of Inventory Status was fully integrated into the business processes for receiving purchase orders and production output (especially the use of quality orders).   The values indicating needed action provided the basis for performing follow-up actions.   Different sales pricing was defined for off-spec material.

Case 16.8: Simplistic Needs for Warehouse Transactions   A manufacturing and distribution company had simplistic needs for warehouse transactions.   They implemented the Basic Inventory approach (without using Inventory Status) at the various warehouses, since they did not require the additional functionality within the Advanced WMS approach.   In addition, they were happy with screen-based approaches for entering warehouse transactions, and did not yet perceive a need for data collection via mobile devices.

Case 16.9: Custom Solution built on Basic Approach   A manufacturing and distribution company had simplistic needs for warehouse transactions, and were implementing the Basic Inventory approach because they did not require the additional functionality within the advanced approach.   For example, they employed order-based picking for sales orders and transfer orders, and used the Picking Workbench to support their wave picking requirements.   A few requirements were being addressed by customizations, such as a customization to support staging/loading steps prior to sales order shipment.

Case 16.10: Support Mobile Devices using 3rd-Party Applications   A manufacturing and distribution company was implementing the Basic Inventory approach (and using Inventory Status) at the various warehouses, since they did not require the additional functionality within the Advanced WMS approach. This meant they could not use the out-of-the-box mobile device transactions, so they employed a third-party solution for these data collection purposes.[3]   The solution supported all variations of transactions within the basic approach, and provided a simpler user interface for the mobile device transactions (relative to the out-of-the-box mobile device transactions).

Case 16.11: Manage Project-related Inventory   A project-oriented business implemented the simpler Basic Inventory approach because they did not require the additional functionality within the Advanced WMS approach.   In

---

[3] RFSmart provides add-on modules to support mobile device transactions for the Basic Inventory approach, and also provide enhancements for using the mobile device transactions within the Advanced WMS approach. See http://www.rfsmart.com for more information.

addition, many of their project-related transactions (such as receipts for project purchase orders and reporting item usage for projects) were not supported by the mobile device transactions within the advanced approach. They are considering a third-party application for supporting their mobile device transactions.

Comparing Approaches The two approaches to warehouse management can be compared in several different ways. In the context of strategic options, the level of complexity in each approach may sway the choice of an option. The comparative level of complexity can be considered from several angles, including (1) the comparative amount of functionality, (2) the comparative complexity in the underlying conceptual models, and (3) the comparative complexity of reservation logic. In summary, the basic approach is simpler for the first two metrics, and the advanced approach is simpler for the third metric.

The advanced approach has approximately twice the aggregate functionality as the basic approach, and its variations for supporting sales order picking/shipping reflect a three-fold increase in functionality. The basic approach is typically simpler in terms of comparable steps for the exact same business process, and substantially simpler in terms of the number of constructs and related life cycles. It also provides a simpler transaction history that does not involve the many additional work order transactions of the advanced approach.

Reservation logic is often one of the more complex aspects of an ERP system, and its significance differs widely between software packages and companies. In the case of AX, the significance and use of reservation logic differs significantly between the basic and advanced approaches to warehouse management. The reservation logic within the advanced approach (based on the concept of a reservation hierarchy assigned to each item) seems to provide a simpler and more effective model for supporting reservation logic.

16.2 Significance of Inventory Status

The significance of Inventory Status is largely determined by user-defined values, and it only applies to WMS-enabled items. Most scenarios employ at least two user-defined values. One value typically indicates good inventory, such as a value of *Available* or *Good*. One or more values can be defined and designated as blocked in order to prevent usage of inventory with the assigned value, and master scheduling logic treats inventory with a blocked value as non-nettable. Examples of these blocked values include *Blocked, Damaged* or *To-Be-Scrapped*.

You define the possible values of Inventory Status, and a value must be assigned to all orders (such as sales order lines and to all supply orders) and inventory transactions. Several characteristics are particularly important for warehouse and quality management purposes, such as the ability to assign a different value during the receiving process, the different approaches of changing the value for existing inventory, and the allowable transactions for existing inventory with a value representing a blocked status. These considerations are reflected in the following topics within the section

◆ Two Different Meanings of the term Inventory Status
◆ Define the Values for Inventory Status
◆ Assign a Value for Inventory Status to Orders
◆ Default Values for Modeling a Purchased Item's Inspection Requirements
◆ Ability to Override a Value for Inventory Status during the Receiving Process
◆ Ability to Change the Value for Inventory Status for Existing Inventory
◆ Allowable Transactions for Inventory with a Blocked Inventory Status

Two Different Meanings of the term Inventory Status   The term "inventory status" has many different meanings in different ERP systems. It has two different meanings in AX. As the primary focus, Inventory Status refers to one of the mandatory dimensions within a Storage Group Dimension that has been enabled to "use warehouse management processes." Related policies indicate whether a value for Inventory Status should be considered for sales pricing, purchase pricing, and/or coverage planning purposes. An additional consideration applies when using the advanced approach to warehouse management, since Inventory Status must be designated in the reservation hierarchy as critical or simply informational for reservation purposes.

The term "inventory status" also refers to the AX viewpoint of inventory transactions, where the status indicates steps in the life cycle of orders for an item. The system-assigned values of an inventory status differ for each type of order. For example, the applicable values for a purchase order line indicate whether the item has been *Ordered*, *Received* or *Purchased*, and the status is automatically updated by different steps in the business process. A subsequent section describes the AX viewpoint of inventory transactions (Section 16.5).

In order to differentiate the two different meanings, this book employs capital letters (for Inventory Status) and lower case letters (for inventory status) for the same term, although the context of the term usually provides sufficient clues about its meaning.

Define the Values for Inventory Status You create a user-defined value and name using the Inventory Status form. One value typically indicates good inventory, such as a user-defined value of *Available* or *Good.* One or more values can be defined and designated as blocked in order to prevent usage of inventory with the assigned value. Master scheduling logic considers the inventory with a blocked value to be non-nettable; it is assumed the inventory cannot be used.

Assign a Value for Inventory Status to Orders A value for Inventory Status must be entered for every type of order. This includes line items on purchase orders, transfer orders and sales orders, as well as production orders and the related lines in a Production BOM. A value is also required on basic inventory transactions. The use of default values for Inventory Status can help streamline data entry, especially for modeling a normal business. The use of default values can also reflect different purposes of Inventory Status.

For most scenarios, a default value of *Available* or its equivalent should be assigned as a companywide policy, and as the default for every site and warehouse involved in normal business. In this way, every transaction will inherit the value unless a different source of the default value applies. For example, the default value for an item can model an item's inspection requirements.

Default Values for Modeling a Purchased Item's Inspection Requirements As one purpose of Inventory Status, it can provide the basis for identifying needed inspection of purchase order receipts. For example, a value of *Needs-Inspection* can be assigned to a purchase order line item so that it is identified when reporting purchase order arrival. A given item that always requires inspection can be assigned a default value of *Needs-Inspection* using the Default Item Status form. In this way, the value will be inherited when creating a purchase order line or firming a planned order.

Ability to Override a Value for Inventory Status during the Receiving Process The ability to override a value for Inventory Status during the receiving process applies to all types of orders except transfer orders. This includes the receiving process for purchase orders, RMAs and production orders. For example, the value of *Available* for a purchase order line can be overridden when reporting arrival, such as changing the value to *Needs-Inspection*, *Return-to-Vendor* or *To-Be-Scrapped*. This approach is illustrated in Case 16.12 for the purchase order receiving process.

The use of automatically-created quality orders may influence how you assign a value during the receiving process. As an additional consideration, you can indicate a scrapped quantity when reporting the finished quantity for a production order, or when reporting receipt of a transfer order line. The value can also be assigned for additions to inventory via inventory adjustments, quantity adjustments or cycle counts.

Ability to Change the Value for Inventory Status for Existing Inventory Several approaches can change the value of Inventory Status. The value can be changed using a mobile device transaction, or using the forms titled Warehouse Inventory Status Change and Change Inventory Status. One form changes status for selected existing inventory with a specified status, and the other form changes status for all existing inventory at a selected location.

A rework order can be used to change the value of Inventory Status. For example, an item's inventory may be assigned an unblocked status of *Needs-Rework*, and you can create a rework order in order to change the status to *Available*.

A quality order can be used to change the value of Inventory Status based on the test results. The quality order can be manually or automatically generated, and the material being tested can have a blocked or unblocked status. As part of the quality order information, you specify the associated value for "fail" and another value for "pass", so that validation of the test results will automatically change the status.

Allowable Transactions for Inventory with a Blocked Inventory Status The allowable transactions include purchase order returns, inventory adjustments, cycle counts, inventory transfers and quality orders. Otherwise, a blocked value prevents inventory transactions.

Case 16.12: Receiving Clerk Assigns Inventory Status when Registering Purchase Order Arrival

The warehouse manager and quality control (QC) manager at a manufacturing company were considering options for reporting quality problems at the time of purchase order arrival. One approach involved the user-defined values for Inventory Status, with possible values of *Good* and *Needs-Inspection* as well as blocked values of *To-Be-Scrapped* and *Return-to-Vendor*. The default value for Inventory Status was typically identified as *Good* on purchase order lines.

If the receiving clerks noticed a quality problem when registering purchase order arrival, they would override the Inventory Status to a value of *Needs-Inspection.* Some purchase order lines were already assigned a value of *Needs-Inspection* so it was not overridden. The two managers prepared a diagram of the proposed business process shown in Figure 16.3.

Figure 16.3 Assign Inventory Status when Registering Purchase Order Arrival

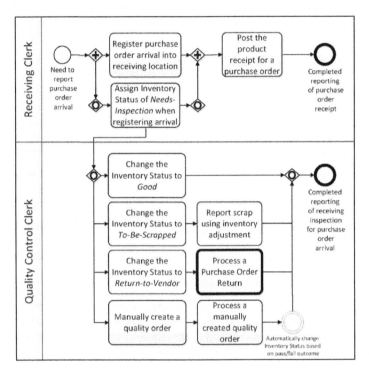

After the receiving clerk identifies received material with a status of *Needs-Inspection,* the quality control clerk subsequently makes a determination by changing the value of Inventory Status to a value of *Good, To-Be-Scrapped,* or *Return-to-Vendor.* As an additional option, the quality control clerk can manually create and process a quality order, and the pass/fail outcome automatically updates the value of Inventory Status. Other roles were typically responsible for the additional steps of processing a purchase order return.

16.3 Basic Approach to Warehouse Management

The basic approach to warehouse management can be summarized, starting with the fundamentals and then covering a typical-yet-basic business process for different types of warehouse transactions.

Fundamentals of the Basic Approach   The fundamentals include the definition of warehouse locations and the use of basic inventory transactions. As part of the setup information for a non-WMS warehouse, you define bin locations within the warehouse and a few item-related policies.   The basic inventory transactions include movements between inventory locations (via the Transfer Journal), adjustments (via the Inventory Adjustment Journal or Quantity Adjustments), and physical counts (via the Counting Journal).

Purchase Order Receiving   As illustrated in Figure 16.4, the receiving clerk uses the Arrival Overview form to review and select open purchase order line items that require receiving, and then generate an arrival journal containing the selected lines.   Alternatively, the receiving clerk can manually create an arrival journal, typically to handle an unplanned receipt.   The receiving clerk registers the actual receipts against each journal line item and then posts the journal to update inventory balances.   The receiving clerk also identifies the vendor's packing list number when posting the product receipt for a purchase order.   For received material with putaway requirements, the warehouse worker uses the Transfer Journal form to report transfers from the receiving location to the putaway location.

Figure 16.4 Typical Process for Purchase Order Receiving
using Basic Inventory Approach

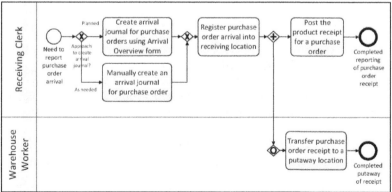

Sales Order Picking/Shipping   The basic approach to warehouse management only supports an order-based approach to sales order picking/shipping, and a sales order picking list represents the key construct to coordinate and report actual picking. As illustrated in Figure 16.5, the shipping clerk uses the Release Sales Order Picking form to review and select open sales order lines that require picking/shipping, and then generate the picking lists for selected orders. The generation of a picking list will reserve the item's inventory for the sales line (if not already reserved). As alternative approaches, a picking list can be generated from a sales order, or the picking lists can be generated from a periodic task or from the Picking Workbench form.

The warehouse worker reports actual picking against a sales order picking list and then posting it. The shipping clerk reports actual shipment by posting the sales order packing slip for picked items.

Figure 16.5 Typical Process for Sales Order Picking/Shipping
using Basic Inventory Approach

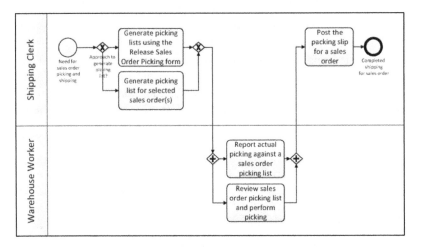

Transfer Order Picking/Shipping   The basic approach to warehouse management only supports an order-based approach to transfer order picking/shipping, and a transfer order picking list represents the key construct to coordinate and report actual picking. As illustrated in Figure 16.6, the shipping clerk uses the Release Transfer Order Picking form to review and select open transfer order lines that require picking/shipping, and then generate the picking lists for selected orders. The generation of a picking list will reserve the item's inventory for the transfer line (if not already reserved).   As alternative approaches, a picking list can be generated from a transfer order, or the picking lists can be generated from a periodic task.

The warehouse worker reports actual picking against a transfer order picking list and then posts it. The shipping clerk reports actual shipment by posting the transfer order shipment for picked items.

Figure 16.6 Typical Process for Transfer Order Picking/Shipping using Basic Inventory Approach

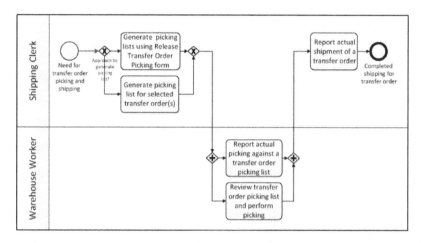

Transfer Order Receiving The order-based approach to transfer order picking/shipping also extends to receiving. As illustrated in Figure 16.7, the receiving clerk uses the Arrival Overview form to review and select shipped transfer order lines, and then create an arrival journal containing the selected lines. The receiving clerk registers the actual receipts against each journal line item and posts the journal to update inventory balances. As a final step, the receiving clerk posts the receipt for a transfer order.

For received material with putaway requirements, the warehouse worker uses the Transfer Journal form to report transfers from the receiving location to the putaway location.

Figure 16.7 Typical Process for Transfer Order Receiving using Basic Inventory Approach

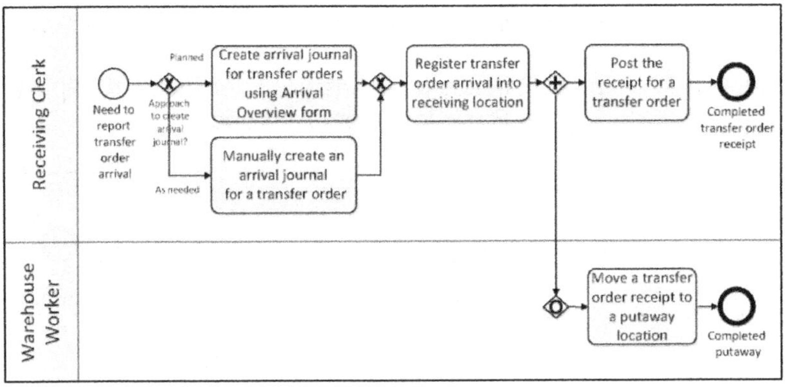

Production Order Picking The basic approach supports an order-based picking approach for production orders. As illustrated in Figure 16.8, the machine operator reports a production order as Started which acts as the trigger for creating a picking list journal based on the Start dialogue policies. The warehouse worker reviews the printed version of the picking list journal, reports actual picking against the picking list journal, and then posts it. The picked material is charged to work in process for the production order, and deducted from inventory. It is typically delivered physically to production but not to a specific location.

In some cases, the machine operator may need to revise actual usage relative to the picked material. The machine operator manually creates a picking list journal containing the adjustments and then posts it.

Production Order Receiving The finished quantity of a production order can be reported using different approaches and delivered to different locations. For example, the finished quantity may be reported multiple times for a given order, or reported once when it represents the entire order quantity. As illustrated in Figure 16.9, the finished quantity can be reported using the Report as Finished form or the Report as Finished Journal, or by using the Route Card Journal for reporting unit completions at the last operation. In addition, the finished quantity may be reported into a production location by the machine operator, or it may be reported into a stocking location by a warehouse worker. The machine operator updates the order status to *Reported as Finished* after all production activities have been reported.

Figure 16.8 Typical Process for Production Order Picking using Basic Inventory Approach

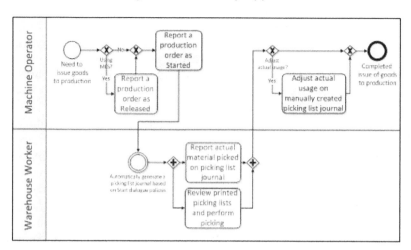

Figure 16.9 Typical Process for Production Order Receiving using Basic Inventory Approach

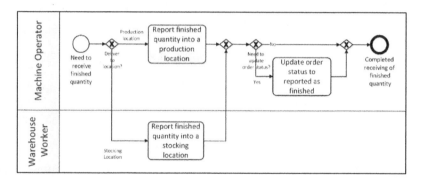

16.4 Advanced Approach to Warehouse Management

The advanced approach to warehouse management can be summarized, starting with the fundamentals and then covering a typical-yet-simple business process for different types of warehouse transactions. The advanced approach supports multiple variations for each business process, and the variations are also summarized.

Fundamentals of the Advanced Approach The fundamentals include the setup information about warehouse locations, item-related policies, and mobile device transactions It also includes the basic inventory transactions, and the significance of license plates and work orders.

A license plate can represent many different physical entities or a logical entity. The significance of a license plate is easiest to conceptualize in terms of a physical pallet, where a standard quantity of the same item is typically placed on a pallet, and a license plate identifier has been assigned to the pallet. The license plate ID provides a convenient way to view inventory balances by pallet, and to report receipts, movement and picking. The concept of a license plate applies to many scenarios, and license plate tracking must be designated for applicable bin locations. However, some scenarios do not want or need license plate tracking, so that applicable bin locations are not enabled for license plate tracking.

Overview of Work Orders Work orders support many different types of warehouse transactions -- ranging from sales order picking to putaway of purchase order arrivals -- and there are different ways to create a work order. For example, some work orders are created by mobile device transactions and other work orders are created by client transactions. The execution of a work order is typically reported via a mobile device transaction. The ability to create and execute work orders via a mobile device transaction requires definition of the corresponding mobile device menu items.

A standard set of work order types are predefined within AX and additional ones can be developed as a customization. Examples of these predefined work order types are illustrated in Figure 16.10 along with a description and the approach for creation of the work order. Grey shading in the figure indicates the use of mobile device transactions. Each work order type requires setup information, such as a work template and location directive.

A work order consists of a header and multiple work lines which represent a set of interrelated warehouse activities identified by a Work ID. You enter or scan the Work ID when reporting various mobile device transactions for a work order. The execution of a work order creates entries for inventory transaction history. When viewing transaction history, a transaction filter can limit the displayed information to "work only" transactions or "omit work" transactions, or you can view "display all" transactions. The "work only" transactions identify the related work order.

Figure 16.10 Examples of Work Order Types

	Work Order Type	Description of Work Order	Example of a Work Order Creation Process
1	Inventory Movement	Move inventory to location	Create move for a selected location
2	Purchase Order	Putaway inventory of a purchase order arrival at receiving location	Register purchase order arrival via mobile device
3	Sales Order	Pick inventory to an outbound dock for a sales order	Release a shipment wave for sales order(s)
4	Transfer Issue	Pick inventory to an outbound dock for a transfer order	Release a shipment wave for transfer order(s)
5	Transfer Receipt	Putaway inventory of a transfer order arrival at a receiving location	Register transfer order arrival via mobile device
6	Raw Material Picking	Pick component inventory to production input location for a production order	Release a production wave for production order components
7	Finished Goods Putaway	Putaway inventory of a finished quantity at a production output location	Report a finished quantity for a production order

Legend: ☐ = Perform transaction via mobile device

Purchase Order Receiving As illustrated in Figure 16.11, the receiving clerk uses the mobile device to register a purchase order arrival into a receiving location (and assign license plate IDs), which automatically creates a work order for putaway. The warehouse worker uses the mobile device to report putaway from the receiving location to a stocking location. A suggested stocking location can reflect location directives, or the warehouse worker can determine and report the stocking location. Alternatively, the receiving clerk registers the arrival and reports putaway as part of a single mobile device transaction. In either case, the receiving clerk subsequently identifies the vendor's packing list number when posting the product receipt for the purchase order.

As an alternative process, the receiving clerk uses the mobile device to register arrival of a purchase load (and related purchase orders) into a receiving location. The purchase load may be previously defined as part of coordinating inbound transportation, or it may be defined at the time of arrival by the receiving clerk. Another alternative involves the use of ASN information provided by the vendor, so that the receiving clerk registers arrival of specific license plate IDs.

Figure 16.11 Typical Process for Purchase Order Receiving using Advanced WMS Approach

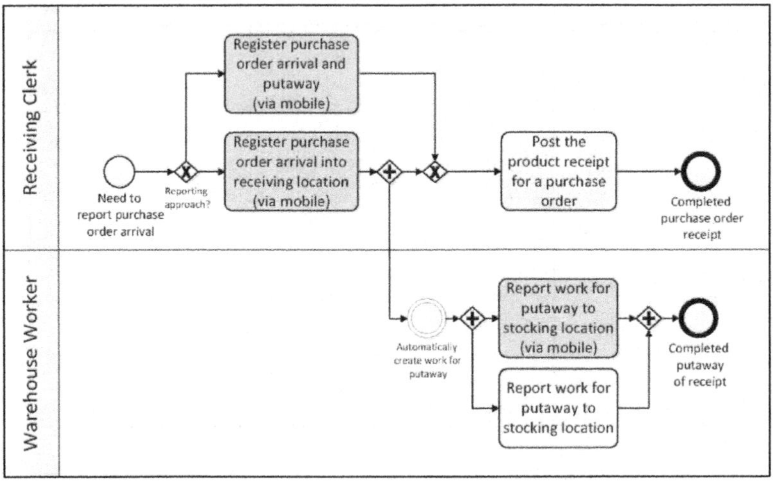

Sales Order Picking/Shipping As illustrated in Figure 16.12, the shipping clerk uses the Release To Warehouse form to review and select open sales order lines that require picking/shipping, and then releases selected orders to the warehouse (which updates the release status for each order). With an order-based picking approach, the release-to-warehouse step can automatically create a shipment and load (with a waved status) and a shipment wave (with a released status) for each sales order. In addition, the released shipment wave automatically creates a picking work order consisting of work lines that identify the pick and put instructions.

The warehouse worker uses the mobile device to report completion of picking work orders with delivery to an outbound dock, which results in a *ready to ship* status for the related shipment and load. The shipping clerk reports actual shipment by confirming the outbound shipments and posting the sales order packing slips for picked items.

In addition to the above-described order-based picking approach, the advanced approach to warehouse management supports other variations of sales order picking/shipping. As described below, these include variations of the release to warehouse step, wave picking, load planning, manual or automated packing, replenishment of picking locations, and staging/loading steps.

Figure 16.12 Typical Process for Sales Order Picking/Shipping using Advanced WMS Approach

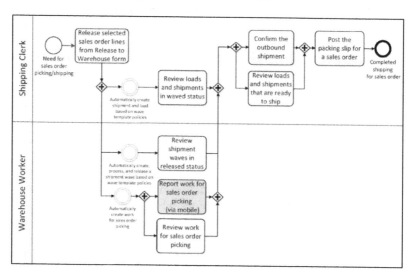

♦ *Release to warehouse for sales orders.* The release to warehouse step represents a key part of any business process for sales order picking/shipping, and it automatically updates the Release Status for a sales order. There are four options for the release to warehouse step. A sales order can be released to the warehouse as part of order entry, or you can use the Release to Warehouse form for releasing selected sales order lines. Both options require reservations before the release to warehouse step, whereas the next two options can defer reservations until the time of release. A third option employs a periodic task to support automatic release to warehouse for sales order lines meeting the selection criteria. A fourth option employs the Load Planning Workbench to support the release to warehouse for all sales orders within a load.

♦ *Wave picking for sales orders.* Wave picking for a grouping of sales order shipments requires a wave planning process after the release to warehouse step. With a manual process, the planner creates a shipment wave and assigns sales order shipments with similar delivery requirements (such as the same ship-from warehouse and ship date). Alternatively, these steps can be performed automatically based on policies within a shipment wave template, such as automatically adding shipments to an existing wave. After releasing the shipment wave, the warehouse worker can use the mobile device to report completion of sales order picking work for the shipment wave.

♦ *Replenishment of Picking Locations.* Some scenarios employ one or more picking lines that contain the most popular items, thereby reducing the time to retrieve inventory from bulk locations. The need for replenishing these picking locations can be manually determined, and the move transactions can be reported via mobile devices. However, the needs can also be automatically determined using three different approaches that also create replenishment work orders for reporting via mobile devices.

- *Wave Demand Approach to Replenishment.* The replenishment work orders reflect the demands related to wave picking, and are automatically created when you process a wave as part of a wave picking process.

- *Load Demand Approach to Replenishment.* This approach reflects demand stemming from selected loads. It employs a separate calculation to create replenishment work orders when the existing quantity for the selected items/locations cannot satisfy the demand for the specified load.

- *Min-Max Approach to Replenishment.* This approach employs min/max quantities for selected items/locations and a separate calculation creates replenishment work when the quantity falls below the minimum. This approach typically applies to scenarios with stable demand and corresponding min/max quantities. The other two options apply to more dynamic scenarios, where suggested replenishment can reflect constant changes in demand.

♦ *Load planning for sales orders.* In a typical load planning process, the Load Planning Workbench is used to view and select open sales order lines. The selected lines are assigned to an existing load or a new load, and you can compare their weight/volume to the maximum allowed for a selected shipping vehicle. The load planning process can serve multiple requirements related to warehouse and transportation management. For example, each load provides an organizing focus for a transportation coordinator to assign the appropriate route and rate, and arrange the transportation appointments. From a warehouse viewpoint, the scheduled departure date/time for a load provides an organizing focus to coordinate sales order picking for a shipment wave.

♦ *Manual packing for sales orders.* Some scenarios require manual packing into containers prior to actual shipment. A container represents the physical structure in which products are packed. Common examples of container types include various sizes of a cardboard box, and a packed container has a unique identifier termed the container ID. However, a container may also reflect other structures or even a reusable object with a permanent container

ID. The nature of a container is one factor among many that result in variations of the manual packing process.

A typical process starts with a warehouse worker picking material for placement at a location representing a packing station, and consists of several steps performed by a warehouse worker or shipping clerk. At the packing station, a worker will select a shipment (or license plate) for manual packing, create a new container id for the desired container type, and identify the items packed into the container. When completed, the worker reports the container as closed, and identifies the weight and destination location as part of the closing process. At that point, the shipping clerk can review shipments that are ready to ship.

◆ *Automated packing for sales orders.* An automated packing process – also termed a containerization process -- provides suggested packing as part of the picking work triggered by a released shipment wave. More specifically, each picking work order contains work lines identifying the suggested container as well as each item and quantity to place in the container. In this way, the warehouse worker can pick the goods directly into the containers with optimal picking routes, and place the material directly at an outbound dock. Each variation of an automated packing process is defined by a container build template with query criteria about the applicable customer, products and/or warehouse.

The use of an automated packing process assumes that the resulting suggestions are 100% correct because they cannot be overridden, and the mobile device transaction simply reports that the work was completed. Under this assumption, the automated packing process can reduce manual reporting and improve efficiency. For example, compared to manual packing, it eliminates the need for moving material to a packing station, and the need for reporting container selection, item assignment and container closing at the packing station.

The two different approaches to packing -- automated packing versus manual packing - represent mutually exclusive options. Containers created from the automated packing process cannot be used or modified in the manual packing process.

◆ *Staging/loading steps for sales orders.* Staging and loading steps often reflect staging material for delivery via truck and then loading the material on the truck prior to reporting actual shipment. In a typical scenario, mobile devices are used by the warehouse worker for reporting completion of sales order picking work to a staging location, and by the shipping clerk for reporting completion of the work order loading.   At that point, you can review shipments and loads that are ready to ship.

Transfer Order Picking/Shipping   As illustrated in Figure 16.13, the shipping clerk uses the Release To Warehouse form to review and select open transfer order lines that require picking/shipping, and then releases selected orders to the warehouse (which updates the release status for each order). With an order-based picking approach, the release-to-warehouse step can automatically create a shipment and load (with a waved status) and a shipment wave (with a released status) for each transfer order. In addition, the released shipment wave automatically creates a picking work order consisting of work lines that identify the pick and put instructions.

The warehouse worker reports actual picking by using the mobile device to report completion of picking work orders. Completion of the picking work to an outbound dock results in shipments and loads that are ready to ship. The shipping clerk reports actual shipment by confirming the outbound shipments.

In addition to the above-described order-based picking approach, the advanced approach to warehouse management supports other variations of transfer order picking/shipping. These include variations of the release to warehouse step, wave picking, load planning, and staging/loading steps. These variations were previously explained for sales order picking/shipping.

Figure 16.13 Typical Process for Transfer Order Picking/Shipping using Advanced WMS Approach

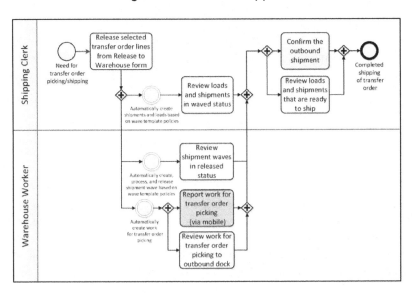

Transfer Order Receiving   The nature of transfer order receiving depends on whether the shipped material has been identified with a license plate ID.   As illustrated in Figure 16.14, the receiving clerk uses the mobile device to receive a license plate ID for a transfer order shipment, which updates inventory balances and automatically creates putaway work.   The warehouse worker uses the mobile device to report putaway from the receiving location to a stocking location.   A suggested stocking location can reflect location directives, or the warehouse worker can determine and report the stocking location.   As an alternative reporting approach, the receiving clerk can report receipt and putaway as part of a single mobile device transaction.

When the shipped material is not identified with a license plate ID, the receiving clerk uses the mobile device to receive a transfer order number, and subsequent receiving steps are the same.

Figure 16.14 Typical Process for Transfer Order Receiving using Advanced WMS Approach

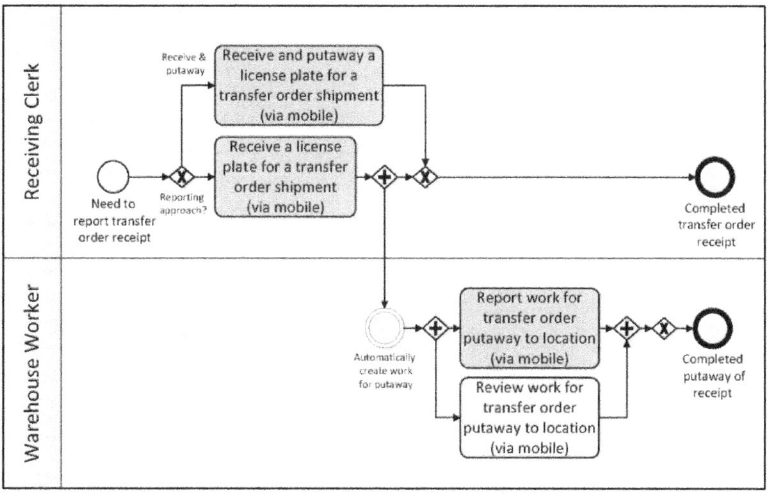

Production Order Picking   A typical process for production order picking using the Advanced WMS approach was previously described (Section 14.5), but is included here for completeness sake.   As illustrated in Figure 16.15 with an order-based picking approach, the machine operator reports a production order as Released, which acts as the trigger for several automatic actions to support actual production.   This includes creating and releasing a production wave for the order, which triggers creation of picking work for delivering components to a production input location when it has insufficient component inventory.

The warehouse worker reviews the released production waves and the associated picking work for raw material. Using the mobile device, the warehouse worker reports completion of the raw material picking work for delivering components to the designated production input location.

When ready, the machine operator reports a production order as Started, which automatically generates a picking list journal based on the Start dialogue policies. The machine operator reports actual material usage on the picking list journal and posts it. In some cases, the machine operator will manually generate a picking list as an alternative to automatic generation, or to identify unexpected component requirements. In either case, the machine operator posts the picking list journal after reporting actual material usage.

Figure 16.15 Typical Process for Production Order Picking using Advanced WMS Approach

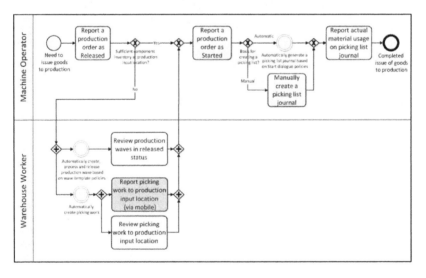

An alternative process employs wave picking, where the content of a production wave consists of raw material picking work orders that have been created for multiple released production orders. The contents of the production wave are defined by a wave planning process, where some of the steps can be performed automatically to reflect normal decision making logic, as modeled by policies within a wave template. For example, a production wave template might be defined so that the raw material picking work created by releases of different production orders at different times will be automatically added to an existing wave. If needed, the planner can manually update the wave contents (such as adding or deleting wave lines) prior to processing and releasing the production wave. At that point in time, the warehouse worker uses the mobile device to report completion of the raw material picking work for delivering components to the designated production input location.

Production Order Receiving The finished quantity of a production order can be reported using different approaches. For example, the finished quantity may be reported multiple times for a given order, or reported once when it represents the entire order quantity. As illustrated in Figure 16.16, the finished quantity can be reported using a mobile device transaction, or using client transactions such as the Report as Finished form or the Report as Finished Journal. The finished quantity can also be identified on the Route Card Journal for reporting unit completions at the last operation. The machine operator updates the order status to *reported as finished* after all production output has been reported.

The finished quantity of a production order can also be placed in different locations. For example, the finished quantity may be reported into a production output location by the machine operator, and a work order for putaway can be created automatically. A warehouse worker can then use the mobile device for reporting completion of the putaway work order. A single mobile device transaction can also be used to report both the finished quantity and its associated putaway to a location.

Figure 16.16 Typical Process for Production Order Receiving using Advanced WMS Approach

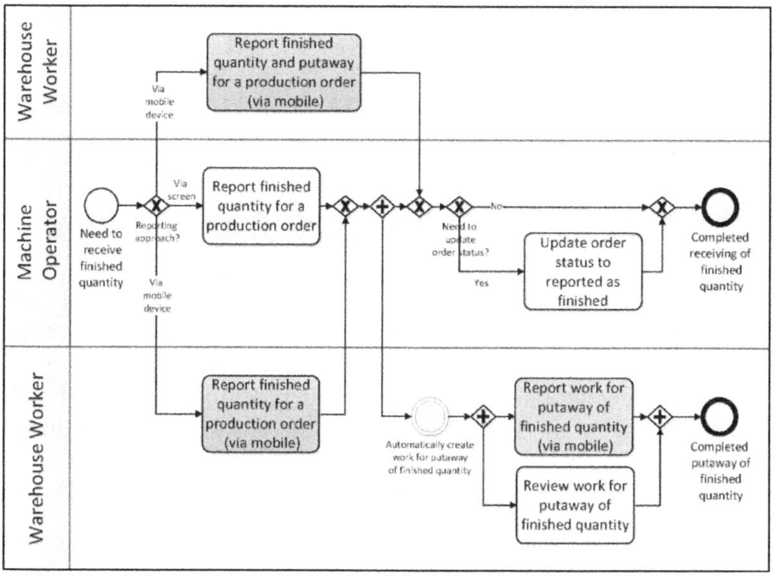

Cycle Counting The advanced approach to warehouse management supports several options for cycle counting. One option involves the use of a cycle count plan for a complete physical inventory or for cycle count purposes, as illustrated in Figure 16.17. A second option supports the ad hoc generation of a cycle count for selected items or locations. The third option involves cycle counting as part of the sales order picking process, so that cycle count work will be automatically created when picking reduces an item's inventory below a specified quantity (aka the cycle counting threshold). Each option generates work orders for counting, and the warehouse worker uses the mobile device to report completion of the picking work. A mobile device transaction also supports a spot count. Cycle counting discrepancies may occur in each variation, which requires a separate process to resolve a discrepancy.

Figure 16.17 Typical Process for Cycle Counting (based on Cycle Count Plan) using Advanced WMS Approach

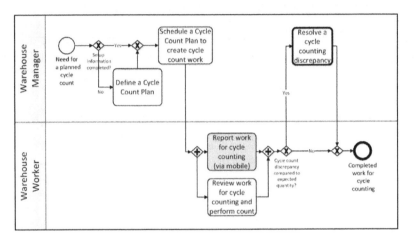

16.5 AX Viewpoint of Inventory Transactions

A key aspect of understanding AX involves the viewpoint of inventory transactions and the associated inventory status. Dynamics AX employs a broader viewpoint of the term inventory transaction since it reflects both actual and anticipated receipts and issues. Additional types of inventory transactions related to work orders are also employed by the Advanced WMS approach to warehouse management.

AX Viewpoint of Inventory Transactions The term inventory transaction normally refers to the actual physical movement of material, such as an inventory adjustment, receipt or shipment. Dynamics AX employs a broader viewpoint because it reflects both actual and anticipated receipts and issues. With orders, for example, it creates an inventory transaction with an associated inventory status that reflects various steps in order processing. Figure 16.18 illustrates this broader viewpoint for several types of inventory transactions and the associated values of inventory status. Previous figures illustrated the values of inventory status in the typical business process for sales orders (Section 11.1), purchase orders (Section 12.1), transfer orders (Section 13.1) and production orders (Section 14.1).

Figure 16.18 AX Viewpoint of Inventory Transactions

	Purchase Order	Sales Order	Inventory Journal*	
			Receipt	Issue
Status of Inventory Transaction	Ordered Create a PO line item	On Order Create a SO line item	Ordered Create a Journal Line	On Order Create a Journal Line
	Received Post the product receipt	Deducted Post the packing slip	Purchased Post the journal	Sold Post the journal
	Purchased Post the vendor's invoice	Sold Post invoice for SO		

	Production Order	
	Parent	Component
Status of Inventory Transaction	Ordered Create a Production Order	On Order
	Received Post report as finished	Sold Post picking list journal
	Purchased Change Status to Ended	N/A

★ = Inventory journals include Inventory Adjustment, Movement, Counting , Transfer and Project Items journals.

As one example within the figure, AX creates an inventory transaction with an inventory status of *Ordered* when you create a purchase order line for an item. This status changes to *Received* after posting the product receipt; it changes to *Purchased* after posting the vendor's invoice. AX also creates inventory transactions for un-posted inventory journals. With an inventory adjustment journal, for example, a journal line item for a positive quantity (a receipt) has an inventory status of *Ordered* item prior to posting, and a status of *Purchased* after posting. You can view these inventory transactions for a selected item, and from any form involving inventory transactions.

Impact of Work Orders on Inventory Transaction History The Advanced WMS approach to warehouse management employs different types of work orders. Examples include a work order for sales order picking and a work order for putaway of a purchase order arrival, as illustrated in a previous figure (Figure 16.10). The execution of a work order creates entries for inventory transaction history. When viewing transaction history, a transaction filter can limit the displayed information to just the work order transactions or just the normal inventory transactions. The "work only" transactions identify the related work order, whereas normal inventory transactions identify the related sales order, purchase order, transfer order, production order or inventory journal.

The execution of work orders has a significant impact on the volume of inventory transaction history. A simple example in a distribution scenario illustrates the increased volume, where an item is purchased and then sold resulting in two normal inventory transactions. This simple example also results in eight work order transactions, which represent a significant increase in transaction history.

This transaction history is also reflected in the Item Trace form for batch tracking of a batch-controlled item. Relative to the above-mentioned example, the work order transactions result in eight additional levels in the multi-level indented format for viewing batch tracking history. The Item Trace form currently provides an option to display only the normal inventory transactions, but they are not displayed in a multi-level indented format.

16.6 Workspaces related to Inventory and Warehouse Management

Several predefined workspaces are related to inventory and warehouse management, as described in the following summary of each workspace and its applicable functionality.

Cost Administration Workspace This workspace includes links to key reports/inquiries about inventory accounting, such as inventory value statements, inventory aging, standard cost transactions, and calculation of ABC classifications.

Cost Analysis Workspace This workspace summarizes inventory turns and inventory accuracy (with drill down to those items with low turns or accuracy) as well as inventory value (with segmentation by item group and also total inventory value over time). The links provide access to key reports/inquiries about inventory accounting, such as inventory value statements, inventory aging, and calculation of ABC classifications.

Outbound Work Planning Workspace This workspace summarizes several aspects of the Advanced WMS approach to sales order picking/shipping as well as transfer order picking/shipping. For example, you can perform the periodic task for automatic release of sales orders or transfer orders. The links provide access to related information such as shipments, waves, and work.

Much of the information applies to the use of wave picking. For a selected warehouse, the workspace identifies shipments not on a wave, and shipment waves that have not been processed or released. It also identifies the open picking work for released waves. If needed, you can manually create a new wave and then manually add selected shipments to the wave.

Some of the information applies to the use of replenishment of picking lines, and it identifies the open replenishment work for the selected warehouse. You can also perform the periodic task to create replenishment work via the replenishment calculations or the load demand replenishment calculations.

Outbound Work Monitoring Workspace   This workspace summarizes several aspects of the Advanced WMS approach to replenishment of picking lines. For a selected warehouse, it identifies the active replenishment work for shipment waves and the unreleased replenishment work.   The links provide access to other types of work orders (such as cycle count work, sales order picking work, transfer order picking work, and inventory movement work), and to information about the shipments (or loads) at a packing station.

16.7 Additional Case Studies

Case 16.13: Indicate the Need for Receiving Inspection using the Item's default value for Inventory Status The quality manager defined a value of *Needs-Inspection* for Inventory Status, and assigned it as the default value for selected items (and a supplying vendor) so that it would inherited by purchase order line items. This approach provided an alternative to using quality orders to communicate the need for inspection at the time of purchase order arrival.

Case 16.14: Identify Off-Spec or Blemished Products using Inventory Status A manufacturing/distribution company of sporting goods occasionally had off spec products that could be sold at a reduced price. They defined two values of Inventory Status to identify products as "Good" and "Off-Spec," and assigned the "Off-Spec" value to finished goods when applicable. They also defined lower sales prices in their sales price trade agreements for items with an Inventory Status of "Off-Spec."   On the occasion, off-spec products were also purchased for their distribution warehouse, and they similarly used purchase price agreements.

16.8 Executive Summary

Inventory and warehouse management involve the physical storage and movement of products within and between inventory locations, as well as handling outbound and inbound shipments with trading partners. One of the fundamentals of modeling inventory locations within AX involves the choice between the basic versus advanced approach to warehouse management, and the choice can be warehouse specific. The two options represent different conceptual models for managing inventory and related business processes, although both options share a high degree of common functionality and can support the Inventory Status capabilities.

This chapter explained the two major options in more detail, and the various strategic options for starting simple and evolving into more sophistication. In particular, it provided illustrative business processes for each option in terms of various warehouse transactions -- such as sales order picking/shipping and purchase order receiving -- and highlighted the major variations for these transactions. It also provided more detailed explanations about the significance of Inventory Status and the AX viewpoint of inventory transactions.

Chapter 17

Quality Management

The concerns of quality management typically extend across every aspect of supply chain management. This broad viewpoint ranges from the definition of item and product structure information through sourcing purchased material, actual production, sales shipments, and returns. These topics have been covered throughout the book. A narrower viewpoint focuses on several aspects of unique functionality for quality management.

The narrower viewpoint includes the definition and enforcement of materials management policies, such as inventory blocking, inspection and product testing, RMA dispositions, and various types of holds. Additional aspects include nonconformance reports, cases about quality-related problems, regulatory reporting requirements, and MSDS documents for hazardous materials. These topics are reflected in the following sections within the chapter.

1. Broad Viewpoint of Quality Management
2. Summary of Inventory Blocking Approaches
3. Variations for Reporting Inspection
4. Quality Orders and Product Testing
5. RMA Disposition Codes
6. Impact of Holds and Stop Flags
7. Nonconformance Reports
8. Using Cases for Quality Management Purposes
9. Coordination of Quality-Related Activities
10. Regulatory Reporting Requirements for Different Countries
11. Sales Order Limitations on Restricted Products
12. Hazardous Materials and MSDS Documents

17.1 Broad Viewpoint of Quality Management

A wide range of quality management considerations are addressed by out-of-the-box capabilities within Dynamics AX. These capabilities have been covered throughout the book, and illustrative examples are summarized below along with the relevant section number in parentheses.

Item and BOM Definition Item and BOM information provide a logical starting point for quality concerns. Some of the major concerns include the following.

◆ Item identification and definition (Section 4.1)
◆ Specify and enforce authorized units of measure for an item (Section 4.6)
◆ Approval of authorized BOM versions for a manufactured item, including the use of electronic signatures for approval (Section 5.1) or product change cases (Section 5.8)
◆ Approval of authorized routing versions for a manufactured item, including the use of electronic signatures for approval (Section 6.6)
◆ Identify quality factors in production, such as planned component scrap for a BOM line and operation scrap percentages in the routing (Sections 5.4 and 6.8)
◆ Identify planned changes reflecting continuous improvements in production, such as planned changes to BOM and routing information (Sections 5.7 and 6.13)
◆ Identify the needed documentation for an item, BOM, routing operation, and other key constructs
◆ Define the BOM and routing for a specific configuration of a configurable item (Section 19.5)

Serial and Batch Tracking Many manufacturing companies require serial or batch tracking for purchased and manufactured items (Sections 8.1 and 8.3). Other considerations include batch attributes and batch disposition codes (Sections 8.5 and 8.6).

Purchasing and Production Several aspects of procurement and production involve quality management concerns, as summarized below.

◆ Specify and enforce approved vendors for a purchased item or subcontracted service (Sections 12.2 and 15.3)
◆ Define and enforce work flow approvals, such as the approval for purchase orders (Section 12.10)

◆ Manage returns to vendor (Section 12.11)

◆ Identify rework for finished production quantities (Section 14.9)

◆ Perform testing and report the test results within different business processes, such as during the receipt for a purchase order or during the production process (Section 17.4)

◆ Identify and track quality problems via nonconformance reports or cases (Sections 17.7 and 17.8)

Sales   The business processes associated with sales orders, shipments and customer returns involve several quality management concerns, as described below.

◆ Employ configuration technologies during entry of a sales order or sales quote to define the valid BOM and routing for a specific configuration of a configurable item (Section 19.1)

◆ Enforce restrictions on sales order processing, such as preventing order entry for stopped items or restricted products (Sections 17.6 and 17.11)

◆ Provide regulatory reports for sales to different countries (Section 17.10)

◆ Identify hazardous materials and their MSDS documents, and ensure compliance for sending MSDS documents to customers (Section 17.12)

◆ Specify RMA disposition codes and related policies for handling customer returns (Section 11.10)

Other quality considerations might include best practices in supply chain management, such as ensuring valid delivery date promises on sales orders (Section 10.10), or the correct assignment of sales prices (Section 11.6).

17.2 Summary of Inventory Blocking Approaches

Inventory blocking represents a key tool for quality management, such as preventing usage and indicating the need for inspection. There are three basic sources or approaches for inventory blocking -- labeled Inventory Status, Quality Order and Manual. Each approach results in an entry on the Inventory Blocking form along with information about the source of blocking. This information can act as a coordination tool for quality management.

One approach employs a blocked value for Inventory Status, as described in a previous chapter (Section 16.2). The second approach employs quality orders, and often works in conjunction with the values of Inventory Status. Quality orders are further explained in a subsequent section (Section 17.4). The third approach involves manual assignment of inventory blocking, which is introduced in this section. The three approaches differ in how the inventory blocking is created and removed, their impact on master scheduling logic, and their allowable transactions. The three approaches are summarized in Figure 17.1 and described below.

Figure 17.1 Summary of Inventory Blocking Approaches

Considerations about Blocking	Type of Inventory Blocking		
	Inventory Status	Quality Order	Manual
Create blocking for the specified inventory of item	Assign a blocked value for Inventory Status	Create a quality order with full blocking	Manually assign inventory blocking
Ability to assign blocking at time of order receipt	Yes	Yes	No
Remove blocking	Change a blocked value for Inventory Status	Delete or complete the quality order	Delete manual assignment of inventory blocking
Impact of blocked inventory on master scheduling logic	Non-nettable	Nettable on expected date	Non-nettable or Nettable on expected date
Allowable transactions for the blocked inventory	Move, adjustment out Cycle count Return to vendor Create quality order	None	None
Description for blocking	None	Yes	Yes
Note/document for blocking	None	Yes	Yes
Additional considerations	Assign to subset of a batch number Different ways to change value of Inventory Status	Block just sample quantity Impact next steps for order Destructive testing Update Inventory Status or Batch Disposition Code	Assign to subset of a batch number

Inventory Blocking based on a blocked value of Inventory Status

This approach reflects a blocked value for Inventory Status which can be assigned at the time of order receipt. The blocking can be viewed on the Inventory Blocking form, and it can only be removed by changing it to a non-blocked value. The inventory is treated as unusable and non-nettable by master scheduling logic. The blocking prevents most inventory transactions with the exception of moves, adjustments, cycle counts, returns to vendor and creation of a quality order. A blocked value can be changed by a quality order or changed directly (via a client or mobile device transaction). A blocked value can also be assigned to a subset of a batch number or to a specific serial number.

Inventory Blocking based on a Quality Order

This approach reflects a quality order with "full blocking" as part of the policies for item sampling. A quality order can be manually created for the specified inventory of an item, including inventory that has already been assigned a blocked value for Inventory Status. Alternatively, an item's quality order can be automatically created based on policies defined on the Quality Association form, such as automatic creation as a result of reporting purchase order arrival or the finished quantity for a production order. Using the Inventory Blocking form, you can optionally define a description and/or notes about blocking related to a quality order.

With full blocking, the inventory associated with a quality order is treated by master scheduling logic as nettable with an expected availability date. This expected outcome is indicated by the automatically-assigned Expected Receipts checkbox. The expected date inherits the creation date and can be manually changed. However, the blocking prevents all inventory transactions.

Blocking based on a quality order has several additional considerations. For example, blocking can just apply to a small sample quantity; so that blocking does not apply to the rest of the inventory associated with the quality order. A quality order may involve destructive testing of the sample. With an automatically generated quality order, the next step(s) for the related order can be prevented until the quality order has been completed, and a validation failure will be identified (via a message) when performing the next step. For example, a quality order stemming from a purchase order arrival can prevent posting of the product receipt until the quality order has been completed. Finally, a quality order can be used to update the value of Inventory Status or the Batch Disposition Code. Batch disposition codes can identify restricted usage policies, and were described in a previous chapter (Section 8.6).

Inventory Blocking based on Manual Assignment This approach reflects a manual assignment of inventory blocking to existing inventory. It can only be created and deleted on the Inventory Blocking form, and you can optionally define a description and/or notes about the manual blocking. When you create manual blocking, you can indicate the expected outcome as non-nettable or as nettable with an expected availability date. You indicate the expected outcome via an Expected Receipts checkbox. The expected date inherits the creation date and can be manually changed. Manual blocking prevents all inventory transactions. For example, the manual blocking must be removed in order to report the inventory as scrapped. Manual blocking can also be assigned to a subset of a batch number or to a specific serial number.

17.3 Variations for Reporting Inspection

Several variations can be employed for reporting inspection, and the variations reflect several factors. One factor includes the different values for Inventory Status and/or the Batch Disposition Code, and a related factor involves the approach and role for reporting a change in value. Other factors include the use of a separate QC location, use of the basic versus advanced approach to warehouse management, and the differences between purchased and manufactured items. This section reviews several variations for reporting inspection and the related factors.

Variations of Inspection using Inventory Status The value for Inventory Status provides one basis for identifying the results of inspection, as well as the need for inspection. The value can be assigned directly by a quality control clerk, or by a non-QC person such as a receiving clerk (for purchase order arrivals) or a machine operator (for production order receipts). A value can also be assigned based on the test results and the pass/fail outcome of a quality order.

Variations of Inspection using Batch Disposition Codes The batch disposition code provides one basis for identifying the results of inspection for a batch-controlled item. The code can be assigned directly to a batch number, or assigned based on the test results and the pass/fail outcome of a quality order.

Separate QC Area for Material requiring Inspection Some scenarios employ a separate QC area for material requiring inspection. For example, a purchase order arrival or the finished quantity for a production order may be placed in the QC area until inspection results have been reported, and then the material is moved to its destination location.

Variations of Inspection using Quarantine Orders A quarantine order provides one basis for identifying the results of inspection when using the Basic Inventory approach.

Capturing Quality-Related Data via Mobile Devices The ability to capture quality-related data via mobile devices involves the assignment of an Audit Template ID when defining the mobile device menu item. Each user-defined ID must be defined beforehand, and there are several capabilities associated with the definition of an Audit Template ID. At its simplest, you define one or more data capture questions (and the trigger for asking the questions) as part of an Audit Template ID. In this way, the worker that reports the mobile device transaction will be automatically prompted to answer the questions. Case 17.1 provides an Illustrative example.

The quality management team at a manufacturing company wanted to capture several aspects of quality-related data at the time of recording finished quantities for production orders. Examples include many of the data elements currently required for their Laboratory Information Management System (LIMS). They were considering the "Audit Template ID" capabilities for the mobile device transaction to receive and putaway finished quantities. They could define the data capture questions (with a trigger based on a different order number) as part of an Audit Template ID, and then assign the Audit Template ID to the mobile device menu item. In this way, the worker will be automatically prompted to answer the questions when reporting the mobile device transaction. The team was also considered a similar application for capturing quality-related data about raw material receipts, so that the receiving clerk will be automatically prompted to answer the questions when reporting the mobile device transaction for purchase order arrivals.

17.4 Quality Orders and Product Testing

Product testing entails the use of quality orders to report test results against a group of predefined tests. The explanation of quality orders can be segmented into three areas: the definition of tests and test groups, the use of quality orders for reporting test results, and the rules for automatic generation of quality orders. Quality orders have been previously discussed as one of the inventory blocking approaches, and as part of the variations for reporting inspection.

Tests and Test Groups   There are two types of predefined tests -- quantitative and qualitative -- and one or more tests can be assigned to a group of tests.

♦ *Quantitative Tests*. Each quantitative test must be assigned a testing unit of measure, so that acceptable values can be assigned when it is included in a test group. A pressure test, for example, might use pounds per square (PSI) as the unit of measure. The units of measure must be predefined along with the desired decimal precision.

♦ *Qualitative Tests*. A qualitative test will have an associated test variable (and its enumerated outcomes) when you assign it to a test group. A taste test, for example, may have one test variable for sweetness (with possible outcomes of sweet, sour and okay) and another test variable for color (with possible outcomes of dark, light and okay). You designate whether an outcome represents a pass or failure of the test.

For both types of tests, you can optionally assign a test instrument and applicable documents that describe the test.

Tests are assigned to a group of tests (termed a *test group*), where the test group has a unique identifier.

◆ *Test Groups.* For each test group, you assign a sampling plan, an acceptable quality level (AQL), and an indication of whether the tests will require destructive testing of the sample. Destructive testing will result in an inventory reduction of the sample quantity.

◆ *Sampling Plan* A sampling plan is used to calculate the sample quantity for a quality order, and it can be expressed as an absolute quantity or as a percentage. For example, a sampling plan of 10% for a purchase order receipt quantity of 500 would result in a sample quantity of 50. The sampling plan can optionally require a different sample for each received batch when receiving multiple batches.

When a quality order has been generated, it also results in inventory blocking -- either for the sample quantity or the entire quantity of related inventory -- until the testing results have been validated. The "full blocking" policy within an Item Sampling plan indicates that the entire quantity should be blocked. As described in a previous section, the Inventory Blocking form displays the blocking with a source of quality order,

◆ *Acceptable Quality Level (AQL)* An acceptable quality level refers to the percentage of tests which must be passed. An AQL of 90%, for example, means that 9 out of 10 tests must be passed, or that 9 out of 10 samples must pass.

◆ *Tests within a Test Group.* When assigning a test to a test group, you define the acceptable measurement values for a quantitative test, or the test variable for a qualitative test. Each test can be assigned a sequence number, validity dates, and documents. You can designate which test results should be included in a certificate of analysis report associated with a quality order. An individual test can have its own AQL, referring to the percentage of passing test results when reported for different samples of the total sample quantity.

The test group assigned to a quality order provides the initial basis for which tests need to be performed. Tests can be added, deleted, or changed on the quality order.

Use of a Quality Order   A quality order defines the tests that need to be performed for an item and a sample quantity of its inventory. It is typically related to a specific order, such as a purchase order, production order or sales order. In addition to communicating the need to perform tests, it provides a mechanism for reporting results against the tests. You can manually create a quality order, or establish quality guidelines within each business process (such as a purchase order receiving process) for automatically creating a quality order. The next subsection explains automatic generation of quality orders.

After reporting the test results for every test within a quality order, you initiate a validation process that assigns a pass or fail status (based on meeting the overall AQL) and closes the quality order. When you try performing the next step in the business process, a message warns you when the quality order has failed or has not yet been closed. In addition, you can optionally reopen the quality order and force the validation process to assign a pass status by accepting any error conditions.

You can view information about a quality order (and its test results) from multiple viewpoints. For example, the quality order can be viewed for the related batch number or from the related sales order, purchase order, production order or quarantine order.

You can optionally generate a certificate of analysis that displays the test results for a quality order. A certificate of analysis, for example, could be printed for a batch of material being shipped to a customer. The printed test results will only be displayed for designated tests within the quality order.

You can optionally create a nonconformance report when a quality order identifies defective material. The nonconformance report provides the basis for further investigation, as described in a subsequent section about nonconformance reports (Section 17.7).

Rules for Automatic Generation of a Quality Order   You can define rules (termed *quality association records*) for automatic generation of a quality order in different business processes. Each rule defines the set of tests, the acceptable quality level (AQL), and the sampling plan that apply to the automatically generated quality orders. Each rule also defines the event and conditions for automatically generating a quality order within a business process for the item. The business process can be related to purchase orders, sales orders or production orders, but not transfer orders. It can also apply to quarantine orders. The rules for automatic generation of a quality order are summarized in Figure 17.2 and described below.

The figure summarizes the events and conditions for generating a quality order for various business processes (termed the *reference type*). An event is expressed in terms of the relevant document and execution timing, such as posting the product receipt for a purchase order. These events reflect variations in AX functionality for modeling different business processes. The figure also identifies the actual event that triggers automatic generation of a quality order.

Figure 17.2 Rules for Automatic Generation of a Quality Order

Business Process (Reference Type)	Label of the event that triggers a quality order — Execution	Label of the event that triggers a quality order — Document	The actual event that triggers a quality order	Conditions — Site	Conditions — Item	Conditions — Other	Destructive Test Allowed
Purchase order	After registration		Register purchase order arrival	Site-specific or companywide	Item-specific, quality group-specific, or all items	Vendor or vendor group	Yes
	Before receipts list		Initial attempt to post receipts list				No
	After receipts list		Post the receipts list				No*
	Before product receipt		Initial attempt to post product receipt				No
	After product receipt		Post the product receipt				Yes
Sales order	Before picking process is scheduled		Create picking list or picking work			Customer or Group	Yes
	Before packing slip		Post packing slip for sales order				Yes
Production or Batch order, or Co-product	After registration		Register production order arrival			N/A	No
	Before report as finished		Initial attempt to report as finished				No
	After report as finished		Update the report as finished				Yes
Route operation	Before report as finished		Create batch/production order	Item-specific, quality group-specific, or all items		Resource or Group Master Operation or Route Group	No
	After report as finished		Report the operation as finished				No
Inventory	None		None				Yes
Quarantine order	Before report as finished		Initial attempt to report as finished			N/A	No
	After report as finished		Report the order as finished				No
	Before end		Initial attempt to report as ended				No
	After end		Report the order as ended				No

The conditions for generating a quality order can be site-specific or companywide, and they can apply to a single item, a group of items (based on the quality group assigned to items) or all items. Other conditions depend on the business process, such as vendor-specific conditions for a purchase order or customer-specific conditions for a sales order. A quality order involving destructive tests can only be generated when inventory exists for the event, as shown in the right-hand column of Figure 17.2. The automatic generation of a quality order can be further described for each business process.

◆ *Purchase Order Process.* The generation of a quality order can occur after registering a purchase order arrival. It can also occur before or after the posting the product receipt for a purchase order. A quality order that requires destructive testing can only be generated after material is on-hand, thereby allowing it to be automatically deducted. The need for a quality order can reflect a particular site, item or vendor, or a combination of these conditions.

◆ *Sales Order Process.* The generation of a quality order can occur before or after the posting of a picking list or packing slip for the material being shipped. A quality order that requires destructive testing can be generated at any step. The need for a quality order can reflect a particular site, item, or customer, or a combination of these conditions.

◆ *Production Order Process.* The generation of a quality order can occur before or after reporting a finished quantity. A quality order that requires destructive testing can only be generated after reporting a finished quantity. The need for a quality order can reflect a particular site or item, or a combination of these conditions.

◆ *Route Operation for a Production Order* When a production order contains a routing operation, the quality order can be generated before or after reporting the operation as finished. The need for a quality order can reflect a particular site, item or quality group, or a combination of these conditions. The need for a quality order can also reflect a specific master operation or the route group assigned to operations.

◆ *Inventory.* A quality order must be manually generated for an item's inventory quantity, and the selected test group determines what tests will be performed. It cannot be generated automatically for an item's existing inventory.

◆ *Quarantine Order Process.* Quarantine orders only apply to the basic approach to warehouse management. The generation of a quality order can occur before or after reporting the quarantine order as finished or ended. A quality order that requires destructive tests cannot be generated for a quarantine order, because it is assumed that the quarantine order functionality will handle scrapping of the destroyed material. The need for a quality order can reflect a particular site, item or vendor, or a combination of these conditions.

A rule must be defined for each variation in a business process requiring automatic creation of a quality order. The validity dates for a quality association record enable you to model planned changes in the business process.

17.5 RMA Disposition Codes

RMA processing builds on sales order functionality, as described in the previous chapter about sales order processing (Section 11.10). In summary, each RMA has an associated sales order (termed the *returned order*) for handling returns, and an optional second sales order (termed the *replacement order*) for handling replacements. Both sales orders have the same order number (but a different order type) with linkage to the originating RMA number. A key aspect of handling an actual return involves the assignment of an RMA disposition code.[1]

This section summarizes the use of various RMA disposition codes, which differs slightly for the two approaches to warehouse management. You can directly assign the RMA disposition code when using the Basic Inventory approach to warehouse management. However, the Advanced WMS approach involves assignment of a "combined disposition code" which reflects the combination of an RMA disposition code and a value for Inventory Status.

RMA Disposition Codes A user-definable RMA disposition code has an assigned action that indicates how to handle a returned item and possible replacement. You can assign an RMA disposition code when registering RMA arrival of the returned items; it can be reassigned as part of the inspection approach. The key point of a RMA disposition code is the assigned action. There are three types of actions that apply to RMA processing (with or without a replacement order):

♦ *Credit [and put in inventory].* This action indicates that inventory balances should be updated by the returned item. For example, you may be able to reuse the item "as is" or refurbish/repair the item to make it usable.

♦ *Scrap.* This action indicates that inventory balances should not be updated by the returned item.

♦ *Return.* This action indicates that the inventory balances should be updated so that the returned item can be sent back to the customer regardless of its condition.

There are two additional types of actions that only apply to RMA processing when use of a replacement order depends on the disposition of returned items.

---

[1] An RMA disposition code represents a different construct than a batch disposition code, which was described in a previous chapter about batch number tracking (Section 8.6).

◆ *Replace and Scrap.* This action indicates that the inventory balances should not be updated by the returned item, and that a replacement order should be automatically created after the returned item has gone through the arrival/inspection process. You must specify the replacement item after recording arrival/inspection of the returned item. This action is not allowed when a replacement order was created for immediate shipment, since it would result in duplicate replacement efforts.

◆ *Replace and Credit.* This action indicates that the inventory balances should be updated by the returned item, otherwise it is exactly the same as the return and scrap action.

The limited number of action types (five) means that you may need a minimum of five RMA disposition codes. Symmetry in naming these RMA disposition codes can simplify explanations, so you can avoid saying things like "the disposition code of Scrap and its related action type of Scrap."

Combined Disposition Code for the Advanced WMS approach. The advanced approach involves selection of a "combined disposition code" when reporting purchase order arrival or RMA arrival via mobile device transactions. A "combined disposition code" reflects the combination of one RMA disposition code and one value for Inventory Status.[2] For example, a combined code of *Needs-Rework* could reflect the combination of the RMA disposition code for *Credit [and put in inventory]* and the Inventory Status value for *Needs-Rework*. An additional combined code would be needed for an Inventory Status of *Return-To-Vendor*.

17.6 Impact of Holds and Stop Flags

The processing of sales orders, supply orders and many warehouse activities can be affected by several types of holds and stop flags. These represent additional restrictions beyond the use of inventory blocking, or the use of batch disposition codes with restricted usage.

---

[2] As a confusing issue, the same form name of "Disposition Codes" is used for two different forms. You define the RMA disposition codes on the Disposition Codes form (as part of the sales and marketing setup information for sales order returns), and you define the "combined disposition code" on the Disposition Codes form (as part of warehouse management setup information for mobile devices). This "combined disposition code" can also be displayed on the mobile device transactions for purchase order arrivals and RMA arrivals, and it is labeled just "disposition code".

Impact of a Customer Hold on Sales Orders   A customer hold status (termed the *Invoicing and Delivery On Hold* policy) can prevent all sales order transactions from being recorded for the customer, or just prevent shipments and invoicing, until it has been removed or changed. It results in a corresponding message when attempting to enter transactions.

Impact of an Order Hold for a Sales Order   Assigning a "hold code" to a sales order will prevent any further processing (such as a confirmation, picking/shipping or invoicing) while still allowing order changes until the hold has been cleared. It results in a corresponding message when attempting to enter transactions.   An additional policy for a hold code determines whether the reservations for a sales order (if any) should be removed after placing it on hold. In either case, the sales order demand will still be recognized by master scheduling logic. One or more hold codes can be assigned to a sales order, and you can then clear a hold code after it has been resolved. A previous chapter about sales order processing provides further explanation about the special considerations related to an order hold (Section 11.3)

A hold code can also be assigned to an RMA to prevent further processing, such as receipts or creation of a replacement order.

Impact of Stopped Sales Activities for an Item   The sales order transactions for an item can be stopped, either as a companywide or site-specific policy within the item's default order policies. The stopped flag prevents further transactions for an item's existing sales orders (including picking/shipping transactions) until it has been removed. It results in a corresponding message when attempting to enter a transaction. A similar stopped flag can be specified for an item's inventory transactions, which also prevents further transactions.

Impact of a Vendor Hold on Purchase Orders   The assignment of a vendor hold for "all" transactions will prevent all purchase order transactions from being recorded for the vendor until it has been removed. It results in a corresponding message when attempting to enter transactions. .

Impact of a Stopped Flag for a Purchase Order Line   A line item on a purchase order can be flagged as stopped. The stopped flag prevents further transactions for the line item (including registration of arrivals and posting of product receipts) until it has been removed. It results in a corresponding message when attempting to enter transactions.

Impact of Stopped Purchasing Activities for an Item   The purchase order transactions for an item can be flagged as stopped, either as a companywide or site-specific policy. The stopped flag prevents further transactions for an item's existing purchase orders (including registration of arrivals and posting of product receipts) until it has been removed. It results in a corresponding message when attempting to enter transactions. A similar stopped flag can be specified for an item's inventory transactions, which also prevents further transactions.

Impact of a Stop Flag for a Production Order The Stop flag primarily serves warehouse management purposes and prevents changes in order status until it has been removed. For example, assigning the Stop flag to a scheduled order prevents a change in order status to Released or Started. By preventing a change to a Started status, it indirectly prevents creation of a picking list journal and reporting of actual picked material. Preventing a change to a Released status impacts the Advanced WMS approach, since it indirectly prevents creation and reporting of raw material picking work. The Stop flag has no impact when assigned after a production order has been started.

No Impact of a Nonconformance Report A quality control clerk can create a nonconformance report in order to identify a problem. The nonconformance report can identify the related inventory, purchase order, sales order, or the related vendor or customer. However, a nonconformance report does not prevent any transactions.

17.7 Nonconformance Reports

A nonconformance report (termed a *nonconformance* within AX) describes an item that has a quality problem, where the descriptive information includes the source and type of problem. The problem source is termed a *nonconformance type*. You assign a problem source and an associated problem type when you create a nonconformance.

Problem Source for a Nonconformance Report There are five types of problem sources (aka nonconformance types) that can be assigned to a nonconformance report, and each type can have optional source information.

◆ *Customer problem.* The source information about a customer problem can include the customer number, sales order number, or a lot number of a sales order transaction. For example, the nonconformance could relate to a specific sales order shipment or to customer feedback about product quality.

◆ *Service Request Problem.* The source information about a service request can include the customer number, sales order number, or lot number of a sales order transaction. For example, the nonconformance could relate to a specific sales order shipment or to a customer's complaint about item quality.

◆ *Vendor Problem.* The source information about a vendor problem can include the vendor number, purchase order number, or a lot number of a purchase order transaction. For example, the nonconformance could relate to a purchase order receipt or to a vendor's concern about a part that it supplies.

◆ *Production Problem.* The source information about a production problem can include the production order number or a lot number of a specific transaction. For example, the nonconformance could relate to a specific batch order.

◆ *Internal Problem.* The source information about an internal problem can include the quality order number or a lot number of a quality order transaction. For example, the nonconformance could relate to the tests that are performed as part of a quality order or to an employee's concern about product quality.

Problem Types for each Problem Source The user-definable problem types provide a classification of quality problems for each nonconformance type. For example, the problem types for service requests could reflect a classification of customer complaints, whereas the problem types for an internal nonconformance could represent a classification of defect codes. A problem type can be authorized for one or more nonconformance types (aka problem sources), as defined in the Nonconformance types form. For example, the problem type concerning a defect code could apply to all nonconformance types. You can change the nonconformance type assigned to a nonconformance, and this may require changing the problem type to a valid value for the new nonconformance type.

Use of a Nonconformance Report A nonconformance is initially created with an approval status of *new*, indicating that it represents a request for action. You can approve or refuse a nonconformance (which changes the approval status to *approved* or *refused*) to indicate that you will or will not take action on the nonconformance.[3] You can also close a nonconformance (as indicated by a separate check box) to indicate that you are finished with it, or reopen a nonconformance to indicate that further consideration is required.

---

[3] A user cannot approve a nonconformance unless the user has been assigned an employee identifier (via the User relations form). The system tracks the nonconformance history in terms of the employees who changed the status.

Comments can be entered for a nonconformance by using the document handling capabilities. It is generally helpful to define a unique document type about nonconformances (by using the Document Type form) so that you can enter notes for the unique document type. You can then use the Report Setup form to define your policy about printing notes for the unique document type on the nonconformance report and tag.

A printed conformance report and nonconformance tag can be used to assist material disposition. You can selectively generate reports and tags based on selection criteria, such as the nonconformance number, item, customer, vendor, or status that are associated with a nonconformance.

◆ *Nonconformance report.* The nonconformance report displays identification information, such as the nonconformance number, item, and problem type. The report displays the related notes based on your report setup policies.

◆ *Nonconformance tag.* The nonconformance tag displays identification information, such as the nonconformance number and item. The tag displays the related notes based on your report setup policies. The tag also displays the quarantine zone and type (such as restricted usage versus unusable) that you assigned to the nonconformance in order to guide disposition of the defective material.

Options for Nonconformance Reports There are several options for handling the business processes pertaining to a nonconformance report, such as corrective actions, the description of work, additional testing, and related nonconformance reports.

◆ *Corrective action for a nonconformance report.* You can optionally define one or more corrections for an approved nonconformance. A correction identifies what type of diagnostic should be performed, who should perform it, and a requested date and a planned date for completing the diagnostic. You predefine the user-defined diagnostic types, and assign one to a corrective action. Indicate that you have finished the diagnostic step by changing the status of a correction to end. The status can be reopened. Comments can be entered for a correction by using the document handling capabilities. It is generally helpful to define a unique document type about corrections (by using the Document type form) so that you can enter notes for the unique document type. Use the Report setup form to define your policy about printing notes for the unique document type on the correction report. A printed correction report displays identification information about the nonconformance and the related nonconformance notes, as well as the correction information (such as the diagnostic) and related correction notes. The report displays the related correction notes based on your report setup policies.

◆ *Description of work for a nonconformance report.* You can optionally define one or more related operations for an approved nonconformance. A related operation describes the work that should be performed, expressed as a selected operation (from a predefined list of user-defined quality operations) and descriptive text about the reason for the work. After defining an operation, you can optionally define the miscellaneous charges, items, and time sheet labor hours that are required to perform the work. The calculated costs are shown for the related operation, and the total calculated costs are shown for the nonconformance. The calculated costs and the underlying detail (about items, labor hours, and miscellaneous charges) represent reference information, and they are only used within the quality management function.

◆ *Defining further tests about a nonconformance report.* You can optionally create a quality order from a nonconformance in order to identify the need for further tests. For example, a quality order may identify the need to test (or retest) the defective material. The newly created quality order displays the linkage to the originating nonconformance.

◆ *Defining related nonconformance reports.* You can optionally link one nonconformance to another, or create a new nonconformance from an existing one. For example, the linkage can reflect the interconnection between quality problems.

17.8 Using Cases for Quality Management Purposes

A quality issue can be identified by a case, and case management provides a multi-faceted approach to manage issues raised by customers, vendors or employees. Each case is uniquely identified by a Case ID. At its simplest, you manually create a case and a description, and then indicate progress (via the case status of opened, in-process, and closed or cancelled) and case resolution (of accept, reject or none). The optional facets of case management serve several different purposes and involve different types of setup information, as illustrated by the following.

◆ *Case Category.* A user-defined hierarchy of case categories will reflect the types of issues in a given business situation, and you must assign a case category to each case. As a simple example, the top of one hierarchy may be labeled sales, and consist of several case categories related to sales issues and customer service issues. For each case category, you can optionally define additional information about the need for creating an activity (for a case that is assigned the case category), and the need for a follow-up activity after changing the case status to closed. An activity can be a task, action, event or appointment. You can also identify an associated case process or knowledge article, as described in the next points.

◆ *Case Process.* A user-defined case process identifies the steps to follow when working on a case. A step can be required or optional. Each step can optionally have a specified activity, priority and responsibility. Linking a case process to a case category enables you to standardize your business processes for different types of issues.

◆ *Case Details about the Associated Customer, Item or Sales Order.* One or more associations can be defined for a case. In the context of sales, for example, the association may reflect a customer, item or sales order, or even a lead, opportunity, prospect or project. The association may reflect a vendor, item, purchase order or invoice in the context of purchasing. An additional case detail involves the source of information, such as a specified customer, vendor or employee.

◆ *Knowledge Article.* A knowledge article represents a file or document, or a link to additional information. It provides information for diagnosing or resolving an issue.

◆ *Service Level Agreement.* A service level agreement can be assigned to a case. It indicates the guaranteed response time to an issue, and may also involve reporting time against a case.

Additional facets of case management have broader applications than just the identification of quality issues. For example, cases can be automatically created to identify audit violations based on audit policies. Audit policies consist of rules about purchase orders and vendor invoices (and expense reports), such as invoices to a certain vendor or exceeding a certain amount. Another example involves a product change case in order to support approval and activation of an item's BOM version or route version. The use of a product change case for maintaining BOM information was described in a previous chapter (Section 5.8).

17.9 Coordination of Quality-Related Activities

Several coordination tools apply to quality management personnel, such as the need to follow-up on quality orders, inventory blocking and cases.

◆ *List of Quality Orders.* Each quality order identifies material that requires inspection, and the (remaining) tests that must be performed. It may also identify a batch number and the related order (such as a purchase or production order).

◆ *List of Inventory Blocking.* The inventory blocking may reflect a quality order, manual assignment, or a blocked value for Inventory Status. Each entry on the Inventory Blocking form identifies the associated source and inventory.

◆ *List of Inventory with an Inventory Status of Needs-Inspection* A value of *Needs-Inspection* or its equivalent indicates the inventory requiring follow-up by a quality control clerk.

◆ *List of Assigned Cases.* The cases assigned to an employee identify the issues raised by customers, vendors and others. The employee can review and take action for each assigned case.

◆ *List of Nonconformances.* Each nonconformance report (termed a nonconformance) describes an item that has a quality problem, where the descriptive information includes the source and type of problem.

◆ *List of Corrective Actions (for a Nonconformance).* Each correction identifies what type of diagnostic should be performed, who should perform it, and a requested date and a planned date for completing the diagnostic.

◆ *Production Schedule for Quality-Related Operations.* The production schedule and job list identify routing operations to be performed by a quality resource. The resource may represent a labor pool of quality control clerks or inspectors, a burn-in area, or other resource under quality management control. This may require time reporting (or unit completions by operation) to correctly reflect progress against the routing, availability for the next operation, and actual costs.

17.10 Regulatory Reporting Requirements for Different Countries

Some countries require reports about regulated products delivered to the country. In order to support these reporting requirements, you must create one or more material reporting lists about the relevant countries and products. More specifically, you use the Material Reporting Lists form to create a user-defined identifier (and name) for a list, and assign one or more countries to the list. You can optionally identify the relevant state/province within a country. Each entry in the list must be flagged for reporting in order for the system to track deliveries. You also identify the item numbers that represent the regulated products for a selected entry within the list, or you can start from a selected item to add it to an existing list.

17.11 Sales Order Limitations on Restricted Products

Restricted products cannot be entered on a sales order line when the customer's delivery address reflects a non-allowed area, and a message warning will be displayed to delete or change the item number on the sales line. In order to support these restrictions, you must create one or more restricted product lists about the relevant countries and products. More specifically, you use the Restricted Products Regional Lists form to create a user-defined identifier (and name) for a list, and assign one or more countries to the list. The list is typically flagged as "exclusive." You also identify the item numbers that represent the restricted products for a selected entry within the list, or you can start from a selected item to add it to an existing list.

When a restricted product applies to a specific state/province within a country, you first define an "inclusive" list for the country and then define a second entry for the state/province as an "exclusive" list. You can then assign the relevant products to this exclusive list.

17.12 Hazardous Materials and MSDS Documents

A regulated item requires a Material Data Safety Sheet (MSDS) that can be sent to the customer. The MSDS document for a purchased item may also be received from a vendor. For a selected item, you can define the associated document by accessing the Product Data Safety Sheet form. This form consists of one or more line items uniquely identified by a system-assigned document number. When you add a line item, you define the related information for the item's MSDS document (such as the effective date, expiry date, version number, and an active flag), and use the document handling capabilities to identify the associated file containing the actual descriptive text. The descriptive text for MSDS documents can also be obtained from a subscription service such as Atrion International.[4]

The requirements for sending an item's MSDS document may apply to all countries or to selected countries. This item-specific information must be defined on the Material Regulated Countries form.

When entering a sales order line for the item, a message warning can be displayed about sending the latest active MSDS document to the customer. This warning warning occurs when the customer has not yet received the item's MSDS document, or when a newer version (defined by the document's effective date) needs to be sent.[5] A message warning can also be generated when an existing MSDS document is about to expire. You can optionally print the relevant MSDS documents when posting the packing list or invoice for the sales order, and even prevent posting when a document's expiry date has been exceeded.[6] The system automatically tracks when an item's MSDS document has been printed for a customer, along with the *last sent date*. The *last sent date* can also be manually entered. The tracking information (about the actual document number, the related sales order number, and the last sent date) can be viewed on the Product Safety Data Sheet Log, accessed from a sales line for the regulated item. The tracking information provides the basis for displaying the message warnings described above.

When entering a purchase order for a hazardous material item, you can view the tracking information about the item's MSDS document. The tracking information (about the actual document number, the related purchase order number, and the last received date) can be viewed on the Product Safety Data Sheet Log, accessed from a purchase order line for the regulated item. A message warning can also be generated when an existing MSDS document is about to expire.

---

[4] See www.atrionintl.com/ for additional information about their subscription service.
[5] In the context of sales order entry, the effective date of an MSDS document can be viewed in terms of the sales order delivery date or the current date, as defined by a companywide policy on the Inventory and Warehouse Management Parameters form.
[6] These two options are displayed on the Posting Packing Slip and Posting Invoice forms, and the values initial default from the companywide policies defined on the Inventory and Warehouse Management Parameters form.

7.13 Additional Case Studies

Several case studies related to quality management were covered in previous chapters. Examples include the identification of inspection requirements using Inventory Status (Case 12.1), vendor invoice matching using quality results (Case 12.6), production inspection by machine operators (Case 14.1), production inspection using quality orders and Inventory Status (Case 14.2), quality orders during the production process (Case 14.3), and production inspection at a separate QC area. Additional examples are provided below.

Case 17.2: Integration with a Laboratory Information Management System   A manufacturer employed a laboratory information management system (LIMS) to track characteristics of their production processes and product quality. The system was uniquely tailored to their environment, and the batch number within AX provided the primary integration point between AX and the LIMS information.

Case 17.3: Certificates of Analysis for Sales Order Shipments   A manufacturer enclosed a certificate of analysis with sales order shipments of selected items. The certificate reflected the test results reported for the item, where test results were captured as part of a quality order. The contents of a certificate of analysis reflected each customer's requirements for selected test results.

Case 17.4: Nonconformance Reports for Purchased Material   The quality manager wanted to track problems related to several purchased items. When a problem was identified, a quality specialist created a nonconformance report that identified the problem source by vendor. The specialist also described the problem (via textual comments), assigned a user-definable problem type that provided a classification of the quality problems, and printed a tag that was attached to the material. When the nonconformance report was approved for further action, it was assigned one or more corrective actions that identified what type of diagnostic should be performed, who should perform it, and the requested date for completion. In some cases, a quality order was also created to capture test results about the material. The status of the nonconformance report was changed to closed after work was completed.

17.14 Executive Summary

This chapter started with a summary of quality management concerns addressed by standard AX capabilities. These concerns range from the definition of item and product structure information through sourcing purchased material, actual production, sales shipments, and returns. In particular, AX supports the definition and enforcement of materials management policies, such as inventory blocking, inspection and product testing, RMA dispositions, and various types of holds. Additional aspects include nonconformance reports, cases about quality-related problems, regulatory reporting requirements, and MSDS documents for hazardous materials. Several types of dispatch lists can help coordinate quality resources to perform inspection and testing. The case studies included certificates of analysis, capturing test results during production and instrument calibration.

Chapter 18

Multicompany Supply Chain

Some manufacturing and distribution businesses have inventory at different physical sites that reflect different companies, and transfers between these sites. The physical sites within a given company can be modeled using AX sites and AX warehouses. The transfers between these sites involve intercompany orders and master scheduling across the multicompany supply chain. These considerations are reflected in the following sections with the chapter.

1. Intercompany orders
2. Variations of creating intercompany orders
3. Master scheduling across a multicompany supply chain

18.1 Intercompany Orders

Trading between two companies involves a customer-to-vendor relationship. Intercompany orders can be used when both companies exist within the same AX instance. Placing a purchase order with an intercompany vendor will automatically create a corresponding sales order in the sister company, and vice versa. The origin of an intercompany order identifies whether it was manually or automatically created, as indicated by the origin field in the order header. The origin field can have a value of *source* or *derived* respectively. The origin field is blank for all other sales orders and purchase orders.

Intercompany orders require setup information about items and also about the vendors and customers representing the sister companies. The setup information will be briefly summarized, and then we'll review several variations of intercompany orders.

Setup Information for Items A product must be released to both companies in order to support intercompany trading, and the item's company-level information must be defined in both companies. In order to support automatic creation of a corresponding order for intercompany orders, several aspects of setup information are critical.

◆ *Default ship-from site/warehouse for an automatically-created sales order.* The default values can be defined for an item or for the customer representing the sister company.

◆ *Default ship-to site/warehouse for an automatically-created purchase order.* The default values can be defined for an item or for the vendor representing the sister company.

◆ *Sales prices and purchase prices.* Item information (at the selling company) should include a standard sales price and/or sales agreements that determine prices on the intercompany sales order and purchase order. Pricing information at the selling company normally dictates the price on the corresponding intercompany purchase order.

Setup Information for an Intercompany Vendor Vendor information is defined within each company. Hence, a vendor number must be defined within the buying company so that you can identify the associated sister company. At the same time, you can also identify the corresponding customer number within the selling company.

Several policies must be defined about the trading practices between a pair of purchasing and selling companies. For example, the policies determine the ability to change prices and discounts on the derived order.

Setup Information for an Intercompany Customer Just like vendors, the customer information is defined within each company. Hence, a customer number must be defined within the selling company so that you can identify the associated sister company. At the same time, you can also identify the corresponding vendor number within the buying company. You can also maintain the policies about the trading practices between the companies.

18.2 Variations of Creating Intercompany Orders

There are several variations of creating intercompany orders, as illustrated by the following examples. The examples involve a distribution company that purchases products from a manufacturing company. Sales orders and purchase orders were previously explained in Chapters 11 and 12 respectively, and intercompany orders reflect the same functionality.

Manually Create an Intercompany Purchase Order A basic scenario consists of a manually created purchase order (in the distribution company) to an intercompany vendor (the manufacturing company). This intercompany purchase order automatically creates an intercompany sales order at the manufacturing company. It is termed a two-legged order because it reflects transactions between the two related companies.

The converse situation involving a manually created sales order will automatically generate an intercompany purchase order when the sales order represents a special order or direct delivery order, as discussed in subsequent examples.

Firm a Planned Intercompany Purchase Order Firming a planned purchase order to an intercompany vendor will automatically create an intercompany purchase order and a corresponding intercompany sales order (at the manufacturing company).

Release an Intercompany Purchase Order from a Blanket Order (aka Purchase Agreement) A purchase agreement can be defined for an intercompany vendor, where the type of commitment must reflect a purchase quantity commitment. Each line item identifies an item, quantity and the purchase price or discount. You can then generate and view the equivalent sales agreement for the company that represents the intercompany vendor. Releasing an order from the purchase agreement (for a specified line item, quantity and date) creates an intercompany purchase order and a corresponding intercompany sales order at the manufacturing company. A previous chapter described purchase agreements (Section 12.6).

Create an Intercompany Purchase Order from a Sales Order (aka Special Order) A special order can be created for a sales order line, which results in an intercompany purchase order when the vendor is a sister company. This is termed a three-legged order because the sales order shipment to an external customer reflects the third leg. Changes on the originating sales order can automatically update the derived order, such as changes to the quantity, delivery date or delivery address. A previous chapter about sales order processing described special orders (Section 11.8).

Create a Direct Delivery Intercompany Purchase Order from a Sales Order (aka Direct Delivery Order) A direct delivery order can be created from a sales order line, which results in an intercompany purchase order (when the vendor is a sister company) that will be directly delivered to the customer. In this case, the sales order shipment at the sister company can automatically update the related orders. That is, the shipment will automatically update the receipt for the intercompany purchase order and the shipment of the related sales order. Several policies in the setup information only apply to this direct delivery scenario. A previous chapter about sales order processing described direct delivery orders (Section 11.7).

18.3 Master Scheduling across a Multicompany Supply Chain

The sequence for performing the master scheduling task becomes important in a multicompany supply chain involving two or more companies. The calculations apply to a single company, which means the master scheduling task should first be performed for the top-tier company. This generates planned intercompany demand that communicates requirements to the second-tier company, which represents an up-stream company within the supply chain.[1] The process must be repeated for additional up-stream companies. The primary coordination approach involves the intercompany master scheduling task.

Intercompany Master Scheduling Task A sequence of companies -- termed an intercompany planning group -- can be defined for performing the intercompany master scheduling task. You also identify the relevant set of master plan data for each company in the sequence. A single intercompany planning group may be sufficient in many scenarios, where the specified sequence often reflects a subset of companies requiring supply chain coordination. You specify the intercompany planning group as part of the dialogue for performing the intercompany master scheduling task.

Some additional information is specified as part of the dialogue for performing the intercompany master scheduling task, such as the number of iterations to correctly support more complex scenarios such as bi-directional trade. The additional information typically specifies regeneration calculations for the first

---

[1] The term upstream provides a relative reference within a supply chain indicating a source of raw material, whereas the term downstream indicates the direction of the end-customer.

iteration and net change calculations for subsequent iterations. The intercompany master scheduling task can be started in any company, since the sequencing will reflect the specified intercompany planning group.

As part of generating planned purchase orders within one company, the master scheduling task generates demand for an up-stream company. This demand is labeled *planned intercompany demand*, which differentiates it from other types of demand.[2]

The generation of planned intercompany demand requires some additional setup information within the master plan policies. That is, you designate that downstream planned intercompany demand should be included, and you also specify all possible companies (and their related set of master plan data) that could be considered. These settings only apply when the downstream company is not included in the same master scheduling run, such as running intercompany master scheduling where the specified intercompany planning group does not include the downstream company.

Planned Intercompany Demand Inquiries The planned intercompany demand can be viewed from two perspectives -- incoming and outbound -- that reflect a company's relative position in the supply chain. The outbound perspective identifies planned purchases (to other companies) for a purchasing company, and the incoming perspective identifies planned sales (to other companies) for a selling company.

Intercompany Supply and Demand Inquiry This form shows all orders -- both planned and actual -- that a company has from upstream and downstream companies. For example, it displays sales order demands and planned intercompany demands for items. Starting from a selected item, you can access a Multilevel Pegging form to view all supplies and demands across the multicompany supply chain and a multilevel product structure.

Intercompany Inventory Inquiry The On-Hand Inquiry form contains a Tab for displaying an item's inventory in multiple companies. The inquiry does not display the quantity of in-transit inventory.

Value of In-Transit Inventory for Intercompany Orders A separate report orders -- termed the Intercompany Goods in Transit Totals report orders -- displays the period beginning balance, period ending balance and net change with a period. Information is grouped by vendor, and provides the basis for manually-

---

[2] The construct for planned intercompany demand replaces the need for firming planned purchase orders to communicate requirements across a multicompany supply chain.

created general ledger entries. An additional report displays the transaction detail about shipments and receipts within a given period.

Example of a Multicompany Supply Chain A simplified example of a global manufacturer illustrates a multicompany supply chain. As shown in Figure 18.1, the simplified example consists of two different companies representing a manufacturing company and a distribution company. In the manufacturing company, an intermediate item (produced at one manufacturing site) was transferred to another site for producing the end item. The manufacturing company sold the end-item to domestic customers. The end-item was also transferred to a different company's distribution center for sales to foreign customers, where replenishment was typically based on demand forecasts for the distribution center. The primary coordination tools across the multicompany supply chain consisted of planned intercompany demand as well as intercompany purchase orders and sales orders.

Figure 18.1 Coordinate a Multicompany Supply Chain

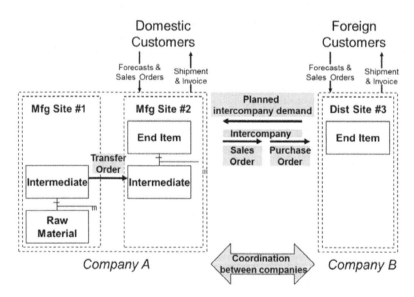

Stocking Levels in a Multicompany Supply Chain The previous example included demand forecasts and stocked products at the manufacturing company and at the distribution company. In a slightly different scenario, the products would only be forecasted and stocked at the manufacturing company, and only sent to the distribution company based on actual sales order demand. A broader viewpoint of this scenario involves the choice of stocking levels in a multicompany supply chain, and considerations about demand forecasts and the appropriate forecast consumption logic.

In the example shown in Figure 18.1, the demand forecasts would only be entered for the site/warehouse representing the manufacturing company. The subset pertaining to the distribution company would be entered as customer-specific forecasts for this same site/warehouse In addition, the forecast consumption logic must consider intercompany sales orders for these customer-specific forecasts. You indicate this forecast consumption logic as part of the coverage group assigned to the relevant items at the manufacturing company. Case 18.1 provides an illustrative example.

18.4 Additional Case Studies

Case 18.1 Stocking Levels in a Multicompany Supply Chain   A manufacturing/distribution business consisted of a distribution network of different inventory locations within different companies. For example, the manufacturing companies produced and delivered products to a regional distribution center (via transfer orders). The products were stocked at the regional distribution center based on demand forecasts and safety stock requirements. The products were then delivered to other inventory locations (in different sister companies) within the distribution network based on actual demand expressed as intercompany sales orders. In order to maintain the correct stocking level at the regional distribution center, the demand forecasts related to each sister company were entered as customer-specific forecasts, and the subsequent intercompany sales orders consumed these forecasts.

Case 18.2: Home Furniture Outlets   A company specializing in home furniture had multiple outlets grouped into various companies. Inventory replenishment was based on outlet-specific min/max quantities. As part of sales order processing, inventory could be checked within a given company's outlets or (if necessary) across all outlets. The system automatically created a transfer order for moving items within a company, or an intercompany order for moving items between companies. When inventory was insufficient, the user could generate a purchase order (to the furniture manufacturer) that was directly linked to the sales order.

18.5 Executive Summary

There are many variations of multicompany operations and the use of intercompany orders. Intercompany orders support the coordination of material transfers between two sites in different companies within a single AX instance. Intercompany orders require setup information in both companies. The chapter described several variations for creating and managing intercompany orders, including special orders and direct orders. It also described master scheduling across a multi-company supply chain and several other multisite variations.

Chapter 19

Configuration Technologies for Custom Products Manufacturing

The nature of custom product manufacturing scenarios can differ significantly. The scenarios can range from the simple to the complex, and from a single-level to a multi-level custom product. They often involve a configure-to-order product built from predefined options. Most of these scenarios can benefit from a configuration technology that simplifies the configuration process and embeds engineering expertise.

Dynamics AX provides several variations of a configuration technology for supporting different custom product scenarios. This chapter summarizes the variations, and provides more detailed explanation of one variation called the constraint-based configuration technology. The chapter also summarizes the use of modular bills of material to support configure-to-order products. The chapter consists of the following sections.

1. Variations of the Configuration Technology
2. Example Product Structure for a Configurable Item
3. Define Item Information for a Configurable Item
4. Define a Product Configuration Model
5. Configuration Process using a Product Configuration Model
6. Considerations about the Constraint-Based Configuration Technology
7. Modular BOMs to Support Configurable Items
8. Workspaces related to Configuration Technologies

19.1 Variations of the Configuration Technology

A configurable item provides the starting point for configuring a custom product, typically in the context of a sales order or sales quote. Dynamics AX provides several different configuration technologies to support configurable items.

The definition of a configurable item shares many similarities to a normal material item. The key differences include the designation as a product master (rather than a product), the use of a product variants (such as the configuration Id) within the product dimension group, and a selected configuration technology. Two major variations of a configuration technology are summarized in Figure 19.1 and described below. [1] The bottom of the figure displays a third configuration technology for modeling custom product scenarios with predefined variant codes rather than using a configurable item.

Figure 19.1 Variations of the Configuration Technology

Configuration Technology	Summarized Description of Approach
Constraint-Based Configuration	Define a Product Configuration Model and assign to the configurable item Use the model to configure an item Automatically create Configuration ID and its BOM/Route Versions
Dimension-Based Configuration (aka Bill of Options Approach)	Define a BOM Version (aka Bill of Options) for the Configurable Item Define a Route Version for the Configurable Item Use the Bill of Options to configure an item Manually assign a Configuration ID
Predefined Variant	Define applicable variant code(s) and the possible values for a variant code and Define valid combinations of values when using multiple variant codes Specify the item and the variant code value(s) on transactions

Constraint-Based Configuration Technology The constraint-based configuration technology requires the definition of a product configuration model. The model provides the dialogue of prompts/responses used in the configuration process, and a mapping of the prompts/responses to the needed components and operations. You can then assign the model to a configurable item along with validity dates.

---

[1] An additional option for a configuration technology was phased out after AX 2012 R3, since it was replaced by the constraint-based configuration technology option. This historical option was termed a "rules-based configuration technology" and the "product builder" approach.

When using the model, such as configuring a line item for a sales order or a sales quotation, the configuration process results in three key outputs from a supply chain perspective. One output consists of an automatically-created configuration Id for the configurable item. The other two outputs consist of the automatically-created BOM version and route version for the configuration id. These three outputs are also created for each configurable component in a multi-level custom product. You can manually maintain these BOM and route versions, which helps when the configuration process results in partially defined information. Additional aspects of the configuration include a calculated ship date and a calculated cost and sales price.

As the model changes, you define a new model and assign it to the configurable item with different validity dates. You typically duplicate the existing model as the starting point for the new model. Hence, a configurable item will ultimately have different assigned models (aka versions) with non-overlapping validity dates. The configuration process automatically uses the relevant model based on the order date.

Dimension-Based Configuration Technology (aka Bill of Options Approach) This configuration technology employs a dramatically different approach to the configuration process in comparison to the above-mentioned configuration technology. Rather than using a model (that defines the mapping between prompts/responses and needed components), you define a BOM version for the configurable item to support option selection of needed components. You also manually assign the configuration Id resulting from the configuration process. The approach represents a historical capability within AX.[2]

The bill of options approach involves a slight reconceptualization for defining and using BOM lines within the BOM version for a configurable item. For example, a group of BOM lines identity the alternatives for a required option (termed a configuration group), where you select one of the alternatives during the option selection process. When the required options or their alternatives change, you define a new BOM version for the configurable item with different validity dates. You typically copy the current BOM version as the starting point for the new BOM version. The configuration process automatically uses the relevant BOM version based on the order date.

The bill of options approach can be employed in reasonably simplistic situations for configuring a custom product via an option selection process. Using the standard AX functionality, it is typically limited to scenarios involving

---

[2] The bill of options approach was previously termed the configurable item approach. This book uses the term "configurable item" as a generic term applicable to the major variations of a configuration technology.

predefined options for 100% of the configuration, where the component quantity for a selected option cannot be manually overridden during the configuration process. The resulting BOM information for a configuration cannot be manually maintained. The route version for the configurable item (if defined) will be inherited by all configurations, and the route version can be manually maintained for a specific configuration. Some simplistic rules can be defined to automatically select an option or prevent selection. The options reflect a one-to-one correspondence to items, and the option selection process displays a list of item numbers, so that the user must be comfortable with the internal item numbers.

Predefined Variant Configuration Technology The use of predefined variants supports item identifiers based on the combination of an item number and one or more variant codes, as described in a previous chapter about item definition (Section 4.16). In summary, you identify the applicable codes (such as color and size) as part of the Product Dimension Group assigned to an item. You also define the possible values for each variant code (such as red/green and large/small), and then define the valid combinations of values. Standard AX includes several variant codes named color, size, style and configuration. You specify the item and the valid value for each applicable variant code as the item identifier for inventory transactions and for other information such as the BOM for a manufactured item.

The predefined variants approach does not support a configuration process in the same way as the other variations of a configuration technology. However, some custom product manufacturing scenarios can employ predefined variants as an alternative for a configuration process.

19.2 Example for a Configurable Item

A simple example of custom equipment can help illustrate the use of configurable items and the constraint-based configuration technology. As shown in Figure 19.2, the simple example consists of a two-level custom product, where the end-item and two variations of a key component have been identified as configurable items. In summary, the configurable "Equipment for Product Line ABC" consists of a configurable "Base Unit" (either Basic or Deluxe), a paint color (either Red or Blue), an optional enhanced control unit, and a set of common parts. Each configurable "Base Unit" consists of a "Power Unit" (either Low or High) and some other parts. This example product structure will be used in the subsequent explanations.

Figure 19.2 Example for Configurable Equipment

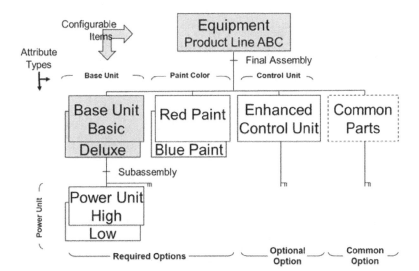

The figure highlights several key aspects. First, the configurable items are highlighted in grey. Second, the major options are identified as "attribute types" (such as base unit or paint color), and each attribute type has an enumerated list of values (such as red and blue for possible paint colors). This approach reflects modularized BOMs, so that the UI prompts/responses can be easily mapped to the relevant item. Third, the bottom of the figure indicates the required, optional and common options. The required and optional options will require mandatory entry of the related UI prompts and responses.

19.3 Define a Configurable Item

The typical process to define a configurable item (for using the constraint-based configuration technology) has many parallels to one for a regular material item. The primary difference involves the designation of a product master (rather than a product) and its configuration technology. The key steps within the typical business process for defining a configurable item are illustrated in Figure 19.3 and described below.

Figure 19.3 Typical Process to Define a Configurable Item

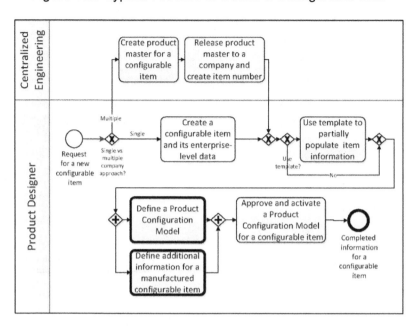

In a multicompany approach, a product designer within a centralized engineering group creates the product master for a configurable item and then releases it to selected companies to create the item number. Alternatively, a single company approach can be used to create the product master and its associated item number. A product designer is also responsible for defining much of the company-level information, typically by using a template to partially populate the item information. The product designer also defines a product configuration model corresponding to the configurable item, and then approves and activates the model for the item. The additional information about a configurable item often involves multiple roles, such as the definition of the item's accounting policies, planning data, testing requirements, and the serial and batch tracking policies.

Use of the Product Configuration Model generates a configuration Id for the configurable item, and the product name for each configuration Id can be maintained as part of the item's enterprise-level information.

19.4 Define a Product Configuration Model

The typical process to define a product configuration model consists of several steps illustrated in Figure 19.4. The first step involves the creation of a new model. You can optionally create a new model by duplicating an existing model, typically in the context of creating an updated version of the model. Information within a model defines the UI prompts and responses needed to configure an item, and consists of several sections. The two key sections for supply chain purposes specify the mapping between these prompts/responses and the needed components and operations. The mapping will populate the automatically-created BOM version and Route version that result from using the model to configure an item. As you define and complete a model, you can validate the model to identify errors, and also test the model to view the end-user experience. After the entire model has been completed and validated, you can approve and activate it for a configurable item. Additional explanation for several key steps is provided below.

Figure 19.4 Typical Process to Define a Product Configuration Model

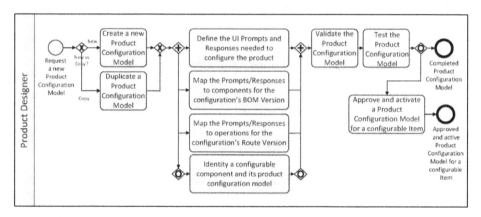

Create a New Product Configuration Model   Each model is uniquely identified by a user-assigned name. The name and description (and their translations) represent properties of the product configuration model, and you can edit these values. The model name frequently reflects the relevant configurable item. For example, the configurable item of "Product XYZ" would have a related model called "Product Configuration Model for Product XYZ."

Duplicate a Product Configuration Model You typically duplicate an existing model in the context of creating a new version, so that you can simply make changes to the newly-created model. You can create a new name and description when duplicating a model, and the system automatically retains the originating source of the model (aka the root component).

Define the UI Prompts and Responses needed to Configure the Product The "Attributes" section of a product configuration model provides the primary basis for defining User Interface (UI) prompts and responses. In particular, it defines each SolverName and SolverValue that represent key constructs within the model. These key constructs reflect the algebraic modeling language called Optimization Modeling Language (OML) used by the Solver Foundation. One example could be a SolverName of "PaintColor" and the two values of "Red" and "Blue" represent a SolverValue. These two key constructs become critical in defining relevant conditions, such as the condition for including a BOM line or an operation.

Map the Prompts/Responses to Components for the Configuration's BOM Version The "BOM Lines" section of a product configuration model defines the mapping for populating an automatically-created BOM version for the item's configuration. The mapping requires a detailed understanding of BOM line information, such as the variations for defining a component's required quantity, the warehouse source of a component, and the BOM line type. You can specify the condition for adding a BOM line. The mapping for each field within a BOM line can reflect a specified value or an attribute, such as an attribute for calculating a component's required quantity. Previous chapters explained a BOM line for a material item (Section 5.4) and for an item representing a subcontracted service (Section 15.4).

Map the Prompts/Responses to Operations for the Configuration's Route Version The "Route Operations" section of a product configuration model defines the mapping for populating an automatically-created route version for the item's configuration. The mapping requires a detailed understanding of information for an operation, such as the variations for defining the required resource and time requirements. You can specify the condition for adding an operation. The mapping for each field within an operation can reflect a specified value or an attribute, such as an attribute for calculating time requirements. Previous chapters explained an internal operation (Section 6.8) as well as an external operation (Section 15.5).

Identify a Configurable Component and its Product Configuration Model In order to support a multi-level custom product, the "Subcomponents" section of a product configuration model defines the configurable components of a configurable item.   Each configurable component requires a product configuration model.

Validate the Product Configuration Model You can validate a model after completion, or at any stage of completion, in order to identity potential errors.

Test the Product Configuration Model You can test a model after completion, or at any stage of completion, in order to view the UI prompts and responses.

Approve and Activate a Product Configuration Model for a Configurable Item You can assign the model to a configurable item along with validity dates, and then approve and activate the assignment.   Each assignment is termed a version.   As the model changes, you define a new model and assign it to the configurable item with different validity dates.   Hence, a configurable item will ultimately have different versions (aka assignments of different models) with non-overlapping validity dates.

19.5 Configuration Process using a Product Configuration Model

A sales order line item provides the typical starting point for configuring a custom product.   A typical process for this starting point is illustrated in Figure 19.5 and summarized below.   In this example, the customer service rep initially enters the sales order line for a configurable item, and then configures the line using the currently-effective Product Configuration Model.   As an alternative, the customer service rep can select an existing configuration id for the item.

Figure 19.5 Typical Process to Enter a Sales Order Line for a Configurable Item

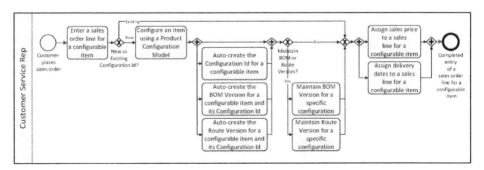

The configuration process results in three key outputs from a supply chain perspective. One output consists of an automatically-created configuration id for the configurable item. The other two outputs consist of the automatically-created BOM version and route version for the configuration id. These three outputs are also created for each configurable component in a multi-level custom product.[3] You can manually maintain these BOM and route versions, which is especially helpful when the configuration process results in partially defined information. Additional aspects of the configuration include a calculated ship date and a calculated cost and sales price.

The calculated sales price for a configured item can reflect a cost-plus-markup approach or attribute-based pricing approach, as designated by a pricing method policy. You designate this pricing method policy when assigning the product configuration model to a configured item.

◆ *Sales Pricing based on Cost Plus Markup.* The cost-plus-markup approach employs order-specific calculations of an item's cost and sales price, as previously described in Section 8.11.

◆ *Sales Pricing based on Attributes.* The attribute-based pricing approach identifies sales prices within the product configuration model. For example, you can define a sales price for each possible response to a prompt (termed the Price Model) and also define the applicable criteria (termed the Price Model Criteria). The applicable criteria can reflect characteristics of the customer and the sales order/quote, and different criteria can be defined for sales orders versus sales quotes. The total sales price reflects an additive model consisting of prices for each response plus a fixed base price. The total sales price is automatically updated and displayed when configuring the item for a sales order or quote.

The additive model for a specific configuration (termed the Price Breakdown) can be viewed in an Excel spreadsheet, and the spreadsheet can be optionally attached to the relevant sales order or quote line.

The typical process varies slightly for other starting points of the configuration process. For example, a promised ship date cannot be calculated for a sales quotation.

---

[3] With the current version of AX, the configuration process results in automatic creation of a configuration Id, and the same configuration id is used for every configurable item in a multi-level custom product.

19.6 Considerations about the Constraint-Based Configuration Technology

Several considerations apply to the constraint-based configuration approach, including the starting points for the configuration process and the use of configuration templates.

Starting Points for the Configuration Process A sales order line item for a configurable item represents one starting point for the configuration process, as described in the previous section. Additional starting points include a sales quotation line item, a replacement order line item for a customer RMA, and a manually-created production order.

Other starting points only apply to project-oriented operations or service orders, such as a project quotation line item, a project-specific item requirement, or an item requirement for a service order.

Configuration Templates as a Short-cut to Populating Values A configuration template represents a partially or completely finished configuration process for a product configuration model. You can create one or more templates for a model, and then use a selected template (when configuring an item) as a short-cut to populating suggested values. The suggested values can be overridden.

Default Value of the Configuration ID for a Configurable Item A default value for an item's configuration id may be defined when it represents the dominant business practice, otherwise it can be left blank.

Release an Existing Configuration to Other Companies An existing configuration is typically released to other companies that represent distributors of the product. After the release step, you must define the company-level information for the item and configuration, just like any other purchased item.

19.7 Modular BOMs to Support Configurable Items

Many manufacturers with multiple variations of similar products can benefit from modularizing their bills of material to support configurable items. There are warning signals for needed modularity: an explosive growth in the numbers of items and BOMs, overly complex bills of material, a perceived need for negative component quantities, difficulties in anticipating demands, and longer-than-necessary delivery lead times. BOM modularization makes it easier for using configurable items to define and sell a custom product.

The definition of modular BOMs starts with a detailed understanding of the product structure. One starting point involves deconstructing the product variations to identify common and unique items, and then restructuring the BOM to reflect the new groupings of common and unique options. This typically results in disentangling an overly complex BOM, isolating the unique items for usage late in the production process, and the use of phantoms for groups of common components. Another starting point involves lead time analysis of the multi-level product structure to identify the highest possible stocking level that supports the desired minimum delivery lead time. The stocking level may be stated in the new groupings of common and unique options, typically leading to a reduction in the number of items to forecast.

Modular BOMs typically impact routing operations. Final assembly operations can be assigned to the configurable end item. Operations can also be embedded in the routings for phantom components.

When modular BOMs and configurable items replace a standard products approach, there are many implications for other aspects of the business. It requires changes to item planning data, and the approach to sales and operations planning. It also requires changes to manufacturing documentation and drawings, sales literature and product pricing, order entry and delivery promises, paperwork (such as confirmations, packing lists and invoices) and sales analysis.

19.8 Workspaces related to Configuration Technologies

The Product Variant Model Definition workspace summarizes several aspects of information about product masters and the three variations of a configuration technology. It identifies the product masters that need to be released, and the product change cases related to them. The nature of additional information differs for the three variations.

◆ *Information about Product Configuration Models.* The workspace identifies configurable items that have not been assigned a product configuration model, and also the configuration models that have not yet been assigned to a configurable item (aka an approved version of the model). The links provide access to information about product configuration models and the related aspects of attribute types and attributes.

◆ *Information about the Bill of Options Approach.* The links provide access to the definition of configuration groups to support the bill of options approach.

◆ *Information about Predefined Variants.* The workspace identifies items that have not yet been assigned the values for predefined variants, and the items where values have been defined but not yet released. The links provide access to information about the variant codes and possible values.

The links provide access to additional information about cases and product masters, including the open product releases. Menu items provide access for defining a new product master or a new case.

19.9 Additional Case Studies

Case 9.1: Custom Windows A manufacturer of custom windows employed a product configurator for each product line. With a window product line, for example, the user dialogue captured information about the dimensions, glass type, casing and other key attributes. The configurator defined the rules for generating the BOM and routing to build the window, including the calculation of glass and wood component quantities and routing operation times. The configurator also calculated the sales price.

Case 19.2: Custom Store Fixtures A manufacturer of store fixtures employed a product configurator to identify the desired options for horizontal racks and vertical supports in a customized store fixture. This involved a two-level custom product, since a customized rack consisted of various subassemblies, and the rack went into a customized store fixture.

Case 19.3: Custom Surgical Kit One product line at a medical products distributor involved a customer-specified kit of components that represented surgical items. For example, a surgical kit was configured based on the requirements to perform a surgery at a hospital. A product configurator provided an option selection process to identify the desired components in the surgical kit. The sales price for a surgical kit reflected the selected components and a cost-plus-markup approach embedded in an order-specific cost calculation.

Case 19.4: Skeleton BOM for an ETO Product One product line at an equipment company involved building customized machines to customer specifications. Every customized machine had a unique identifier, and its product structure consisted of the same type of customized subassemblies (such as a power unit, a horizontal table, and a vertical column) with unique item identifiers. Each customized subassembly required several unique components with long purchasing lead times, and subassembly production was initiated prior to receipt of these unique components. Substantial engineering time was required to define the unique item identifiers, initiate purchases of the long lead time components, and ultimately define each machine's product structure (with unique components correctly placed in BOMs). Any delays in these engineering efforts impacted the purchasing and production activities, and the delayed definition of the product structure information made it difficult to coordinate requirements. As a solution approach, the company employed a product configurator to automatically create the unique item numbers and the product structure skeleton, with the unique purchased components correctly placed in the subassembly BOMs. The solution approach resulted in significant reductions in engineering time and the number of delays.

Case 19.5: Custom Overhead Crane One product line at an equipment company involved a customized overhead crane for moving heavy material around a factory floor. The user dialogue in the product configurator identified usage characteristics, such as maximum load weight, mounting height, and the factory floor dimensions. The product configurator translated the usage characteristics into the required materials and operations to produce the customized overhead crane.

Case 19.6: Custom Plastic Assembly One product line at a fabricated products company involved customized plastic assemblies that reflected a two-level custom product. Plastic components were produced to custom specifications, and then assembled into a customized plastic product. A product configurator provided the user dialogue to capture the customer specifications, and also provided a mapping to the required materials and operations. The two-level custom product enabled warehouse personnel to find the customized plastic components that were prepared for final assembly.

Case 19.7: Using a Legacy Product Configurator A manufacturer of customized kitchen countertops and cabinets wanted to use two previously-developed product configurators as part of AX, since these configurators provided continuity for usage by salesmen/dealers and contained extensive engineering knowledge about product design. One of these legacy configurators -- for kitchen countertops -- already employed .net user control, so that usage within AX required a few changes to some of the exposed methods and dropping it onto an AX form. The second legacy configurator – for cabinets – was written in Delphi. In order to support usage within AX, it required creation of a .net user control as a wrapper layer with exposed methods, and then dropping it onto an AX form.

19.10 Executive Summary

The nature of custom products manufacturing can differ significantly, ranging from special one-time items to a configure-to-order product built from pre-defined components. Dynamics AX provides several options for a configuration technology to support custom products manufacturing. The chapter summarized these variations of a configuration technology, and provided more detail about the variation for a Constraint-Based Configuration Technology. Several case studies illustrated how to handle custom products for windows, store fixtures, surgical kits and overhead cranes.

Chapter 20

Summary

This book focused on how Microsoft Dynamics AX provides an integrated ERP system to support supply chain management in discrete manufacturing and distribution. This focus guided the prior research and the scope of book topics that were described at the beginning of the book. In particular, this book covered the embedded conceptual models and business processes within AX. The book contents apply to use of AX 2012 R3 and to the new Dynamics AX because these versions share the same business logic.

The book contents were segmented to support several categories of targeted readers, so that you can focus on just the relevant chapters and sections for your learning objectives. Some typical learning objectives are summarized in Figure 20.1, along with the number of estimated pages to accomplish the objective.

Initially Learn AX New users can benefit from a quick overview of how the whole system fits together, especially in a linear sequence of topics that build on each other. Appendix A summarized the suggested chapters and sections.

Learn Business Processes and their Variations Numerous business processes were illustrated throughout the book, as summarized in the first chapter (Section 1.7). The explanation of each business process started with a basic model that reflects the key constructs and embedded conceptual models within AX. The typical steps and role responsibilities were illustrated using BPM diagrams. The basic model provided a baseline for explaining key considerations and variations in the business process, thereby supporting a "+1" learning approach.

Reference Book to Confirm/Extend AX Knowledge This book attempted to explain most of the SCM-related capabilities within AX. Many readers find it useful as a reference book to confirm or extend their AX knowledge. It is often helpful to read another viewpoint to complement your hands-on learning and research into the user documentation, blogs and other sources of information.

Readers of my previous books have commented about their usefulness as reference information, and it is hoped the current book serves a similar purpose.

Figure 20.1 Typical Learning Objectives about
Supply Chain Management using AX

Learning Objective	Estimated Pages
Initially Learn AX	100-130
Learn Business Processes and their Variations	
Selectively Learn AX Capabilities	
- SCM for a Manufacturing Business	80-180
- SCM for a Distribution Business	70-170
- S&OP Scenarios and Master Scheduling Logic	50
- Warehouse Management	30-40
- Quality Management	25
Reference Book to Confirm/Extend AX Knowledge	
Incrementally Learn the New Capabilities	
- Starting from AX 2012	30-40
- Starting from AX 2012 R3	5-10

For AX Veterans

Incrementally Learn the new Capabilities in AX The incremental learning depends on the starting point of the knowledgeable reader, such as a starting point of the older version of AX 2012. Appendix B summarized the incremental differences between AX 2012 and the newer versions, and identified the relevant sections providing more detailed explanations. For those already familiar with AX 2012 R3, Appendix C summarized just the differences in the new Dynamics AX.

Concluding Remarks When learning any ERP software package, it is important to understand its underlying conceptual models and how it supports variations in business processes. It is easy to get bogged down in the navigational details. This book summarized how Microsoft Dynamics AX can support supply chain management in manufacturing and distribution businesses. It also addressed the learning objectives for those new to AX as well as those already familiar with AX.

Appendix A
Initially Learn AX

New users can benefit from a quick overview of how the whole system fits together, especially in a linear sequence of topics that build on each other. This quick overview consists of approximately 100 to 130 pages, although this can vary based on type of business and level of user interest. As a starting point, you may want to read about common scenarios that reflect your dominant business models, including the description of a baseline model of operations (Section 2.2).

The linear sequence starts with several foundation topics. This includes the definition of inventory locations, material items, BOMs and routings for manufactured items, product costing, and the coverage planning data to model SCM decision-making. The sequence continues with the definition of S&OP game plans and the use of master scheduling logic to coordinate supply chain activities in several business processes. Subsequent chapters cover these key business processes related to sales orders, purchase orders, transfer orders, production orders, warehouse management and quality management. The magnitude of these initial learning efforts for each book chapter (relative to total book content) are graphically summarized in Figure A.1 and the related text provides suggested guidelines.

Fundamentals of Modeling Inventory Locations The definition of inventory locations represents a key part of modeling any supply chain, and this short chapter introduces the fundamental options for modeling these locations within AX. These options include the use of AX sites and AX warehouses to model inventory locations with a legal entity, and the locations may reflect more than one legal entity. For a given AX warehouse, another option concerns the basic versus advanced approach to warehouse management.

The model of inventory locations has multiple impacts. It impacts the definition of items, the BOM/routing for manufactured items, product costs, coverage planning data and S&OP game plans. It also impacts the business processes related to inventory, such as sales orders, purchase orders, transfer orders and production orders. These impacts are covered throughout the book, and a separate chapter provides more detailed explanations about inventory and warehouse management.

Figure A.1 Initially Learn AX

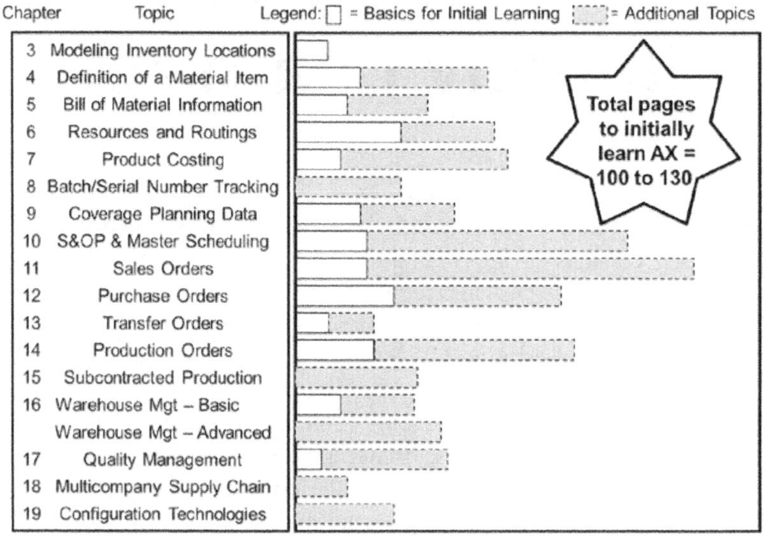

Definition of a Material item   Information about material items provides the foundation for managing supply chain activities in distribution and manufacturing environments. In terms of initially learning AX, it is critical to understand the enterprise- versus company-level information and the typical process to define a material item. It is also helpful to gain an overview of the differences between purchased and manufactured items, and the company versus site/warehouse information for an item.

Bill of Material Information   The typical process to define an item's BOM requires a basic understanding about Master BOMs and BOM Versions, the BOM Version policies for an item, and several key fields in the BOM line for a component.

Resources and Routings   The typical process to define an item's routing requires a basic understanding about Master Routings and Route Versions, the Route Version policies for an item, and several key aspects of defining a routing operation and its resource requirements. The prerequisite information includes the definition of production resources and master operations, and the optional use of resource capabilities to model the scheduling logic about preferred machines. This chapter also introduces the two basic options for scheduling logic -- termed job scheduling and operation scheduling.

Product Costing The primary variations in product costing involve the use of standard versus actual costs for valuing an item's inventory, and the differences between purchased and manufactured items. A basic understanding starts with the foundation of costing versions which contain the cost records about items, labor rates and overheads. These cost records are used in the cost calculations for manufactured items based on their BOM and routing information. Product costing often represents one of the more complex aspects of an integrated ERP system, and the responsibility of cost accounting specialists. A cursory understanding is sufficient for most readers.

Batch Number and Serial Number Tracking Some scenarios require tracking of serial numbers or batch numbers for a material item, or both. Hence, this chapter represents optional information for many readers, and the topics are not included in Figure A.1 as part of the basics for initial learning.

Coverage Planning Data to Model SCM Decision Making Coverage planning data (or planning data for short) represents a model of decision making about coordinating the supply chain, and the planning data differs for purchased items, manufactured items and transfers. The key planning data includes the coverage group assigned to an item and warehouse. Each user-defined coverage group consists of multiple policies such as the applicable coverage code (e.g., period lot sizing for planned orders) and use of action messages. For initial learning purposes, you can focus on the key planning data and optionally skim the special cases and the in-depth explanations of related policies.

S&OP and Master Scheduling S&OP game plans represent a cornerstone for effective supply chain management, and build on the models of the organization's supply chain and decision-making. Most businesses have several different scenarios requiring a different approach to the S&OP game plans. For initial learning purposes, you can focus on the common scenarios applicable to your organization, and the typical process to maintain the S&OP game plans. The additional topics – such as demand forecasts, safety stock requirements, sales order promise dates and master scheduling logic -- are probably more applicable to the master scheduler role.

Sales Order Processing Sales order processing often involves a wide spectrum of considerations and many variations in business practices. For initial learning purposes, it is easiest to start with a basic model of sales order processing. The basic model provides a foundation for a cursory review of the key considerations and major variations applicable to your organization. Examples of major variations include sales prices, sales quotations, direct delivery orders, customer returns and commissions.

Purchase Order Processing The coordination of purchasing activities for material items are normally driven by a firm's S&OP game plans. For initial learning purposes, it is easiest to start with a basic model of purchase order processing. The basic model provides a foundation for a cursory review of the key considerations and major variations applicable to your organization. Examples of major variations include purchase prices, purchasing RFQs and receiving inspection. A cursory review of the key coordination tools -- such as planned purchase orders -- is also suggested.

Transfer Order Processing Some businesses require transfers between sites where transfers are normally driven by the firm's S&OP game plans. A basic model of transfer order processing provides a foundation for a cursory review of several key considerations and coordination tools.

Production Order Processing Production order processing often involves a wide spectrum of considerations and many variations in business practices. For initial learning purposes, it is easiest to start with a basic model of production order processing and an understanding of order status. The basic model provides a foundation for a cursory review of the key considerations and the additional topics about picking, labor reporting, finished quantities, scheduling logic and costing. A cursory review of the key coordination tools -- such as planned production orders and production schedules -- is also suggested.

Subcontracted Production Some scenarios employ an outside operation for production orders and supply material to the vendor. There are many similarities to production orders for internal manufacturing but several unique aspects and different variations. For initial learning purposes, it is easiest to start with a basic model of production order processing for subcontracted production. The basic model provides the foundation for a cursory review of the unique aspects (such as BOM and routing information) and the different variations. This chapter represents optional information for many readers, and the topics are not included in Figure A.1 as part of the basics for initial learning.

Inventory and Warehouse Management Many aspects of inventory and warehouse management have already been covered in previous chapters, such as the fundamentals of modeling inventory locations and the typical business processes for sales orders and supply orders. Hence, most readers can focus on just the incremental topics related to Inventory Status and the AX viewpoint of inventory transactions.

The chapter summarizes a companion book about Warehouse Management using AX and actually consists of three parts. One part of the chapter summarizes the basic approach to warehouse management, and another part summarizes the advanced WMS approach. A third part compares the two approaches and may be valuable in making a decision.

Quality Management In terms of the basics for initially learning AX, the key topics include the summary of quality management concerns and the inventory blocking approaches. The other topics generally apply to quality specialists, such as the use of quality orders and nonconformance reports.

Multicompany Supply Chain Some scenarios require transfers between sites in different companies. The transfers involve the use of intercompany orders and master scheduling across the multicompany supply chain. This represents optional information for many readers, and the topics are not included in Figure A.1 as part of the basics for initial learning.

Configuration Technologies for Custom Product Manufacturing
Some scenarios involve a configuration technology to support configure-to-order products. Standard AX supports several approaches, and a typical process for using a constraint-based configuration technology provides a foundation for understanding the key considerations and variations. However, this chapter represents optional information for many readers, and the topics are not included in Figure A.1 as part of the basics for initial learning.

Appendix B
Incrementally Learn AX

One purpose of the book is to assist knowledgeable AX readers so they can focus on incremental learning of new SCM-related topics. For example, those readers familiar with the previous AX 2012 version can build on what they already know, since it comprises the majority of SCM functionality within the newer version of AX 2012 R3. In addition, the same business logic within AX 2012 R3 functionality is embedded within the new Dynamics AX.

The incremental learning efforts of knowledgeable users are supported by Microsoft's documentation about "What's New." However, it is difficult to gauge the relative amount of functionality and incremental learning. This appendix quantifies the incremental learning and the proportionate amount of change between AX 2012 and the newer versions. The comparison focuses on the SCM-related topics covered within the book.

B.1 Metrics about the Amount of AX Functionality

The amount of AX functionality and the associated incremental learning are difficult to measure. A helpful starting point involves a rough measure of the previous versus new functionality which indicates the proportionate amount of change. One rough measure can be based on a page count analysis of this book. The heat map displayed in Figure B.1 summarizes the book topics, and a yardstick portrayal of previous functionality in AX 2012 (shown in white) and the incrementally new functionality within AX 2012 R3 or the new Dynamics AX (shown in light grey). It also identifies just the differences between AX 2012 R3 and the new Dynamics AX (shown in dark grey). The entire length of a yardstick represents the book's attempt to provide a complete walkthrough of the topic using AX so you get a proportionate sense of magnitude.

Figure B.1 Incremental Learning of AX

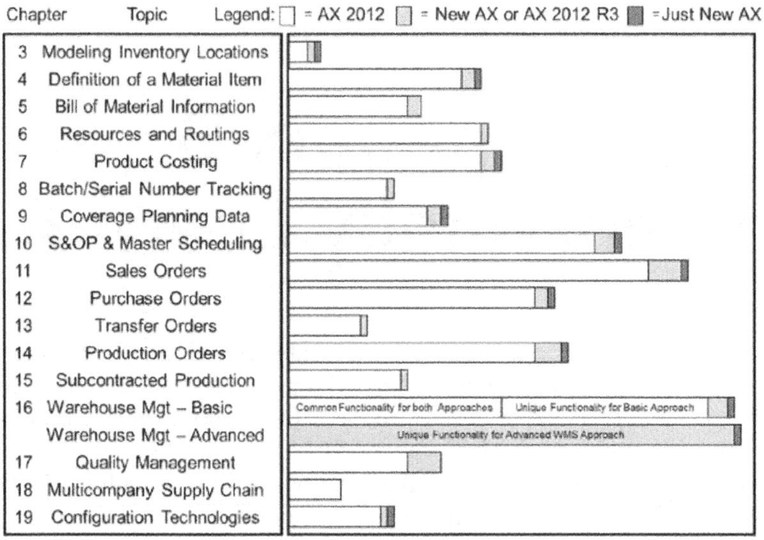

Chapter　　　Topic　　Legend: ☐ = AX 2012 ☐ = New AX or AX 2012 R3 ■ = Just New AX

Chapter	Topic	
3	Modeling Inventory Locations	
4	Definition of a Material Item	
5	Bill of Material Information	
6	Resources and Routings	
7	Product Costing	
8	Batch/Serial Number Tracking	
9	Coverage Planning Data	
10	S&OP & Master Scheduling	
11	Sales Orders	
12	Purchase Orders	
13	Transfer Orders	
14	Production Orders	
15	Subcontracted Production	
16	Warehouse Mgt – Basic	Common Functionality for both Approaches | Unique Functionality for Basic Approach
	Warehouse Mgt – Advanced	Unique Functionality for Advanced WMS Approach
17	Quality Management	
18	Multicompany Supply Chain	
19	Configuration Technologies	

As you can see by the yardsticks within Figure B.1, the most significant changes involve the unique functionality for the Advanced WMS approach to warehouse management, which was introduced in AX 2012 R3. The Advanced WMS topic would not apply to scenarios using just the basic approach to warehouse management. The yardsticks about warehouse management reflect a page count of the companion book "Warehouse Management using AX," and the length simply indicates a large number (rather than a proportionate page count).

Almost every topic had changes stemming from AX 2012 R3, and most topics were also affected by the slight differences in the new Dynamics AX. The next section provides a brief description of key changes in AX 2012 R3. It also describes some of the new Dynamics AX changes, and Appendix C provides a more complete description.

In summary, the amount of incremental learning differs based on whether you need to understand the Advanced WMS approach to warehouse management. When using just the basic approach to warehouse management, the incremental learning represents a 5-10% change in overall functionality compared to AX 2012.

The Advanced WMS approach requires a significantly higher amount of incremental learning. A rough estimate of incremental learning would be 200+ pages based on a page count analysis of my companion book about "Warehouse Management using AX."

Several caveats apply to this heat map and the estimates of incremental learning. The topics reflect the book's SCM focus on manufacturing and distribution. It does not include topics related to accounting and human resources. Book length considerations precluded other relevant topics, such as lean manufacturing, projects, service orders, and possibly retail-oriented operations. With these limitations in mind, the analysis can still provide rough yardsticks of incremental learning.

B.2 Summarizing the Changes in AX Functionality

The previous section quantified the incremental learning and the proportionate amount of change between AX 2012 and the newer versions of AX 2012 R3 and the new Dynamics AX. The analysis focused on the SCM-related topics covered within the book. This section summarizes some of the major changes for the SCM-related topics; it is not an exhaustive list of "What's New." The book chapters provide an organizing focus for the explanation.

Fundamentals of Modeling Inventory Locations   The item- and warehouse-specific policies that support use of the basic versus advanced approach to warehouse management represent the biggest change for modeling inventory locations.

An additional change within the new Dynamics AX affects the approach to intercompany trade when using an additional AX instance or a different ERP package. In these scenarios, you handle intercompany trade using the new Data Import/Export framework rather than the previous approach using the Application Integration Framework (AIF).

Definition of a Material item   Several changes in item definition stem from use of the Advanced WMS approach to warehouse management, starting with additional policies within the Storage Dimension Group assigned to items (Section 4.4). Use of the Advanced WMS approach also impacts the essential data for an item, which requires two additional fields about a reservation hierarchy and unit sequence group (Section 4.3). It impacts the item's enterprise-level data about an NMFC code which provides information for the new bill of lading format. The values for four different item filter codes can be defined, and you assign the relevant value to an item to support Advanced WMS purposes such as directed putaway based on the item characteristic.

Bill of Material Information The BOM versions for manufactured items can be optionally maintained via product change cases (Section 5.8).

As part of supporting the Advanced WMS approach, an additional option was introduced for defining the warehouse source of components in BOM/routing information so that raw material picking work can deliver components to a production input location (Section 5.5).

Resources and Routings As part of supporting the Advanced WMS approach to production order picking and receiving, you can define a production input location for a resource group (or a resource) and a production output location.

Product Costing One change involved a new capability related to a costing version for planned costs, where the item cost records for purchased items can be automatically populated based on purchase prices within purchase trade agreements (Section 7.9). These item cost records can then be used to calculate the planned costs for manufactured items.

A new Compare Item Prices report enables a comparison of costs within a selected costing version (1) to the pending costs in a specified costing version or (2) to the active costs as per an effective date. It can also calculate the net change in inventory value for a set of standard cost data.

Batch Number and Serial Number Tracking An additional option for serialized items supports the deferred assignment of serial numbers until sales order shipment (Section 8.2). A new Item Trace inquiry provides more comprehensive information for batch (and serial) number tracking purposes, and it can identify the customers that received products containing a component with a bad batch.

An additional option for merging batches was also introduced, but the topic was not included because it does not generally apply to discrete manufacturing and distribution.

Coverage Planning Data to Model SCM Decision Making A graphical analysis of related action messages termed the Action Graph was introduced (Section 9.10), where you can apply the suggested action for a selected message. This capability was enhanced in the new Dynamics AX, so that the Action Graph still displays reference information after applying the suggested action for an action message.

S&OP and Master Scheduling   An additional option for forecast consumption logic supports demand forecasts for stocked components so that any demand consumes the forecast (Section 10.8). This same logic applies to demand forecasts for stocked end-items at different levels of a distribution network, so that transfer order demands consume the forecast.

A new option supports demand forecasts by customer and the associated forecast consumption logic by sales orders for the customer (Section 10.5). It also applies to demand forecasts for a customer group.

A new capability involves an explanation of master scheduling logic, which can be provided as part of a net change explosion (Section 10.12). You specify the calculation of this "trace" information as part of the dialogue for performing the net change explosion, and then view the results on the "Explanation" tab. The explanation applies to the multi-level product structure for a manufactured item. It provides a detailed breakdown of the coverage planning calculations, and the generation of action messages and messages about delayed dates.

A small refinement was made to the CTP logic for sales orders, so that it can first consider an item's supply orders that meet the required date before considering on-hand inventory (Section 10.10).

One approach to statistical forecasting was introduced in AX 2012 R3, where the forecast models in Microsoft SQL Server Analysis Services were used to create demand forecast predictions. It was replaced by a different approach in the new Dynamics AX, where future demand can be estimated using the Microsoft Azure Learning cloud service (Section 10.6).

Sales Order Processing Several new aspects of sales order processing were introduced. These include placing a sales order on hold, creating sales lines via copying from an Item List, identifying changes to sales orders via order events, and enforcing the start and end dates for selling an item (Section 11.3). Other aspects include a new item-specific reservation policy that will be inherited by sales order lines, such as a policy of Automatic versus Manual.

The new Direct Delivery form can help coordinate the sales order and purchase order involved in a direct delivery (Section 11.8). A new item-related policy identifies those items typically sold as a direct delivery, so that the policy will be inherited by sales lines for the item.

The assignment of serial numbers to a serialized item can be deferred until sales order shipment (Section 8.2).

The basic model of sales order processing includes an additional option for using the Advanced WMS approach to sales order picking/shipping and the related use of mobile device transactions (Section 11.1). The Advanced WMS approach has multiple impacts, such as different reservation logic and different options for the release-to-warehouse step.

The basic approach to warehouse management also has an additional option (termed the Picking Workbench) to support the wave picking concept for sales order picking lists.

Purchase Order Processing   An approval process (termed change management) can be used for a manually-created purchase order for trade goods. An associated policy (termed activate change management) can enforce the approval process as a companywide, vendor-specific or order-specific policy (Section 12.8).

The Vendor Portal capabilities apply to AX 2012 R3 but were deprecated in the new Dynamics AX. When using AX 2012 R3, for example, the vendor portal can be used to reply to vendor-specific RFQs (Section 12.7).

An additional step in the basic model of purchase order processing supports external review prior to confirming an order (Section 12.1). Another change to the basic model entails the additional option for using the Advanced WMS approach to purchase order receiving and the related use of mobile device transactions.

Transfer Order Processing The basic model of transfer order processing includes the additional option for using the Advanced WMS approach to transfer order picking/shipping and receiving (Section 13.1).   The basic approach to warehouse management also has an additional option (termed the Picking Workbench) to support the wave picking concept for transfer order picking lists.

Production Order Processing The only major change entails the additional options within the Advanced WMS approach for production order picking and receiving, and the related use of mobile device transactions (Section 14.1). The new capabilities support raw material picking work and wave picking, and the picking list journal is used to report actual consumption of components.

A new capability enables you to assign (and remove) a Stop flag for a production order. The Stop flag primarily serves warehouse management purposes and prevents changes in order status prior to starting a production order.   For example, assigning the Stop flag to a scheduled order prevents a change in order status to Released (which prevents creation of raw material picking work) and to Started (which prevents reporting of labor and material).

Subcontracted Production The major change entails the additional options within the Advanced WMS approach to support production orders and transfer orders, as noted in the previous point.

Inventory and Warehouse Management The new capabilities within the Advanced WMS approach represent the largest change in functionality in comparison to the basic approach supported by previous AX versions. They involve consideration of the strategic options for warehouse management (Section 16.1), the new Inventory Status capabilities (Section 16.2) and the impact of work orders on inventory transactions (Section 16.5).

The summarized explanations of the basic and advanced approaches to warehouse management (Sections 16.3 and 16.4) do not adequately reflect the magnitude of incremental learning. A more realistic estimate of magnitude can be based on the companion book about Warehouse Management using AX, and the yardsticks within Figure B.1 reflect this different basis of page count metrics. The text within each yardstick indicates the common and unique functionality related to the basic and advanced approaches.

Quality Management The major changes include the use of Inventory Status and cases for quality management purposes. For example, the user-defined values for Inventory Status provide an additional option for inventory blocking (Section 17.2), reporting inspection (Section 17.3), and indicating inspection requirements for purchased items. An additional consideration only applies to the Advanced WMS approach, where you define a combined disposition code (with an associated Inventory Status and RMA disposition code) in order to report exceptions during mobile device transactions for receiving purchase orders and RMAs (Section 17.5).

Cases can be used to identify a quality issue (Section 17.8), and case management provides a multi-faceted approach to manage issues raised by customers, vendors or employees. A special variation of cases -- termed a product change case -- can also support maintenance of BOM and route information (Section 5.8).

The minor changes for quality management include two new options for holds and stop flags (Section 17.6). That is, you can place a sales order on hold, and also assign a stop flag to a production order. In addition, the use of quarantine orders (and a quarantine warehouse) only applies to the basic approach to warehouse management.

Multicompany Supply Chain   No major changes were introduced for managing a multicompany supply chain.

Configuration Technologies for Custom Product Manufacturing   One change involved a new capability within a Product Configuration Model in order to calculate a configuration's sales price based on responses. This provides an alternative to the cost-plus-markup calculation (based on BOM/routing information) of a suggested sales price.

Appendix C
Differences between
the new Dynamics AX
and AX 2012 R3

This appendix summarizes some of the differences between AX 2012 R3 and the new Dynamics AX, and focuses on the SCM-related topics covered within the book.

Changes in User Experience The standard menu structure and user-defined favorites provide commonly used approaches for navigation in both versions. However, there are significant changes in the menu structure and in the approach to maintain favorites when using the new Dynamics AX. For example, the menu structure is flatter, a Cost Management menu has been introduced, and the topics within the Product Information Management menu now include a broader set of relevant information. Based on my experience, those users familiar with the previous menu structure will initially struggle to determine "where is it?" However, an additional approach to navigation -- termed "search for a page" -- enables you to specify the desired topic, review a list of applicable forms, and then navigate to a selected form.

Workspaces represent one variation in the user experience when using the new Dynamics AX, as further described in the next point. The links within workspaces support navigation to commonly used tasks.

Some aspects of the displayed information have changed, such as a "yes/no switch" (rather than a checkbox) and a message bar and message box (rather than an infolog about warnings and errors). Several changes in AX terminology were also introduced, as described in a subsequent point.

Workspaces Workspaces represent one variation in the user experience when using the new Dynamics AX. Workspaces provide an aggregation of tasks related to a specific role or business process. Almost half of the 30+ predefined workspaces apply to the SCM-related topics within the book, as previously summarized at the beginning of the book (Section 1.6). Separate sections described the workspaces related to item definition (Section 4.18), product costing (Section 7.14), master scheduling (Section 10.18), sales orders (Section 11.17), purchase orders (Section 12.14), production orders (Section 14.16), warehouse management (Section 16.6) and configuration technologies (Section 19.8). Other workspaces were mentioned in the context of defining resources (Section 6.2) and employee competencies (Section 6.4). It is anticipated that additional workspaces and related functionality will become available as the software evolves.

Calculate Demand Forecasts based on Historical Usage A different approach for calculating demand forecasts was introduced using the Microsoft Azure Machine Learning cloud service. The service performs best match model selection and offers key performance indicators for calculating forecast accuracy. These capabilities were explained as one of the options for calculating demand forecasts (Section 10.6).

Analyze Delivery Alternatives for a Sales Order Line The delivery alternatives for meeting a customer's requested delivery date and quantity can reflect product availability at different ship-from warehouses and different modes of delivery. It may also reflect different product variants (such as size or color) in some scenarios. You can evaluate these options for a sales line using the Delivery Alternatives information, and select the desired option for updating the promised dates, ship-from warehouse and mode of delivery on the sales line. You can also choose to ship a smaller quantity than ordered (based on availability) and ship the remainder at a later date, which results in a delivery schedule for the sales line. These capabilities were highlighted in the typical process for entering a sales order (Section 11.2), and explained as one of the key considerations in sales order processing (Section 11.3).

Changes in AX Terminology A number of changes in SCM-related terminology were introduced in the new Dynamics AX, such as changes in the names of fields and forms. As one example, the term "futures message" has been changed to "calculated delays message" to more accurately indicate its purpose. A comprehensive list of these changes was not yet available at the time of book publication. However, these changes in AX terminology did not affect functionality.

This book covers two options for using AX so that the choice of AX terminology and its consistent use become an important consideration. For explanatory purposes, this book employs the new term (within the new Dynamics AX) whenever it is known.

Changes in Technology Technology considerations generally fall outside the book's scope, but some of the changes can be briefly summarized.

The workspace functionality replaces several capabilities in previous AX versions, such as role-centered pages and the enterprise portal. The role-centered pages were built on the deprecated Enterprise Portal capabilities which have been replaced by the new web client platform. This new web client improves usability across multiple platforms and devices.

The Data Import/Export framework replaces the Application Integration Framework (AIF) capabilities in previous AX versions.

Other technology changes include improved integration with Microsoft Office; enhanced use of business intelligence (BI) reports and visualizations; improvements in the "Help" system; and improvements in electronic documents via the Generic Electronic Reporting tool.

Other Minor Changes Minor changes were introduced for displaying information on the Action Graph and Gantt chart. A new Fleet Management module supports rental purposes.

Deprecated Functionality This includes the "old WMS II" capabilities for warehouse management (replaced by the Advanced WMS capabilities), the "product builder" capabilities (replaced by the constraint-based configuration technology); and the shipping carrier interface (partially replaced by the advanced transportation management capabilities).

List of Figures

List of Cases

About the Author

Scott Hamilton has specialized in ERP/SCM information systems for manufacturing and distribution for three decades as a consultant, developer, user and researcher. He has consulted worldwide with over a thousand firms, conducted several hundred executive seminars, helped design several influential ERP packages, and taught ERP/SCM as an MBA professor at universities in North America, Europe and the Pacific Rim. Scott earned a doctorate in information systems specializing in manufacturing, and has been a multiyear winner of the rarely given Microsoft MVP Award for Dynamics AX. Scott has authored nine books about Dynamics AX as well as two textbooks about ERP/SCM for APICS and McGraw-Hill. His regular column "The AX Solution Architect" is published in MSDynamicsWorld.com. He lives in Minnesota, a place where people still build ice castles.

About UXC Eclipse

Scott Hamilton has become the "go to" authority on Microsoft Dynamics AX in the manufacturing space. His books provide valuable insights into the market place we serve, which gives us all the opportunity to expand our thinking and see beyond the software features and functions.

UXC Eclipse is widely recognized as a global leader in industry solutions built on the Dynamics AX platform. We have a depth of experience across the horizontal global ERP market with specific focus on industry solutions for Retail, Wholesale and Distribution, Manufacturing and the surrounding supply chain.

We help organizations streamline their business and operational processes to bring the best from their organizational experience to the best of our Dynamics AX solutions; the result is 'win-win'. From their Dynamics AX solutions, our customers realize operational efficiencies, improve business performance and heighten their supply chain collaboration. At UXC Eclipse we use a combination of old-fashioned service with ISO-9001 accredited quality systems and controls to ensure our implementations deliver to our customers' expectations – on time and on budget. Our happy customers are the true indication of our success. With a global team of over 650 people, some 2,700 customer sites rely on UXC Eclipse for their project implementation services and everyday support.

We trust you find this book to be a useful insight into Microsoft Dynamics AX. If UXC Eclipse can be of service on your supply chain journey, then please get in touch with us at _www.uxceclipse.com_

Bradley Stroop
Chief Executive Officer
UXC Eclipse Group

Made in the USA
Middletown, DE
23 December 2019